INTRODUCTION

This guide has been produced with the sole aim of assisting airband listeners to quickly find details of a flight - once they have identified an aircraft's call sign

We have attempted to include most of the flights to ;
details of many of the overflights with aircraft f
Particulars of scheduled, charter, freight and mail fl

CW00815755

This thirteenth edition has been completely revised
airlines themselves. These schedules are being cc
charter flights, there may be changes to the details p
services, whilst others stop operations.

Once again, we should like to express our sincere appreciation to the airlines, airport directors, traffic controllers, handling agents, etc. etc. Without their assistance, the publication of this guide would not have been possible.

We must also thank the many readers, who kindly send corrections, additions and information which may be of interest in future editions of the guide.

Airlines are listed alphabetically in order of their 'Call Signs'. Shown alongside these, is the name of the company, their 2 and/or 3 number designator, and the country of registration. There is also an index of the airline companies. This year we have deleted the unusual call signs section - there are many dedicated publications which list far more of these than we could possibly show.

Also included are details of the alpha/numerical call signs introduced by British Airways, their franchised companies, British Midland, British Regional and KLM UK. The majority of these have been supplied by fellow enthusiasts, and we cannot guarantee their accuracy.

The heading on each page are similar:-

Flight number   (The Flight Identification Number)
Departure Time   (UK time)
Departure Airport
Arrival Time   (UK time)
Arrival Airport
Type of aircraft normally operating the flight
Day (s) of operation. (1 = Monday, 2 = Tuesday, etc.)
Notes

All the charter flights, and some scheduled services have the outbound and inbound details of their flights on one line, e.g. on page 22 'Britannia 136A' departs from East Midlands at 1930Hrs for Rhodes, returning from there as 'Britannia 136B' landing at East Midlands at 0445 Hrs The day of operation shown is the departure day from the UK, in this instance the flight leaves the UK on a Wednesday, returning on a Thursday.

T.T. & S.J. Williams,
"Greenfields",
126, Haven Road,
HAVERFORDWEST.
Pembs.
SA61 1DP

ISBN 0-9535339-0-5

AIRLINES   INDEX

63 -	FEDERAL EXPRESS	120 -	PAKISTAN INTERNATIONAL AIRWAYS
63 -	FINNAIR	154 -	PEGASUS HAVA TASIMACILIK
64 -	FLIGHTLINE	120 -	POLAR AIR CARGO
43 -	FLYING COLOURS	166 -	PREMAIR
76 -	GARUDA	121 -	QANTAS AIRWAYS
69 -	GB AIRWAYYS	121 -	QATAR AIRWAYS
70 -	GEMINI AIR CARGO	51 -	QUICK AIR SERVICE
71 -	GHANA AIRWAYS CORPORATION		
71 -	GILL AVIATION	122 -	REGIONAL AIRLINES
72 -	GO (BRITISH AIRWAYS)	122 -	RIGA AIRLINES
74 -	GULF AIR	121 -	ROYAL AIR FORCE
		104 -	ROYAL AIR MAROC
75 -	HAPAG LLOYD	122 -	ROYAL AIRLINES
75 -	HEAVYLIFT CARGO AIRLINES	32 -	ROYAL BRUNEI AIRLINES
75 -	HUNTING AIR CARGO	87 -	ROYAL JORDANIAN AIRLINES
75 -	IBERIA	123 -	ROYAL NEPAL AIRLINES
		123 -	RYANAIR
76 -	IBERWORLD		
76 -	ICEBIRD AIRLINE CO.	153 -	S.A.S.
76 -	ICELANDAIR	126 -	SABENA
76 -	IRAN NATIONAL AIRLINES	151 -	SABRE AIRWAYS
129 -	ISLE OF SCILLY SKYBUS	152 -	SAUDIA ARABIAN AIRLINES
76 -	ISRAIR	152 -	SERVICO ACOREANO DE TRANSPORTES
76 -	ISTANBUL AIRLINES	135 -	SINGAPORE AIRLINES
		150 -	SOUTH AFRICAN AIRWAYS
		154 -	SPANAIR
77 -	JAPAN AIRLINES	168 -	STAR AIR AS
77 -	JERSEY EUROPEAN AIRWAYS	150 -	STERLING EUROPEAN AIRWAYS
77 -	JUGOSLOVENSKI AEROTRANSPORT	150 -	STREAMLINE AVIATION
		150 -	SUCKLING AIRWAYS
88 -	KENYA AIRWAYS LTD.	154 -	SUDAN AIRWAYS
93 -	KLM	154 -	SUN-AIR OF SCANDINAVIA
160 -	KLM U.K.	155 -	SWISSAIR
95 -	KOREAN AIRLINES	156 -	SYRIAN ARAB AIRLINES
95 -	KUWAIT AIRWAYS CORPORATION		
		157 -	TAROM
95 -	LAUDA AIR	157 -	TAT EUROPEAN AIRLINES
96 -	LITHUANIAN AIRLINES	157 -	THAI AIRWAYS INTERNATIONAL
96 -	LOGANAIR	169 -	TITAN AIRWAYS
121 -	LOT	118 -	TNT INTERNATIONAL AVIATION
97 -	LTU LUFTTRANS UNTER GMBH	157 -	TOWER AIR
97 -	LUFTHANSA	156 -	TRANS MEDITERRANEAN AIRWAYS
100 -	LUXAIR	159 -	TRANSAERO AIRLINES
		159 -	TRANSAVIA HOLLAND B.V.
101 -	MACEDONIAN AIRLINES	158 -	TRANSBRASIL SA LINHAS AEREAS
101 -	MAERSK I/S	158 -	TRANSLIFT AIRWAYS LTD.
17 -	MAERSK AIR LTD.	9 -	TRANSPORTES AEREOS PORTUGUESES
101 -	MALAYSIAN AIRLINE SYSTEM	159 -	TUNIS AIR
101 -	MALEV	159 -	TURKISH AIRLINES
102 -	MANX AIRLINES	159 -	TWA TRANS WORLD AIRLINES
104 -	MARTINAIR HOLLAND BV	159 -	TYROLEAN AIRLINES
105 -	MERIDANA SPA		
40 -	MIDDLE EAST AIRLINES	165 -	U.S. AIR
112 -	MK AIR CARGO	164 -	UNITED AIRLINES
17 -	MNG AIRLINES	165 -	UNITED PARCEL SERVICE
113 -	MONARCH AIRLINES	166 -	UZBEKISTAN AIRWAYS
117 -	NAMIB AIR (PTY) LTD.	166 -	VARIG
118 -	NIPPON CARGO AIRLINES	166 -	VIRGIN ATLANTIC AIRWAYS
118 -	NORTH FLYING	74 -	VIRGIN EXPRESS (IRELAND)
118 -	NORTHWEST AIRLINES	17 -	VIRGIN EXPRESS AIRWAYS (BELGIUM)
119 -	NOUVELAIR AIR TUNISIE	166 -	VIRGIN EXPRESS AIRWAYS
		123 -	VLAAMSE LUCHTTRANSPORT
119 -	OLYMPIC AIRWAYS		
120 -	ONUR HAVA TASIMACILIK	168 -	WIDEROE'S FLYVESELSKAP
169 -	ORBI GEORGIAN AIRWAYS	168 -	WOODGATE AIR CHARTER
		168 -	YEMEN AIRWAYS

ADRIA — ADRIA AIRWAYS   JP/ADR   SLOVENIA

1626		LJUBLJANA	0915	HEATHROW	DC9/A320	1 3 56	ARR 1315 5
		LJUBLJANA	1910	HEATHROW	DC9/A320	2 4 7	
1627	1000	HEATHROW		LJUBLJANA	DC9/A320	1 3 56	DEP 1415 5
	2000	HEATHROW	1730	LJUBLJANA	DC9/A320	2 4 7	
1628		LJUBLJANA	1535	MANCHESTER	A.320	3	
1629	1620	MANCHESTER		LJUBLJANA	A.320	3	

AER ARANN — AER ARANN   RE/REA   EIRE

121F	2140	DUBLIN	2255	COVENTRY	SH-360	1234
122F	0130	COVENTRY	0245	DUBLIN	SH-360	2345

AEROFLOT — AEROFLOT   SU/AFL   RUSSIAN FEDERATION

241	0820	MOSCOW	1210	HEATHROW	A310/ILW	1234567	
242	1330	HEATHROW	1710	MOSCOW	A310/ILW	1234567	
243	0555	MOSCOW	0945	HEATHROW	IL-86/A310	5 7	1005/1345 7
244	0940	HEATHROW	1325	MOSCOW	IL-86/A310	4 7	1455/2035 7
245	1800	MOSCOW	2200	HEATHROW	B.737	3 5 7	
246	2245	HEATHROW	0245	MOSCOW	B.737	3 5 7	
247	0540	MOSCOW	0930	HEATHROW	IL-86	6	
248	1100	HEATHROW	1240	MOSCOW	IL-86	6	
301	0905	MOSCOW		TORONTO	A.310	2 5	
302		MONTREAL	0810	MOSCOW	A.310	3 6	
303	0910	MOSCOW		TORONTO	A.310	7	
304		TORONTO	0620	MOSCOW	A.310	1	
315	0740	MOSCOW		NEW YORK	B777/A310	1234567	
316		NEW YORK	0500	MOSCOW	B777/A310	1234567	
317	0805	MOSCOW		WASHINGTON	A.310	1 5	
318		WASHINGTON	0635	MOSCOW	A.310	2 6	
319	0735	ST.PETERSBERG		NEW YORK	A.310	5 7	
320		NEW YORK	0400	ST.PETERSBERG	A.310	1 6	
321	0715	MOSCOW		SEATTLE	IL.96/B767	12 456	
322		SEATTLE	1425	MOSCOW	IL.96/B767	23 567	
323	0855	MOSCOW		SEATTLE	IL.96/B767	3 5 7	DEP 1205 7
324		SAN FRANCISCO	1445	MOSCOW	IL.96/B767	1 6	
325	0925	MOSCOW	1350	SHANNON	A.310	5	TO MIAMI
326	1140	SHANNON	1550	MOSCOW	A.310	6	EX MIAMI
329	0835	MOSCOW	1250	SHANNON	B.767	1	TO CHICAGO
	1105	MOSCOW		CHICAGO	B.767	3 6	NON STOP
330	0830	SHANNON	1225	MOSCOW	B.767	4	EX CHICAGO
		CHICAGO	0955	MOSCOW	B.767	2 7	NON STOP
332		SEATTLE	0605	MOSCOW	IL-96	5	
333	2255	MOSCOW		HAVANA	IL-96	1	
334		HAVANA	0140	MOSCOW	IL-96	3	
335	2255	MOSCOW		HAVANA	IL-96	3 6	
336		HAVANA	1835	MOSCOW	IL-96	5	
341	2300	MOSCOW	0325	SHANNON	A.310	2	TO MIAMI
342	1030	SHANNON	1425	MOSCOW	A.310	4	EX MIAMI
581	1100	HEATHROW	1440	MOSCOW	A.310	2 5 7	DEP 0840 2
582	1555	MOSCOW	1945	HEATHROW	A.310	1 3 6	ARR 1805 3
637	1010	ST. PETERSBURG	1325	HEATHROW	TU-154	6	
638	1425	HEATHROW	1740	ST. PETERSBURG	TU-154	6	
661	1015	ST. PETERSBURG	1325	GATWICK	TU-154	3 5 7	
662	1425	GATWICK	1735	ST. PETERSBURG	TU-154	3 5 7	
909	1715	MOSCOW	2115	STANSTED	DC-10	3 5	
910	1025	STANSTED		MOSCOW	DC-10	4 6	

AEROLYON — AEROLYON   4Q/AEY   FRANCE

964	1100	TOULOUSE		POINTE-A-PITRE	DC-10	2
965		POINTE-A-PITRE	0620	MARSEILLES	DC-10	3
967		POINTE-A-PITRE	0705	LYON	DC-10	7

AEROMEXICO — AEROVIAS DE MEXICO S.A.   AM/AMX   MEXICO

003		MEXICO	1115	HEATHROW	B.767	2 5 7
004	1315	HEATHROW		MEXICO	B.767	2 5 7
005		MEXICO	0725	PARIS CDG	B.767	1234567
006	0930	PARIS CDG		MEXICO	B.767	1234567

8038	1245	PARIS CDG		MEXICO	A.340	1234567	
8039		MEXICO	1340	PARIS CDG	A.340	1234567	

AFRO   *AFFRETAIR   ZL/AFM   ZIMBABWE*

2	1450	AMSTERDAM	1600	GATWICK	DC-10	1	
	1900	GATWICK		HARARE	DC-10	1	
4	1450	AMSTERDAM	1600	GATWICK	DC-10	2	
	1900	GATWICK		HARARE	DC-10	2	
6	1450	AMSTERDAM	1600	GATWICK	DC-10	4	
	1900	GATWICK		HARARE	DC-10	4	
8	1450	AMSTERDAM	1600	GATWICK	DC-10	6	
	1900	GATWICK		HARARE	DC-10	6	

AIR ALGERIE   *AIR ALGERIA   AH/DAH   ALGERIA*

2054		ALGIERS	1345	HEATHROW	A300/B737	2 5 7	
2055	1450	HEATHROW		ALGIERS	A300/B737	2 5 7	
2218		ALGIERS	1800	HEATHROW	HERCULES	6	
2219	1900	HEATHROW		ALGIERS	HERCULES	6	
2626		ALGIERS	1130	GATWICK	B.737	3 5	
2627	1300	GATWICK		ALGIERS	B.737	3 5	DEP 1330 3

AIR CANADA   *AIR CANADA   AC/ACA   CANADA*

840		TORONTO	0915	MANCHESTER	B.767	1234567	
841	1100	MANCHESTER		TORONTO	B.767	1234567	
848		TORONTO	0745	HEATHROW	B.767	7	06.06-26.09
849	1415	HEATHROW		TORONTO	B.767	67	DEP 1145 6
850		CALGARY	1330	HEATHROW	A.340	1234567	
851	1520	HEATHROW		CALGARY	A.340	1234567	
854		VANCOUVER	1425	HEATHROW	B767/A340	1 34567	ARR 1215 1 4 6
		VANCOUVER	1305	HEATHROW	B.767	2	
855	1505	HEATHROW		VANCOUVER	B.767	1 3 56	DEP 2105 5
	1705	HEATHROW		VANCOUVER	B.767	2 4	
856		TORONTO	0650	HEATHROW	B.747	1234567	
857	1300	HEATHROW		TORONTO	B.747	1234567	
858		TORONTO	1205	HEATHROW	B.767	1234567	
859	2105	HEATHROW		TORONTO	B.767	1234567	DEP 2035 3
860		ST. JOHN'S	0820	HEATHROW	B.767	1234567	ARR 0650 257
861	1200	HEATHROW		ST. JOHN'S	B.767	1234567	
862		TORONTO	1010	HEATHROW	B747/B767	1234567	ARR 1105 3
863	1645	HEATHROW		TORONTO	B747/B767	1234567	
864		MONTREAL	0655	HEATHROW	A.340	1234567	
865 •	1255	HEATHROW		MONTREAL	A.340	1234567	
866		OTTAWA	0640	HEATHROW	B747/B767	1234567	
867	1255	HEATHROW		MONTREAL	B747/B767	1234567	
868		TORONTO	2105	HEATHROW	B.767	1234567	
869	0740	HEATHROW		TORONTO	B.767	1234567	
870		MONTREAL	0705	PARIS	A.340	1234567	
871	1040	PARIS		MONTREAL	A.340	1234567	
872		TORONTO	0620	FRANKFURT	A.340	1234567	
873	1210	FRANKFURT		TORONTO	A.340	1234567	
874		MONTREAL	0650	FRANKFURT	B.767	1234567	
875	1700	FRANKFURT		MONTREAL	B.767	1234567	
878		TORONTO	0825	ZURICH	B.767	1234567	
879	1150	ZURICH		TORONTO	B.767	1234567	
880		TORONTO	0725	PARIS	B.767	1234567	
881	1020	PARIS		TORONTO	B.767	1234567	
884		MONTREAL	1355	TEL AVIV	B.767	123 56	
885	2230	TEL AVIV		MONTREAL	B.767	123 56	
888		OTTAWA	0735	HEATHROW	B.767	1234567	0905 2 / 1005 5
889	1445	HEATHROW		OTTAWA	B.767	1234567	1155 2 / 1605 5
896		VANCOUVER	1025	HEATHROW	A340/B767	1234567	
	1145	HEATHROW		DELHI	A.340	2 4 67	
897		DELHI	1200	HEATHROW	A.340	1 3 5 7	
	1330	HEATHROW		VANCOUVER	A340/B767	1234567	

3

AIR CHINA

AIR CHINA   CA/CCA   CHINA

937		BEIJING	1750	HEATHROW	B.747	2 4 7	
938	2030	HEATHROW		SHARJAH	B.747	2 4 7	

AIR EUROPE

AIR EUROPE SPA   PE/AEL   ITALY

2906	0925	ROME		HAVANA	B.767	1	
2907		HAVANA	0920	ROME	B.767	2	
2908	1300	MILAN		HAVANA	B.767	2 7	DEP 1635 2
2909		HAVANA	1125	MILAN	B.767	1 3	ARR 1530 3
2928	1230	MILAN		HAVANA	B.767	4	
2929		HAVANA	1355	MILAN	B.767	5	

AIRFRANS

AIR FRANCE   AF/AFR   FRANCE

001		NEW YORK	1645	PARIS	CONCORDE	1234567	
002	1000	PARIS		NEW YORK	CONCORDE	1234567	
003		NEW YORK	0525	PARIS	B.747	1234567	
004	0925	PARIS		NEW YORK	B.747	1234567	
006	1215	PARIS		NEW YORK	B.777	1234567	
007		NEW YORK	0750	PARIS	B.747	1234567	
008	1800	PARIS		NEW YORK	B.747	1234567	
009		NEW YORK	1050	PARIS	B.747	1234567	
010	1500	PARIS		NEW YORK	B.747	1234567	
011		NEW YORK	0530	PARIS	B.777	1234567	
026	1530	PARIS CDG		WASHINGTON	A.310	1234567	
027		WASHINGTON	1050	PARIS CDG	A.310	1234567	
028	1210	PARIS		WASHINGTON	B.777	1234567	
029		WASHINGTON	0710	PARIS	B.777	1234567	
033		HOUSTON	0750	PARIS	B.757	1234567	
036	0930	PARIS		HOUSTON	B.777	1234567	
051		CHICAGO	1035	PARIS	B.767	1234567	
054	1505	PARIS		CHICAGO	B.767	1234567	
056	0915	PARIS CDG		CHICAGO	B.767	1234567	
057		CHICAGO	0745	PARIS CDG	B.767	1234567	
061		LOS ANGELES	1340	PARIS	B.747	1234567	
062	1220	PARIS		LOS ANGELES	B.747	12	
068	1540	PARIS CDG		LOS ANGELES	B.747	3456	
070	1840	PARIS		LOS ANGELES	B.747	1 567	
071		LOS ANGELES	1555	PARIS	B.747	1234567	
083		SAN FRANCISCO	1300	PARIS	B.747	1234567	
084	1225	PARIS		SAN FRANCISCO	B.747	1234567	
090	0945	PARIS		MIAMI	B.747	12 7	
091		MIAMI	1255	PARIS CDG	B.747	1 67	
092	1540	PARIS CDG		MIAMI	B.747	1234567	
095		MIAMI	0715	PARIS CDG	B.747	5	
272	2230	PARIS CDG		TOKYO	B.747	1234 6	
273		TOKYO	0325	PARIS	B.747	12 67	
274	2215	PARIS		TOKYO	B.747	1234567	
275		TOKYO	1610	PARIS	B.747	1234567	
276	1220	PARIS		TOKYO	B.747	4	
288	1505	PARIS CDG		TOKYO	B.747	5	
289		TOKYO	1710	PARIS CDG	B.747	1 34567	
291		OSAKA	1600	PARIS	A.340	234567	
292	1210	PARIS		OSAKA	A.340	1234567	
300	1455	PARIS CDG		ATLANTA	A.340	1234567	
307		ATLANTA	1050	PARIS CDG	A.340	1234567	
321		BOSTON	1045	PARIS CDG	B.767	1234567	
344	1230	PARIS		MONTREAL	B.747	1234567	
345		MONTREAL	0530	PARIS	B.747	1234567	21.06-11.09
346	1545	PARIS		MONTREAL	B.747	1234567	
347		MONTREAL	0745	PARIS	B.747	1234567	
358	1220	PARIS		TORONTO	A.340	1234567	
359		TORONTO	0750	PARIS	A.340	1234567	
438	1245	PARIS CDG		MEXICO	B.747	1234567	
439	2055	MEXICO	1340	PARIS CDG	A.340	2 567	
470	0925	PARIS CDG		CARACAS	A.340	23 67	
471		CARACAS	0730	PARIS CDG	A.340	1 3 67	
1070	0605	PARIS CDG	0710	HEATHROW	A.320	1234567	
1071	0815	HEATHROW	0920	PARIS CDG	A.320	1234567	

Flight	Dep	From	Arr	To	Aircraft	Days	Notes
1170	0720	PARIS CDG	0830	HEATHROW	A.320	123456	
1171	0915	HEATHROW	1020	PARIS	A.320	123456	
1180	1805	PARIS CDG	1905	LONDON CITY	BAE-146	12345	
1181	1935	LONDON CITY	2035	PARIS CDG	BAE-146	12345	
1270	0820	PARIS	0925	HEATHROW	B.737	12345	
1271	1015	HEATHROW	1120	PARIS	B.737	12345	
1368	1935	PARIS CDG	2100	MANCHESTER	A.320	1234567	
1369	0640	MANCHESTER		PARIS CDG	A.320	1234567	
1370	0920	PARIS CDG	1025	HEATHROW	A.320	1234567	
1371	1115	HEATHROW	1220	PARIS CDG	A.320	1234567	
1388	1945	PARIS CDG	2130	EDINBURGH	BAE-146	1234567	JERSEY EUR. A/C
1389	1725	EDINBURGH	1910	PARIS CDG	BAE-146	1234567	JERSEY EUR. A/C
1470	1020	PARIS CDG	1110	HEATHROW	A.320	7	
1471	1215	HEATHROW	1320	PARIS CDG	A.320	7	
1560	0700	PARIS CDG	0845	DUBLIN	BAE-146	1234567	CITY-JET A/C
1570	1110	PARIS CDG	1215	HEATHROW	A.320	12345 7	
1571	1305	HEATHROW	1410	PARIS CDG	A.320	1234567	1715/1820 6
1660	1000	CDG	1145	DUBLIN	BAE-146	1234567	CITY-JET A/C
1661	0640	DUBLIN	0830	PARIS CDG	BAE-146	1234567	CITY JET A/C
1668		PARIS CDG	0815	MANCHESTER	A.320	1234567	
1669	0915	MANCHESTER		PARIS CDG	A.320	1234567	
1670	1205	PARIS	1310	HEATHROW	A320/B737	1234567	
1671	1400	HEATHROW	1410	PARIS CDG	B.737	1234567	
1680	0650	PARIS CDG	0750	LONDON	BAE-146	12345	
1681	0815	LONDON CITY	0915	PARIS CDG	BAE-146	12345	
1864	0950	TOULOUSE	1150	BIRMINGHAM	BAE-146	2345	JERSEY EUR. A/C
	1020	TOULOUSE	1220	BIRMINGHAM	BAE-146	1	JERSEY EUR. A/C
1867	1230	BIRMINGHAM	1435	TOULOUSE	BAE-146	2345 7	JERSEY EUR. A/C
	1300	BIRMINGHAM	1605	TOULOUSE	BAE-146	1	JERSEY EUR. A/C
1868	1515	TOULOUSE	1715	BIRMINGHAM	BAE-146	7	JERSEY EUR. A/C
1870	1405	PARIS	1510	HEATHROW	A.320	1234567	
1871	1600	HEATHROW	1705	PARIS	A.320	1234567	
1970	1505	PARIS	1610	HEATHROW	A.320	1234567	
1971	1700	HEATHROW	1805	PARIS CDG	A.320	1234567	1815/1920 1 4
1988	0900	PARIS CDG	1045	EDINBURGH	BAE-146	1234567	JERSEY EUR. A/C
1989	0535	EDINBURGH	0710	PARIS CDG	BAE-146	1234567	JERSEY EUR. A/C
2070	1600	PARIS CDG	1710	HEATHROW	A.320	123456	
2071	1800	HEATHROW	1905	PARIS	A.320	123456	
2170	1705	PARIS CDG	1810	HEATHROW	A.320	1234567	
2171	1915	HEATHROW	2020	PARIS	A.320	1234567	
2180	1100	PARIS CDG	1200	LONDON CITY	BAE-146	12345	
2181	1245	LONDON CITY	1345	PARIS CDG	BAE-146	12345	
2268		PARIS CDG	1325	MANCHESTER	A.320	1234567	
2269	1515	MANCHESTER		PARIS CDG	A.320	1234567	
2270	1815	PARIS	1920	HEATHROW	A.320	1234567	
2271	2015	HEATHROW	2120	PARIS	A.320	1234567	2030/2135 6
2370	1910	PARIS	2020	HEATHROW	A.320	1234567	
2460	1500	PARIS CDG	1645	DUBLIN	BAE-146	1234567	CITY-JET A/C
2461	1225	DUBLIN	1405	PARIS CDG	BAE-146	1234567	CITY-JET A/C
2471	0655	HEATHROW	0800	PARIS CDG	A.320	1234567	
2488	1430	PARIS CDG	1615	EDINBURGH	BAE-146	12345 7	JERSEY EUR A/C
	1340	PARIS CDG	1525	EDINBURGH	BAE-146	6	JERSEY EUR. A/C
2489	1140	EDINBURGH	1325	PARIS CDG	BAE-146	1234567	JERSEY EUR. A/C
2561	1855	DUBLIN	2040	PARIS CDG	BAE-146	1234567	CITY-JET A/C
2568		PARIS CDG	1620	MANCHESTER	B.737	1234567	
2569	1715	MANCHESTER		PARIS CDG	B.737	1234567	
2570	1845	PARIS CDG	1950	HEATHROW	B.737	1234567	
2571	2045	HEATHROW	2150	PARIS CDG	B.737	1234567	
2580	1435	PARIS CDG	1535	LONDON city	BAE-146	12345	
2581	1620	LONDON CITY	1720	PARIS CDG	BAE-146	12345	
2670	0650	PARIS CDG	0755	HEATHROW	A.320	123456	
2671	0845	HEATHROW	0950	PARIS CDG	A.320	123456	
2760	1955	PARIS CDG	2140	DUBLIN	BAE-146	1234567	CITY JET A/C
2761	1735	DUBLIN	1905	PARIS CDG	BAE-146	1234567	CITY-JET A/C
2768	1745	PARIS CDG	1910	MANCHESTER	B.737	1234567	
2769	2010	MANCHESTER	2035	PARIS CDG	B.737	1234567	
3212	0600	STRASBOURG	0730	LONDON CITY	?	123456	
3213	0755	LONDON CITY	0925	STRASBOURG	?	123456	

3214	1130	STRASBOURG	1300	LONDON CITY	?	12345	
3215	1445	LONDON CITY	1615	STRASBOURG	?	12345	
3216	1700	STRASBOURG	1830	LONDON CITY	BAE-146	12345 7	
3217	1900	LONDON CITY	2030	STRASBOURG	?	12345 7	
3220	1130	NICE	1330	HEATHROW	B.737	1234567	
3221	0850	HEATHROW	1045	NICE	B.737	1234567	
3222	1910	NICE	2110	HEATHROW	B.737	1234567	1645/1845 6
3223	1630	HEATHROW	1825	NICE	B.737	1234567	1405/1600 6
3415		FORT DE FRANCE	0750	PARIS ORLY	B.747	12345667	
3450	1540	PARIS CDG		FORT DE FRANCE	B.747	123 567	
3453		FORT DE FRANCE	1050	PARIS CDG	B.747	1234567	
3520	1100	PARIS ORLY		POINTE-A-PITRE	B.747	1234567	
3523		POINTE-A-PITRE	0645	PARIS ORLY	B.747	1234567	
3527		POINTE A PITRE	0555	PARIS ORLY	B.747	1234567	
3531		POINTE A PITRE	1035	PARIS CDG	B.747	123 56	
3532	1505	PARIS CDG		POINTE-A-PITRE	B.747	12 4567	
3539		ST. DENIS	0515	PARIS ORLY	B.747	1234567	
3694	0950	PARIS CDG		ST.MAARTEN	B.747	1 3	
		SAN DOMINGO	0705	PARIS CDG	B.747	4 6	
3696	0945	PARIS CDG		ST. MAARTEN	B.747	2 4 6	
		SANTO DOMINGO	0700	PARIS CDG	B.747	3 5 7	
3698	0945	PARIS CDG		ST. MAARTEN	B.747	7	
3699		SANTO DOMINGO	0700	PARIS CDG	B.747	1	
5100	1000	PARIS CDG	1130	NEWCASTLE	F-100	123456	
5101	0700	NEWCASTLE	0840	PARIS CDG	F-100	123456	
5102	1425	PARIS CDG	1555	NEWCASTLE	F-100	12345 7	
5103	1205	NEWCASTLE	1345	PARIS CDG	F-100	12345 7	
5104	1910	PARIS CDG	2040	NEWCASTLE	F-100	12345 7	
5105	1640	NEWCASTLE	1815	PARIS CDG	F-100	12345 7	
5134	1020	PARIS CDG	1210	TEESSIDE	BAE-146	123456	
5135	0710	TEESSIDE	0910	PARIS CDG	BAE-146	123456	
5136	1525	PARIS CDG	1725	TEESSIDE	BAE-146	12345 7	
5137	1240	TEESSIDE	1430	PARIS CDG	BAE-146	12345 7	
5144	1015	PARIS CDG	1200	HUMBERSIDE	BAE-146	123456	
5145	0735	HUMBERSIDE	0920	PARIS CDG	BAE-146	123456	
5146	1525	PARIS CDG	1710	HUMBERSIDE	BAE-146	12345 7	
5147	1240	HUMBERSIDE	1445	PARIS CDG	BAE-146	12345 7	
5200	0650	PARIS CDG	0805	BIRMINGHAM	BAE-146	123456	JERSEY EUR.A/C
5201	0640	BIRMINGHAM	0755	PARIS CDG	BAE-146	1234567	JERSEY EUR.A.C
5202	0900	PARIS CDG	1015	BIRMINGHAM	BAE-146	1234567	JERSEY EUR.A.C
5203	0900	BIRMINGHAM	1015	PARIS CDG	BAE-146	123456	JERSEY EUR.A/C
5204	1310	PARIS CDG	1425	BIRMINGHAM	BAE-146	123456	JERSEY EUR.A/C
5205	1220	BIRMINGHAM	1340	PARIS CDG	BAE-146	1234567	JERSEY EUR.A/C
5206	1430	PARIS CDG	1545	BIRMINGHAM	BAE-146	1234567	JERSEY EUR.A/C
5207	1525	BIRMINGHAM	1640	PARIS CDG	BAE-146	12345 7	JERSEY EUR.A/C
5208	1805	PARIS CDG	1920	BIRMINGHAM	BAE-146	12345 7	JERSEY EUR.A/C
5209	1825	BIRMINGHAM	1940	PARIS CDG	BAE-146	1234567	JERSEY EUR.A/C
5210	2015	PARIS CDG	2130	BIRMINGHAM	BAE-146	12345 7	JERSEY EUR.A/C
5211	1955	BIRMINGHAM	2110	PARIS CDG	BAE-146	12345 7	JERSEY EUR.A/C
5222	0610	PARIS CDG	0855	GLASGOW	EMB-145	1234567	JERSEY EUR. A/C
5223	0910	GLASGOW	1050	PARIS	EMB-145	1234567	JERSEY EUR A/C
5224	1145	PARIS CDG	1330	GLASGOW	EMB-145	1234567	JERSEY EUR. A/C
5225	1435	GLASGOW	1615	PARIS CDG	EMB-145	1234567	JERSEY EUR. A/C
5226	1655	PARIS CDG	1840	GLASGOW	EMB-145	1234567	JERSEY EUR. A/C
5227	1935	GLASGOW	2115	PARIS CDG	EMB-145	1234567	JERSEY EUR. A/C
5238	0630	TOULOUSE	0840	HEATHROW	BAE-146	1234567	JERSEY EUR.A/C
5239	0920	HEATHROW	1110	TOULOUSE	BAE-146	1234567	JERSEY EUR.A/C
5240	1150	TOULOUSE	1345	HEATHROW	BAE-146	1234567	JERSEY EUR.A/C
5241	1505	HEATHROW	1655	TOULOUSE	BAE-146	1234567	JERSEY EUR.A/C
5242	1735	TOULOUSE	1930	HEATHROW	BAE-146	1234567	JERSEY EUR.A/C
5243	2010	HEATHROW	2200	TOULOUSE	BAE-146	1234567	JERSEY EUR.A/C
5244	0600	LYON	0755	HEATHROW	BAE-146	123456	JERSEY EUR.A/C
5245	0850	HEATHROW	1030	LYON	BAE-146	123456	JERSEY EUR.A/C
5246	1135	LYON	1320	HEATHROW	BAE-146	1234567	JERSEY EUR.A/C
5247	1410	HEATHROW	1555	LYON	BAE-146	1234567	JERSEY EUR.A/C
5248	1645	LYON	1835	HEATHROW	BAE-146	12345 7	JERSEY EUR.A/C
5249	1915	HEATHROW	1915	LYON	BAE-146	12345 7	JERSEY EUR.A/C
5850	0610	NANTES	0715	GATWICK	CANADAIR	123456	

Flight	Dep	From	Arr	To	Aircraft	Days	Notes
5851	0755	GATWICK	0905	NANTES	CANADAIR	123456	
5852	1125	NANTES	1230	GATWICK	CANADAIR	1234567	
5853	1330	GATWICK	1440	NANTES	CANADAIR	1234567	
5854	1740	NANTES	1845	GATWICK	CANADAIR	1234567	
5855	1925	GATWICK	2035	NANTES	CANADAIR	1234567	
5856	0800	GATWICK	0845	LE HAVRE	BAE-146	123456	
5857	0645	LE HAVRE	0730	GATWICK	BAE-146	123456	
5858	1930	GATWICK	2020	LE HAVRE	BAE-146	12345 7	
5859	1705	LE HAVRE	1750	GATWICK	BAE-146	12345 7	
5865	0700	PARIS CDG	0815	SOUTHAMPTON	ATR-42	123456	
5866	0845	SOUTHAMPTON	0955	PARIS CDG	BAE-146	123456	
5867	1650	PARIS CDG	1800	SOUTHAMPTON	ATR-42	12345 7	
5868	1825	SOUTHAMPTON	1935	PARIS CDG	BAE-146	12345 7	
6400	1910	PARIS		CHICAGO	B.747	3	
6402	1515	PARIS		MONTREAL	B.747	3	
6403		MONTREAL	2030	PARIS	B.747	7	
6404	1515	PARIS		MONTREAL	B.747	6	
6405		CHICAGO	1410	PRESTWICK	B.747	1	
	1610	PRESTWICK		PARIS CDG	B.747	1	
6406	2100	PARIS CDG		CHICAGO	B.747	6	
6407		CHICAGO	1405	PARIS CDG	B.747	4	
6414	1730	PARIS CDG		NEW YORK	B.747	2	
6416	0605	PARIS CDG		NEW YORK	B.747	3	
6417		MONTREAL	1435	PARIS CDG	B.747	4	
6418	1635	PARIS		MIAMI	B.747	6	
6421		NEW YORK	1050	PARIS CDG	B.747	3	
6422	0800	PARIS CDG		ATLANTA	B.747	1	
6423		ATLANTA	0415	PARIS CDG	B.747	2	
6428	1825	PARIS CDG		CHICAGO	B.747	2	
6429		CHICAGO	1405	PARIS CDG	B.747	3	
6430	1730	PARIS CDG		NEW YORK	B.747	5	
6433		NEW YORK	1050	PARIS	B.747	5	
6434	1715	PARIS		NEW YORK	B.747	6	
6435		HOUSTON	2355	PARIS	B.747	7	
6443		MONTREAL	2230	PARIS	B.747	7	
6450	1925	PARIS CDG		CHICAGO	B.747	7	
6452	1820	PARIS ORLY		CHICAGO	B.747	4	
6453		CHICAGO	1310	PRESTWICK	B.747	5	
	1440	PRESTWICK	1620	PARIS CDG	B.747	5	
6457	1535	SHANNON	1720	PARIS	B.747	6	EX. CHICAGO
6458	1925	PARIS ORLY		CHICAGO	B.747	5	
6467		CHICAGO	1700	PARIS CDG	B.747	7	
6491		NEW YORK	1050	PARIS	B.747	7	
6492	1730	PARIS		NEW YORK	B.747	6	
6495		MONTREAL	2220	PARIS CDG	B.747	4	
6497		NEW YORK	0905	PRESTWICK	B.747	1	
	1205	PRESTWICK	1345	PARIS CDG	B.747	1	
6498	1730	PARIS		NEW YORK	B.747	7	
6700	1720	PARIS CDG		FAIRBANKS	B.747	2	
6760	1720	PARIS CDG		FAIRBANKS	B.747	3	
6765		ANCHORAGE	0700	PARIS CDG	B.747	7	
6766	1000	PARIS CDG		ANCHORAGE	B.747	7	
6768	1720	PARIS CDG		FAIRBANKS	B.747	1	
6786	1815	PARIS CDG		FAIRBANKS	B.747	4	
6838	0910	PARIS CDG		POINTE-A-PITRE	DC-10	5	
6843		POINTE-A-PITRE	1215	STANSTED	DC-10	6	
	1415	STANSTED	1520	PARIS	DC-10	6	
6844	0720	PARIS CDG		POINTE-A-PITRE	B.747	3	
6883		POINTE-A-PITRE	1825	STANSTED	DC-10	4	
	2015	STANSTED	2120	PARIS	DC-10	4	

AIR HONG KONG			*AHK AIR HONG KONG*	*LD/AHK*	*HONG KONG.*		
1		HONG KONG	1030	MANCHESTER	B.747	1234567	VIA DUBAI
2	1210	MANCHESTER		HONG KONG	B.747	1234567	VIA BRUSSELS

AIR INDIA — AIR INDIA AI/AIC INDIA

Flight	Dep	From	Arr	To	Aircraft	Days
101		BOMBAY	1130	HEATHROW	B.747	2 456
	1315	HEATHROW		NEW YORK	B.747	2 456
102		NEW YORK	0800	HEATHROW	B.747	3 567
	0945	HEATHROW		BOMBAY	B.747	3 567
111		DELHI	1130	HEATHROW	B.747	1 3 7
	1315	HEATHROW		NEW YORK	B.747	1 3 7
112		NEW YORK	0800	HEATHROW	B.747	12 4
	0945	HEATHROW		BOMBAY	B.747	2 4 6
122		CHICAGO	1015	HEATHROW	B.747	3
	1200	HEATHROW		DELHI	B.747	3
123		BOMBAY	1015	HEATHROW	B.747	2
	1205	HEATHROW		CHICAGO	B.747	2
124		CHICAGO	1105	HEATHROW	B.747	1
	1240	HEATHROW		BOMBAY	B.747	1
125		BOMBAY	1425	HEATHROW	B.747	7
	1610	HEATHROW		CHICAGO	B.747	7
128		CHICAGO	1015	HEATHROW	B.747	6
	1200	HEATHROW		BOMBAY	B.747	6
129		BOMBAY	1015	HEATHROW	B.747	5
	1200	HEATHROW	1310	CHICAGO	B.747	5
130	1430	MANCHESTER	1705	ROME	A.310	1
131	1020	ROME	1305	MANCHESTER	A.310	1
132	1715	MANCHESTER	1950	ROME	A.310	6
133	1315	ROME	1600	MANCHESTER	A.310	6
134	1430	MANCHESTER	1705	ROME	A.310	3
135	1020	ROME	1305	MANCHESTER	A.310	3
138	1430	MANCHESTER	1705	ROME	A.310	5
139	1020	ROME	1305	MANCHESTER	A.310	5
150		CHICAGO	1040	FRANKFURT	B.747	6
151	1515	FRANKFURT		CHICAGO	B.747	6
152	2150	CHICAGO	1305	FRANKFURT	B.747	1
153	1405	FRANKFURT		CHICAGO	B.747	1

AIRKIRBIS — KIBRIS TURK HAVA KYV TURKEY

Flight	Dep	From	Arr	To	Aircraft	Days	Notes
801		ISTANBUL	1230	STANSTED	A.310	5	-02.07 / 01.10-
		ISTANBUL	1530	STANSTED	B.727	5	09.07-24.09
802	1400	STANSTED		ISTANBUL	A.310	5	-02.07 / 01.10-
	1700	STANSTED		ISTANBUL	B.727	5	09.07-24.09
941		ANTALYA	1230	STANSTED	A310/B727	3 7	
942	1400	STANSTED		ANTALYA	A310/B727	3 7	
945		ADB	1015	STANSTED	B.727	1	19.07-20.09
946	1145	STANSTED		ADB	B.727	1	19.07-20.09
947		ANTALYA	1230	STANSTED	A310/B727	456	24.06-25.09
948	1400	STANSTED		ANTALYA	A310/B727	456	24.06-25.09
949		DALAMAN	1155	STANSTED	B.727	3 7	ARR 1830 7
950	1345	STANSTED		DALAMAN	B.727	3 7	DEP 2015 7
4801		ISTANBUL	1230	STANSTED	A.310	2	
4802	1400	STANSTED		ISTANBUL	A.310	2	

AIR LANKA — AIR LANKA UL/ALK SRI LANKA

Flight	Dep	From	Arr	To	Aircraft	Days	Notes
503		COLOMBO	1540	HEATHROW	A.340	3 5	ARR 1540 5
504	2130	HEATHROW	1505	AMSTERDAM	A.340	3 5	DEP 2205 5
505		COLOMBO	0925	HEATHROW	A.340	4567	ARR 1200 4
		COLOMBO	1335	HEATHROW	A.340	12	ARR 1450 1
506	1055	HEATHROW		COLOMBO	A.340	567	DEP 1150 56
	1400	HEATHROW		COLOMBO	A.340	2 4	DEP 1515 2
	1705	HEATHROW		COLOMBO	A.340	1	

AIR LIBERTE — AIR LIBERTE IJ/LIB FRANCE

Flight	Dep	From	Arr	To	Aircraft	Days
800	1305	PARIS ORLY		POINTE-A-PITRE	DC-10	1 3 7
800		POINTE-A-PITRE	0910	PARIS ORLY	DC-10	12 4
803	1230	PARIS ORLY		POINTE-A-PITRE	DC-10	456
804		POINTE-A-PITRE	0650	PARIS ORLY	DC-10	567
811	1210	PARIS ORLY		FORT DE FRANCE	DC-10	4 6
815	1305	PARIS ORLY		FORT DE FRANCE	DC-10	2
		POINTE-A-PITRE	0910	PARIS ORLY	DC-10	3

857	2355	TOULOUSE		ST.DENIS	DC-10	4	
880	1240	PARIS ORLY		FORT-DE-FRANCE	DC-10	5	
		ST. LUCIA	0845	PARIS ORLY	DC-10	6	

AIR MALTA

AIR MALTA   KM/AMC   MALTA

??	2015	CARDIFF	1930	MALTA	B.737	2	
070		MALTA	2030	BRISTOL	B.737	4	
	2115	BRISTOL	2200	EAST MIDLANDS	B.737	4	
071	2245	EAST MIDLANDS		MALTA	B.737	4	-30.09
100		MALTA	0945	HEATHROW	A320/B737	1234567	
101	1045	HEATHROW		MALTA	A320/B737	1234567	
102		MALTA	1935	HEATHROW	A320/B737	1234567	ARR 1825 5
103	2045	HEATHROW		MALTA	A320/B737	1234567	DEP 1920 5
106		MALTA	1910	HEATHROW	B.737	5	23.07-03.09
107	2100	HEATHROW		MALTA	B.737	5	23.07-03.09
116		MALTA	1030	GATWICK	B.737	1234567	
117	1130	GATWICK		MALTA	B.737	1234567	
118		MALTA	1910	GATWICK	A320/B737	1 456	ARR 2125 56
119	2000	GATWICK		MALTA	B.737	1 456	DEP 2230 56
122		MALTA	2215	GATWICK	B.737	6	26.06-25.09
123	2300	GATWICK		MALTA	B.737	6	22.06-25.09
138		MALTA	1005	MANCHESTER	B.737	567	ARR 1120 6
139	1100	MANCHESTER		MALTA	B.737	567	DEP 1205 6
146		MALTA	2355	MANCHESTER	B.737	5	23.07-03.09
147	0040	MANCHESTER		MALTA	B.737	6	23.07-03.09
154		MALTA	2045	MANCHESTER	B.737	6	
155	2135	MANCHESTER		MALTA	B.737	6	
164		MALTA	1050	STANSTED	B.737	2 4	ARR 1640 4
165	1135	STANSTED		MALTA	B.737	2 4	DEP 1735 4
172		MALTA	0110	BIRMINGHAM	B.737	2	27.07-07.09
		MALTA	1135	BIRMINGHAM	B.737	4 7	ARR 0915 7
173	1220	BIRMINGHAM		MALTA	B.737	4 7	DEP 1005 7
	0155	BIRMINGHAM		MALTA	B.737	2	27.07-07.09
194		MALTA	1825	GLASGOW	B.737	4 7	ARR 1840 4
195	1910	GLASGOW		MALTA	B.737	4 7	DEP 1925 4

EVEN NUMBERS - FLIGHTS INTO THE U.K.   UNEVEN NUMBERS - FLIGHTS LEAVING THE U.K.

3118/9	2130	GATWICK	2045	MALTA	B.737	2		20.07-05.10
3120/1	2120	GATWICK	2030	MALTA	B.737		6	
3124/5	2155	GATWICK	2100	MALTA	B.737	2		20.07-05.10
3126/7	2355	GATWICK	2310	MALTA	B.737		6	17.07-02.10
3128/9	2330	GATWICK	2245	MALTA	B.737	4		22.07-30.09
3130/1	0105	GATWICK	0020	MALTA	B.737		7	-03.10
3134/5	0015	GATWICK	2330	MALTA	B.737		6	17.07-02.10
4136/7	2130	MANCHESTER	2045	MALTA	B.737	1		
4138/9	0005	MANCHESTER	2320	MALTA	A.320		6	
4146/7	0215	MANCHESTER	0130	MALTA	B.737		7	27.06-03.10
4152/3	2045	MANCHESTER	2000	MALTA	B.737	2		20.07-28.09
	0140	MANCHESTER	0055	MALTA	B.737		7	25.07-26.09
5158/9	2105	EDINBURGH	2020	MALTA	B.737	1		26.07-02.08
5159/0	VAR	LIVERPOOL	VAR	MALTA	B.737	1		
5160/1	1950	ABERDEEN	1905	MALTA	B.737	1		07.06-27.09
5168/9	VAR	NORWICH	VAR	MALTA	B.737		5	
5170/1	0150	BIRMINGHAM	0105	MALTA	B.737	1		19.07-27.09
5174/5	1045	BIRMINGHAM	1000	MALTA	B.737		5	
5186/7	0140	GLASGOW	0055	MALTA	B.737		7	
5192/3	1045	GLASGOW	1000	MALTA	B.737	1		
5194/5	2000	GLASGOW	1915	MALTA	B.737	2		
5202/3	1215	LEEDS	1130	MALTA	B.737	2		
5214/5	0915	EDINBURGH	0830	MALTA	B.737	2		6.7-27.7

AIRMAURITIUS

AIR MAURITIUS   MK/MAU   MAURITIUS

42		MAURITIUS	0730	HEATHROW	A.340	5 7	
53	1700	HEATHROW		MAURITIUS	A.340	5 7	
66		MAURITIUS	1750	MANCHESTER	B.767	1	
77	1935	MANCHESTER		MAURITIUS	B.767	1	

AIR MOLDOVA

AIR MOLDOVA   9U/MLD   REPUBLIC OF MOLDOVA

885		KISHINEV	1140	GATWICK	TU-134	4 7	ARR 1500 7
886	1225	GATWICK		KISHINEV	TU-134	4 7	DEP 1400 4

AIR PORTUGAL

TRANSPORTES AEREOS PORTUGUESES E.P.   TP/TAP   PORTUGAL

5151	0830	HEATHROW	1100	LISBON	A.320	1234567	
5152	0810	LISBON	1045	HEATHROW	A.340	1234567	
5153	1150	HEATHROW	1420	LISBON	A.340	1234567	
5156	1435	LISBON	1710	HEATHROW	A31/320/340	1234567	
5157	1810	HEATHROW	2045	LISBON	A310/320/340	1234567	
5168	1910	LISBON	2145	HEATHROW	A.320	1234567	
5171	0640	HEATHROW	0925	FARO	A.320	1234567	
5178	1820	FARO	2105	HEATHROW	A.320	1234567	
5182	1030	OPORTO	1245	HEATHROW	A.320	1234567	
5183	1345	HEATHROW	1600	OPORTO	A.320	1234567	
5186	1600	OPORTO	1820	HEATHROW	A.320	1234567	
5187	1920	HEATHROW	2140	OPORTO	A.320	1234567	2000/2220 5
5194	1150	FUNCHAL	1535	HEATHROW	B.737	4 7	
5195	1630	HEATHROW	2010	FUNCHAL	B.737	4 7	
9282	0640	LISBON	1005	DUBLIN	A.340	6	
9283	1105	DUBLIN	1440	FARO	A.340	6	
9284	1400	FARO	1735	DUBLIN	A.340	6	
9285	1835	DUBLIN	2200	LISBON	A.340	6	

AIRSCAN

AIR SCANDIC   SCY   U.K.

752		TENERIFE	1650	BIRMINGHAM	A.300	5	
753	1805	BIRMINGHAM		TENERIFE	A.300	5	

AIR TOULOUSE

AIR TOULOUSE   TLE   FRANCE

506		NANTES	1910	SHANNON	B.737	6	03.07-04.09
507	1955	SHANNON		NANTES	B.737	6	03.07-04.09
580		TOULOUSE	0700	SHANNON	B.737	6	-25.09
581	0915	SHANNON		TOULOUSE	B.737	6	-25.09
582		BORDEAUX	1230	SHANNON	B.737	6	03.07-28.09
583	1320	SHANNON		BORDEAUX	B.737	6	03.07-28.09
588		LYON	0900	CORK	B.737	5	
589	1000	CORK		TOULOUSE	B.737	5	

AIR UKRAINE

AIR UKRAINE   PS/UKR   UKRAINE

501		KIEV	1100	GATWICK	B.737	1 34 7	
502	1230	GATWICK		KIEV	B.737	1 34 67	
1551		LVOV, UKRAINE	0840	MANCHESTER	B.737	6	3 WEEKLY
1552	2100	MANCHESTER		LVOV	B.737	5	3 WEEKLY
1553	1915	GATWICK	2005	MANCHESTER	B.737	5	25.06-27.08
1554	0945	MANCHESTER	1035	GATWICK	B.737	6	26.06-28.08
2551		IVANO-FRANKOVSK	0840	MANCHESTER	B.737	6	3 WEEKLY
2552	2100	MANCHESTER		IVANO-FRANKOVSK	B.737	5	3 WEEKLY
2553	1915	GATWICK	2005	MANCHESTER	B.737	5	11.06-13.08
2554	0945	MANCHESTER	1035	GATWICK	B.737	6	12.06-14.08

AIR ZIMBABWE

AIR ZIMBABWE   UM/AZW   ZIMBABWE

720		HARARE	0415	GATWICK	B.767	5
721	0540	GATWICK		HARARE	B.767	5
722		HARARE	1710	GATWICK	B.767	7
723	2000	GATWICK		HARARE	B.767	7
724		HARARE	0740	GATWICK	B.767	2 6
725	1900	GATWICK		HARARE	B.767	2 4 6
728		HARARE	0740	GATWICK	B.767	4

AKHAL

AKHAL   T5/AKH   TURKMENISTAN

421		ASHGABAT	0825	BIRMINGHAM	B.757	4
422	0955	BIRMINGHAM		ASHGABAT	B.757	4
423		ASHGABAT	2105	HEATHROW	B.757	2
424	2230	HEATHROW		ASHGABAT	B.757	2
425		ASHGABAT	1040	BIRMINGHAM	B.757	5

AKHAL   (Cont.)

426	1210	BIRMINGHAM		ASHGABAT	B.757	5		
427		ASHGABAT	1450	HEATHROW	B.757	6		
428	1635	HEATHROW		ASHGABAT	B.757	6		
429		ASHGABAT	1750	BIRMINGHAM	B.757	7		
430	1920	BIRMINGHAM		ASHGABAT	B.757	7		

ALITALIA   *ALITALIA   AZ/AZA   ITALY*

200	0725	ROME	0920	HEATHROW	A.320	1234567	
201	0705	HEATHROW	0945	ROME	A.320	1234567	
202	0830	ROME	1120	HEATHROW	A.320	1234567	
203	1020	HEATHROW	1255	ROME	MD-80	1234567	
204	1355	ROME	1635	HEATHROW	MD-80	1234567	
205	1215	HEATHROW	1445	ROME	A.320	1234567	
207	1720	HEATHROW	2000	ROME	MD-80	1234567	
208	1630	ROME	1905	HEATHROW	A.320	1234567	
209	2000	HEATHROW	2240	ROME	A.320	1234567	
210	1650	ROME	1930	HEATHROW	A.320	6	
218		TURIN	1800	GATWICK	MD-80	1234567	ARR 2115 357
219	1850	GATWICK		TURIN	MD-80	1234567	DEP 2205 357
222		TURIN	1815	STANSTED	BAE-146	12345 7	
223	1855	STANSTED		TURIN	BAE-146	12345 7	
226	0605	MILAN	0835	HEATHROW	A.320	1234567	
227	0625	HEATHROW	0905	MILAN	MD-80	1234567	
228	0920	MILAN	1150	HEATHROW	A.320	1234567	
229	0705	HEATHROW		MILAN	A.320	1234567	
236	1315	MILAN	1530	HEATHROW	A.320	1234567	
237	0930	HEATHROW	1145	MILAN	A.320	1234567	
238	1510	MILAN	1725	HEATHROW	A.320	1234567	
239	1245	HEATHROW	1500	MILAN	A.320	1234567	
241	1630	HEATHROW	1845	MILAN	A320/MD80	1234567	
242	1545	MILAN	1000	HEATHROW	A.320	1234567	
243	1810	HEATHROW	2020	MILAN	A.320	1234567	
244	1610	MILAN	1835	HEATHROW	A.320	1234567	
245	1850	HEATHROW	2110	MILAN	A.320	1234567	
246	1900	MILAN	2100	HEATHROW	MD-80	1234567	
247	1935	HEATHROW	2135	MILAN	A.320	1234567	
248	1930	MILAN	2140	HEATHROW	A.320	1234567	
252	1900	ROME	2110	HEATHROW	A.320	1234567	
253	2015	HEATHROW	2230	ROME	MD-80	6	
256	0655	MILAN	0855	LONDON CITY	??	12345	
257	0940	LONDON CITY	1140	MILAN	??	12345	
258	1520	MILAN	1720	LONDON CITY	??	12345 7	
259	1810	LONDON CITY	2010	MILAN	??	12345 7	
262	0930	BOLOGNA	1100	GATWICK	MD-80	1234567	
263	1200	GATWICK	1400	BOLOGNA	MD-80	1234567	
264	1445	BOLOGNA	1655	GATWICK	MD-80	1234567	
265	1755	GATWICK	2005	BOLOGNA	MD-80	1234567	
266	1820	PISA	2020	GATWICK	MD-80	1234567	
267	1515	GATWICK	1715	PISA	MD-80	1234567	
272	0625	VENICE	0825	GATWICK	MD-80	1234567	
273	0910	GATWICK	1110	VENICE	MD-80	1234567	
274	1210	VENICE	1420	GATWICK	MD-80	1234567	
276	1715	ROME	1925	GATWICK	MD-80	1234567	
277	2010	GATWICK	2220	ROME	MD-80	1234567	
279	2100	GATWICK	2310	VENICE	MD-80	1234567	
294	1205	MILAN	1435	DUBLIN	MD-80	1 3 56	
295	1525	DUBLIN	1750	MILAN	MD-80	1 3 56	
296	1445	ROME	1750	DUBLIN	MD-80	3 67	1540/1845 3
297	1840	DUBLIN	2135	ROME	MD-80	3 67	1935/2230 3
600	1000	MILAN		NEW YORK	DC-10	1234567	
601		NEW YORK	0655	MILAN	DC-10	1234567	
602	1320	MILAN		NEW YORK	B.747	1234567	
603		NEW YORK	0700	MILAN	B.747	1234567	
604	0900	MILAN		NEW YORK	DC-10	1234567	
605		NEW YORK	0645	MILAN	DC-10	1234567	
608	0915	ROME		NEW YORK	B.767	1234567	
609		NEW YORK	0600	ROME	B.767	1234567	
610	1200	ROME		NEW YORK	B.747	1234567	

Flight	Dep	From	Arr	To	Aircraft	Days
611		NEW YORK	0835	ROME	B.747	1234567
618	1310	MILAN		BOSTON	B.767	1234567
619		BOSTON	0645	MILAN	B.767	1234567
622	0925	MILAN		LOS ANGELES	MD-11	1234567
623		LOS ANGELES	1100	MILAN	MD-11	1234567
626	0915	MILAN		CHICAGO	B.767	1234567
627		CHICAGO	0625	MILAN	B.767	1234567
628	0920	MILAN		DETROIT	B.767	1234567
629		DETROIT	0625	MILAN	MD-11	1234567
630	0850	ROME		MIAMI	B.747	3 7
631		MIAMI	0650	ROME	B.747	1 3
636	0915	MILAN		MIAMI	B.747	1 5
637		MIAMI	0630	MILAN	B.747	5 7
640	0840	ROME		NEW YORK	DC-10	1234567
641		NEW YORK	0640	ROME	DC-10	1234567
642	1355	ROME		NEW YORK	DC-10	1234567
643		NEW YORK	1045	ROME	DC-10	1234567
650	1220	ROME		TORONTO	DC-10	1234567
651		TORONTO	0855	ROME	DC-10	1234567
652	0930	MILAN		TORONTO	B.767	1234 6
653		TORONTO	0555	MILAN	B.767	2345 7
656	0900	ROME		MONTREAL	DC-10	1 7
657		TORONTO	0645	ROME	DC-10	67
666	0900	MILAN		CARACAS	B.767	1 3 567
667		CARACAS	0645	MILAN	B.767	12 4 67
786	1315	MILAN		TOKYO	B.747	2 6
787		TOKYO	1635	MILAN	B.747	1 3
788	1315	MILAN		TOKYO	B.747	45 7
789		TOKYO	1635	MILAN	B.747	567
794	1305	MILAN		OSAKA	MD-11	1 3 5
795		OSAKA	1700	MILAN	MD-11	2 4 7
9090	1525	AMSTERDAM		TOKYO	B.747	4 6
9124	2030	MILAN		NEW YORK	B.747	7
9125		ATLANTA	2045	MILAN	B.747	1
9162	1115	MILAN		CHICAGO	B.747	4
9163		CHICAGO	0805	MILAN	B.747	5
9168	1215	MILAN		NEW YORK	B.747	3
9169		NEW YORK	0825	MILAN	B.747	3
9204	1900	MILAN		NEW YORK	B.747	6
9205		NEW YORK	1005	MILAN	B.747	7
9206	1800	MILAN		CHICAGO	B.747	6
9207		CHICAGO	1530	MILAN	B.747	7
9208	2200	MILAN		CHICAGO	B.747	7
9209		CHICAGO	1905	ROME	B.747	1
9212	1500	MILAN		NEW YORK	B.747	5
9213		ATLANTA	1435	MILAN	B.747	6

ALL NIPPON			*ALL NIPPON AIRWAYS*		*NH/ANA*	*JAPAN*
201		TOKYO	1540	HEATHROW	B.747	1234567
202	1800	HEATHROW		TOKYO	B.747	1234567
205		TOKYO	1510	PARIS CDG	B.747	1234567
206	1900	PARIS CDG		TOKYO	B.747	1234567
207		TOKYO	1415	VIENNA	B.747	3
208	1955	VIENNA		TOKYO	B.747	2
209		TOKYO	1535	FRANKFURT	B.747	2 4 67
210	1715	FRANKFURT		TOKYO	B.747	2 4 67
285		TOKYO	1510	VIENNA	B.747	1 6
286	1230	VIENNA		TOKYO	A.340	5 7
921		OSAKA	1615	HEATHROW	B.747	234 67
922	1845	HEATHROW		OSAKA	B.747	234 67 DEP 2005 2
931		OSAKA	1615	ROME	B.747	2 7 ARR 2140 7
932	1750	ROME		OSAKA	B.747	2 4 7
939		OSAKA	1630	HEATHROW	B.747	4

23	1020	BIRMINGHAM		CHICAGO	B.767	1234567	
24		CHICAGO	0815	BIRMINGHAM	B.767	1234567	
37	0915	ZURICH		CHICAGO	B.767	1234567	
38		CHICAGO	0655	ZURICH	B.767	1234567	
41	1250	PARIS ORLY		CHICAGO	B.767	1234567	
42		CHICAGO	0700	PARIS ORLY	B.767	1234567	
46		CHICAGO	1035	HEATHROW	B.777	1234567	
47	1355	HEATHROW		CHICAGO	B.777	1234567	
48		DALLAS	0935	PARIS ORLY	B.767	1234567	
49	0925	PARIS ORLY		DALLAS	B.767	1234567	
50		DALLAS	0900	GATWICK	B.777	1234567	
51	1000	GATWICK		DALLAS	MD-11	1234567	
52		CHICAGO	1015	GLASGOW	B.767	1234567	
53	1400	GLASGOW		CHICAGO	B.767	1234567	
54		CHICAGO	0825	MANCHESTER	B.767	1234567	
55	1035	MANCHESTER		CHICAGO	B.767	1234567	
56		MIAMI	0905	HEATHROW	MD-11	1234567	
57	1055	HEATHROW		MIAMI	MD-11	1234567	
62		MIAMI	0930	PARIS ORLY	B.767	1234567	
63	1015	PARIS ORLY		MIAMI	B.767	1234567	
66		CHICAGO	0845	HEATHROW	B.767	1234567	
67	1320	HEATHROW		CHICAGO	B.767	1234567	
78		DALLAS	0650	GATWICK	MD-11	1234567	
79	1305	GATWICK		DALLAS	B.777	1234567	
80		CHICAGO	0740	STOCKHOLM	B.767	1234567	
81	0955	STOCKHOLM		CHICAGO	B.767	1234567	
83	0935	FRANKFURT		CHICAGO	B.767	1234567	
84		CHICAGO	0730	FRANKFURT	B.767	1234567	
86		CHICAGO	0620	HEATHROW	B.777	1234567	
87	1030	HEATHROW		CHICAGO	B747/MD11	1234567	
88		CHICAGO	1100	BRUSSELS	B.767	1234567	
89	1255	BRUSSELS		CHICAGO	B.767	1234567	
90		CHICAGO	2235	HEATHROW	B767/MD11	1234567	
91	2005	HEATHROW		CHICAGO	MD-11	1234567	
92		NEW YORK	0655	HEATHROW	B.767	1234567	
93	1300	HEATHROW		NEW YORK	B.767	1234567	
95	1200	MILAN		CHICAGO	B.767	1234567	
96		CHICAGO	0925	MILAN	B.767	1234567	
98		CHICAGO	1155	GATWICK	B.767	1234567	02.06-07.09
99	1630	GATWICK		CHICAGO	B.767	1234567	02.06-07.09
100		NEW YORK	0625	HEATHROW	B.767	1234567	
101	0955	HEATHROW		NEW YORK	B.767	1234567	
104		NEW YORK	0740	HEATHROW	B.767	1234567	
105	1200	HEATHROW		NEW YORK	A.300	1234567	
106		NEW YORK	2135	HEATHROW	A.300	1234567	
107 ●	1830	HEATHROW		NEW YORK	A.300	1234567	
108		BOSTON	0640	HEATHROW	A.300	1234567	
109	1130	HEATHROW		BOSTON	A.300	1234567	
110		DALLAS	0845	MANCHESTER	B.767	1234567	
111	1025	MANCHESTER		DALLAS	B.767	1234567	
112		MIAMI	0725	GATWICK	B.767	1234567	
113	1100	GATWICK		MIAMI	B.767	1234567	
115	0800	HEATHROW		NEW YORK	B.767	1234567	
116		NEW YORK	1135	HEATHROW	A.300	1234567	
120		BOSTON	0555	GATWICK	B.767	1234567	
121	1130	GATWICK		BOSTON	B.767	1234567	
131	1600	HEATHROW		NEW YORK	B.767	1234567	
132		NEW YORK	0915	HEATHROW	A.300	1234567	
136		LOS ANGELES	1305	HEATHROW	B.767	1234567	
137	1105	HEATHROW		LOS ANGELES	B.767	1234567	
141	2005	HEATHROW		NEW YORK	A.300	1234567	
142		NEW YORK	2030	HEATHROW	B.767	1234567	
146		BOSTON	0605	PARIS ORLY	A.300	1234567	
147	1210	PARIS ORLY		BOSTON	A.300	1234567	
155	1805	HEATHROW		BOSTON	A.300	1234567	
156		BOSTON	2045	HEATHROW	A.300	1234567	
173	1400	GATWICK		RALEIGH	B.767	1234567	
174		RALEIGH	0825	GATWICK	B.767	1234567	

AMTRAN — AMERICAN TRANS AIR INC.   TZ/AMT   U.S.A.

Flt	Dep	From	Arr	To	Aircraft	Days	Period
302		NEW YORK	0730	SHANNON	757	1 4 6	04.06-25.09
307	1115	SHANNON		NEW YORK	757	1 4 6	04.06-25.09
7022	1500	EDINBURGH		MANCHESTER	L10	7	18.7-25.7
7025		GANDER	1100	EDINBURGH	L10	6	3.7-10.7
8444		DETROIT	0730	SHANNON	757	3	23.06-25.08
8445	0930	SHANNON		DETROIT	757	3	23.06-25.08
8446		DETROIT	0915	GATWICK	B.757	6	05.06-11.09
8447	1205	GATWICK		DETROIT	B.757	6	05.06-11.09
8700		GANDER	1045	GATWICK	L-1011	5	16.07-
8701	1145	GATWICK		GANDER	L-1011	4	01.07-
8702		GANDER	1125	GATWICK	L-1011	6	31.07-
8703	1245	GATWICK		GANDER	L-1011	5	16.07-
8704		GANDER	1335	GATWICK	L-1011	7	01.08-
8705	1240	GATWICK		GANDER	L-1011	6	07.07-
8708		GANDER	1045	GATWICK	L-1011	2	03.08-
8709	1200	GATWICK		GANDER	L-1011	1	26.07-
8718		GANDER	0900	MANCHESTER	L-1011	5	23.07-
8719	0930	MANCHESTER		GANDER	L-1011	4	01.07-
8720		GANDER	0915	MANCHESTER	L-1011	2	20.07-
8721	0935	MANCHESTER		GANDER	L-1011	1	05.07-
8722		GANDER	1300	MANCHESTER	L-1011	7	01.08-
8722		GANDER	1400	EDINBURGH	L10	7	18.7-25.7
8723	1255	MANCHESTER		GANDER	L-1011	6	17.07-
8723	1300	EDINBURGH		GANDER	L10	6	3.7-10.7
8724		GANDER	1100	MANCHESTER	L-1011	6	17.07-
8725	1100	MANCHESTER		GANDER	L-1011	5	02.07-
8880		BOSTON	0735	SHANNON	B.757	4	24.06-16.09
8881	1200	SHANNON		BOSTON	B.757	4	24.06-16.09
8884		BOSTON	0735	SHANNON	B.757	7	-10.10
8885	0935	SHANNON		BOSTON	B.757	7	-10.10

ARKIA — ARKIA ISRAELI INLAND AIRLINES   IZ./AIZ   ISRAEL

Flt	Dep	From	Arr	To	Aircraft	Days	Period
911		TEL AVIV	1920	GATWICK	B.757	4	01.07-30.09
912	2100	GATWICK		TEL AVIV	B.757	4	01.07-30.09
913		TEL AVIV	1525	HEATHROW	B.757	3	
914	2230	HEATHROW		TEL AVIV	B.757	3	

ARMENIAN — ARMENIAN INTL. AIRLINES   RME   ARMENIA

Flt	Dep	From	Arr	To	Aircraft	Days	Period
155		AMSTERDAM	0735	GATWICK	A.310	6	
		YEREVAN	0850	GATWICK	A.310	12 4 7	ARR 1350 1
156	1110	GATWICK		AMSTERDAM	A.310	12 4	DEP 1525 1
	0910	GATWICK		YEREVAN	A.310	67	DEP 1110 7

ASIANA — ASIANA AIRLINES   OZ/AAR   SOUTH KOREA

Flt	Dep	From	Arr	To	Aircraft	Days	Period
588		NEW YORK	1440	BRUSSELS	B.747	2	
589		TASHKENT	1600	STANSTED	B.747	5 7	ARR 1610 7
590	1755	STANSTED	1805	BRUSSELS	B.747	5 7	DEP 1910 7

ATLANTA — ATLANTA   CC/ABD   ICELAND

Flt	Dep	From	Arr	To	Aircraft	Days	Period
790		REYKJAVIK	1330	STANSTED	B.747	4	10.06-04.10
		REYKJAVIK	1300	GATWICK	B.747	4	
791	1000	STANSTED		REYKJAVIK	B.747	7	10.06-04.10
	1000	GATWICK		REYKJAVIK	B.747	1	

AUSTRIAN — AUSTRIAN AIRLINES   OS/AUA   AUSTRIA

Flt	Dep	From	Arr	To	Aircraft	Days	Period
451	0625	VIENNA	0905	HEATHROW	A320/MD80	1234567	
452	0935	HEATHROW	1145	VIENNA	A320/MD80	1234567	
453	1000	VIENNA	1215	HEATHROW	F70/MD80	567	
454	1250	HEATHROW	1510	VIENNA	F70/MD87	567	
455	1605	VIENNA	1840	HEATHROW	A320/MD80	1234567	
456	1930	HEATHROW	2150	VIENNA	A320/MD80	1234567	
457	1500	VIENNA	1700	HEATHROW	MD-81	4 7	
458	2115	HEATHROW	2345	VIENNA	MD-81	4 7	
459	1850	VIENNA	2110	HEATHROW	A.320	1234567	
460	0635	HEATHROW	1100	VIENNA	A.320	1234567	

501	1050	VIENNA		NEW YORK	A.330	1234567	
502		NEW YORK	0820	VIENNA	A.330	1234567	
503	1615	VIENNA		NEW YORK	A.310	1 3 6	
504		NEW YORK	1150	VIENNA	A.310	2 5 7	
555	1230	VIENNA		TOKYO	A.340	5 7	
556		TOKYO	1510	VIENNA	A.340	1 6	
3761		VIENNA	1420	SHANNON	MD-83	6	-02.10
3762	1510	SHANNON		VIENNA	MD-83	6	-02.10

AUSTRIAN CHARTER   *AUSTRIAN AIR TRANSPORT   AAT   AUSTRIA*

2801		VIENNA	2025	STANSTED	MD-83	4	17.06-
2802	2125	STANSTED		VIENNA	MD-83	4	17.06-
2803		VIENNA	2130	STANSTED	MD-83	7	30.05-
2804	2220	STANSTED		VIENNA	MD-83	7	30.05-

AVIANCA   *AEROVIAS NACIONALES DE COLUMBIA   AV/AVA   COLUMBIA*

14		BOGOTA	0930	PARIS CDG	B.767	2 4 6
15	1145	PARIS CDG		BOGOTA	B.767	2 4 6
16		BOGOTA	1100	HEATHROW	B.767	2 4 6
17	1400	HEATHROW		BOGOTA	B.767	2 4 6
18		CARACAS	0900	FRANKFURT	B.767	1
19	1110	FRANKFURT		CARACAS	B.767	1

AYLINE   *AURIGNY AIR SERVICES   GR/AUR   U.K.*

112	0815	GUERNSEY	0845	DINARD	BN.TRIS.	123456
113	0900	DINARD	0930	GUERNSEY	BN.TRIS.	123456
182	1740	GUERNSEY	1810	DINARD	BN.TRIS.	1234567
183	1825	DINARD	1855	GUERNSEY	BN.TRIS.	1234567
208	0745	GUERNSEY	0800	ALDERNEY	BN.TRIS.	1234567
209	0745	ALDERNEY	0800	GUERNSEY	BN.TRIS.	123456
218	0955	GUERNSEY	1010	ALDERNEY	BN.TRIS.	123456
221	1025	ALDERNEY	1040	GUERNSEY	BN.TRIS.	1234567
222	1055	GUERNSEY	1110	ALDERNEY	BN.TRIS.	1234567
229	1230	ALDERNEY	1245	GUERNSEY	BN.TRIS.	1234567
234	1330	GUERNSEY	1345	ALDERNEY	BN.TRIS.	1234567
239	1600	ALDERNEY	1615	GUERNSEY	BN.TRIS.	1234567
240	1645	GUERNSEY	1700	ALDERNEY	BN.TRIS.	12345 7
247	1715	ALDERNEY	1730	GUERNSEY	BN.TRIS.	1234567
248	1745	GUERNSEY	1800	ALDERNEY	BN.TRIS.	6
250	1755	GUERNSEY	1810	ALDERNEY	BN.TRIS.	1234
259	1830	ALDERNEY	1845	GUERNSEY	BN.TRIS.	1234567
260	1905	GUERNSEY	1920	ALDERNEY	BN.TRIS.	567
341	0900	ALDERNEY	0915	JERSEY	BN.TRIS.	123456
344	0940	JERSEY	0955	ALDERNEY	BN.TRIS.	123456
346	0945	JERSEY	1000	ALDERNEY	BN.TRIS.	6
355	1230	ALDERNEY	1245	JERSEY	BN.TRIS.	6
356	1300	JERSEY	1315	ALDERNEY	BN.TRIS.	6
369	1630	ALDERNEY	1645	JERSEY	BN.TRIS.	6
373	1715	ALDERNEY	1730	JERSEY	BN.TRIS.	12 45 7
376	1745	JERSEY	1800	ALDERNEY	BN.TRIS.	12 45 7
420	0725	JERSEY	0745	DINARD	BN.TRIS.	6
421	0800	DINARD	0820	JERSEY	BN.TRIS.	6
422	0800	JERSEY	0820	DINARD	BN.TRIS.	12345
423	0835	DINARD	0855	JERSEY	BN.TRIS.	12345
466	1715	JERSEY	1735	DINARD	BN.TRIS.	1234567
467	1750	DINARD	1810	JERSEY	BN.TRIS.	1234567
501	0820	ALDERNEY	0905	SOUTHAMPTON	BN.TRIS.	123456
502	0920	SOUTHAMPTON	1005	ALDERNEY	BN.TRIS.	123456
521	1015	ALDERNEY	1100	SOUTHAMPTON	BN.TRIS.	6
522	1120	SOUTHAMPTON	1205	ALDERNEY	BN.TRIS.	6
529	1115	ALDERNEY	1200	SOUTHAMPTON	BN.TRIS.	1234567
530	1220	SOUTHAMPTON	1305	ALDERNEY	BN.TRIS.	1234567
547	1330	ALDERNEY	1415	SOUTHAMPTON	BN.TRIS.	6
548	1330	SOUTHAMPTON	1415	ALDERNEY	BN.TRIS.	6
551	1400	ALDERNEY	1445	SOUTHAMPTON	BN.TRIS.	1234567
552	1510	SOUTHAMPTON	1555	ALDERNEY	BN.TRIS.	1234567

559	1500	ALDERNEY	1545	SOUTHAMPTON	BN.TRIS.	567	
560	1600	SOUTHAMPTON	1645	ALDERNEY	BN.TRIS.	567	
569	1615	ALDERNEY	1700	SOUTHAMPTON	BN.TRIS.	1234567	
570	1730	SOUTHAMPTON	1815	ALDERNEY	BN.TRIS.	1234567	
612	1935	JERSEY	2040	GATWICK	SH-360	12345	
613	2230	GATWICK	2330	EAST MIDLANDS	SH-360	12345	
614	0005	EAST MIDLANDS	0055	GATWICK	SH-360	23456	
615	0425	GATWICK	0530	JERSEY	SH-360	23456	
630		GUERNSEY	0900	STANSTED	SAAB-340	123456	
631	0930	STANSTED		GUERNSEY	SAAB-340	123456	
642		GUERNSEY	1300	STANSTED	SAAB-340	1234567	
643	1330	STANSTED		GUERNSEY	SAAB-340	1234567	
648		GUERNSEY	1755	STANSTED	SAAB-340	12345 7	
649	1830	STANSTED		GUERNSEY	SAAB-340	12345 7	
652	1315	JERSEY	1350	CAEN	BN.TRIS.	1 45 7	
653	1410	CAEN	1445	JERSEY	BN.TRIS.	1 45 7	
800	0730	GUERNSEY	0745	JERSEY	BN.TRIS.	123456	
801	0730	JERSEY	0745	GUERNSEY	BN.TRIS.	6	
803	0745	JERSEY	0800	GUERNSEY	BN.TRIS.	12345	
804	0800	GUERNSEY	0815	JERSEY	BN.TRIS.	6	
806	0815	GUERNSEY	0830	JERSEY	BN.TRIS.	12345	
807	0815	JERSEY	0830	GUERNSEY	BN.TRIS.	123456	
810	0845	GUERNSEY	0900	JERSEY	BN.TRIS.	1234567	
811	0845	JERSEY	0900	GUERNSEY	BN.TRIS.	1234567	
814	0915	GUERNSEY	0930	JERSEY	BN.TRIS.	1234567	
815	0915	JERSEY	0930	GUERNSEY	BN.TRIS.	1234567	
818	0945	GUERNSEY	1000	JERSEY	BN.TRIS.	1234567	
819	0945	JERSEY	1000	GUERNSEY	BN.TRIS.	12345	
822	1015	GUERNSEY	1030	JERSEY	BN.TRIS.	12345	
823	1015	JERSEY	1030	GUERNSEY	BN.TRIS.	1234567	
828	1100	GUERNSEY	1115	JERSEY	BN.TRIS.	1234567	
833	1130	JERSEY	1145	GUERNSEY	BN.TRIS.	1234567	
836	1200	GUERNSEY	1215	JERSEY	BN.TRIS.	1234567	
841	1230	JERSEY	1245	GUERNSEY	BN.TRIS.	1234567	
844	1300	GUERNSEY	1315	JERSEY	BN.TRIS.	1234567	
849	1330	JERSEY	1345	GUERNSEY	BN.TRIS.	1234567	
852	1400	GUERNSEY	1415	JERSEY	BN.TRIS.	1234567	
857	1430	JERSEY	1445	GUERNSEY	BN.TRIS.	1234567	
860	1500	GUERNSEY	1515	JERSEY	BN.TRIS.	1234567	
865	1530	JERSEY	1545	GUERNSEY	BN.TRIS.	12345	
868	1600	GUERNSEY	1615	JERSEY	BN.TRIS.	1234567	
872	1630	GUERNSEY	1645	JERSEY	BN.TRIS.	6	
873	1630	JERSEY	1645	GUERNSEY	BN.TRIS.	1234567	
876	1700	GUERNSEY	1715	JERSEY	BN.TRIS.	123457	
877	1700	JERSEY	1715	GUERNSEY	BN.TRIS.	1234567	
880	1730	GUERNSEY	1745	JERSEY	BN.TRIS.	1234567	
881	1730	JERSEY	1745	GUERNSEY	BN.TRIS.	1234567	
884	1800	GUERNSEY	1815	JERSEY	BN.TRIS.	1234567	
885	1800	JERSEY	1815	GUERNSEY	BN.TRIS.	1234567	
888	1830	GUERNSEY	1845	JERSEY	BN.TRIS.	1234567	
889	1830	JERSEY	1845	GUERNSEY	BN.TRIS.	1234567	
891	1845	JERSEY	1900	GUERNSEY	BN.TRIS.	1234567	
892	1900	GUERNSEY	1915	JERSEY	BN.TRIS.	1234567	
896	1930	GUERNSEY	1945	JERSEY	BN.TRIS.	1234567	
897	1930	JERSEY	1945	GUERNSEY	BN.TRIS.	1234567	
1142		JERSEY	1130	BOURNEMOUTH	SH-360	5	24.09-
1143	1145	BOURNEMOUTH		JERSEY	SH-360	5	24.09-
1144		JERSEY	1055	BOURNEMOUTH	SH-360	7	-19.09
1145	1110	BOURNEMOUTH		JERSEY	SH-360	7	-19.09
1146		JERSEY	1610	BOURNEMOUTH	SH-360	7	26.09-
1147	1630	BOURNEMOUTH		JERSEY	SH-360	7	26.09-

AZTEC AIR   *AB AIRLINES*   *7L/AZX*   *UK*

204	1730	GATWICK		NICE	BAC1-11	12345	DEP 1655 3
	1615	GATWICK		NICE	BAC1-11	67	
205		NICE	2155	GATWICK	BAC1-11	12345	
		NICE	2055	GATWICK	BAC1-11	67	

331	2000	GATWICK		BERLIN	B.737	6	
501	0620	LIVERPOOL	0720	HEATHROW	B.737	1234567	
502	1040	HEATHROW	1140	LIVERPOOL	B.737	1234567	
503	0955	LIVERPOOL	1055	HEATHROW	B.737	1234567	
504	1520	HEATHROW	1620	LIVERPOOL	B.737	1234567	
505	1335	LIVERPOOL	1435	HEATHROW	B.737	1234567	
506	1900	HEATHROW	2000	LIVERPOOL	B.737	1234567	
507	1715	LIVERPOOL	1815	HEATHROW	B.737	1234567	
510	0910	HEATHROW	1040	INVERNESS	B.737	1234567	
511	0655	INVERNESS	0825	HEATHROW	B.737	1234567	
512	1420	HEATHROW	1550	INVERNESS	B.737	1234567	
513	1205	INVERNESS	1335	HEATHROW	B.737	1234567	
514	1910	HEATHROW	2040	INVERNESS	B.737	1234567	
715	1655	INVERNESS	1825	HEATHROW	B.737	1234567	
736		BERLIN	1800	GATWICK	B.737	7	
771		BEAUVAIS	2015	GATWICK	B.737	12345	
772	2045	GATWICK		BEAUVAIS	B.737	12345	
801		SHANNON	1000	GATWICK	B.737	123456	
802	1045	GATWICK		SHANNON	B.737	123456	
803		SHANNON	1355	GATWICK	B.737	123456	ARR 1415 6
805		SHANNON	1140	GATWICK	B.737	7	
806	1515	GATWICK		SHANNON	B.737	12345 7	DEP 1445 7
807		SHANNON	1825	GATWICK	B.737	12345 7	ARR 1900 7
808	1910	GATWICK		SHANNON	B.737	123456	DEP 2015 5
810	2045	GATWICK		SHANNON	B.737	7	
830	1200	GATWICK		KNOCK	BAC1-11	12345 7	DEP 1130 7
831		KNOCK	1640	GATWICK	BAC1-11	12345	
832	1500	GATWICK		KNOCK	BAC1-11	67	DEP 1600 7
833		KNOCK	1950	GATWICK	BAC1-11	12345 7	ARR 1930 7
876		BELFAST	2030	GATWICK	BAE-146	1234	

AZZURRA AIR   *AZZURRA AIR   ZS/AZI   ITALY*

218	0645	TURIN	0845	STANSTED	BAE-146	1234567	FLIGHTLINE A/C
219	0915	STANSTED	1115	TURIN	BAE-146	1234567	FLIGHTLINE A/C
222	1615	TURIN	1815	STANSTED	BAE-146	12345 7	FLIGHTLINE A/C
223	1855	STANSTED	2055	TURIN	BAE-146	12345 7	FLIGHTLINE A/C

BALKAN   *BALKAN-BULGARIAN AIRLINES   LZ/LAZ   BULGARIA*

495		SOFIA	1300	HEATHROW	737/767/TU5	1 3 567	
496	1445	HEATHROW		SOFIA	737/767/TU5	1 3 567	
601	1000	SOFIA	1235	SHANNON	A.310	12 5	1205/1440 2
	1325	SHANNON		NEW YORK	A.310	12 5	DEP 1530 2
602		NEW YORK	1140	SOFIA	B.767	23 6	NON-STOP

EVEN NUMBERS - FLIGHTS LEAVING THE U.K.   UNEVEN NUMBERS - FLIGHTS INTO THE U.K.

903/4	2025	MANCHESTER	1925	BOURGAS	TU-154	6	-02.10
969/0	0915	BELFAST	0825	VAR	TU-154	6	05.06-25.09
7901/2	1730	GATWICK	1630	BOURGAS	TU-154	6	-02.10
7959/0	1845	GATWICK	1735	VARNA	TU-154	6	-02.10
7961/2	0930	MANCHESTER	0710	VARNA	TU-154	6	-02.10

BANGLADESH   *BANGLADESH BIMAN   BG/BBC   BANGLADESH*

001	0705	FRANKFURT	0830	HEATHROW	DC-10	2	
002	1355	HEATHROW		DHAKA	DC-10	2	VIA FRANKFURT
003		DHAKA	1115	HEATHROW	DC-10	6	VIA PARIS
004	1630	HEATHROW		DHAKA	DC-10	6	VIA PARIS
005		DHAKA	0915	HEATHROW	DC-10	7	VIA DUBAI
006	1630	HEATHROW		DHAKA	DC-10	7	
007		DHAKA	1100	HEATHROW	DC-10	4	VIA ROME
008	1315	HEATHROW		DHAKA	DC-10	4	VIA ROME
015		KUWAIT	1315	MANCHESTER	DC-10	3	
	1450	MANCHESTER	1550	HEATHROW	DC-10	3	
016	2105	HEATHROW		DHAKA	DC-10	3	
055		DHAKA	1115	HEATHROW	DC-10	1	VIA ABU DHABI
056	1430	HEATHROW		DHAKA	DC-10	1	VIA ABU DHABI

BEE MED — *BRITISH MEDITERRANEAN AIRWAYS   KJ/LAJ   UK*

A BA FRANCHISEE COMPANY.

Flight					Aircraft	Days	Notes
6701	1425	HEATHROW		BEIRUT	A.320	1234567	
6702		BEIRUT	1320	HEATHROW	A.320	1234567	
6703	1605	HEATHROW		BEIRUT	A.320	6	
6704		BEIRUT	1145	HEATHROW	A.320	7	
6705	1705	HEATHROW		AMMAN	A.320	3 5 7	DEP 2120 57
6706		AMMAN	1135	HEATHROW	A.320	1 4 6	ARR 1300 4
6707	1705	HEATHROW		DAMASCUS	A.320	12 6	DEP 2105 2
	2005	HEATHROW		DAMASCUS	A.320	4	
6708		DAMASCUS	1220	HEATHROW	A.320	23 5 7	
6721	1305	HEATHROW		TBILSI	A.320	1 3	DEP 1605 1
	2100	HEATHROW		TBILSI	A.320	5	
6722		TBILSI	1230	HEATHROW	A.320	2 4 6	
6723	1450	HEATHROW		YEREVAN	A.320	4 7	DEP 1615 7
6724		YEREVAN	1215	HEATHROW	A.320	1 5	ARR 1300 5

BELARUS AVIA — *BELAVIA   B2/BRU   BELARUS*

851		MINSK	1300	GATWICK	TU-134	3 5 7
852	1400	GATWICK		MINSK	TU-134	3 5 7

BELSTAR — *VIRGIN EXPRESS AIRWAYS   TV/VEX   BELGIUM*

EVEN NUMBERS - FLIGHTS LEAVING THE UK   UNEVEN NUMBERS - - FLIGHTS INTO THE UK

304/5	2245	GATWICK	0440	MALAGA	B.737	3	21.07-07.10
500/1	2245	GATWICK	0405	ALICANTE	B.737	5	02.07-02.10
680/1	2245	GATWICK	0345	PALMA	B.737	6	-26.09
700/1	2245	GATWICK	0535	CORFU	B.737	7	18.07-03.10

BLACK SEA — *MNG AIRLINES CARGO   MB/MNB   TURKEY*

123		HAHN (GERMANY)	2145	STANSTED	A.300	1
124	2310	STANSTED		ISTANBUL	A.300	1
223		HAHN	2355	STANSTED	A.300	2
224	0130	STANSTED		ISTANBUL	A.300	3
321		ISTANBUL	1300	STANSTED	A.300	3
322	1430	STANSTED		ISTANBUL	A.300	3
323		HAHN	2355	STANSTED	A.300	3
324	0130	STANSTED		ISTANBUL	A.300	4
423		HAHN	2355	STANSTED	A.300	4
424	0130	STANSTED		ISTANBUL	A.300	5
523		HAHN	2145	STANSTED	A.300	5
524	2310	STANSTED		ISTANBUL	A.300	5
621		ISTANBUL	1300	STANSTED	A.300	6
622	1430	STANSTED		ISTANBUL	A.300	6
623		HAHN	2355	STANSTED	A.300	6
624	0130	STANSTED		ISTANBUL	A.300	7
723		HAHN	2355	STANSTED	A.300	7
724	0130	STANSTED		ISTANBUL	A.300	1

BLUE STAR — *MAERSK AIR LTD.   MSK /VB   U.K.*

A BRITISH AIRWAYS FRANCHISEE COMPANY

EVEN NUMBERS - FLIGHTS LEAVING THE UK   UNEVEN NUMBERS - FLIGHTS INTO THE UK

102/3	0745	BIRMINGHAM	2155	FARO	B.737	6
106/7	1535	STANSTED	1415	FARO	B.737	6
202/3	0745	BIRMINGHAM	1420	MALAGA	B.737	7
204/5	1500	BIRMINGHAM	2100	PALMA	B.737	6
500/1	0810	BIRMINGHAM	1415	MURCIA	B.737	6
604/5	0815	BIRMINGHAM	1450	MALAGA	B.737	7
702/3	1630	BIRMINGHAM	2305	PALMA	B.737	6
850/1	0645	BIRMINGHAM	1205	VENICE	B.737	7
920/1	1515	BIRMINGHAM	2250	CORFU	B.737	6

SCHEDULED SERVICES. THE FIGURE 8 IS DELETED FROM THEIR CALL SIGN E.G. 300 REFERS TO FLIGHT NO 8300

8300	0900	BIRMINGHAM	1045	LYONS	B737/CAN	1234567	1310/1455 7
8301	1130	LYONS	1315	BIRMINGHAM	B737/CAN	1234567	1535/1720 7
8322	1200	BIRMINGHAM	1345	BERLIN	B737/CAN	12345 7	

8323	1430	BERLIN	1625	BIRMINGHAM	B737/CAN	12345 7	
8340	0700	BIRMINGHAM	0755	BELFAST	B.737	12345	
8341	0840	BELFAST	0940	BIRMINGHAM	B737/CAN	12345 7	
8342	0945	BIRMINGHAM	1045	BELFAST	CANADAIR	1234567	
8343	1125	BELFAST	1225	BIRMINGHAM	CANADAIR	1234567	
8344	1305	BIRMINGHAM	1405	BELFAST	B737/CAN	1234567	
8345	1445	BELFAST	1545	BIRMINGHAM	B737/CAN	1234567	
8346	1805	BIRMINGHAM	1905	BELFAST	B737/CAN	1234567	
8347	1945	BELFAST	2045	BIRMINGHAM	B737/CAN	1234567	
8348	2010	BIRMINGHAM	2110	BELFAST	B737/CAN	1234567	2125/2225 5
8349	0700	BELFAST	0800	BIRMINGHAM	B.737	123456	
8350	1315	BIRMINGHAM	1420	AMSTERDAM	CANADAIR	1 4567	01.09-
8351	1500	AMSTERDAM	1610	BIRMINGHAM	CANADAIR	1 4567	01.09-
8352	0645	BIRMINGHAM	0800	AMSTERDAM	B.737	12345	
8353	0855	AMSTERDAM	1010	BIRMINGHAM	B.737	12345	
8354	1020	BIRMINGHAM	1125	AMSTERDAM	B737/CAN	1234567	
8355	1205	AMSTERDAM	1315	BIRMINGHAM	B737/CAN	1234567	
8356	1415	BIRMINGHAM	1520	AMSTERDAM	B737/CAN	1234567	
8357	1610	AMSTERDAM	1720	BIRMINGHAM	B737/CAN	1234567	
8358	1625	BIRMINGHAM	1735	AMSTERDAM	B737/CAN	1234567	
8359	1815	AMSTERDAM	1925	BIRMINGHAM	B737/CAN	1234567	
8360	2030	BIRMINGHAM	2030	COPENHAGEN	CANADAIR	12345 7	
8361	0700	COPENHAGEN	0900	BIRMINGHAM	CANADAIR	123456	
8362	0645	BIRMINGHAM	0850	COPENHAGEN	B.737	12345	
8363	0945	COPENHAGEN	1145	BIRMINGHAM	B.737	12345	
8364	1305	BIRMINGHAM	1505	COPENHAGEN	B.737	12345 7	
8365	1550	COPENHAGEN	1750	BIRMINGHAM	CANADAIR	12345 7	
8368	1600	BIRMINGHAM	1800	COPENHAGEN	B.737	12345 7	
8369	1850	COPENHAGEN	2040	BIRMINGHAM	B.737	12345 7	
8370	0845	BIRMINGHAM	1100	MILAN	B.737	123456	
8371	1145	MILAN	1350	BIRMINGHAM	B.737	123456	
8372	1220	BIRMINGHAM	1425	MILAN	CANADAIR	12345	
8373	1520	MILAN	1725	BIRMINGHAM	CANADAIR	12345	
8374	1625	BIRMINGHAM	1840	MILAN	B737/CAN	12345 7	
8375	1920	MILAN	2125	BIRMINGHAM	B737/CAN	12345 7	
8380	0715	BIRMINGHAM	0855	STUTTGART	CANADAIR	12345	
8381	0935	STUTTGART	1125	BIRMINGHAM	CANADAIR	12345	
8384	1655	BIRMINGHAM	1845	STUTTGART	B.737	12345 7	
8385	1915	STUTTGART	2105	BIRMINGHAM	B.737	12345 7	
8388	1850	BIRMINGHAM	2030	STUTTGART	CANADAIR	12345 7	
8389	0615	STUTTGART	0805	BIRMINGHAM	CANADAIR	12345	
8390	0725	BIRMINGHAM	0825	NEWCASTLE	J'STREAM 41	12345	
8391	0850	NEWCASTLE	0950	BIRMINGHAM	J'STREAM 41	12345	
8392	1015	BIRMINGHAM	1115	NEWCASTLE	J'STREAM 41	12345	
8393	1140	NEWCASTLE	1240	BIRMINGHAM	J'STREAM 41	12345	
8394	1600	BIRMINGHAM	1700	NEWCASTLE	J'STREAM 41	12345 7	
8395	1725	NEWCASTLE	1825	BIRMINGHAM	J'STREAM 41	12345 7	
8396	1850	BIRMINGHAM	1950	NEWCASTLE	J'STREAM 41	12345	
8397	2015	NEWCASTLE	2115	BIRMINGHAM	J'STREAM 41	12345	
8399	0655	NEWCASTLE	0755	BIRMINGHAM	CANADAIR	12345	
8402	0705	BIRMINGHAM	0920	VIENNA	CANADAIR	123456	
8403	0955	VIENNA	1225	BIRMINGHAM	CANADAIR	123456	
8404	1440	BIRMINGHAM	1655	VIENNA	CANADAIR	12345 7	
8405	1725	VIENNA	1955	BIRMINGHAM	CANADAIR	12345 7	
8412	0900	BIRMINGHAM	1045	GENEVA	B737/CAN	123456	
8413	1120	GENEVA	1305	BIRMINGHAM	B737/CAN	123456	
8414	1340	BIRMINGHAM	1525	GENEVA	CANADAIR	12345 7	
8415	1600	GENEVA	1745	BIRMINGHAM	CANADAIR	12345 7	

EVEN NUMBERS - FLIGHTS LEAVING THE U.K.   UNEVEN NUMBERS - FLIGHTS INTO THE U.K.

102/3	0745	BIRMINGHAM	2210	FARO	B.737	6	
106/7	1535	STANSTED	1415	FARO	B.737	6	
202/3	0745	BIRMINGHAM	1420	MALAGA	B.737	7	
204/5	1500	BIRMINGHAM	2100	PALMA	B.737	6	
264/5	0815	BIRMINGHAM	1450	MALAGA	B.737	7	
500/1	0810	BIRMINGHAM	1415	MURCIA	B.737	6	
604/5	0815	BIRMINGHAM	1450	MALAGA	B.737	7	
702/3	1630	BIRMINGHAM	2305	PALMA	B.737	6	-09.10

850/1	0645	BIRMINGHAM	1205	VENICE	B.737	7	-26.09
920/1	1445	BIRMINGHAM	2235	CORFU	B.737	6	10.07-25.09

		BRAATHENS		*BRAATHENS S.A.F.E.*	*AIR TRANSPORT*	*BU/BRA*	*NORWAY*
551	0720	STAVANGER	0825	ABERDEEN	B.737	123456	
552	0905	ABERDEEN	1005	STAVANGER	B.737	123456	
555	1720	STAVANGER	1820	ABERDEEN	B.737	12345 7	
556	1900	ABERDEEN	2000	STAVANGER	B.737	12345 7	
561	0920	OSLO	1100	NEWCASTLE	B.737	12345	
563	0930	OSLO	1110	NEWCASTLE	B.737	7	
564	1200	NEWCASTLE	1335	OSLO	B.737	7	
568	1855	NEWCASTLE	2030	OSLO	B.737	12345	
574	1135	NEWCASTLE	1245	STAVANGER	B.737	12345 7	1745/1900 7
575	1705	STAVANGER	1820	NEWCASTLE	B.737	12345	
578	1935	NEWCASTLE	2045	STAVANGER	B.737	7	
583	0825	OSLO	1030	STANSTED	B.737	123456	
584	1105	STANSTED	1315	OSLO	B.737	123456	
585	0930	OSLO	1140	STANSTED	B.737	7	
586	1230	STANSTED	1445	OSLO	B.737	7	
587	1620	OSLO	1810	STANSTED	B.737	1234567	
588	1855	STANSTED	2100	OSLO	B.737	1234567	
595		BERGEN	2000	STANSTED	B.737	1234567	
596	2100	STANSTED		BERGEN	B.737	1234567	
771	0910	MALMO	1105	LONDON CITY	??	12345	
772	1135	LONDON CITY	1320	MALMO	??	12345	
773	1050	MALMO	1245	LONDON CITY	??	7	
774	1315	LONDON CITY	1500	MALMO	??	7	
775	1635	MALMO	1830	LONDON CITY	??	12345 7	
776	1910	LONDON CITY	2010	MALMO	??	12345 7	

		BRINTEL		*BRITISH INTERNATIONAL HELICOPTERS*	*BS/BIH*	*U.K.*
312	1015	PENZANCE	1035	TRESCO, IOS	SIKORSKY	123456
313	1040	TRESCO, IOS	1100	PENZANCE	SIKORSKY	123456
319	1345	TRESCO, IOS	1405	PENZANCE	SIKORSKY	123456
324	1605	PENZANCE	1625	TRESCO, IOS	SIKORSKY	123456
325	1630	TRESCO, IOS	1650	PENZANCE	SIKORSKY	123456
418	1420	PENZANCE	1340	TRESCO, IOS	SIKORSKY	123456
730	0730	PENZANCE	0750	ST MARY'S, IOS	SIKORSKY	1 6
755	0755	ST MARY'S, IOS	0815	PENZANCE	SIKORSKY	1 6
825	0825	PENZANCE	0845	ST MARY'S, IOS	SIKORSKY	123456
850	0850	ST MARY'S, IOS	0910	PENZANCE	SIKORSKY	123456
920	0920	PENZANCE	0940	ST MARY'S, IOS	SIKORSKY	123456
945	0945	ST MARY'S, IOS	1005	PENZANCE	SIKORSKY	123456
1110	1110	PENZANCE	1130	ST MARY'S, IOS	SIKORSKY	23456
1135	1135	ST MARY'S, IOS	1155	PENZANCE	SIKORSKY	123456
1205	1205	PENZANCE	1225	ST MARY'S, IOS	SIKORSKY	23456
1230	1230	ST MARY'S, IOS	1250	PENZANCE	SIKORSKY	23456
1415	1415	PENZANCE	1435	ST MARY'S, IOS	SIKORSKY	1
1440	1430	ST MARY'S, IOS	1500	PENZANCE	SIKORSKY	1
1510	1510	PENZANCE	1530	ST MARY'S, IOS	SIKORSKY	123456
1535	1535	ST MARY'S, IOS	1555	PENZANCE	SIKORSKY	123456
1700	1700	PENZANCE	1720	ST MARY'S, IOS	SIKORSKY	123456
1725	1725	ST MARY'S, IOS	1745	PENZANCE	SIKORSKY	123456
1755	1755	PENZANCE	1815	ST MARY'S, IOS	SIKORSKY	123456
1820	1820	ST MARY'S, IOS	1840	PENZANCE	SIKORSKY	123456
5008	0945	PENZANCE	1005	ST MARY'S, IOS	SIKORSKY	123456
5009	1010	ST MARY'S, IOS	1030	PENZANCE	SIKORSKY	123456
5022	1635	PENZANCE	1655	ST MARY'S, IOS	SIKORSKY	123456
5023	1700	ST MARY'S, IOS	1720	PENZANCE	SIKORSKY	123456
6010	1040	PENZANCE	1100	TRESCO, IOS	SIKORSKY	12345
6021	1605	TRESCO, IOS	1625	PENZANCE	SIKORSKY	12345

03P	POSITIONING FLIGHTS STANSTED - DUBLIN. BAC1-11 AIRCRAFT WITH DIFFERING TIMES & DAYS							
04P	POSITIONING FLIGHTS DUBLIN - STANSTED. BAC1-11 AIRCRAFT WITH DIFFERING TIMES & DAYS							
101/2	FLIGHTS STANSTED-LOURDES-STANSTED. USING BAC 1-11 A/C WITH DIFFERING TIMES/DAYS							
111/2	0830	STANSTED	1435	PALMA	BAC1-11		6	01.05-09.10
115/6	FLIGHTS STANSTED-LOURDES-STANSTED USING BAC 1-11 A/C WITH DIFFERING TIMES/DAYS							
141/2	0920	STANSTED	1430	VENICE	BAC1-11		7	02.05-26.09
203	FLIGHTS FROM DUBLIN TO LOURDES.			BAC1-11 AIRCRAFT WITH DIFFERING TIMES AND DAYS				
204	FLIGHTS FROM LOURDES TO DUBLIN.			BAC1-11 AIRCRAFT WITH DIFFERING TIMES AND DAYS				
210 - 287	FLIGHTS TO LOURDES FROM VARIOUS UK AIRPORTS USING BAC1-11 AIRCRAFT. TIMES/DAYS VARY							
231/2	1110	GATWICK	1615	LOURDES	BAC1-11		5	
241/2	FLIGHTS STANSTED-EXETER-LOURDES-EXETER-STANSTED. BAC 1-11 A/C. VARIOUS TIMES/DAYS							
247/8	FLIGHTS STANSTED-LIVERPOOL-LOURDES-LIVERPOOL-STANSTED. BAC 1-11 A/C. TIMES/DAYS VARY							
295/6	0825	GATWICK	1315	LOURDES	BAC1-11		7	
501	0650	ABERDEEN	0750	SUMBURGH	ATR-72	123456	0830/0930 6	
502	0810	SUMBURGH	0910	ABERDEEN	ATR-72	123456	1430/1530 6	
503	0935	ABERDEEN	1035	SUMBURGH	ATR-72	12345		
504	1055	SUMBURGH	1155	ABERDEEN	ATR-72	12345		
505	1230	ABERDEEN	1330	SUMBURGH	ATR-72	12345		
506	1350	SUMBURGH	1450	ABERDEEN	ATR-72	12345		
507	1515	ABERDEEN	1615	SUMBURGH	ATR-72	12345		
508	1635	SUMBURGH	1735	ABERDEEN	ATR-72	12345		
557/8	1545	GATWICK	2055	VENICE	BAC1-11	1		
559/0	1015	GATWICK	1500	VERONA	BAC1-11		6	
567/8	1510	GATWICK	1955	VERONA	BAC1-11		4	

'A' - FLIGHTS LEAVING THE U.K.   'B' - FLIGHTS INTO THE U.K.

001	0625	MANCHESTER	1445	ZAKINTHOS	B.757	1	
003	0710	GATWICK	1230	MAHON	B.767	3	
004	0635	STANSTED	1205	PALMA	B.757	4	
005	0605	EAST MIDLANDS	1405	ZAKINTHOS	B.757	5	
006	0705	BRISTOL	1235	MAHON	B.757	6	
007	0800	STANSTED	1425	MALAGA	B.757	7	
008	0835	LUTON	1745	LAS PALMAS	B.757	1	
009	1805	GATWICK	2340	ALICANTE	B.767	2	
010	0700	GATWICK	1620	DALAMAN	B.757	3	
011	0730	BRISTOL	1630	KOS	A.320	4	
012	1720	GATWICK	2210	VENICE	B.757	5	
013	1405	BRISTOL	1900	REUS	B.757	6	
014	1615	LUTON	2230	MALAGA	B.757	7	
015	1535	BIRMINGHAM	2120	IBIZA	B.757	1	
017	1745	MANCHESTER	0325	RHODES	B.767	3	
018	0630	GLASGOW	1305	PALMA	B.757	5	
019	0700	LUTON	1610	TENERIFE	B.757	5	
021	2010	CARDIFF	0125	PALMA	A.320	7	
022	1505	MANCHESTER	2110	IBIZA	B.767	1	
023	0745	EAST MIDLANDS	1955	REUS	B.757	2	
024	0605	NEWCASTLE	1220	MAHON	B.757	3	
025	0730	LUTON	1505	KEFALLINIA	B,757	4	
026	0840	MANCHESTER	1510	ALICANTE	B.767	6	
027	0940	GATWICK	1710	KEFALLINIA	B.757	4	
028	1145	LUTON	2200	LARNACA	B.757	7	
029	1825	CARDIFF	2355	IBIZA	B.757	1	
032	1800	BRISTOL	0255	HERAKLION	A.320	4	
033	1535	EAST MIDLANDS	2200	NAPLES	B.757	5	
035	1805	BRISTOL	0435	LARNACA	B.757	7	
036	0030	TEESSIDE	2255	ALICANTE	B.757	3	
037	1745	BIRMINGHAM	2345	ALICANTE	B.757	2	
040	2225	MANCHESTER	0530	PALMA	B.767	5	
044	0730	NEWCASTLE	1710	FUERTVENTURA	B.757	2	
046	1850	NEWCASTLE	0145	MALAGA	B.757	4	
047	0630	GATWICK	1235	NAPLES	B.767	5	
048	0745	EAST MIDLANDS	1800	PAPHOS	B.757	6	
049	0600	MANCHESTER	1205	PALMA	B.767	7	
051	1725	GATWICK	2220	REUS	B.767	2	
052	0730	BRISTOL	1300	IBIZA	B.757	3	
053	1505	EAST MIDLANDS	2040	PALMA	B.757	4	

054	0820	MANCHESTER	1420	MAHON	B.757	5
055	1835	GATWICK	2320	GERONA	B.757	6
056	0830	CARDIFF	1700	LANZAROTE	B.757	7
057	1855	BIRMINGHAM	0405	BODRUM	A.320	1
058	2125	EAST MIDLANDS	0230	GERONA	B.757	2
059	1800	EAST MIDLANDS	2345	IBIZA	B.757	3
061	2330	GLASGOW	0615	IBIZA	B.757	5
062	2220	GATWICK	0345	IBIZA	B.767	6
063	2250	GLASGOW	0445	GERONA	B.757	2
064	0800	MANCHESTER	1745	BODRUM	B.757	1
065	0850	BIRMINGHAM	1755	FUERTVENTURA	B.757	2
066	0730	BIRMINGHAM	2105	MAHON	B.757	3
067	1045	EAST MIDLANDS	1830	KEFALLINIA	B.757	4
068	0730	MANCHESTER	1545	ZAKINTHOS	B.757	5
069	0555	GATWICK	1125	MAHON	B.757	6
072	1520	BRISTOL	2010	GERONA	A.320	2
074	2000	EAST MIDLANDS	0220	MALAGA	B.757	4
075	1555	STANSTED	2125	PALMA	B.757	5
076	1400	LEEDS	2005	MAHON	A.320	6
077	1825	MANCHESTER	0515	LARNACA	B.757	7
078	2255	BIRMINGHAM	0635	THESSALONIKI	B,757	1
079	1930	BIRMINGHAM	0450	TENERIFE	B.757	2
080	1925	MANCHESTER	0515	DALAMAN	B.767	3
081	0050	GLASGOW	0755	ALICANTE	A.320	5
083	2045	BRISTOL	0205	PALMA	B.757	6
084	1800	BIRMINGHAM	0320	TENERIFE	B.757	7
	1835	STANSTED	0350	DALAMAN	B.757	6
085	0650	GATWICK	1300	NAPLES	B.757	1
086	1415	BIRMINGHAM	2350	ANTALYA	B.757	2
088	0900	GATWICK	0655	ORLANDO	B.767	4
089	0625	LEEDS	1420	CORFU	A.320	5
091	0730	EAST MIDLANDS	1305	PALMA	B.757	7
092	1940	GLASGOW	0540	HERAKLION	B.757	1
093	1500	EAST MIDLANDS	2050	ALICANTE	B.757	2
095	1525	MANCHESTER	2130	PALMA	B.767	4
096	1515	LUTON	2220	CORFU	B.757	5
097	1345	GATWICK	1905	PALMA	B.767	6
098	1800	LUTON	2325	PALMA	B.757	7
099	2140	STANSTED	0655	LAS PALMAS	B.757	1
101	2050	BIRMINGHAM	0620	DALAMAN	B.757	3
102	1335	STANSTED	2215	HERAKLION	B.757	4
104	0055	GATWICK	0630	ALICANTE	B.757	7
105	2335	NEWCASTLE	0455	PALMA	B.757	7
106	0735	MANCHESTER	1335	MAHON	B.767	1
107	0730	CARDIFF	1250	PALMA	B.757	2
108	0730	BIRMINGHAM	1645	RHODES	B.757	3
109	0605	LUTON	1825	PALMA	B.757	4
110	0935	BELFAST INTL.	1750	CORFU	B.757	5
111	0820	GATWICK	1740	DALAMAN	B.767	6
112	0715	MANCHESTER	1355	FARO	B.767	7
113	1220	GATWICK	1740	PALMA	B.757	1
114	1245	LUTON	1810	PALMA	B.757	2
117	1540	BRISTOL	2110	IBIZA	B.757	5
118	1800	BIRMINGHAM	2305	REUS	B.757	6
119	1235	CARDIFF	1830	FARO	A.320	7
121	0715	GATWICK	1610	FUERTVENTURA	B.767	2
122	1745	BIRMINGHAM	0405	PAPHOS	B.757	3
123	2120	GATWICK	0610	KOS	B.757	4
125	1930	EAST MIDLANDS	0425	KOS	B.757	6
127	0825	LUTON	1735	BODRUM	B.757	1
128	1215	GATWICK	2135	ANTALYA	B.757	2
129	1730	GATWICK	0235	RHODES	B.767	3
130	0755	MANCHESTER	1735	LAS PALMAS	B.767	4
131	0545	LUTON	1320	ZAKINTHOS	B.757	5
132	0700	STANSTED	1240	IBIZA	B.757	6
133	1045	GATWICK	2000	LANZAROTE	B.767	7
134	0640	EAST MIDLANDS	2015	IBIZA	B.757	1
135	0600	LUTON	1055	REUS	B.757	2

136	1930	EAST MIDLANDS	0445	RHODES	B.757	3	
137	1620	NEWCASTLE	0705	ALICANTE	B.757	2	
138	1415	MANCHESTER	2155	CORFU	B.767		5
139	1755	LUTON	2320	MAHON	B.757		6
140	0630	NEWCASTLE	1325	MALAGA	B.757		7
141	2155	EAST MIDLANDS	0330	PALMA	B.757	1	
142	2315	MANCHESTER	0535	ALICANTE	B.767	2	
143	1755	STANSTED	2335	IBIZA	B.757	3	
144	2210	EAST MIDLANDS	0400	ALICANTE	B.757		4
145	1740	NEWCASTLE	1825	MANCHESTER	B.757		5
	1925	MANCHESTER	0305	MALTA	B.757		5
146	2140	LEEDS	0410	IBIZA	A.320		6
147	2245	GATWICK	0550	CORFU	B.767		7
148	0805	CARDIFF	1645	LAS PALMAS	B.757	1	
	2250	GATWICK	0540	MALTA	B.757		5
149	0715	MANCHESTER	1245	REUS	B.767	2	
150	1430	BRISTOL	0005	DALAMAN	B.757	3	
151	0630	BRISTOL	1150	PALMA	B.757		4
152	1105	MANCHESTER	0645	ORLANDO	B.767		5
153	0700	BIRMINGHAM	1630	DALAMAN	B.757		6
154	0855	MANCHESTER	1635	CORFU	B.767		7
155	1915	LUTON	0410	HERAKLION	B.757	1	
156	2310	MANCHESTER	0515	PALMA	B.757	2	
157	1255	LUTON	1825	IBIZA	B.757	3	
158	1405	EDINBURGH	1235	PALMA	B.757		4
159	1500	GATWICK	2025	IBIZA	B.767		5
160	1350	BELFAST INTL.	2030	IBIZA	B.757		6
161	1515	MANCHESTER	2155	MALAGA	B.767		7
162	0915	GLASGOW	1630	NAPLES	B.757	1	
163	0825	LUTON	1720	FUERTVENTURA	B.757	2	
164	2040	GLASGOW	0325	IBIZA	B.757	3	
165	1840	GATWICK	0055	FARO	B.757		4
166	0700	NEWCASTLE	1440	CORFU	B.757		5
167	2335	BIRMINGHAM	0430	GERONA	B.757		6
168	0045	GLASGOW	0720	PALMA	B.757		7
169	1805	GLASGOW	0400	LAS PALMAS	B.757	1	
170	0825	MANCHESTER	1420	PULA	B.757	2	
171	0835	EAST MIDLANDS	1800	DALAMAN	B.757	3	
172	1115	BIRMINGHAM	0645	ORLANDO	B.767		4
173	1030	GATWICK	1550	PALMA	B.757		5
174	0820	MANCHESTER	1425	PALMA	B.767		6
175	0510	CARDIFF	1105	MALAGA	A.320		7
176	1015	GATWICK	0815	BRIDGETOWN	B.767	1	
177	1055	GATWICK	0615	PUERTO PLATA	B.767	2	
178	1855	CARDIFF	0515	PAPHOS	B.757	3	
179	1320	BRISTOL	1915	MALAGA	B.757		4
180	1445	LUTON	2015	PALMA	B.757		5
181	1400	GATWICK	1855	REUS	B.757		6
182	1725	NEWCASTLE	2105	PALMA	B.757		7
183	0030	GATWICK	0550	PALMA	B.767	2	
184	2255	GATWICK	0555	MALTA	B.757	2	
185	1055	BIRMINGHAM	2020	SKIATHOS	A.320	3	
186	2210	BIRMINGHAM	0710	KOS	B.757		4
187	2320	MANCHESTER	0715	THESSALONIKI	B.757		5
188	2335	MANCHESTER	0500	IBIZA	B.767		6
190	0745	MANCHESTER	1720	LAS PALMAS	B.767	1	
191	0750	MANCHESTER	1710	FUERTVENTURA	B.767	2	
192	1400	NEWCASTLE	2325	LANZAROTE	B.757	3	
194	0915	GATWICK	1050	ORLANDO	B.767		5
195	0755	EAST MIDLANDS	1330	MAHON	B.757		6
196	0835	BRISTOL	1700	LANZAROTE	B.757		7
197	2015	GATWICK	0505	HERAKLION	B.757	1	
198	1420	CARDIFF	1915	REUS	B.757	2	
199	1600	LUTON	0120	DALAMAN	B.757	3	
200	1520	MANCHESTER	2155	ALMERIA	B.757		4
201	0935	MANCHESTER	2025	LARNACA	B.767		5
202	1840	LUTON	0320	KOS	B.757		6
203	1550	STANSTED	2220	FARO	B.757		7

No.	Dep	From	Arr	To	Aircraft	Day	Notes
206	0710	EAST MIDLANDS	1630	TENERIFE	B.757	3	
207	2345	MANCHESTER	0605	ALICANTE	B.767	4	
208	2315	GATWICK	0440	IBIZA	B.757	5	
209	0050	BIRMINGHAM	0630	PALMA	B.757	7	
211	0810	BIRMINGHAM	1355	MAHON	B.757	1	
212	0625	BIRMINGHAM	1140	REUS	B.757	2	
214	0910	GATWICK	1800	HERAKLION	B.767	4	
215	0625	GATWICK	1330	CORFU	B.767	5	
216	0620	CARDIFF	1205	ALICANTE	B.757	6	
217	1650	GLASGOW	0355	LARNACA	A.320	7	
219	1950	MANCHESTER	0330	CORFU	B.757	2	
220	2135	MANCHESTER	0500	MONASTIR	B.767	3	
221	1615	GLASGOW	2340	MALAGA	A.320	4	
222	1435	GLASGOW	2150	NAPLES	B.757	5	
223	1320	CARDIFF	1855	MAHON	B.757	6	
224	1425	LUTON	2150	THESSALONIKI	B.757	1	
225	0650	MANCHESTER	1255	PALMA	B.767	1	
226	2045	CARDIFF	0135	GERONA	B.757	2	
227	1845	BRISTOL	0400	RHODES	A.320	3	
228	2245	NEWCASTLE	0500	PALMA	B.757	4	
229	1610	NEWCASTLE	2225	PALMA	B.757	5	
230	2155	BELFAST INTL.	0430	PALMA	B.757	6	
231	2045	NEWCASTLE	0630	TENERIFE	B.757	7	
232	0540	GATWICK	1225	MAHON	B.767	1	
233	0830	STANSTED	1330	REUS	B.757	2	
234	0600	LUTON	1125	MAHON	B.757	3	
235	0745	NEWCASTLE	1720	HERAKLION	B.757	4	
236	0650	LUTON	1300	NAPLES	B.757	5	
237	0710	LUTON	1710	PAPHOS	B.757	6	
238	0810	GLASGOW	0515	SANTO DOMINGO	B.767	7	VIA M'CHESTER
	0615	GLASGOW	0700	MANCHESTER	B.767	1	
239	1605	MANCHESTER	2255	NAPLES	B.757	1	
241	1740	LEEDS	0430	DALAMAN	A.320	3	
243	1035	GLASGOW	0525	ORLANDO	B.767	5	
244	1105	MANCHESTER	0655	ORLANDO	B.767	6	
245	1505	BIRMINGHAM	2130	MALAGA	B.757	7	
246	0830	NEWCASTLE	1450	IBIZA	B.757	1	
247	0055	GATWICK	0540	GERONA	B.767	3	
248	2350	LUTON	0520	IBIZA	B.757	5	
251	2240	GLASGOW	0515	PALMA	B.757	6	
252	2255	BIRMINGHAM	0435	PALMA	B.757	7	
253	0715	GATWICK	1620	LAS PALMAS	B.767	1	
254	0710	GATWICK	1530	CORFU	B.757	2	
255	1245	BIRMINGHAM	0815	PUERTO PLATA	B.767	3	
256	0655	GATWICK	1330	ALMERIA	B.767	4	
257	0730	MANCHESTER	1335	PALMA	B.767	5	
258	0840	BIRMINGHAM	1425	MAHON	B.757	6	
259	1055	GATWICK	0625	SANTO DOMINGO	B.767	7	
262	2135	BIRMINGHAM	0440	MONASTIR	A.320	3	
263	1405	BIRMINGHAM	2025	ALMERIA	B.757	4	
264	1600	GATWICK	2120	PALMA	B.757	5	
265	1830	MANCHESTER	0420	DALAMAN	B.757	6	
266	1920	MANCHESTER	0450	TENERIFE	B.767	7	
267	1620	NEWCASTLE	0210	LAS PALMAS	B.757	1	
268	1540	LEEDS	2225	ALICANTE	A.320	2	
269	2105	NEWCASTLE	0325	IBIZA	B.757	3	
271	2255	STANSTED	0435	IBIZA	B.757	5	
272	1430	NEWCASTLE	2005	GERONA	B.757	6	
274	1300	EAST MIDLANDS	2215	BODRUM	B.757	1	
275	0825	MANCHESTER	1825	ANTALYA	B.757	2	
276	0900	GLASGOW	1910	DALAMAN	B.757	3	
277	0645	LEEDS	1250	PALMA	A.320	4	
278	0700	STANSTED	2250	CORFU	B.757	5	
279	0730	GLASGOW	1340	REUS	B.757	6	
281	1450	MANCHESTER	2245	THESSALONIKI	B.767	1	
282	1800	BIRMINGHAM	0315	LAS PALMAS	B.757	4	
283	1835	GLASGOW	0440	RHODES	B.757	3	
284	0830	CARDIFF	1350	PALMA	B.757	4	

No.	Dep	From	Arr	To	Aircraft	1	2	3	4	5	6	7	Notes
285	1550	MANCHESTER	2115	VENICE	B.757					5			
286	1410	STANSTED	0220	GERONA	B.757						6		
287	1905	EAST MIDLANDS	0425	TENERIFE	B.757							7	
289	1845	LUTON	0030	ALICANTE	B.757		2						
291	1250	NORWICH	1135	PALMA	B.757				4				
292	2145	LUTON	0310	PALMA	B.757					5			
293	1405	STANSTED	1945	IBIZA	B.757						6		
295	0730	LEEDS	1715	LAS PALMAS	A.320	1							
296	0700	GATWICK	1610	TENERIFE	B.767		2						
297	0725	LUTON	1725	PAPHOS	B.757			3					
298	0715	MANCHESTER	1640	HERAKLION	B.757				4				
299	1920	BELFAST INTL.	0455	TENERIFE	B.757					5			
301	0900	GATWICK	1740	SAMOS	B.757							7	
302	1740	GATWICK	2305	IBIZA	B.767	1							
303	0755	GLASGOW	1440	PALMA	B.757		2						
304	0655	GATWICK	1305	ALMERIA	B.757							7	
305	1755	MANCHESTER	0330	LAS PALMAS	B.757				4				
306	0825	BIRMINGHAM	1555	CORFU	B.757					5			
307	1355	BIRMINGHAM	1900	QBS???	B.757						6		
308	1435	GATWICK	2230	KAVALA	B.757							7	
309	0825	BIRMINGHAM	1720	FANTAIL	A.320	1							
311	2300	BIRMINGHAM	0455	IBIZA	B.757			3					
312	2300	MANCHESTER	0505	PALMA	B.767				4				
313	2255	BRISTOL	0415	PALMA	B.757					5			
314	1910	GATWICK	0415	RHODES	B.767						6		
315	1435	EAST MIDLANDS	2200	CORFU	B.757							7	
316	0730	BRISTOL	1515	THESSALONIKI	B.757	1							
317	0600	GLASGOW	2110	ALICANTE	B.757		2						
318	0730	LUTON	1420	MONASTIR	B.757			3					
319	0805	EAST MIDLANDS	1340	PALMA	B.757				4				
321	1455	GLASGOW	2135	MAHON	B.757						6		
322	0830	LUTON	1445	FARO	B.757							7	
324	1605	GLASGOW	1700	EAST MIDLANDS	B.757		2						
	1800	EAST MIDLANDS	2210	MALTA	B.757		2						
	0225	EAST MIDLANDS	0320	GLASGOW	B.757			3					
326	2010	LUTON	0135	PALMA	B.757				4				
327	0035	BIRMINGHAM	0615	PALMA	B.757						6		
328	1600	MANCHESTER	2200	MAHON	B.767						6		
329	0645	BELFAST INTL.	1400	MALAGA	B.757							7	
332	0645	BIRMINGHAM	1225	PALMA	B.757						6		
333	0035	BELFAST	0705	ALICANTE	B.757					5			
335	2040	BIRMINGHAM	0240	ALICANTE	B.757						6		
336	1735	MANCHESTER	1630	MOMBASSA	B.767							7	VIA GATWICK
337	0805	CARDIFF	1610	ZAKINTHOS	A.320	1							
338	1900	NEWCASTLE	0115	PALMA	B.757		2						
339	0715	STANSTED	1615	LANZAROTE	B.757			3					
341	0650	GATWICK	1420	ZAKINTHOS	B.757					5			
342	0705	LUTON	1620	DALAMAN	B.757						6		
343	2320	MANCHESTER	0430	PALMA	B.757							7	
344	1740	CARDIFF	0240	BODRUM	A.320	1							
345	1620	MANCHESTER	2140	GERONA	B.757		2						
346	1920	MANCHESTER	0140	ALICANTE	B.767				4				
347	1545	GATWICK	2105	PALMA	B.767				4				
348	0600	MANCHESTER	1245	NAPLES	B.767					5			
349	1620	BIRMINGHAM	2205	IBIZA	B.757						6		
352	1835	MANCHESTER	0430	ABU DHABI	B.767		2						VIA GATWICK
353	1740	EAST MIDLANDS	0300	LAS PALMAS	B.757	1							
354	0740	MANCHESTER	1345	PALMA	B.767				4				
356	2120	EAST MIDLANDS	0305	IBIZA	B.757						6		
357	2100	GATWICK	0220	PALMA	B.767							7.	
358	0735	STANSTED	1305	PALMA	B.757	1							
359	1420	EDINBURGH	1250	ALICANTE	B.757		2						
361	0545	MANCHESTER	1355	KEFALLINIA	B.757				4				
362	1510	TEESSIDE	1325	PALMA	B.757				4				
363	0615	GATWICK	1140	IBIZA	B.767						6		
364	1335	MANCHESTER	2010	ALMERIA	B.767							7	
365	0600	LEEDS	1205	PALMA	A.320							7	
366	1815	GATWICK	1540	PULA	A.320		2						

367	0825	NEWCASTLE	1855	PAPHOS	B.757	3	
368	1425	LEEDS	2105	MALAGA	A.320	4	
369	1730	BIRMINGHAM	0400	LARNACA	B.757		5
374	1650	EAST MIDLANDS	0305	PAPHOS	B.757	3	
376	2335	MANCHESTER	0455	GERONA	B.767		6
377	2030	GATWICK	0150	PALMA	B.757		6
378	2325	MANCHESTER	0530	PALMA	B.767		7
379	0550	EAST MIDLANDS	1125	MAHON	B.757	1	
382	0600	GLASGOW	2045	PALMA	B.757	4	
383	0710	BRISTOL	1330	NAPLES	B.757		5
384	0700	NEWCASTLE	1315	MAHON	B.757		6
385	0705	EAST MIDLANDS	1735	LARNACA	B.757		7
386	1415	GATWICK	2145	ZAKINTHOS	B.757	1	
387	1500	STANSTED	0015	TENERIFE	B.757	2	
388	1510	MANCHESTER	1315	MAHON	B.757	3	
390	1505	MANCHESTER	2105	IBIZA	B.767		5
392	1305	CARDIFF	1855	ALICANTE	A.320		6
393	1915	MANCHESTER	0115	PALMA	B.757	1	
394	0725	EAST MIDLANDS	1655	FUERTVENTURA	B.757	2	
395	2310	MANCHESTER	0510	IBIZA	B.757	3	
397	2330	LEEDS	0535	PALMA	A.320		5
398	0730	GATWICK	1700	KOS	B.757		6
399	0730	LUTON	1620	LANZAROTE	B.757		7
401	0930	MANCHESTER	0545	ST. LUCIA	B.767	1	
402	0930	MANCHESTER	1615	PAPHOS	B.767	3	
403	0710	EAST MIDLANDS	1615	HERAKLION	B.757	4	
404	1505	BIRMINGHAM	2305	ZAKYNTHOS	B.757		5
405	0845	NEWCASTLE	1830	DALAMAN	B.757		6
406	0625	BIRMINGHAM	1210	PALMA	B.757		7
407	1955	MANCHESTER	0530	LAS PALMAS	B.767	1	
408	2320	LUTON	0450	IBIZA	B.757	1	
409	2015	LUTON	0505	RHODES	B.757	3	
411	2155	MANCHESTER	0730	TENERIFE	B.767		5
412	1415	LUTON	0015	PAPHOS	B.757		6
413	1010	MANCHESTER	1925	SAMOS	B.757		7
414	1540	LUTON	0100	LAS PALMAS	B.757	4	
417	2215	GLASGOW	0450	PALMA	B.757	4	
418	0630	EAST MIDLANDS	1215	IBIZA	B.757		5
419	0830	MANCHESTER	1910	PAPHOS	B.767		6
421	0930	MANCHESTER	1045	ORLANDO	B.767	1	
422	0930	MANCHESTER	0420	BRIDGETOWN	B.767	2	
423	0755	LEEDS	1715	LANZAROTE	A.320	3	
424	0830	MANCHESTER	1750	KOS	B.767	4	
425	1750	LUTON	0405	LARNACA	B.757		5
426	1100	NEWCASTLE	0610	ORLANDO	B.767		6
427	0945	MANCHESTER	0505	ORLANDO	B.767		7
428	1645	BRISTOL	0125	LAS PALMAS	B.757	1	
429	2355	LEEDS	0600	PALMA	A.320	2	
431	1415	GATWICK	2020	MALAGA	B.757	4	
432	1700	CARDIFF	0050	THESSALONIKI	A.320		5
433	0800	BIRMINGHAM	1820	PAPHOS	B.757	3	
434	2135	NEWCASTLE	0410	ALICANTE	B.757		6
435	1920	MANCHESTER	0445	HERAKLION	B.767	1	
439	2115	CARDIFF	0305	IBIZA	B.757		5
442	0720	NEWCASTLE	1530	ZAKINTHOS	B.757	1	
443	1230	LUTON	1945	MALTA	B.757	2	
444	0700	MANCHESTER	1640	RHODES	B.767	3	
445	0605	BIRMINGHAM	1130	FARO	B.757	4	
446	0720	CARDIFF	1240	PALMA	B.757		5
447	0800	STANSTED	1655	RHODES	B.757		6
449	1420	GATWICK	2150	THESSALONIKI	B.767	1	
450	0045	BIRMINGHAM	0625	PALMA	B.757	3	
451	0830	GLASGOW	1825	BODRUM	B.757	1	
452	0725	GATWICK	1245	PALMA	B.757	4	
453	1725	MANCHESTER	0005	PALMA	B.757		5
454	2025	CARDIFF	0550	RHODES	B.757		6
455	1540	BELFAST INTL.	0105	LANZAROTE	B.757		7
456	2320	GATWICK	0445	IBIZA	B.767	1	

Flt	Dep	Origin	Arr	Destination	Aircraft	Day
457	0630	BRISTOL	1350	MALTA	A.320	2
460	2110	MANCHESTER	0630	KOS	B.767	6
461	0720	MANCHESTER	1700	RHODES	B.757	6
462	0730	GLASGOW	2325	MALAGA	B.757	7
465	0740	GLASGOW	1725	LANZAROTE	B.757	3
466	0745	BIRMINGHAM	1325	PALMA	B.757	4
467	0900	STANSTED	1425	MAHON	B.757	5
468	0650	LEEDS	1230	REUS	A.320	6
469	1300	STANSTED	2215	TENERIFE	B.757	7
471	1945	LUTON	0245	CORFU	B.757	2
472	1755	MANCHESTER	0435	PAPHOS	B.757	3
473	0830	BIRMINGHAM	1615	KEFALLINIA	B.757	4
474	0800	CARDIFF	1530	CORFU	A.320	5
475	0800	NEWCASTLE	1610	THESSALONIKI	B.757	5
476	1335	LEEDS	2330	TENERIFE	A.320	7
478	2140	BRISTOL	0300	PALMA	A.320	2
481	2355	NEWCASTLE	0615	IBIZA	B.757	5
482	2100	CARDIFF	0220	PALMA	A.320	6
484	0845	BIRMINGHAM	1645	ZAKINTHOS	B.757	1
485	0905	NEWCASTLE	1455	REUS	B.757	2
486	0640	MANCHESTER	1550	LANZAROTE	B.757	3
488	1545	LEEDS	2205	IBIZA	A.320	5
490	0710	GATWICK	1315	MALAGA	B.767	7
493	1710	NEWCASTLE	0300	BODRUM	B.757	1
494	1535	MANCHESTER	2215	FARO	B.767	4
495	1350	EAST MIDLANDS	2115	CORFU	B.757	5
496	0945	GLASGOW	1820	ZAKYNTHOS	A.320	5
497	1340	BIRMINGHAM	2235	LANZAROTE	B.757	7
499	2335	GATWICK	0505	PALMA	B.767	2
500	1015	GATWICK	2030	PAPHOS	B.767	3
501	0745	BELFAST	1415	PALMA	B.757	4
502	2115	MANCHESTER	0655	RHODES	B.757	6
504	0600	STANSTED	1130	PALMA	B.757	7
505	0505	LUTON	1030	MAHON	B.757	1
506	0825	LEEDS	1400	GERONA	A.320	2
507	0700	EAST MIDLANDS	1550	LANZAROTE	B.757	3
508	1520	CARDIFF	0030	HERAKLION	B.757	4
509	0720	BIRMINGHAM	1350	NAPLES	B.757	5
510	1300	GATWICK	0900	ORLANDO	B.767	6
511	0840	MANCHESTER	1750	LANZAROTE	B.767	7
514	0800	BRISTOL	1700	TENERIFE	A.320	3
515	2015	GATWICK	0520	LAS PALMAS	B.767	4
516	0010	MANCHESTER	0610	IBIZA	B.757	6
517	1640	MANCHESTER	2210	REUS	B.767	6
518	1435	GATWICK	2050	FARO	B.767	7
521	2350	GATWICK	0545	IBIZA	B.757	3
522	2045	BRISTOL	0230	ALICANTE	B.757	4
523	1410	CARDIFF	1930	PALMA	B.757	5
526	1905	BIRMINGHAM	0420	LAS PALMAS	B.757	1
527	0700	BRISTOL	1540	FUERTENTURA	B.757	2
528	0710	CARDIFF	1650	DALAMAN	B.757	3
529	0945	MANCHESTER	0655	ORLANDO	B.767	4
530	2300	BIRMINGHAM	0445	PALMA	B.757	4
531	0625	BELFAST INTL.	1235	REUS	B.757	6
532	0755	BIRMINGHAM	1555	KAVALLINIA	B.757	7
533	1450	STANSTED	2015	MAHON	B.757	1
534	1745	BRISTOL	0105	CORFU	B.757	2
535	1200	GATWICK	2105	RHODES	B.767	3
536	1500	BIRMINGHAM	2145	MALAGA	B.757	4
537	1440	GATWICK	1955	MAHON	B.767	5
538	1430	EAST MIDLANDS	2005	PALMA	B.757	6
540	0830	EAST MIDLANDS	1610	THESSALONIKI	B.757	1
543	1605	BELFAST	2305	FARO	B.757	4
544	2130	GATWICK	0640	TENERIFE	B.767	5
546	1605	EDINBURGH	1430	MALAGA	B.757	7
548	0615	LUTON	1110	GERONA	B.757	2
549	0815	MANCHESTER	1805	DALAMAN	B.767	3
550	0800	GLASGOW	1515	FARO	A.320	4

Flight	Dep	From	Arr	To	Aircraft	Day	Notes
551	1535	NORWICH	1415	CORFU	B.757	5	
552	0730	LUTON	1300	IBIZA	B.757	6	
553	0850	MANCHESTER	1710	KAVALA	B.757	7	
555	1410	MANCHESTER	2200	MALTA	B.767	2	
556	1900	GATWICK	0455	PAPHOS	B.757	3	
	1945	NEWCASTLE	0530	RHODES	B.757	6	
559	1020	GLASGOW	0515	ORLANDO	B.767	6	
560	1835	CARDIFF	0320	TENERIFE	B.757	7	
562	1900	EAST MIDLANDS	0120	FARO	B.757	4	
564	1120	BIRMINGHAM	0650	ORLANDO	B.767	5	
565	0050	GATWICK	0455	CORFU	B.767	5	
567	0815	GLASGOW	1500	IBIZA	A.320	6	
568	0610	MANCHESTER	1440	ORLANDO	B.767	1	VIA GATWICK
569	1250	MANCHESTER	0815	PUERTO PLATA	B.767	2	
571	0800	LUTON	1420	ALMERIA	B.757	4	
573	0700	CARDIFF	1155	REUS	A.320	6	
574	0850	NEWCASTLE	1935	LARNACA	B.757	7	
575	2250	MANCHESTER	0450	IBIZA	B.767	1	
576	1000	BIRMINGHAM	2345	PULA	A.320	2	
579	1615	BIRMINGHAM	2155	PALMA	B.757	5	
580	2105	GLASGOW	0700	TENERIFE	A.320	5	
581	1630	GLASGOW	0240	DALAMAN	A.320	6	
583	2335	GATWICK	0640	CORFU	B.757	2	
585	0800	EAST MIDLANDS	1335	PALMA	B.757	2	
588	0655	GLASGOW	1525	CORFU	A.320	7	
589	0830	BIRMINGHAM	1735	HERAKLION	B.757	1	
590	0805	BIRMINGHAM	1535	CORFU	B.757	2	
591	1045	GATWICK	2239	LUXOR	B.757	3	
592	0710	NEWCASTLE	2120	PALMA	B.757	4	
593	0830	BIRMINGHAM	1420	IBIZA	B.757	5	
594	0930	MANCHESTER	1920	DALAMAN	B.757	6	
595	0715	BIRMINGHAM	1335	ALMERIA	B.757	7	
596	1415	HUMBERSIDE	1250	IBIZA	B.757	1	
597	1440	HUMBERSIDE	1310	REUS	B.757	2	
598	0930	MANCHESTER	2150	LUXOR	B.757	3	
609	1925	GATWICK	0440	TENERIFE	B.757	7	
612	1415	GATWICK	2300	LANZAROTE	B.767	3	
628	2020	DUBLIN	0240	IBIZA	B.767	5	
629	2230	DUBLIN	0830	HERAKLION	B.767	6	
636	0730	DUBLIN	1315	REUS	B.767	6	
637	1100	DUBLIN	1140	SHANNON	B.767	7	
638	1045	DUBLIN	1135	ORLANDO	B.767	1	
639	1450	DUBLIN	0905	BRIDGETOWN	B.767	2	
639	1450	DUBLIN	0905	BRIDGETOWN	B.767	2	
640	1215	DUBLIN	0105	LUXOR	B.767	3	
641	0845	DUBLIN	1845	ABU DHABI	B.767	4	
643	1440	DUBLIN	2105	FARO	B.767	6	
660	1655	GATWICK	2215	PALMA	B.757	2	
689	1910	GATWICK	0115	MALAGA	B.767	3	

EVEN NOS:- FLIGHTS INTO EUROPE   UNEVEN NOS:- FLIGHTS LEAVING EUROPE

Flight	Dep	From	Arr	To	Aircraft	Day
801/2	0415	OSLO	0325	PUERTO PLATO	B.767	2
901/2	1310	MUNICH	1030	VARADERO	B.767	1
903/4	1420	BERLIN	1140	VARADERO	B.767	1
905/6	1500	COLOGNE	1220	VARADERO	B.767	2
907/8	1520	HANOVER	1240	VARADERO	B.767	3
911/2	1120	FRANKFURT	0340	VARADERO	B.767	4
913/4	1150	HAMBURG	0910	VARADERO	B.767	5
915/6	1220	BASLE	0940	VARADERO	B.767	6
919/0	1015	STUTTGART	0715	PUERTO PLATO	B.767	1
921/2	0640	BERLIN	0720	PUERTO PLATO	B.767	2
923/4	1600	FRANKFURT	0340	PUERTO PLATO	B.767	3
925/6	1615	ZURICH	1230	GENEVA	B.767	4
927/8	1540	MUNICH	1310	PUERTO PLATO	B.767	5
929/0	0540	BASLE	0240	PUERTO PLATO	B.767	6
931/2	1015	MUNICH	0235	COLOGNE	B.767	7
933/4	1220	BERLIN	0920	PUERTO PLATO	B.767	1
935/6	0920	KARLSHRUHE	0750	KARLSHRUHE	B.767	2

937/8	0330	FRANKFURT	1510	PUERTO PLATO	B.767	3	
939/0	0535	BERLIN	0405	PUERTO PLATO	B.767	4	
941/2	0550	MUNICH	0250	PUERTO PLATO	B.767	5	
943/5	0540	BASLE	0240	PUERTO PLATO	B.767	6	
945/6	1015	MUNICH	0300	PUERTO PLATO	B.767	7	
947/8	0650	MUNICH	0745	PUNTA CANA	B.767	2	
949/0	0730	BERLIN	0430	PUNTA CANA	B.767	3	
951/2	0740	MUNICH	0440	PUNTA CANA	B.767	4	
953/4	0600	HAMBURG	0300	PUERTO PLATO	B.767	5	
955/6	1525	COLOGNE	1225	PUERTO PLATO	B.767	6	
957/8	1500	HANOVER	1200	PUERTO PLATO	B.767	7	
959/0	0715	COLOGNE	1130	PUERTO PLATO	B.767	1	
963/4	0715	COLOGNE	0415	PUERTO PLATO	B.767	3	
967/8	1140	FRANKFURT	0330	PUNTA CANA	B.767	4	
969/0	1115	HAMBURG	0815	PUNTA CANA	B.767	5	
971/2	1150	BASLE	0735	PUNTA CANA	B.767	6	
973/4	1040	DUSSELDORF	0805	PUNTA CANA	B.767	7	
983/4	0735	MUNICH	0505	MONTEGO BAY	B.767	7	
985/6	1125	COLOGNE	0915	MONTEGO BAY	B.767	1	
987/8	1540	FRANKFURT	1240	MONTEGO BAY	B.767	2	

FLIGHT NOS. 901F - 999F ARE POSITIONING FLIGHTS, USED ON VARIOUS DAYS BETWEEN ENTIRELY DIFFERENT SETS OF AIRPORTS.

BRITISH   *BRITISH REGIONAL AIRLINES   TH/BRT U.K.*

ROUTES FLOWN BY MANX AIRLINES (B.A. FRANCHISEE) AIRCRAFT. BRITISH REGIONAL AIRLINES AND MANX AIRLINES COMPRISE THE BRITISH REGIONAL AIRLINES GROUP.

101	0655	LEEDS	0805	SOUTHAMPTON	J'STREAM41	12345		
102	0825	SOUTHAMPTON	0930	LEEDS	J'STREAM41	12345		
103	0950	LEEDS	1115	ABERDEEN	J'STREAM41	12345		
107	1910	SOUTHAMPTON	2015	LEEDS	J'STREAM41	12345		
108	1600	ABERDEEN	1725	LEEDS	J'STREAM41	12345		
109	1745	LEEDS	1850	SOUTHAMPTON	J'STREAM41	12345		
112	1435	LEEDS	1540	SOUTHAMPTON	J'STREAM41	12345		
114	1610	SOUTHAMPTON	1715	LEEDS	J'STREAM41	12345		
116	0650	LEEDS	0815	ABERDEEN	J'STREAM41	12345		
117	0835	ABERDEEN	0955	LEEDS	J'STREAM41	12345		
118	1740	LEEDS	1905	ABERDEEN	J'STREAM41	12345		
118	1740	LEEDS	1905	ABERDEEN	J'STREAM41		7	
119	1925	ABERDEEN	2050	LEEDS	J'STREAM41	12345	7	
201	0705	CARDIFF	0825	GLASGOW	J'STREAM41	12345		
202	0850	GLASGOW	1015	CARDIFF	J'STREAM41	12345		
209	1330	CARDIFF	1450	GLASGOW	J'STREAM41	12345		
211	1515	GLASGOW	1640	CARDIFF	J'STREAM41	12345	7	1615/1740 7
212	1710	CARDIFF	1835	GLASGOW	J'STREAM41	12345	7	1810/1935 7
216	1500	CARDIFF	1615	BELFAST	J'STREAM41		7	
217	1635	BELFAST	1740	ABERDEEN	J'STREAM41		7	
218	1810	ABERDEEN	1915	BELFAST	J'STREAM41		7	
219	1935	BELFAST	2050	CARDIFF	J'STREAM41		7	
221	1905	GLASGOW	2030	CARDIFF	J'STREAM41	12345		
227	0700	CARDIFF	0835	PARIS CDG	J'STREAM41	12345		
228	0900	PARIS CDG	1035	CARDIFF	J'STREAM41	12345		
229	1105	CARDIFF	1220	BELFAST	J'STREAM41	12345		
234	1720	CARDIFF	1855	PARIS CDG	J'STREAM41		7	
236	1925	PARIS CDG	2100	CARDIFF	J'STREAM41	12345	7	
237	0845	CARDIFF	1000	BELFAST	J'STREAM41	6		
238	1030	BELFAST	1145	CARDIFF	J'STREAM41	6		
241	1200	CARDIFF	1255	GUERNSEY	J'STREAM41		7	
242	1320	GUERNSEY	1415	CARDIFF	J'STREAM41		7	
243	0650	CARDIFF	0835	BRUSSELS	J'STREAM41	12345.		
244	0900	BRUSSELS	1035	CARDIFF	J'STREAM41	12345		
246	1255	CARDIFF	1430	PARIS CDG	J'STREAM41	12345		
247	1455	PARIS CDG	1630	CARDIFF	J'STREAM41	12345		
248	1700	CARDIFF	1835	BRUSSELS	J'STREAM41	12345	7	
249	1905	BRUSSELS	2040	CARDIFF	J'STREAM41	12345	7	
251	1240	BELFAST	1345	ABERDEEN	J'STREAM41	12345		
252	1410	ABERDEEN	1515	BELFAST	J'STREAM41	12345		
253	1535	BELFAST	1650	CARDIFF	J'STREAM41	12345		

254	1720	CARDIFF	1855	PARIS CDG	J'STREAM41	12345		
257	1045	CARDIFF	1140	GUERNSEY	J'STREAM41	12345		
258	1205	GUERNSEY	1300	CARDIFF	J'STREAM41	12345		
323	0650	BELFAST CITY	0815	SOUTHAMPTON	J'STREAM41	12345		
324	0840	SOUTHAMPTON	1010	BELFAST CITY	J'STREAM41	123456	1340/1505 6	
339	1340	BELFAST CITY	1505	SOUTHAMPTON	J'STREAM41	123456	1025/1150 6	
341	1530	SOUTHAMPTON	1700	BELFAST CITY	J'STREAM41	12345		
342	1530	BELFAST CITY	1655	SOUTHAMPTON	J'STREAM41	7		
342	1730	BELFAST CITY	1855	SOUTHAMPTON	J'STREAM41	12345		
343	1920	SOUTHAMPTON	2050	BELFAST CITY	J'STREAM41	12345 7	1730/1900 7	
346	1500	BELFAST CITY	1545	GLASGOW	J'STREAM41	7		
349	2000	GLASGOW	2045	BELFAST CITY	J-STREAM41	7		
361	0700	BELFAST CITY	0800	MANCHESTER	BAE-ATP	123456		
362	0850	MANCHESTER	0955	BELFAST CITY	BAE-ATP	123456		
363	1030	BELFAST CITY	1130	MANCHESTER	BAE-ATP	12345		
383	0740	BELFAST CITY	0830	EDINBURGH	J'STREAM41	6		
384	0900	EDINBURGH	0950	BELFAST CITY	J'STREAM41	6		
422	0710	SOUTHAMPTON	0815	BRUSSELS	EMB-145	12345		
423	0840	BRUSSELS	0950	SOUTHAMPTON	EMB-145	12345		
424	1025	SOUTHAMPTON	1140	GLASGOW	EMB-145	12345		
425	1215	GLASGOW	1330	SOUTHAMPTON	EMB-145	12345		
426	1405	SOUTHAMPTON	1520	GLASGOW	EMB-145	12345		
427	1555	GLASGOW	1710	SOUTHAMPTON	EMB-145	12345		
428	1740	SOUTHAMPTON	1845	BRUSSELS	EMB-145	12345 7		
429	1920	BRUSSELS	2025	SOUTHAMPTON	EMB-145	12345 7		
433	0700	SOUTHAMPTON	0815	EDINBURGH	EMB-145	12345		
434	0850	EDINBURGH	1005	SOUTHAMPTON	EMB-145	12345		
435	1050	SOUTHAMPTON	1205	EDINBURGH	EMB-145	12345		
436	1250	EDINBURGH	1405	SOUTHAMPTON	EMB-145	12345		
437	1700	SOUTHAMPTON	1815	EDINBURGH	EMB-145	12345		
438	1850	EDINBURGH	2005	SOUTHAMPTON	EMB-145	12345		
445	0745	SOUTHAMPTON	0900	GLASGOW	EMB-145	67	1300/1415 7	
446	0930	GLASGOW	1000	EDINBURGH	EMB-145	67	1445/1515 7	
447	1030	EDINBURGH	1145	SOUTHAMPTON	EMB-145	67	1545/1700 7	
451	0650	SOUTHAMPTON	0805	GLASGOW	EMB-145	12345		
452	0840	GLASGOW	0955	SOUTHAMPTON	EMB-145	12345		
453	1030	SOUTHAMPTON	1145	DUBLIN	EMB-145	12345		
454	1215	DUBLIN	1325	SOUTHAMPTON	EMB-145	12345		
455	1400	SOUTHAMPTON	1515	EDINBURGH	EMB-145	12345		
456	1545	EDINBURGH	1700	SOUTHAMPTON	EMB-145	12345 7	1710/1845 7	
457	1730	SOUTHAMPTON	1845	GLASGOW	EMB-145	12345 7		
458	1920	GLASGOW	2035	SOUTHAMPTON	EMB-145	12345 7		
468	1220	SOUTHAMPTON	1335	DUBLIN	EMB-145	6		
469	1410	DUBLIN	1525	SOUTHAMPTON	EMB-145	6		
472	1350	SOUTHAMPTON	1505	DUBLIN	EMB-145	7		
473	1535	DUBLIN	1645	SOUTHAMPTON	EMB-145	7		
511	0710	EDINBURGH	0805	BELFAST CITY	BAE-ATP	12345		
512	0840	BELFAST CITY	0930	EDINBURGH	BAE-ATP	12345		
513	1200	EDINBURGH	1255	BELFAST CITY	BAE-ATP	12345		
514	1330	BELFAST CITY	1420	LIVERPOOL	BAE-ATP	12345		
515	1500	LIVERPOOL	1555	BELFAST CITY	BAE-ATP	12345		
516	1630	BELFAST CITY	1720	EDINBURGH	ATP/J'S41	123456	1655/1745 6	
517	1810	EDINBURGH	1905	BELFAST CITY	ATP/J'S41	1234567		
518	1940	BELFAST CITY	2030	EDINBURGH	BAE-ATP	12345 7		
521	0715	EDINBURGH	0900	PARIS CDG	EMB-145	123456		
522	0945	PARIS CDG	1130	EDINBURGH	EMB-145	123456		
523	1200	EDINBURGH	1345	PARIS CDG	EMB-145	1234567		
524	1415	PARIS CDG	1600	EDINBURGH	EMB-145	1234567		
525	1715	EDINBURGH	1900	PARIS CDG	EMB-145	12345 7		
526	1940	PARIS CDG	2125	EDINBURGH	EMB-145	12345 7		
528	1035	EDINBURGH	1125	BELFAST	J'STREAM41	12345		
529	1200	BELFAST	1250	EDINBURGH	J'STREAM41	12345		
530	1320	EDINBURGH	1445	CARDIFF	J'STREAM41	12345		
531	1510	CARDIFF	1635	EDINBURGH	J'STREAM41	12345		
532	0650	EDINBURGH	0815	CARDIFF	J'STREAM41	12345		
533	0840	CARDIFF	1005	EDINBURGH	J'STREAM41	12345		
538	1710	EDINBURGH	1835	CARDIFF	J'STREAM41	12345		
539	1900	CARDIFF	2025	EDINBURGH	J'STREAM41	12345		

540	1430	EDINBURGH	1520	BELFAST	J'STREAM41		7	
541	1550	BELFAST	1640	EDINBURGH	J'STREAM41		7	
542	1910	SOUTHAMPTON	2045	EDINBURGH	J'STREAM41		7	
545	1510	JERSEY	1645	MANCHESTER	BAE-ATP		6	-25.09
	1310	JERSEY	1445	MANCHESTER	BAE-ATP		7	
546	1720	MANCHESTER	1850	JERSEY	BAE-ATP		6	-25.09
596	2035	LEEDS	2140	SOUTHAMPTON	J'STREAM41		5	
597	1900	SOUTHAMPTON	2005	LEEDS	J'STREAM41		7	
598	1900	GLASGOW	2010	MANCHESTER	BAE-ATP	12345		-24.09
599	1320	MANCHESTER	1430	GLASGOW	BAE-ATP		7	-26.09
615	0750	SUMBURGH	0850	ABERDEEN	BAE-ATP	12345		
616	0930	ABERDEEN	1030	SUMBURGH	BAE-ATP	12345		
620	1440	GLASGOW	1530	ABERDEEN	BAE-ATP		7	
621	1350	GLASGOW	1440	ABERDEEN	BAE-ATP	12345		
	1510	ABERDEEN	1610	SUMBURGH	BAE-ATP	12345 7		1600/1700 7
622	1645	SUMBURGH	1745	ABERDEEN	BAE-ATP	12345		
623	1825	ABERDEEN	1925	SUMBURGH	BAE-ATP	123456		1600/1700 6
624	0910	SUMBURGH	1010	ABERDEEN	BAE-ATP		67	
641	0700	INVERNESS	0845	GATWICK	BAE-146	1234567		
642	0930	GATWICK	1115	INVERNESS	BAE-146	1234567		
645	1155	INVERNESS	1340	GATWICK	BAE-146	1234567		
646	1500	GATWICK	1645	INVERNESS	BAE-146	1234567		
647	1730	INVERNESS	1915	GATWICK	BAE-146	1234567		
648	2000	GATWICK	2145	INVERNESS	BAE-146	1234567		
688	0710	ABERDEEN	0755	KIRKWALL	SAAB-340	12345		
689	0825	KIRKWALL	0910	ABERDEEN	SAAB-340	12345		
690	0950	ABERDEEN	1035	KIRKWALL	SAAB-340	123456		0845/0930 6
691	1110	KIRKWALL	1155	ABERDEEN	SAAB-340	123456		1010/1055 6
692	1245	ABERDEEN	1345	SUMBURGH	SF3/ATP	1234567		1100/1200 67
693	1415	SUMBURGH	1515	ABERDEEN	SF3/ATP	123456		1300/1400 6
694	1555	ABERDEEN	1640	KIRKWALL	SAAB-340	123456		1130/1215 6
695	1710	KIRKWALL	1755	ABERDEEN	SAAB-340	123456		1245/1330 6
698	1400	ABERDEEN	1445	KIRKWALL	SAAB-340		6	
699	1515	KIRKWALL	1600	ABERDEEN	SAAB-340		6	
700	0715	GLASGOW	0800	BELFAST CITY	BAE-ATP	123456		0805/0850 6
701	0845	BELFAST CITY	0930	GLASGOW	BAE-ATP	123456		0920/1005 6
702	1020	GLASGOW	1120	STORNOWAY	BAE-ATP	123456		
703	1155	STORNOWAY	1235	INVERNESS	BAE-ATP	123456		
704	1310	INVERNESS	1350	STORNOWAY	BAE-ATP	123456		
705	1430	STORNOWAY	1530	GLASGOW	BAE-ATP	123456		
706	1600	GLASGOW	1645	BELFAST CITY	BAE-ATP	1234567		1700/1745 6
707	1715	BELFAST CITY	1800	GLASGOW	BAE-ATP	1234567		1815/1900 6
708	1830	GLASGOW	1915	BELFAST CITY	BAE-ATP	12345 7		
709	1945	BELFAST CITY	2030	GLASGOW	BAE-ATP	12345 7		
712	0640	GLASGOW	0725	INVERNESS	BAE-ATP	1		
713	0755	INVERNESS	0835	STORNOWAY	BAE-ATP	12345		
714	0920	STORNOWAY	1015	GLASGOW	BAE-ATP	12345		
715	1100	GLASGOW	1200	BENBECULA	BAE-ATP	123456		
716	1240	BENBECULA	1340	GLASGOW	BAE-ATP	123456		
717	1450	GLASGOW	1550	STORNOWAY	BAE-ATP	12345		
718	1630	STORNOWAY	1705	INVERNESS	BAE-ATP	12345		
718	1750	INVERNESS	1835	GLASGOW	BAE-ATP		5	
721	1450	GLASGOW	1550	STORNOWAY	BAE-ATP		6	22.05-25.09
722	0920	STORNOWAY	1015	GLASGOW	BAE-ATP		6	22.05-25.09
723	1600	SUMBURGH	1700	ABERDEEN	BAE-ATP		7	
724	1735	ABERDEEN	1825	GLASGOW	BAE-ATP		7	
725	1115	SUMBURGH	1215	ABERDEEN	BAE-ATP	12345		
726	1245	ABERDEEN	1335	GLASGOW	BAE-ATP	12345		
739	0935	GLASGOW	1025	BELFAST	J'STREAM41	4 7		1200/1250 7
740	1100	BELFAST	1150	GLASGOW	J'STREAM41	4 7		1315/1405 7
741	1530	GLASGOW	1620	BELFAST	J'STREAM41	12345		
742	1645	BELFAST	1735	GLASGOW	J'STREAM41	12345		
743	0700	GLASGOW	0750	BELFAST	J'STREAM41	123456		0715/0805 6
744	0815	BELFAST	0905	GLASGOW	J'STREAM41	123456		0830/0925 6
745	1800	GLASGOW	1850	BELFAST	J'STREAM41	1234567		1730/1820 67
746	1920	BELFAST	2010	GLASGOW	J'STREAM41	1234567		1850/1940 67
800	0650	MANCHESTER	0750	STANSTED	J'STREAM41	12345		
801	0820	STANSTED	0920	MANCHESTER	J'STREAM41	12345		

802	1035	MANCHESTER	1135	STANSTED	J'STREAM41	12345 7		
803	1200	STANSTED	1330	WATERFORD	J'STREAM41	12345 7		
804	1400	WATERFORD	1530	STANSTED	J'STREAM41	12345 7		
805	1600	STANSTED	1700	MANCHESTER	J'STREAM41	12345 7		
806	1740	MANCHESTER	1840	STANSTED	J'STREAM41	12345		
807	1910	STANSTED	2010	MANCHESTER	J'STREAM41	12345		
815	1825	BELFAST CITY	1915	LIVERPOOL	BAE-ATP	7		
819	0700	MANCHESTER	0810	CORK	EMB/J'ST41	123456	0755/0920 6	
820	0845	CORK	0955	MANCHESTER	EMB/J'ST41	123456	0945/1105 6	
821	1740	MANCHESTER	1850	CORK	EMB-145	12345		
822	1925	CORK	2035	MANCHESTER	EMB-145	12345 7		
823	0700	LIVERPOOL	0755	BELFAST CITY	J'STREAM41	12345		
824	0820	BELFAST CITY	0910	LIVERPOOL	J'STREAM41	12345		
825	0935	LIVERPOOL	1030	BELFAST CITY	J'STREAM41	123456	1150/1240 6	
826	1100	BELFAST CITY	1150	LIVERPOOL	J'STREAM41	123456	1030/1120 6	
827	1520	LIVERPOOL	1615	BELFAST CITY	J'STREAM41	12345 7	1405/1500 7	
828	1645	BELFAST CITY	1735	LIVERPOOL	J'STREAM41	12345		
829	1805	LIVERPOOL	1900	BELFAST CITY	J'STREAM41	12345 7	1945/2035 7	
830	1930	BELFAST CITY	2020	LIVERPOOL	J'STREAM41	12345 7		
833	1145	MANCHESTER	1300	WATERFORD	J'STREAM41	6		-25.09
834	1330	WATERFORD	1500	STANSTED	J'STREAM41	6		-25.09
835	1530	STANSTED	1700	WATERFORD	J'STREAM41	6		-25.09
836	1730	WATERFORD	1845	MANCHESTER	J'STREAM41	6		-25.09
843	1130	MANCHESTER	1300	HANOVER	EMB-145	123456	1330/1500 6	
844	1330	HANOVER	1520	MANCHESTER	EMB-145	123456	1535/1725 6	
845	1240	MANCHESTER	1435	BERLIN	EMB-145	12345 7		
846	1510	BERLIN	1700	MANCHESTER	EMB-145	12345 7		
852	0705	MANCHESTER	0830	SHANNON	J'STREAM41	12345		
853	0855	SHANNON	1015	MANCHESTER	J'STREAM41	12345		
854	1045	MANCHESTER	1200	LONDONDERRY	J'STREAM41	12345		
855	1225	LONDONDERRY	1340	MANCHESTER	J'STREAM41	12345		
858	0800	MANCHESTER	0925	SHANNON	J'STREAM41	6		
859	0950	SHANNON	1110	MANCHESTER	J'STREAM41	6		
862	1145	MANCHESTER	1300	LONDONDERRY	J'STREAM41	6		
863	1330	LONDONDERRY	1445	MANCHESTER	J'STREAM41	6		
864	1515	MANCHESTER	1640	CORK	J'STREAM41	6		
865	1715	CORK	1835	MANCHESTER	J'STREAM41	6		
867	0955	MANCHESTER	1110	KNOCK	EMB-145	6		
868	1145	KNOCK	1300	MANCHESTER	EMB-145	6		
874	1750	MANCHESTER	1905	LONDONDERRY	J'STREAM41	7		
875	1930	LONDONDERRY	2045	MANCHESTER	J'STREAM41	7		
878	1730	MANCHESTER	1855	SHANNON	J'STREAM41	12345 7		
879	1925	SHANNON	2045	MANCHESTER	J'STREAM41	12345 7		
900	0700	MANCHESTER	0800	BELFAST	BAE146/ATP	123456		
901	0840	BELFAST	0940	MANCHESTER	BAE146/ATP	123456		
902	1020	MANCHESTER	1120	BELFAST	BAE-146	12345		
903	1150	BELFAST	1250	MANCHESTER	BAE-ATP	12345		
904	1430	MANCHESTER	1530	BELFAST	BAE146/ATP	12345 7	1400/1500 7	
905	1600	BELFAST	1700	MANCHESTER	BAE-146	12345		
906	1750	MANCHESTER	1850	BELFAST	BAE146/EMB	1234567	1800/1900 6	
907	1920	BELFAST	2020	MANCHESTER	BAE146/EMB	1234567	1930/2030 6	
908	1010	MANCHESTER	1145	JERSEY	BAE-ATP	12345		
909	1220	JERSEY	1355	MANCHESTER	BAE-ATP	12345		
911	0655	MANCHESTER	0755	SOUTHAMPTON	BAE-ATP	12345		
912	0830	SOUTHAMPTON	0930	MANCHESTER	BAE-ATP	12345		
915	1430	MANCHESTER	1530	SOUTHAMPTON	BAE-ATP	12345		
916	1600	SOUTHAMPTON	1700	MANCHESTER	BAE-ATP	12345		
919	1020	MANCHESTER	1155	GUERNSEY	BAE-ATP	6		
920	1230	GUERNSEY	1405	MANCHESTER	BAE-ATP	6		
921	1455	MANCHESTER	1630	GUERNSEY	BAE-ATP	6	22.05-25.09	
922	1710	GUERNSEY	1845	MANCHESTER	BAE-ATP	6	22.05-25.09	
925	1710	MANCHESTER	1840	KNOCK	BAE-ATP	7		
926	1910	KNOCK	2035	MANCHESTER	BAE-ATP	7		
929	1200	MANCHESTER	1330	KNOCK	BAE-ATP	12345		
930	1400	KNOCK	1530	MANCHESTER	BAE-ATP	12345		
934	1530	BELFAST	1630	MANCHESTER	BAE-ATP	7		
935	1730	MANCHESTER	1830	SOUTHAMPTON	BAE-ATP	12345		
936	1905	SOUTHAMPTON	2005	MANCHESTER	BAE-ATP	12345		

937	0920	MANCHESTER	1055	GUERNSEY	BAE-ATP	7	23,05-26.09
938	1135	GUERNSEY	1310	MANCHESTER	BAE-ATP	7	23.05-26.09
941	0815	MANCHESTER	0950	JERSEY	BAE-ATP	6	-02.10
	1055	MANCHESTER	1230	JERSEY	BAE-ATP	7	
942	1355	JERSEY	1530	MANCHESTER	BAE-ATP	6	-02.10
943	1550	MANCHESTER	1700	JERSEY	BAE-146	6	-02.10
944	1750	JERSEY	1900	MANCHESTER	BAE-146	6	-02.10
947	0730	MANCHESTER	0905	JERSEY	BAE-ATP	12345	
948	0930	JERSEY	1000	GUERNSEY	BAE-ATP	12345	
949	1025	GUERNSEY	1200	MANCHESTER	BAE-ATP	12345	
952	1600	MANCHESTER	1735	GUERNSEY	BAE-ATP	12345	
953	1800	GUERNSEY	1830	JERSEY	BAE-ATP	12345	
954	1855	JERSEY	2030	MANCHESTER	BAE-ATP	12345	
960	0750	MANCHESTER	0900	JERSEY	BAE-146	6	
961	0950	JERSEY	1100	MANCHESTER	BAE-146	6	
962	1150	MANCHESTER	1300	JERSEY	BAE146/EMB	67	0900/1015 7
963	1350	JERSEY	1500	MANCHESTER	BAE146/EMB	67	1050/1205 7
964	1250	MANCHESTER	1350	BELFAST CITY	BAE-ATP	12345 7	1640/1740 7
965	1425	BELFAST CITY	1525	MANCHESTER	BAE-ATP	12345	
	1330	BELFAST CITY	1430	MANCHESTER	BAE-ATP	67	1500/1600 7
966	1605	MANCHESTER	1705	BELFAST CITY	BAE-ATP	12345	
	1500	MANCHESTER	1600	BELFAST CITY	BAE-ATP	67	1525/1625 7
967	1740	BELFAST CITY	1840	MANCHESTER	BAE-ATP	1234567	1655/1755 7
968	1920	MANCHESTER	2025	BELFAST CITY	BAE-ATP	1234567	1825/1930 7
969	2000	BELFAST CITY	2100	MANCHESTER	BAE-ATP	7	
990 - 998		TRAINING FLIGHTS					

BRITTANY   *BRITAIR S.A.*   *BZH*   *FRANCE*

5850		NANTES	0720	GATWICK	CANADAIR	123456	
5851	0800	GATWICK		NANTES	CANADAIR	123456	
5852		NANTES	1200	GATWICK	CANADAIR	1234567	ARR 1230 6
5853	1315	GATWICK		NANTES	CANADAIR	1234567	
5854		NANTES	1845	GATWICK	CANADAIR	1234567	ARR 1825 12
5855	1925	GATWICK		NANTES	CANADAIR	1234567	
5856	0800	GATWICK		RENNES	CANADAIR	123456	
5857		RENNES	0730	GATWICK	ATR-42	123456	
5858	1930	GATWICK		RENNES	ATR-42	12345 7	
5859		RENNES	1750	GATWICK	ATR-42	12345 7	
8840		NANTES	0715	HEATHROW	CANADAIR	123456	
8841	0745	HEATHROW		NANTES	CANADAIR	123456	
8842		NANTES	1500	HEATHROW	CANADAIR	1234567	
8843	1530	HEATHROW		NANTES	CANADAIR	1234567	
8844		NANTES	1845	HEATHROW	CANADAIR	1234567	
8845	1920	HEATHROW		NANTES	CANADAIR	1234567	
8858A	1330	GATWICK		DEAUVILLE	ATR-42	12345	02.08-03.09
8859A		DEAUVILLE	1300	GATWICK	ATR-42	12345	02.08-03.09

BROADSWORD   *AIR FOYLE CHARTER AIRWAYS LTD*   *UPD*   *U.K.*

EVEN NUMBERS - FLIGHTS INTO THE UK   UNEVEN NUMBERS - FLIGHTS LEAVING THE U.K.

711/2	0755	MANCHESTER	1815	DALAMAN	A.300	1	
713/4	1930	MANCHESTER	0625	BODRUM	A.300	1	
731/2	0745	MANCHESTER	1655	RHODES	A.300	3	
733/4	1830	MANCHESTER	0515	PAPHOS	A.300	3	21.07-
741/2	1000	MANCHESTER	1915	LANZAROTE	A.300	4	
743/4	0945	MANCHESTER	1545	MALAGA	A.300	4	01.07-
745/6	1655	MANCHESTER	0240	LAS PALMAS	A.300	4	01.07-
751/2	0715	MANCHESTER	1715	TENERIFE	A.300	5	
753/4	1800	MANCHESTER	0350	TENERIFE	A.300	5	
761/2	0555	MANCHESTER	1155	ALICANTE	A.300	6	
763/4	1330	MANCHESTER	2000	ALICANTE	A.300	6	
765/6	2100	MANCHESTER	0320	ALICANTE	A.300	6	03.07-
771/2	0500	MANCHESTER	1255	KEFALLINIA	A.300	7	
773/4	1425	MANCHESTER	0110	LARNACA	A.300	7	

093		BANDER SERI	0625	HEATHROW	B.767	12	6	VIA ABU DHABI
094	1150	HEATHROW		BANDER SERI	B.767	12		DEP. 1330 2
	1450	HEATHROW		BANDER SERI	B.767		6	
095		BANDER SERI	0755	HEATHROW	B.767		5	VIA DUBAI
096	1330	HEATHROW		BANDER SERI	B.767		5	VIA DUBAI
097		BANDER SERI	0630	HEATHROW	B.767	3	7	ARR 0700 7
		BANDER SERI	0850	HEATHROW	B.767	4		
098	1330	HEATHROW		BANDER SERI	B.767	3	7	DEP. 1605 7
	1415	HEATHROW		BANDER SERI	B.767	4		

BRYMON   *BRYMON EUROPEAN AIRWAYS   BC/BRY   U.K.*

A BRITISH AIRWAYS FRANCHISEE. AIRCRAFT ARE PAINTED IN BA COLOURS. THE FIGURE 4 IS NORMALLY DELETED FROM THE CALL SIGN, WHILST THE LETTER REFERS TO THE SECTOR BEING FLOWN, E.G. FLIGHT 010A REFERS TO THE BRISTOL - PLYMOUTH SECTOR, WHILST FLIGHT NO. 010B REFERS TO THE PLYMOUTH - GATWICK SECTOR.

109	1520	JERSEY	1655	PRESTWICK	DHC-8	6	
110	1725	PRESTWICK	1900	JERSEY	DHC-8	6	
112	0800	ABERDEEN	0945	JERSEY	DHC-8	6	-09.10
113	1825	JERSEY	2010	ABERDEEN	DHC-8	6	-09.10
114	0800	MANCHESTER		JERSEY	DHC-8	6	-02.10
115		JERSEY	2055	MANCHESTER	DHC-8	6	-02.10
205	1410	SOUTHAMPTON	1450	JERSEY	DHC-8	6	22.05-25.09
206	1300	JERSEY	1340	SOUTHAMPTON	DHC-8	6	22.05-25.09
1600	1355	ABERDEEN	1520	MANCHESTER	DHC-8	12345	
1607	1715	MANCHESTER	1940	ABERDEEN	DHC-8	12345	
1608	1355	ABERDEEN	1520	MANCHESTER	DHC-8	12345	
1615	0900	MANCHESTER	1005	GLASGOW	DHC-8	123456	
1622	1800	GLASGOW	1905	MANCHESTER	DHC-8	7	
1641	1525	MANCHESTER	1630	GLASGOW	DHC-8	7	
1655	1700	MANCHESTER	1805	EDINBURGH	DHC-8	12345	
1660	1150	GLASGOW	1255	MANCHESTER	DHC-8	123456	
1705	0850	MANCHESTER	0955	EDINBURGH	DHC-8	6	
1714	1710	EDINBURGH	1815	MANCHESTER	DHC-8	7	
1840	0705	MANCHESTER	0810	GLASGOW	DHC-8	12345	
1843	0940	GLASGOW	1045	MANCHESTER	DHC-8	12345	
1844	1350	MANCHESTER	1455	GLASGOW	DHC-8	12345	
1847	1625	GLASGOW	1730	MANCHESTER	DHC-8	12345	
1848	1700	MANCHESTER	1805	GLASGOW	DHC-8	12345	
1849	1905	GLASGOW	2010	MANCHESTER	DHC-8	12345	
1864	0700	MANCHESTER	0805	EDINBURGH	DHC-8	12345	
1867	0840	EDINBURGH	0945	MANCHESTER	DHC-8	12345	
1868	1350	MANCHESTER	1455	EDINBURGH	DHC-8	12345	
1869	1525	EDINBURGH	1630	MANCHESTER	DHC-8	12345	
1873	1835	EDINBURGH	1940	MANCHESTER	DHC-8	12345	
1874	1530	MANCHESTER	1635	EDINBURGH	DHC-8	7	
1875	1355	EDINBURGH	1500	MANCHESTER	DHC-8	6	
4002	0650	PLYMOUTH	0835	GATWICK	DHC-8	1234567	VIA NEWQUAY
4003	0910	GATWICK	1020	PLYMOUTH	DHC-8	1234567	
	1035	PLYMOUTH	1215	GATWICK	DHC-8	1234567	VIA NEWQUAY
4005	1245	GATWICK	1425	NEWQUAY	DHC-8	1234567	VIA PLYMOUTH
	1405	PLYMOUTH	1545	GATWICK	DHC-8	67	VIA NEWQUAY
4006	1440	NEWQUAY	1545	GATWICK	DHC-8	12345	
4007	1615	GATWICK	1725	NEWQUAY	DHC-8	1234567	
	1740	NEWQUAY	1915	GATWICK	DHC-8	1234567	
	1615	GATWICK	1800	PLYMOUTH	DHC-8	67	
	1815	PLYMOUTH	1915	GATWICK	DHC-8	67	
4008	1405	BRISTOL	1440	PLYMOUTH	DHC-8	12345	
	1455	PLYMOUTH	1600	GATWICK	DHC-8	12345	
4009	1630	GATWICK	1735	PLYMOUTH	DHC-8	1234567	1945/2125 67
	1750	PLYMOUTH	1825	BRISTOL	DHC-8	12345	
4010	1815	PLYMOUTH	1915	GATWICK	DHC-8	12345	
4011	1945	GATWICK	2125	PLYMOUTH	DHC-8	12345	
4017	0700	GLASGOW	0830	BRISTOL	DHC-8	12345	
4019	2150	GLASGOW	2320	BRISTOL	DHC-8	5	
4020	0630	PLYMOUTH	0705	BRISTOL	DHC-8	12345	
	0730	BRISTOL	0855	GLASGOW	DHC-8	123456	
4021	0925	GLASGOW	1055	BRISTOL	DHC-8	123456	
	1125	BRISTOL	1220	JERSEY	DHC-8	6	

4022	0930	BRISTOL	1100	GLASGOW	DHC-8	12345 7	0850/1020 7
4023	1130	GLASGOW	1300	BRISTOL	DHC-8	12345 7	1045/1215 7
4024	1325	BRISTOL	1455	GLASGOW	DHC-8	12345	
4025	1520	GLASGOW	1650	BRISTOL	DHC-8	12345	
4026	1600	BRISTOL	1730	GLASGOW	DHC-8	12345 7	1540/1705 7
4027	1800	GLASGOW	1930	BRISTOL	DHC-8	12345 7	1735/1905 7
	2000	BRISTOL	2035	PLYMOUTH	DHC-8	12345	
4028	1530	JERSEY	1625	BRISTOL	DHC-8	6	
	1720	BRISTOL	1850	GLASGOW	DHC-8	1234567	1655/1825 6
4029	1920	GLASGOW	2050	BRISTOL	DHC-8	1234567	1850/2020 6
4030	1955	BRISTOL	2125	GLASGOW	DHC-8	12345 7	1935/2105 7
4031	0700	EDINBURGH	0830	BRISTOL	DHC-8	12345	
	0855	BRISTOL	0930	PLYMOUTH	DHC-8	12345	
	0950	PLYMOUTH	1030	JERSEY	DHC-8	12345	
	1055	JERSEY	1205	PARIS CDG	DHC-8	12345	
4032	0725	BRISTOL	0855	EDINBURGH	DHC-8	123456	
4033	0920	EDINBURGH	1045	BRISTOL	DHC-8	123456	
	1115	BRISTOL	1150	PLYMOUTH	DHC-8	6	
	1210	PLYMOUTH	1250	JERSEY	DHC-8	6	
	1315	JERSEY	1425	PARIS CDG	DHC-8	6	
4034	0935	BRISTOL	1105	EDINBURGH	DHC-8	12345	
	0745	PLYMOUTH	0820	BRISTOL	DHC-8	7	
	0845	BRISTOL	1015	EDINBURGH	DHC-8	7	
4035	1130	EDINBURGH	1300	BRISTOL	DHC-8	12345 7	1040/1210 7
4035	1130	EDINBURGH	1300	BRISTOL	DHC-8	1 3 5 7	1200/1330 7
	1330	BRISTOL	1425	JERSEY	DHC-8	1 3 5 7	1235/1330 7
	1450	JERSEY	1505	GUERNSEY	DHC-8	1 3 5 7	
4036	1145	BRISTOL	1315	EDINBURGH	DHC-8	12345	
4037	1345	EDINBURGH	1515	BRISTOL	DHC-8	12345	
	1330	BRISTOL	1505	GUERNSEY	DHC-8	1 3 5	
4038	1350	JERSEY	1405	GUERNSEY	DHC-8	7	
	1430	GUERNSEY	1520	BRISTOL	DHC-8	7	
	1545	BRISTOL	1715	EDINBURGH	DHC-8	1234567	1625/1755 6
4039	1740	EDINBURGH	1910	BRISTOL	DHC-8	1234567	1825/1955 6
4040	1350	PARIS CDG	1500	JERSEY	DHC-8	12345	
	1525	JERSEY	1605	PLYMOUTH	DHC-8	12345	
	1620	PLYMOUTH	1655	BRISTOL	DHC-8	12345	
	1730	BRISTOL	1900	EDINBURGH	DHC-8	12345 7	
4041	1925	EDINBURGH	2055	BRISTOL	DHC-8	12345 7	
4042	1955	BRISTOL	2125	EDINBURGH	DHC-8	12345 7	1940/2110 7
4043	2150	EDINBURGH	2320	BRISTOL	DHC-8	5	
4051	0630	ABERDEEN	0730	NEWCASTLE	DHC-8	12345	
	0750	NEWCASTLE	0905	BRISTOL	DHC-8	12345	
4052	0745	BRISTOL	0900	NEWCASTLE	DHC-8	123456	0800/0915 6
	0925	NEWCASTLE	1025	ABERDEEN	DHC-8	123456	0935/1035 6
4053	1100	ABERDEEN	1200	NEWCASTLE	DHC-8	123456	1115/1215 6
	1220	NEWCASTLE	1335	BRISTOL	DHC-8	123456	1235/1350 6
4054	1850	BRISTOL	2040	ABERDEEN	DHC-8	7	
4055	1245	ABERDEEN	1345	NEWCASTLE	DHC-8	7	
	1405	NEWCASTLE	1520	BRISTOL	DHC-8	7	
4056	1345	BRISTOL	1500	NEWCASTLE	DHC-8	12345 7	1245/1400 7
	1525	NEWCASTLE	1625	ABERDEEN	DHC-8	12345 7	1420/1520 7
4057	1655	ABERDEEN	1755	NEWCASTLE	DHC-8	12345 7	1545/1645 7
	1815	NEWCASTLE	1930	BRISTOL	DHC-8	12345 7	1705/1820 7
4058	1850	BRISTOL	2005	NEWCASTLE	DHC-8	12345 7	1600/1715 7
	2025	NEWCASTLE	2125	ABERDEEN	DHC-8	12345 7	1735/1835 7
4059	2040	ABERDEEN	2230	BRISTOL	DHC-8	5	
4060	0710	BRISTOL	0805	JERSEY	DHC-8	6	
4062	0805	BRISTOL	0900	JERSEY	DHC-8	67	
4063	1530	JERSEY	1625	BRISTOL	DHC-8	67	1955/2050 6
4067	1330	JERSEY	1345	GUERNSEY	DHC-8	6	
	1410	GUERNSEY	1450	PLYMOUTH	DHC-8	6	
	1510	PLYMOUTH	1545	BRISTOL	DHC-8	6	
4068	1615	BRISTOL	1650	PLYMOUTH	DHC-8	6	
	1710	PLYMOUTH	1750	GUERNSEY	DHC-8	6	
	1815	GUERNSEY	1830	JERSEY	DHC-8	6	
4069	1915	JERSEY	2010	BRISTOL	DHC-8	6	

4070	1445	JERSEY	1500	GUERNSEY	DHC-8	1 3 5	
	1525	GUERNSEY	1615	BRISTOL	DHC-8	1 3 5	
4075	0820	BRISTOL	0855	PLYMOUTH	DHC-8	7	
	0915	PLYMOUTH	0955	JERSEY	DHC-8	7	
	1020	JERSEY	1130	PARIS CDG	DHC-8	7	
4076	1200	PARIS CDG	1315	JERSEY	DHC-8	67	1455/1605 6
	1340	JERSEY	1420	PLYMOUTH	DHC-8	67	1630/1710 6
	1440	PLYMOUTH	1515	BRISTOL	DHC-8	7	
4082	0730	BRISTOL	0905	PARIS CDG	DHC-8	1234567	
4083	0940	PARIS CDG	1110	BRISTOL	DHC-8	1234567	
4084	1150	BRISTOL	1320	PARIS CDG	DHC-8	1234567	1205/1335 67
4085	1245	PARIS CDG	1415	BRISTOL	DHC-8	1234567	1410/1540 67
4086	1655	BRISTOL	1825	PARIS CDG	DHC-8	12345 7	
4087	1935	PARIS CDG	2105	BRISTOL	DHC-8	12345 7	1910/2040 7
4093	0830	ABERDEEN	0930	NEWCASTLE	DHC-8	6	
4095	1330	ABERDEEN	1430	NEWCASTLE	DHC-8	12345	
	1455	NEWCASTLE	1615	SOUTHAMPTON	DHC-8	12345	
	0830	ABERDEEN	0930	NEWCASTLE	DHC-8	67	1415/1700 7
	0955	NEWCASTLE	1115	SOUTHAMPTON	DHC-8	67	1540/1700 7
4096	1645	SOUTHAMPTON	1930	ABERDEEN	DHC-8	12345	
	1200	SOUTHAMPTON	1320	NEWCASTLE	DHC-8	6	
	1345	NEWCASTLE	1445	ABERDEEN	DHC-8	6	
4098	1645	SOUTHAMPTON	1805	NEWCASTLE	DHC-8	12345 7	1730/1850 7
	1830	NEWCASTLE	1930	ABERDEEN	DHC-8	12345 7	1915/2015 7
4106	0745	PLYMOUTH	0820	BRISTOL	DHC-8	7	
	0845	BRISTOL	1000	CORK	DHC-8	7	
4108	1055	CORK	1210	BRISTOL	DHC-8	7	
	1130	BRISTOL	1205	PLYMOUTH	DHC-8	2 4	
	1225	PLYMOUTH	1330	CORK	DHC-8	2 4	
	1240	BRISTOL	1315	PLYMOUTH	DHC-8	67	1420/1455 6
	1330	PLYMOUTH	1435	CORK	DHC-8	67	1515/1620 6
4109	1400	CORK	1505	PLYMOUTH	DHC-8	2 4	67 1650/1755 6
	1525	PLYMOUTH	1600	BRISTOL	DHC-8	2 4 6	1815/1850 6
	1620	PLYMOUTH	1655	BRISTOL	DHC-8	7	
4120	0750	ABERDEEN	1000	OSLO	DHC-8	12345 7	0845/1055 7
4121	1035	OSLO	1250	ABERDEEN	DHC-8	12345 7	1130/1345 7
4130	0650	NEWCASTLE	0745	BELFAST	DHC-8	12345	
	0730	NEWCASTLE	0825	BELFAST	DHC-8	67	0820/0915 7
4131	0810	BELFAST	0905	NEWCASTLE	DHC-8	12345	
	0855	BELFAST	0950	NEWCASTLE	DHC-8	67	0950/1045 7
	0935	NEWCASTLE	1155	COPENHAGEN	DHC-8	12345 7	1110/1330 7
4132	1230	COPENHAGEN	1500	NEWCASTLE	DHC-8	12345 7	1410/1640 7
	1525	NEWCASTLE	1620	BELFAST	DHC-8	12345 7	1710/1805 7
	1230	COPENHAGEN	1620	BELFAST	DHC-8	12345 7	1410/1805 7
4133	1650	BELFAST	1745	NEWCASTLE	DHC-8	12345 7	1835/1930 7
4134	1815	NEWCASTLE	1910	BELFAST	DHC-8	12345	
4135	1935	BELFAST	2030	NEWCASTLE	DHC-8	12345	
4140	0650	ABERDEEN	0820	MANCHESTER	DHC-8	123456	0700/0825 6
4141	0730	MANCHESTER	0855	ABERDEEN	DHC-8	12345	
	0850	MANCHESTER	1015	ABERDEEN	DHC-8	67	0800/0925 7
4142	0920	ABERDEEN	1045	MANCHESTER	DHC-8	12345 7	1000/1125 7
	1115	MANCHESTER	1210	BRISTOL	DHC-8	12345	
4143	1015	MANCHESTER	1140	ABERDEEN	DHC-8	12345	
4144	1155	ABERDEEN	1320	MANCHESTER	DHC-8	12345	
4145	1200	MANCHESTER	1325	ABERDEEN	DHC-8	12345 7	1250/1415 7
4146	1715	ABERDEEN	1840	MANCHESTER	DHC-8	12345	
	1525	ABERDEEN	1650	MANCHESTER	DHC-8	67	1625/1750 6
4147	1250	BRISTOL	1345	MANCHESTER	DHC-8	12345	
	1420	MANCHESTER	1545	ABERDEEN	DHC-8	123456	1400/1525 6
	1720	MANCHESTER	1845	ABERDEEN	DHC-8	7	
4148	1910	ABERDEEN	2035	MANCHESTER	DHC-8	12345 7	
4149	1910	MANCHESTER	2035	ABERDEEN	DHC-8	12345	
4170	0640	ABERDEEN	0820	BIRMINGHAM	DHC-8	12345 7	0800/0940 7
4171	0845	BIRMINGHAM	1025	ABERDEEN	DHC-8	12345 7	1010/1150 7
4172	1300	ABERDEEN	1440	BIRMINGHAM	DHC-8	12345	
4173	1510	BIRMINGHAM	1750	ABERDEEN	DHC-8	12345	
4174	1625	ABERDEEN	1805	BIRMINGHAM	DHC-8	12345 7	1600/1740 7
4175	1830	BIRMINGHAM	2010	ABERDEEN	DHC-8	12345 7	1805/1945 7

4176	1040	ABERDEEN	1220	BIRMINGHAM	DHC-8	6	
4177	1245	BIRMINGHAM	1425	ABERDEEN	DHC-8	6	

CALEDONIAN   *CALEDONIAN AIRWAYS LTD.*   *KT/CKT*   *U.K.*

FIRST NUMBER - FLIGHTS LEAVING THE U.K.   SECOND NUMBER - FLIGHTS INTO THE U.K.

Flight	Dep	From	Arr	To	Type	Days	Dates
34/5	1920	GATWICK	0610	LARNACA	DC-10	7	
36/7	2000	GATWICK	0615	LARNACA	L.1011	3	
38/9	1030	GATWICK	2050	LARNACA	L.1011	3	
42/3	1700	GATWICK	0305	LARNACA	L.1011	6	
46/7	1030	MANCHESTER	2110	LARNACA	L.1011	7	
48/9	1425	MANCHESTER	0115	PAPHOS	A.320	3	21.07-
56/7	1055	MANCHESTER	2155	PAPHOS	L.1011	7	
54/5	1130	GATWICK	2125	PAPHOS	L.1011	7	
58/9	0730	GATWICK	1725	PAPHOS	L.1011	7	
60/1	0725	GATWICK	1740	LARNACA	L.1011	7	
63/4	1015	GATWICK	0710	ST. LUCIA	DC-10	5	
65/6	0930	GATWICK	0625	GRENADA	DC-10	3	
71/2	0555	GATWICK	0625	TOBAGO	DC-10	2	
73/4	1115	GATWICK	0625	ST. LUCIA	DC-10	7	
77/8	1030	GATWICK	0655	BRIDGETOWN	DC-10	6	
81/2	0930	GATWICK	0625	ANTIGUA	DC-10	1	
83	0930	GATWICK		ST. THOMAS IS.	DC-10	4	
84		MAHON	0610	GATWICK	DC-10	5	
106/7	0500	GATWICK	1300	CORFU	A.320	1	
108/9	1255	GATWICK	2255	PAPHOS	L.1011	3	21.07-
112/3	1500	GATWICK	0115	LARNACA	A.320	3	21.07-
116/7	1030	GATWICK	2115	LARNACA	L.1011	7	
120/1	0615	GATWICK	1530	DALAMAN	L.1011	1	19.07-04.10
128/9	0555	GATWICK	1540	FARO	L.1011	4	22.07-07.10
131/2	1030	GATWICK	0630	ORLANDO	DC-10	4	
135/6	0600	GATWICK	0625	ORLANDO	DC-10	5	23.07-
143/4	1200	GATWICK	0710	ORLANDO	DC-10	6	
144/5	1205	MANCHESTER	2310	LARNACA	L.1011	3	21.07-
164/5	1355	MANCHESTER	2245	THIRA	A.320	2	
172/3	2000	MANCHESTER	0610	DALAMAN	A.320	1	26.07-05.10
176/7	0715	MANCHESTER	1715	BODRUM	L.1011	1	
178/9	0700	GATWICK	1200	SALZBURG	A.320	5	
180/1	0625	MANCHESTER	1150	INN	A.320	3	-22.09
182/3	0625	MANCHESTER	1200	SALZBURG	A.320	6	-25.09
184/5	1220	MANCHESTER	1740	SALZBURG	A.320	6	-02.10
186/7	1515	MANCHESTER	2355	KALAMATA	A.320	7	-03.10
194/5	2345	MANCHESTER	0925	IZMIR	A.320	1	-05.10
206/7	0600	MANCHESTER	1115	MILAN	A.320	6	-02.10
216/7	0540	MANCHESTER	1310	KAVALA	A.320	3	
220/1	1825	MANCHESTER	0425	DALAMAN	L.1011	5	-09.10
224/5	1015	MANCHESTER	1655	FARO	L.1011	4	
226/7	1445	MANCHESTER	2155	FARO	L.1011	6	
228/9	1355	MANCHESTER	0210	LUXOR	A.320	4	
230/1	1730	MANCHESTER	0035	MALAGA	A.320	7	
234/5	0615	MANCHESTER	1245	MALAGA	A.320	4	
236/7	1030	MANCHESTER	1300	ALICANTE	A.320	2	
250/1	2345	GATWICK	0510	IBIZA	A.320	7	
252/3	1930	GATWICK	0715	IBIZA	A.320	7	
254/5	0625	MANCHESTER	1540	TENERIFE	L.1011	5	
256/7	0700	GATWICK	2250	ALICANTE	A.320	2	
258/9	0745	MANCHESTER	1720	TENERIFE	L.1011	5	
268/9	0715	MANCHESTER	1645	TENERIFE	L.1011	2	
276/7	2030	MANCHESTER	0555	LAS PALMAS	A.320	1	
294/5	0615	MANCHESTER	1315	FARO	L.1011	6	
302/3	1755	MANCHESTER	0040	MALAGA	A.320	2	
308/9	0555	MANCHESTER	1250	MALAGA	L.1011	6	

CALEDONIAN (Cont.)

Flight	Dep	From	Arr	To	Aircraft	Days	Dates
318/9	1030	GATWICK	2215	TENERIFE	L.1011	5	
324/5	1615	GATWICK	2250	MALAGA	L.1011	6	
334/5	1025	MANCHESTER	2005	LANZAROTE	L.1011	4	
344/5	1245	MANCHESTER	1100	MAHON	L.1011	5	
346/7	0625	GATWICK	1540	RHODES	L.1011	3	
348/9	2255	MANCHESTER	0835	RHODES	L.1011	6	
352/3	1655	GATWICK	0220	RHODES	L.1011	3	21.07-
356/7	0540	MANCHESTER	1140	MAHON	A.320	5	
358/9	1130	MANCHESTER	2100	SKIATHOS	A.320	4	
362/3	0925	MANCHESTER	1855	SKIATHOS	A.320	1	
364/5	1910	MANCHESTER	0440	HERAKLION	A.320	5	
366/7	0015	GATWICK	0940	RHODES	L.1011	6	24.07-
372/3	1940	MANCHESTER	0550	ANTALYA	A.320	6	
374/5	2350	MANCHESTER	0600	PALMA	A.320	2	
378/9	1450	MANCHESTER	2105	PALMA	L.1011	6	
382/3	1930	MANCHESTER	0500	HERAKLION	L.1011	5	
386/7	2055	MANCHESTER	0655	HERAKLION	L.1011	2	
388/9	0930	MANCHESTER	1845	HERAKLION	L.1011	2	
394/5	1255	MANCHESTER	2225	KOS	A.320	3	
396/7	0620	MANCHESTER	1420	ZAKYNTHOS	A.320	7	
398/9	1310	MANCHESTER	2025	CATANIA	A.320	6	-25.09
402/3	0445	MANCHESTER	1225	CORFU	A.320	1	
404/5	2345	MANCHESTER	0725	CORFU	A.320	1	
408/9	2000	MANCHESTER	0345	CORFU	A.320	5	
410/1	2135	MANCHESTER	0510	CORFU	A.320	6	
412/3	0800	MANCHESTER	1610	ZAKYNTHOS	A.320	7	
414/5	1630	GATWICK	2255	MALAGA	L.1011	1	19.07-04.10
424/5	1255	MANCHESTER	1815	GERONA	A.320	5	
428/9	2345	MANCHESTER	0900	KOS	L.1011	6	-02.10
432/3	0715	MANCHESTER	1645	CHANIA	A.320	2	
436/7	0740	MANCHESTER	1745	MIKONOS	A.320	5	-08.10
440/1	1740	GATWICK	0305	MALAGA	L.1011	5	
445		MALAGA	1600	GATWICK	L.1011	5	23.07-
454/5	1355	MANCHESTER	2230	FUNCHAL	A.320	1	
460/1	0640	GATWICK	2045	TENERIFE	A.320	2	
462/3	1110	GATWICK	2030	TENERIFE	L.1011	5	
476/7	0640	GATWICK	1615	TENERIFE	L.1011	5	23.07-
480/1	0555	GATWICK	2115	LANZAROTE	L.1011	1	19.07-
486/7	1200	GATWICK	2055	LANZAROTE	L.1011	4	
496/7	0600	GATWICK	1110	AJACCIO	A.320	7	
506/7	0640	GATWICK	1330	ALICANTE	A.320	4	
508/9	1715	GATWICK	2315	ALICANTE	L.1011	1	19.07-04.10
510/1	2355	GATWICK	0540	ALICANTE	A.320	2	20.07-
512/3	1645	GATWICK	2120	ALICANTE	A.320	4	
514/5	0625	GATWICK	2215	ALICANTE	L.1011	6	
518/9	0610	GATWICK	1230	ALICANTE	A.320	2	20.07-05.10
520/1	1530	GATWICK	2120	ALICANTE	L.1011	6	
526/7	0930	GATWICK	1615	MURCIA	A.320	6	
528/9	1600	GATWICK	2245	ALMERIA	A.320	4	
534/5	1630	GATWICK	2130	MILAN	A.320	6	
538/9	1755	GATWICK	0025	FARO	L.1011	4	22.07-04.10
550/1	0710	GATWICK	1415	FARO	L.1011	6	
552/3	0810	GATWICK	1615	FARO	L.1011	4	
554/5	0540	GATWICK	1245	FARO	A.320	6	
558/9	1030	GATWICK	2000	FARO	L.1011	4	22.07-04.10
560/1	1430	GATWICK	2055	FARO	L.1011	6	
568/9	1400	GATWICK	1955	FARO	A.320	6	
572/3	1740	GATWICK	0305	HERAKLION	L.1011	6	
578/9	1225	GATWICK	1845	MALAGA	A.320	7	
580/1	1645	GATWICK	2305	MALAGA	A.320	4	
582/3	2130	GATWICK	0350	MALAGA	A.320	5	

Flt	Time	Origin	Dep	Destination	Type	1	2	3	4	5	6	7	Dates
584/5	0555	GATWICK	0615	MALAGA	L.1011		2						
586/7	0615	GATWICK	1500	MALAGA	L.1011						6		
588/9	1655	GATWICK	2325	MALAGA	A.320							7	
592/3	0025	GATWICK	0540	MALAGA	A.320							7	03.07-
601		MAHON	1820	GATWICK	A.320					5			
604/5	0500	GATWICK	1900	MAHON	L.1011					5			
610/1	1100	GATWICK	1640	MAHON	L.1011					5			
618/9	1145	GATWICK	1710	MAHON	L.1011	1							19/07-20.09
622/3	0700	GATWICK	1255	PALMA	L.1011						6		
636/7	2320	GATWICK	0440	PALMA	A.320		2						
638/9	1555	GATWICK	1740	PALMA	A.320					5			
656/7	1355	GATWICK	2220	FUNCHAL	A.320	1							
668/9	1055	GATWICK	1835	FUNCHAL	A.320	1							
692/3	1630	GATWICK	2120	GERONA	A.320					5			
698/9	1500	GATWICK	0015	LAS PALMAS	A.320	1							
700/1	1500	GATWICK	0225	SHARM EL SHEIKH	A.320				4				
704/5	1355	GATWICK	0115	LUXOR	A.320				4				
711/2	1710	NORWICH	1620	ALICANTE	A.320		2						
722/3	1600	GLASGOW	1325	ALICANTE	L.1011						6		
752/3	1225	GLASGOW	1125	SALZBURG	A.320						6		
736/7	0630	GATWICK	1755	SALZBURG	A.320			3					-22.09
740/1	1920	GATWICK	0420	BODRUM	A.320						6		
742/3	2045	GATWICK	0540	IZMIR	A.320	1							
746/7	2020	GATWICK	0545	BODRUM	A.320	1							
750/1	0555	GATWICK	1815	SALZBURG	A.320						6		
760/1	0730	GATWICK	1230	INNSBRUCK	A.320			3					-22.09
764/5	1555	GATWICK	2045	INNSBRUCK	A.320			3					
778/9	1900	GATWICK	0315	ATHENS	A.320					5			
786/7	2030	GATWICK	0530	DALAMAN	A.320					5			
788/9	1030	GATWICK	2015	BODRUM	L.1011	1							
792/3	1040	GATWICK	2015	DALAMAN	DC-10	1							
794/5	2015	GATWICK	0440	DALAMAN	A.320					5			
796	2055	GATWICK		DALAMAN	L.1011	1							
797		BODRUM	0625	GATWICK	L.1011		2						20.07-
802/3	1750	GATWICK	0010	DUBROVNIK	A.320							7	25.07-10.10
812/3	1255	GATWICK	2200	SKIATHOS	A.320					5			
818/9	1030	GATWICK	1545	PISA	A.320						6		
834/5	2115	GATWICK	0800	KOS	L.1011						6		
838/9	0625	GATWICK	1525	KOS	L.1011			3					
840/1	2105	GATWICK	0610	KOS	A.320			3					21.07-07.10
842/3	1645	GATWICK	2310	PALERMO	A.320						6		
844/5	0625	GATWICK	1245	MAP	A.320					5			
846/7	0645	GATWICK	1400	NAPLES	L.1011						6		
848/9	0800	GATWICK	1345	OLBIA	A.320				4				
854/5	1810	GATWICK	2310	VERONA	A.320				4				17.06-
860/1	0820	GATWICK	1655	KEFALLINIA	A.320							7	
868/9	2140	GATWICK	0440	MALTA	A.320						6		
872/3	1200	GATWICK	1925	KEFALLINIA	L.1011							7	
880/1	1015	GATWICK	1910	CHANIA	L.1011		2						
884/5	1345	GATWICK	2215	THIRA	A.320		2						
886/7	0640	GATWICK	1555	CHANIA	A.320		2						
888/9	0610	GATWICK	1450	MIKONOS	A.320			3					
890/1	0655	GATWICK	1530	MIKONOS	A.320					5			
892/3	0700	GATWICK	1615	SKIATHOS	A.320	1							
894/5	0700	GATWICK	1615	SKIATHOS	A.320				4				
896/7	2225	GATWICK	0600	CORFU	A.320					5			
900/1	0545	GATWICK	1245	CORFU	A.320	1							
902/3	2255	GATWICK	0625	CORFU	A.320					5			
904/5	2245	GATWICK	0625	CORFU	A.320						6		
906/7	2040	GATWICK	0330	CORFU	A.320							7	
910/1	2100	GATWICK	0420	CORFU	A.320	1							19.07-05.10

916/7	0555	GATWICK	1430	LAS VEGAS	A.320	4	
918/9	0545	GATWICK	1500	KOS	A.320	3	
924/5	0915	GATWICK	1650	PREVEZZA	DC-10	7	
938/9	0545	GATWICK	2230	ZAKYNTHOS	A.320	7	
940/1	0725	GATWICK	1530	KALAMATA	A.320	7	
948/9	0625	GATWICK	1600	HERAKLION	L.1011	2	
952/3	1100	GATWICK	2000	HERAKLION	L.1011	2	
944/5	2000	GATWICK	0510	HERAKLION	A.320	5	
958/9	1755	GATWICK	0300	HERAKLION	A.320	2	20.07-06.10
964/5	1315	GATWICK	2230	RHODES	DC-10	3	
966/7	2250	GATWICK	0755	RHODES	L.1011	6	
968/9	0915	GATWICK	1840	RHODES	L.1011	3	
972/3	1745	GATWICK	0440	TEL AVIV	A.320	2	13.07-
974/5	1715	GATWICK	0410	TEL AVIV	A.320	3	14.07-
976/7	1700	GATWICK	0425	TEL AVIV	A.320	7	
980/1	2015	GATWICK	0445	ATHENS	L.1011	5	
984/5	2200	GATWICK	0630	ATHENS	L.1011	7	25.07-04.10
986/7	0115	GATWICK	0925	ATHENS	A.320	1	
3114/5	0925	GLASGOW	2055	LARNACA	A.300	7	
3274/5	0900	GLASGOW	1645	FARO	A.300	4	
3304/5	0500	GLASGOW	1220	MALAGA	A.300	6	
3472/3	0555	GLASGOW	0330	TENERIFE	A.300	5	
3474/5	1745	MANCHESTER	1545	TENERIFE	A.300	5	23.07-
3518/9	2155	GLASGOW	0600	IBIZA	A.300	6	-25.09
3628/9	1355	GLASGOW	2055	PALMA	A.300	6	
3778/9	0955	GLASGOW	2035	DALAMAN	A.300	1	
3972/3	1025	GLASGOW	2225	PAPHOS	A.300	3	

CAM-AIR   CAMEROON AIRLINES   UY/UYC   CAMEROON

72		DOULA	0455	GATWICK	B.747	2
	0540	GATWICK		PARIS CDG	B.747	2
75		PARIS CDG	2000	GATWICK	B.747	2
	2100	GATWICK		DOULA	B.747	2

CANADIAN   CANADIAN AIRLINES INTERNATIONAL   CP/CDN   CANADA

040		TORONTO	0900	ROME	DC-10	12345	
041	1220	ROME		TORONTO	DC-10	23456	
044		MONTREAL	0645	ROME	B.767	1 7	ARR 0940 1
045	0900	ROME		MONTREAL	B.767	1 7	
076		OTTAWA	0930	HEATHROW	DC-10	1 3 5 7	
077	1610	HEATHROW		TORONTO	B.767	2 4 6	DEP 1705 2 6
	1805	HEATHROW		OTTAWA	B.767	7	
082		TORONTO	2015	HEATHROW	B.767	1234567	
083	1425	HEATHROW		TORONTO	DC-10	1234567	
086		TORONTO	0705	HEATHROW	DC-10	1234567	
087	1610	HEATHROW		TORONTO	B.767	1 345	
088		TORONTO	0930	HEATHROW	B.767	2 456	
089	2145	HEATHROW		TORONTO	B.767	1234567	
090		VANCOUVER	1345	HEATHROW	DC-10	1234567	
091	2105	HEATHROW		VANCOUVER	DC-10	123456	DEP 1705 6
	1905	HEATHROW		VANCOUVER	DC-10	7	
094		CALGARY	1425	HEATHROW	B.767	67	
095	1730	HEATHROW		CALGARY	B.767	67	DEP 1905 7
096		CALGARY	1115	HEATHROW	DC-10	1234567	
097	1530	HEATHROW		CALGARY	DC-10	1234567	

CARGOLUX   CARGOLUX AIRLINES INTERNATIONAL   CV/CLX   LUXEMBOURG

6024	1900	LUXEMBURG		MEXICO CITY	B.747	4
6046	1900	LUXEMBURG		MEXICO CITY	B.747	6
7045	1830	LUXEMBOURG		MEXICO	B.747	5
7056		HOUSTON	0915	PRESTWICK	B.747	7
	1045	PRESTWICK	1230	LUXEMBOURG	B.747	7

7721	0945	LUXEMBOURG	1130	PRESTWICK	B.747	1	
	1230	PRESTWICK		SEATTLE	B.747	1	
7723	0600	LUXEMBOURG	0745	MANCHESTER	B.747	3	
	0915	MANCHESTER		SEATTLE	B.747	3	
7732		SEATTLE	0735	PRESTWICK	B.747	2	
	0845	PRESTWICK	1020	LUXEMBURG	B.747	2	
7733		SEATTLE	0525	MANCHESTER	B.747	4	
	0625	MANCHESTER	0800	LUXEMBOURG	B.747	3	
7742	0600	LUXEMBOURG		MEXICO CITY	B.747	2	TO SEATTLE
7743	1545	LUXEMBOURG		LOS ANGELES	B.747	3	
7744	0830	LUXEMBURG		SAN FRANCISCO	B.747	4	
7745	1100	LUXEMBOURG	1300	PRESTWICK	B.747	5	
	1400	PRESTWICK		SEATTLE	B.747	5	
7746	1730	LUXEMBOURG		LOS ANGELES	B.747	6	
7747	0730	LUXEMBOURG		SAN FRANCISCO	B.747	7	
7751		SAN FRANCISCO	0740	LUXEMBOURG	B.747	1	
7753		SEATTLE	0655	LUXEMBOURG	B.747	3	
7754		LOS ANGELES	1615	LUXEMBOURG	B.747	4	
7755		SAN FRANCISCO	0530	SHANNON	B.747	5	
	0700	SHANNON	0845	LUXEMBURG	B.747	5	
7756		SAN FRANCISCO	1500	LUXEMBOURG	B.747	6	
7757		LOS ANGELES	1800	LUXEMBOURG	B.747	7	
7783	1330	LUXEMBOURG		REYKJAVIK	B.747	3	TO NEW YORK
7787	0800	LUXEMBOURG		REYKJAVIK	B.747	7	TO NEW YORK
7794		HOUSTON	1600	PRESTWICK	B.747	4	
	1725	PRESTWICK	1900	LUXEMBOURG	B.747	4	
7797		REYKJAVIK	0640	LUXEMBOURG	B.747	1	EX NEW YORK

CATHAY   *CATHAY PACIFIC AIRWAYS   CX/CPA   U.K.*

007		HONG KONG	0620	HEATHROW	B.747	5 7	ARR 1900 5
008	0850	HEATHROW		HONG KONG	B.747	5 7	DEP 2155 5
037		BAHRAIN	0620	HEATHROW	B.747	1 4	ARR 0605 4
038	0850	HEATHROW		HONG KONG	B.747	1 4	DEP 1000 1
250	1845	HEATHROW		HONG KONG	B.747	1234567	
251		HONG KONG	0540	HEATHROW	B.747	1234567	
254	2230	HEATHROW		HONG KONG	B.747	1234567	
255		HONG KONG	0625	HEATHROW	B.747	1234567	
260	1000	MANCHESTER	1125	PARIS	B.747	2 4 7	
261	0625	PARIS	0755	MANCHESTER	B.747	2 4 7	0555/0725 4
270	1100	MANCHESTER	1220	AMSTERDAM	B.747	1 3 56	
271	0625	AMSTERDAM	0745	MANCHESTER	B.747	1 3 56	

CAVREL   *AIR CAVREL   ACL   U.K.*

| 500 | 2030 | DUBLIN | 2150 | COVENTRY | SH-330 | 12345 | |
| 501 | 0450 | COVENTRY | 0510 | DUBLIN | SH-330 | 23456 | |

CEDARJET   *MIDDLE EAST AIRLINES   ME/MEA   LEBANON*

201		BEIRUT	1115	HEATHROW	A.310	234 67	
202	1300	HEATHROW		BEIRUT	A.310	234 67	
215		BEIRUT	1530	HEATHROW	A.320	1 45 7	ARR 1655 1
216	2245	HEATHROW		BEIRUT	A.320	1 45 7	

CHANNEX   *CHANNEL EXPRESS (AIR SERVICES) LTD.   LS/EXS   U.K.*

461	1900	BOURNEMOUTH	1930	BRISTOL	F-27/HERALD	7	
	1950	BRISTOL	2050	EAST MIDLANDS	F27/HERALD	7	
462	2145	EAST MIDLANDS	2245	BRISTOL	F27/HERALD	7	
	2315	BRISTOL	2345	BOURNEMOUTH	F27/HERALD	7	
463	1925	BIGGIN HILL	2025	EAST MIDLANDS	F-27	7	
464	2150	EAST MIDLANDS	2250	GATWICK	F-27	7	
470	2225	BOURNEMOUTH	2255	EXETER	F27/HERALD	12345	SKYNET 19
471	2315	EXETER	0020	LIVERPOOL	F27/HERALD	12345	SKYNET 19
472	2355	LIVERPOOL	0105	GATWICK	F27/HERALD	12345	SKYNET 14
473	2235	GATWICK	2345	LIVERPOOL	F27/HERALD	12345	SKYNET 28
474	0025	LIVERPOOL	0130	BOURNEMOUTH	F27/HERALD	23456	SKYNET 28
484	2040	STANSTED	2205	EDINBURGH	ELECTRA	12345	SKYNET 36

485	2250	EDINBURGH	0010	STANSTED	ELECTRA	12345	SKYNET 36
486	2335	STANSTED	0055	EDINBURGH	ELECTRA	12345	SKYNET 5
487	2040	EDINBURGH	2200	STANSTED	ELECTRA	12345	SKYNET 5
501	2300	COVENTRY	0045	COLOGNE	F-27	12345 7	2030/2215 7
502	2200	COLOGNE	03500	COVENTRY	F-27	123456	0540/0730 1
570	2215	LIEGE	2330	PARIS CDG	F-27	12345	
571	0100	PARIS CDG	0215	LIEGE	F-27	23456	
580	2005	ISLE OF MAN	2100	COVENTRY	F-27	12345	
581	0520	COVENTRY	0620	ISLE OF MAN	F-27	23456	
595P	0110	EAST MIDLANDS	0150	STANSTED	A.300	6	
609		???		COVENTRY	F-27	23456	STANDBY A/C
610		COVENTRY		???	F-27	12345	STANDBY A/C
720	0445	BOURNEMOUTH	0530	JERSEY	F27/HERALD	12345	
721F	1100	JERSEY	1145	BOURNEMOUTH	F27/HERALD	1	
721P	0600	JERSEY	0645	BOURNEMOUTH	F27/HERALD	2345	
722	0535	BOURNEMOUTH	0615	GUERNSEY	F-27	6	
723P	0645	GUERNSEY	0835	DUBLIN	F-27	6	
724	0430	STANSTED	0530	JERSEY	ELECTRA	6	
725P	0630	JERSEY	0730	STANSTED	ELECTRA	6	
730	0430	STANSTED	0530	JERSEY	ELECTRA	7	
731P	0630	JERSEY	0730	STANSTED	ELECTRA	7	
740	0535	BOURNEMOUTH	0615	GUERNSEY	F27/HERALD	3456	
	0500	STANSTED	0615	GUERNSEY	F-27	7	
741P	0645	GUERNSEY	0725	BOURNEMOUTH	F-27	7	
750	2130	DUBLIN	2310	STANSTED	F-27	6	
820	0455	GATWICK	0600	GUERNSEY	F-27	123456	
821	1920	GUERNSEY	2030	GATWICK	F-27	12345 7	1720/1825 7
6513	1940	CORK	2020	DUBLIN	ELECTRA	12345	
	2110	DUBLIN	2315	COLOGNE	ELECTRA	12345	
6514	0145	COLOGNE	0350	DUBLIN	ELECTRA	12345	
	0645	DUBLIN	0730	CORK	ELECTRA	12345	
6525	1950	SHANNON	2030	DUBLIN	ELECTRA	12345	
	2100	DUBLIN	2245	COLOGNE	ELECTRA	12345	
6526	0300	COLOGNE	0505	DUBLIN	ELECTRA	12345	
	0705	DUBLIN	0745	SHANNON	ELECTRA	12345	
6533	2020	EDINBURGH	2135	STANSTED	A.300	234	
	2245	STANSTED	2350	COLOGNE	A.300	1234	
	2115	EDINBURGH	2250	COLOGNE	A.300	5	
6534	0215	COLOGNE	0325	EAST MIDLANDS	A.300	2345	
	0530	EAST MIDLANDS	0630	EDINBURGH	A.300	12345	
	0235	COLOGNE	0335	STANSTED	A.300	6	
6582	0715	STANSTED	0920	STOCKHOLM	A.300	7	
6583	1650	STOCKHOLM	1910	STANSTED	A.300	7	
7040	1800	DUBLIN	1940	STANSTED	F-27	1234 6	1815/1955 6
8040	2130	STANSTED	2310	DUBLIN	F-27	1234 6	2145/2325 6

CHARTER   *EUROPEAN AVIATION AIR CHARTER   YE/EAF   U.K.*

EVEN NUMBERS - FLIGHTS LEAVING THE U.K.   UNEVEN NUMBERS - FLIGHTS INTO THE U.K

322/3	0915	MANCHESTER	1430	LOURDES	BAC1-11	1	
324/5	0915	MANCHESTER	1430	LOURDES	BAC1-11	5	-08.10
500/1	1100	STANSTED	1425	MUNSTER	BAC1-11	1	
502/3	1525	STANSTED	1845	BGN??	BAC1-11	1 5	1450/1810 5
504/5	1100	STANSTED	1450	HANOVER	BAC1-11	2 5	1000/1350 5
506/7	1100	STANSTED	1445	PADERBORN	BAC1-11	4	
3200/1	1455	BOURNEMOUTH	1930	GERONA	BAC1-11	6	22.05-25.09
2000/1	0915	BELFAST	2040	GATWICK	BAC1-11	1234567	
2000/1	1130	GATWICK	1700	BERLIN	BAC1-11	1234567	
3002/3	0730	MANCHESTER	1330	BASTIA	BAC1-11	7	-03.10
3160/1	1530	MANCHESTER	2120	PISA	BAC1-11	7	
3174/5	0730	MANCHESTER	1310	PISA	BAC1-11	6	-02.10
3176/7	0655	GATWICK	1255	PISA	BAC1-11	6	
3210/1	0800	MANCHESTER	1350	PISA	BAC1-11	4	
3272/3	0915	MANCHESTER	2125	VERONA	BAC1-11	3	-29.09
3274/5	1550	CARDIFF	1450	VERONA	BAC1-11	3	-29.09
3304/5	1130	GATWICK	1630	BASTIA	BAC1-11	7	23.05-03.10
3356/7	1150	GATWICK	1810	ROME	BAC1-11	6	-02.10
3386/7	0925	GATWICK	1225	VERONA	BAC1-11	7	06.09-03.10

CHARTER   (Cont.)

3390/1	0830	STANSTED	1410	FIGARI	BAC1-11		7	-03.10
3416/7	1000	STANSTED	1550	ALGHERO	BAC1-11		6	-02.10
3426/7	1000	GATWICK	1440	MILAN	BAC1-11		4	
3428/9	1800	GATWICK	2240	MILAN	BAC1-11		7	
3440/1	1615	GATWICK	2105	VERONA	BAC1-11		6	-02.10
3442/3	1545	GATWICK	2055	LOURDES	BAC1-11	1		-27.09
3446/7	1000	GATWICK	2110	MILAN	BAC1-11		3	-06.10
3448/9	1605	MANCHESTER	1505	MILAN	BAC1-11		3	-06.10
3454/5	1410	MANCHESTER	2010	NICE	BAC1-11		6	-02.10
3456/7	1700	STANSTED	2240	OLBIA	BAC1-11		6	-02.10
3460/1	0900	STANSTED	1455	GLASGOW	BAC1-11		3	
3461/2	1950	VERONA	1850	STANSTED	BAC1-11		3	-06.10
3462/3	1555	GLASGOW	1455	VERONA	BAC1-11		3	-06.10
3494/5	1530	GATWICK	2150	ROME	BAC1-11		4	
3498/9	1530	GATWICK	2150	ROME	BAC1-11		7	

CITY-IRELAND   *CITY JET   WX/BCY   IRELAND*

502	0710	DUBLIN	0810	EAST MIDLANDS	BAE-ATP	12345	
503	0845	EAST MIDLANDS	0945	DUBLIN	BAE-ATP	12345	
504	1055	DUBLIN	1155	EAST MIDLANDS	BAE-ATP	12345 7	
505	1230	EAST MIDLANDS	1330	DUBLIN	BAE-ATP	12345 7	
506	1440	DUBLIN	1540	EAST MIDLAND	BAE-ATP	12345 7	
507	1615	EAST MIDLANDS	1715	DUBLIN	BAE-ATP	12345 7	
508	1810	DUBLIN	1819	EAST MIDLANDS	BAE-ATP	12345 7	
509	1945	EAST MIDLANDS	2045	DUBLIN	BAE-ATP	12345 7	
510	0845	DUBLIN	0945	EAST MIDLANDS	BAE-ATP	6	
511	1015	EAST MIDLANDS	1115	DUBLIN	BAE-ATP	6	
512	1210	DUBLIN	1310	EAST MIDLANDS	BAE-ATP	6	
513	1345	EAST MIDLANDS	1445	DUBLIN	BAE-ATP	6	
802	0715	DUBLIN	0825	LONDON CITY	BAE-146	12345	
803	0900	LONDON CITY	1010	DUBLIN	BAE-146	12345	
804	0815	DUBLIN	0930	LONDON CITY	BAE-146	123456	
805	1000	LONDON CITY	1115	DUBLIN	BAE-146	123456	
806	1050	DUBLIN	1200	LONDON CITY	BAE-146	12345	
807	1230	LONDON CITY	1340	DUBLIN	BAE-146	12345	
808	1115	DUBLIN	1230	LONDON CITY	BAE-146	12345 7	
809	1300	LONDON CITY	1415	DUBLIN	BAE-146	12345 7	
810	1315	DUBLIN	1430	LONDON CITY	BAE-146	12345 7	
811	1500	LONDON CITY	1615	DUBLIN	BAE-146	12345 7	
812	1515	DUBLIN	1630	LONDON CITY	BAE-146	12345 7	
813	1700	LONDON CITY	1815	DUBLIN	BAE-146	12345 7	
814	1705	DUBLIN	1820	LONDON CITY	BAE-146	12345 7	
815	1855	LONDON CITY	2010	DUBLIN	BAE-146	12345 7	
816	1815	DUBLIN	2000	LONDON CITY	BAE-146	12345	
817	2030	LONDON CITY	2145	DUBLIN	BAE-146	12345	
818	1900	DUBLIN	2015	LONDON CITY	BAE-146	7	
819	2045	LONDON CITY	2200	DUBLIN	BAE-146	7	

COASTRIDER   *BASE REGIONAL AIRLINES   5E/BRO   NETHERLANDS*

253		COLOGNE	0900	MANCHESTER	EMB-120	12345	
254	0930	MANCHESTER		COLOGNE	EMB-120	12345	
257		COLOGNE	1815	MANCHESTER	EMB-120	12345	ARR 1640 1
258	1845	MANCHESTER		COLOGNE	EMB-120	12345	DEP 1930 3
303	0655	EINDHOVEN	0755	GATWICK	EMB-120	123456	
304	0820	GATWICK	0920	EINDHOVEN	EMB-120	123456	
305	1300	EINDHOVEN	1400	GATWICK	EMB-120	12345 7	1400/1500 7
306	1430	GATWICK	1530	EINDHOVEN	EMB-120	12345 7	1525/1625 7
307	1900	EINDHOVEN	2000	GATWICK	EMB-120	12345 7	
308	1930	GATWICK	2030	EINDHOVEN	EMB-120	12345 7	
334	0655	HEATHROW	0755	EINDHOVEN	EMB-120	12345	
335	1235	EINDHOVEN	1335	HEATHROW	EMB-120	1234 6	
336	1400	HEATHROW	1500	EINDHOVEN	EMB-120	1234 6	
337	2105	EINDHOVEN	2205	HEATHROW	EMB-120	1234 7	
384	0700	GATWICK	0800	EINDHOVEN	EMB-120	1234567	
385	0900	EINDHOVEN	1000	GATWICK	EMB-120	1234567	
386	1100	GATWICK	1200	EINDHOVEN	EMB-120	1234567	

503		ROTTERDAM	0750	BIRMINGHAM	EMB-120	12345	
504	0815	BIRMINGHAM		ROTTERDAM	EMB-120	12345	
507		ROTTERDAM	1815	BIRMINGHAM	EMB-120	12345	7
508	1850	BIRMINGHAM		ROTTERDAM	EMB-120	12345	7
603		ROTTERDAM	0805	MANCHESTER	EMB-120	12345	
604	0830	MANCHESTER		ROTTERDAM	EMB-120	12345	
605		ROTTERDAM	1520	MANCHESTER	J'STREAM31	12345	
606	1600	MANCHESTER		ROTTERDAM	J'STREAM31	12345	
607		ROTTERDAM	1825	MANCHESTER	EMB-120	12345	
608	1850	MANCHESTER		ROTTERDAM	EMB-120	12345	

COAST CENTRE   *COAST AIR K/S   CST   NORWAY*

223		HAUGESUND	1000	ABERDEEN	J'STREAM 31	12345
226	1430	ABERDEEN		HAUGESUND	J'STREAM 31	12345
251		HAUGESUND	1605	ABERDEEN	J'STREAM 31	7
252	1640	ABERDEEN		HAUGESUND	J'STREAM 31	7

COLOURS   *FLYING COLOURS   FCL   U.K.*

1ST NUMBER - FLIGHTS LEAVING THE U.K.   2ND NUMBER - FLIGHTS INTO THE U.K.

1/2	1815	MANCHESTER	0335	LAS PALMAS	A.320	1		
3		CARDIFF	0930	GATWICK	B.757	2		POSITIONING
4	0540	GATWICK		CARDIFF	B.757		4	POSITIONING
13/4	2210	MANCHESTER	0545	MALTA	A.320		4	
18/9	2010	GLASGOW	0605	TENERIFE	B.757		5	
20/1	1335	GATWICK	1225	FARO	B.757			7
22/3	1400	MANCHESTER	2310	HERAKLION	B.757	2		
31/2	0900	GATWICK	1905	LARNACA	B.757	3		
33/4	0120	GLASGOW	0755	PALMA	B.757	3		
38/9	2100	GATWICK	0600	ANTALYA	A.320	2		
43/4	0610	MANCHESTER	1110	GERONA	A.320			7
50/1	2245	MANCHESTER	0400	GERONA	B.757		4	
52/3	0700	GATWICK	1655	LARNACA	B.757	3		
63/4	0945	MANCHESTER	1905	DALAMAN	A.320	1		
67/8	2230	GATWICK	0530	CORFU	B.757		5	
71/2	2230	GATWICK	0505	DALAMAN	B.757	1		
76/7	0055	MANCHESTER	0700	IBIZA	B.757			7
78/9	1555	MANCHESTER	0055	LANZAROTE	B.757		4	
81/2	1915	MANCHESTER	0445	TENERIFE	A.320		5	
83/4	1655	MANCHESTER	2200	REUS	A.320	3		
86/7	0625	MANCHESTER	1440	ATHENS	A.320		5	
88/9	1545	MANCHESTER	0210	LARNACA	A.320			7
92/3	0555	GATWICK	1650	PAPHOS	B.757	2		
96/7	1435	GATWICK	1950	PALMA	B.757	1		
98/9	2255	GLASGOW	0545	IBIZA	B.757	3		
102/3	0715	MANCHESTER	1305	MAHON	B.757		5	
104/5	0805	MANCHESTER	1435	MALAGA	B.757			7
107/8	0655	GATWICK	1350	CORFU	B.757		5	
116/7	0700	GATWICK	1615	TENERIFE	B.757	2		
118/9	1945	MANCHESTER	0505	DALAMAN	A.320		5	
122/3	1530	MANCHESTER	2150	ALMERIA	A.320		4	
126/7	0750	MANCHESTER	1950	DALAMAN	B.757	1		
128/9	1545	GATWICK	1730	IBIZA	A.320			7
134/5	1155	GATWICK	2110	DALAMAN	B.757			7
137/8	2100	TENERIFE	0540	BRISTOL	B.757		5	
142/3	0800	MANCHESTER	1835	LARNACA	B.757	3		
152/3	0735	MANCHESTER	1350	ALICANTE	B.757	2		
154/5	1235	MANCHESTER	2005	PREVEZA	A.320			7
157/8	1300	MANCHESTER	2235	ANTALYA	A.320	2		
161/2	0745	MANCHESTER	1535	ZAKYNTHOS	A.320		4	
168/9	0730	MANCHESTER	1635	THESSALONIKI	A.320	3		
173/4	0900	BIRMINGHAM	1905	LARNACA	B.757	3		
177/8	0815	MANCHESTER	2045	REUS	B.757	3		
181/2	0950	BRISTOL	1735	ZAKYNTHOS	B.757	2		
183/4	0945	GLASGOW	1650	MALAGA	B.757			7
185/6	1625	MANCHESTER	0135	FUERTVENTURA	B.757	3		
188/9	1530	BIRMINGHAM	2110	PALMA	B.757	1		

Route	Dep	Origin	Arr	Destination	Aircraft	No.	
191/2	1650	GATWICK	2130	GERONA	B.757	5	
197/8	0905	MANCHESTER	1455	MAHON	B.757	4	
201/2	2230	MANCHESTER	0800	DALAMAN	A.320	5	
202/3	1555	CARDIFF	2125	PALMA	??	1	
204/5	2225	CARDIFF	0755	DALAMAN	??	1	
206/7	0615	CARDIFF	1145	MAHON	??	5	
2067	1115	MANCHESTER	1215	GATWICK	A.320	2	POSITIONING
208/9	0600	CARDIFF	1455	IBIZA	??	1	
211/2	2025	BRISTOL	0550	ANTALYA	B.757	7	
212/3	0700	CARDIFF	1230	PALMA	??	6	
213/4	1500	GLASGOW	1400	REUS	B.757	3	
214/5	2040	CARDIFF	0540	TENERIFE	??	5	
218/9	0605	CARDIFF	2000	FARO	??	7	
218/9	1015	MANCHESTER	2020	PAPHOS	A.320	2	
221/2	1740	BRISTOL	0430	LANZAROTE	B.757	4	
225/6	0820	MANCHESTER	1740	BODRUM	B.757	1	
226/7	1300	CARDIFF	1900	MALAGA	??	5	
232/4	1410	CARDIFF	1950	ALICANTE	??	6	
234/5	2235	CARDIFF	0425	IBIZA	??	6	
236/7	2125	CARDIFF	0325	MALAGA	??	7	
240/1	0635	CARDIFF	1455	ZAKYNTHOS	??	4	
242/3	1615	CARDIFF	0105	LANZAROTE	??	4	
242/3	2250	GATWICK	0725	HERAKLION	B.757	2	
248/9	0055	MANCHESTER	0710	ALICANTE	B.757	2	
252/3	1740	BRISTOL	0340	PAPHOS	B.757	3	
258/9	0940	BIRMINGHAM	1900	TENERIFE	B.757	5	
263/4	0020	BIRMINGHAM	0815	ZAKYNTHOS	B.757	5	
278/9	1615	GATWICK	2120	MAHON	B.757	3	
283/4	2255	MANCHESTER	0815	RHODES	A.320	3	
288/9	2050	MANCHESTER	0245	PALMA	B.757	2	
306/7	0745	GLASGOW	1735	LANZAROTE	B.757	4	
308/9	0835	BRISTOL	1620	ZAKYNTHOS	B.757	4	
312/3	1755	GATWICK	0255	RHODES	B.757	3	
314/5	0730	BRISTOL	1555	FUERTVENTURA	B.757	3	
331/2	2035	GATWICK	0530	LAS PALMAS	B.757	6	
337/8	0715	MANCHESTER	1620	RHODES	A.320	3	
339/0	0730	MANCHESTER	1355	FARO	A.320	7	
341/2	2110	GATWICK	0455	DALAMAN	A.320	5	
343/4	0630	GATWICK	1130	PALMA	A.320	7	
345/6	0730	MANCHESTER	1525	ZAKYNTHOS	A.320	7	
347/8	1450	GATWICK	2045	MAHON	B.757	5	
349/0	1330	BIRMINGHAM	1910	PALMA	B.757	7	
353/4	0900	MANCHESTER	1755	CHANIA	A.320	2	
363/4	0055	MANCHESTER	0650	PALMA	B.757	3	
365/6	2150	GLASGOW	0555	CORFU	B.757	1	
368/9	0620	GATWICK	1525	LAS PALMAS	B.757	1	
372/3	0705	GLASGOW	1645	HERAKLION	B.757	2	
374/5	0810	MANCHESTER	1730	TENERIFE	B.757	5	
376/7	1535	MANCHESTER	2050	VENICE	A.320	4	
382/3	0905	GLASGOW	2015	LARNACA	B.757	3	
388/9	0700	BRISTOL	1615	DALAMAN	B.757	1	
392/3	1700	MANCHESTER	2335	FARO	B.757	4	
398/9	0700	GATWICK	1600	LAS VEGAS	A.320	4	
401/2	0605	MANCHESTER	1430	MYTILENE	A.320	4	
404/5	0725	GLASGOW	1400	PALMA	B.757	6	
406/7	0620	BRISTOL	1825	MAHON	B.757	5	
408/9	1900	MANCHESTER	0340	IZMIR	A.320	4	
410/1	0555	GATWICK	1305	CORFU	B.757	1	
412/3	0700	MANCHESTER	1445	KEFALLINIA	A.320	7	
414/5	1240	GATWICK	2100	ATHENS	A.320	5	
416/7	2255	GLASGOW	0845	LAS PALMAS	B.757	6	
419/0	1510	MANCHESTER	2130	MALAGA	A.320	6	
421/2	2110	GATWICK	0615	TENERIFE	A.320	5	
425/6	0900	MANCHESTER	1820	LAS PALMAS	B.757	1	
428/9	2005	MANCHESTER	0720	LAS PALMAS	B.757	7	
431/2	2130	MANCHESTER	0625	HERAKLION	A.320	2	
434/5	0010	MANCHESTER	0600	IBIZA	A.320	6	
442/3	0735	MANCHESTER	1650	FUERTVENTURA	B.757	3	

COLOURS   (Cont.)

Code	Dep	From	Arr	To	Aircraft		
446/7	2140	MANCHESTER	0700	LAS PALMAS	B.757		6
448/9	1615	MANCHESTER	2355	MALTA	B.757		6
450/1	0740	MANCHESTER	1335	PALMA	B.757	2	
452/3	2015	MANCHESTER	0535	DALAMAN	A.320	1	
454/5	1655	MANCHESTER	2230	PALMA	A.320	1	
459/0	0620	GATWICK	1199	GERONA	B.757		7
463/4	2355	GATWICK	0810	IZMIR	A.320	1	
467/8	1335	MANCHESTER	1910	PALMA	A.320	1	
469/0	1920	BRISTOL	0235	MALTA	B.757	2	
471/2	2245	GATWICK	0410	IBIZA	B.757		6
474/5	0640	GATWICK	1415	ZAKYNTHOS	B.757		4
477/8	0815	MANCHESTER	1715	LANZAROTE	B.757		4
479/0	0725	MANCHESTER	0725	KAVALA	A.320	3	
483/4	2245	MANCHESTER	0755	TENERIFE	B.757		5
486/7	1530	GATWICK	0130	LARNACA	B.757		7
495/6	1635	MANCHESTER	2250	ALMERIA	A.320		4
498/9	1755	GATWICK	0225	KOS	B.757	3	
503/4	1500	GATWICK	2000	REUS	B.757	3	
505/6	1655	GATWICK	0205	ANTALYA	B.757	2	
507/8	2045	MANCHESTER	0555	LAS PALMAS	A.320		6
512/3	2120	BIRMINGHAM	0630	LAS PALMAS	B.757		6
516/7	1845	MANCHESTER	0030	MAHON	B.757	1	
519/0	2355	MANCHESTER	0835	IZMIR	A.320	1	
525/6	1725	MANCHESTER	2315	IBIZA	A.320	3	
529/0	2210	BIRMINGHAM	0725	DALAMAN	B.757	1	
532/3	0700	GATWICK	1655	PAPHOS	B.757	3	
535/6	1255	GATWICK	1915	FARO	B.757		6
537/8	2235	GATWICK	0540	MALTA	B.757		4
541/2	2000	MANCHESTER	0505	KOS	A.320	3	
543/4	1445	MANCHESTER	2040	PALMA	B.757		6
548/9	0700	BIRMINGHAM	1325	FARO	B.757		6
551/2	2010	BIRMINGHAM	0540	ANTALYA	B.757	1	
554/5	1700	BIRMINGHAM	2320	ALMERIA	B.757		4
557/8	2140	GATWICK	0625	LAS PALMAS	B.757		7
560/1	0745	MANCHESTER	1405	FARO	A.320		4
562/3	0630	GATWICK	1210	ALICANTE	B.757		6
564/5	0730	BIRMINGHAM	1230	GERONA	B.757		7
568/9	1835	GLASGOW	0110	MAHON	B.757		4
572/3	0700	MANCHESTER	1235	PALMA	A.320		6
574/5	1030	GATWICK	1755	FUNCHAL	A.320	2	
576/7	0610	GATWICK	1130	PALMA	B.757	2	
581/2	0855	MANCHESTER	1530	MALAGA	B.757		5
583/4	2225	MANCHESTER	0755	ANTALYA	A.320		7
585/6	0700	MANCHESTER	1600	LANZAROTE	B.757		4
590/1	2300	MANCHESTER	0450	IBIZA	A.320		6
592/3	0700	MANCHESTER	1245	PALMA	A.320	2	
598/9	1250	LEEDS	1150	MAHON	B.757		5
603/4	1630	MANCHESTER	2220	MAHON	A.320		5
6030/1	1715	GATWICK	1140	PALMA	A.320		6
605/6	0700	GATWICK	1415	KEFALLINIA	B.757		7
607/8	1230	BIRMINGHAM	2150	LAS PALMAS	B.757	1	
615/6	0655	BIRMINGHAM	1420	CORFU	B.757	1	
617/8	1750	GATWICK	2250	PALMA	A.320	1	
620/1	1940	GATWICK	0440	DALAMAN	B.757	1	
623/4	0900	GLASGOW	1855	TENERIFE	B.757		5
626/7	2255	BRISTOL	0425	IBIZA	B.757		6
628/9	2145	MANCHESTER	0710	RHODES	B.757	3	
632/3	0005	MANCHESTER	0600	IBIZA	A.320		4
634/5	2030	GATWICK	0510	KOS	B.757	3	
640/1	1600	GATWICK	2205	ALMERIA	B.757		4
642/3	1425	BIRMINGHAM	2020	ALICANTE	B.757		6
644/5	2110	GATWICK	0410	MALTA	A.320		6
647/8	2200	MANCHESTER	0720	LAS PALMAS	B.757		7
651/2	0915	MANCHESTER	1950	LARNACA	B.757	2	
653/4	0035	MANCHESTER	0845	ZAKYNTHOS	B.757		5
655/6	0940	MANCHESTER	1610	FARO	A.320		6
657/8	2015	GATWICK	0520	LAS PALMAS	B.757		6
659/0	0045	GLASGOW	0925	ZAKYNTHOS	B.757	1	

COLOURS (Cont.)

661/2	0700	MANCHESTER	1335	FARO	B.757	6
663/4	0620	MANCHESTER	1155	PALMA	A.320	6
666/7	0600	MANCHESTER	1230	MALAGA	B.757	6
670/1	0540	GATWICK	1150	MALAGA	A.320	5
672/3	1615	GATWICK	1930	PALMA	B.757	6
674/5	0640	GATWICK	1400	KAVALA	B.757	3
681/2	1635	GATWICK	0110	FUERTVENTURA	A.320	3
684/5	0700	BIRMINGHAM	1555	LANZAROTE	B.757	4
686/7	1625	MANCHESTER	2140	VENICE	A.320	7
688/9	0900	MANCHESTER	1515	ALICANTE	B.757	6
691/2	0625	MANCHESTER	1540	BODRUM	A.320	1
698/9	0600	MANCHESTER	1135	PALMA	A.320	2
702/3	1725	GATWICK	0140	IZMIR	A.320	4
708/9	1310	MANCHESTER	1920	ALICANTE	A.320	6
718/9	0600	BRISTOL	1910	FARO	B,757	7
732/3	0930	MANCHESTER	1725	ZAKYNTHOS	A.320	4
734/5	1625	GATWICK	2130	MAHON	B.757	1
736/7	2050	MANCHESTER	0600	KOS	B.757	3
738/9	2230	GATWICK	0455	CORFU	B.757	5
740/1	1740	GATWICK	0205	HERAKLION	B.757	2
742/3	1550	GATWICK	0020	LANZAROTE	B.757	4
746/7	2100	GATWICK	0545	BODRUM	B.757	1
748/9	0705	MANCHESTER	1855	GERONA	B.757	7
751/2	1810	GATWICK	0320	ANTALYA	A.320	7
753/4	1810	MANCHESTER	0010	IBIZA	B.757	3
755/6	0935	MANCHESTER	1655	CORFU	A.320	1
760/1	0945	MANCHESTER	1900	TENERIFE	B.757	5
764/5	1430	GATWICK	1955	MURCIA	A.320	6
773/4	1350	BRISTOL	1910	PALMA	B.757	6
775/6	1750	GLASGOW	2345	GERONA	B.757	7
778/9	1540	BIRMINGHAM	0145	LARNACA	B.757	2
780/1	2315	MANCHESTER	0625	CORFU	A.320	5
785/6	2210	GATWICK	0520	LAS PALMAS	B.757	7
792/3	2335	MANCHESTER	0510	PALMA	A.320	2
796/7	1720	BRISTOL	2240	PALMA	B.757	1
808/9	0640	GATWICK	1530	LAS PALMAS	A.320	1
812/3	2330	MANCHESTER	0740	ZAKYNTHOS	B.757	7
815/6	0600	GATWICK	1305	PREVEZA	B.757	7
817/8	0630	GATWICK	1435	MURCIA	B.757	4
819/0	1045	GATWICK	1555	PALMA	B.757	2
822/3	0900	BIRMINGHAM	1440	PALMA	B.757	2
828/9	2015	BIRMINGHAM	0535	TENERIFE	B.757	5
835/6	0800	MANCHESTER	1720	TENERIFE	A.320	5
838/9	0835	MANCHESTER	1410	PALMA	A.320	6
843/4	2045	MANCHESTER	0605	BODRUM	B.757	6
849/0	0700	GATWICK	1535	SKIATHOS	A.320	3
851/2	1930	MANCHESTER	0505	ANTALYA	A.320	2
855/6	0540	GATWICK	1140	PALMA	B.757	6
861/2	2010	MANCHESTER	0320	CORFU	A.320	1
864/5	1435	MANCHESTER	2350	TENERIFE	A.320	2
866/7	0800	MANCHESTER	1405	IBIZA	B.757	7
868/9	0625	GATWICK	1515	LANZAROTE	B.757	4
874/5	2030	BIRMINGHAM	0545	RHODES	B.757	3
884/5	2010	MANCHESTER	0520	LAS PALMAS	A.320	6
888/9	1020	MANCHESTER	1830	FUNCHAL	A.320	1
890/1	1500	GLASGOW	2155	ALICANTE	B.757	6
892/3	1610	GATWICK	2130	MAHON	B.757	5
894/5	1315	GATWICK	1915	MALAGA	B.757	6
8978	11630	MANCHESTER	2145	GERONA	B.757	5
901/2	1535	MANCHESTER	2210	FARO	B.757	7
903/4	0710	GATWICK	1310	MALAGA	B.757	6
906/7	0700	GATWICK	1515	ATHENS	B.757	5
908/9	0935	MANCHESTER	1840	SKIATHOS	A.320	5
910/1	2350	BRISTOL	0830	IZMIR	B.757	1
914/5	1545	MANCHESTER	0120	ANTALYA	A.320	7
916/7	1330	MANCHESTER	1945	ALICANTE	B.757	7
920/1	1745	GLASGOW	0020	PALMA	B.757	2
923/4	0715	MANCHESTER	1730	PAPHOS	A.320	3

COLOURS (Cont.)

925/6	1615	GATWICK	1330	ALICANTE	A.320		6
927/8	1045	GLASGOW	2050	DALAMAN	B.757	1	
937/8	2335	MANCHESTER	0740	ZAKYNTHOS	A.320		4
939/0	0735	GATWICK	1635	DALAMAN	B.757	1	
943/4	1715	MANCHESTER	2315	PALMA	A.320		6
945/6	1500	GATWICK	2045	MONASTIR	B.757		7
958/9	0055	MANCHESTER	0700	IBIZA	A.320		4
961/2	0030	MANCHESTER	0545	REUS	A.320		3
966/7	1450	MANCHESTER	2040	MAHON	A.320		5
972/3	1230	GATWICK	2140	TENERIFE	B.757	2	
978/9	0640	GATWICK	1550	TENERIFE	B.757		5
980/1	2115	GATWICK	0240	IBIZA	B.757	3	
985/6	0710	BRISTOL	1240	ALICANTE	B.757		6
988/9	1505	MANCHESTER	2100	PALMA	B.757		7
991/2	1450	MANCHESTER	2355	HERAKLION	B.757	2	
993/4	2255	MANCHESTER	0630	CORFU	B.757	1	

COMEX   *COMED AVIATION LTD.   5W/CDE   U.K.*

201	0800	BLACKPOOL	0830	ISLE OF MAN	EMB-110	12345
202	0900	ISLE OF MAN	0930	BLACKPOOL	EMB-110	12345
203	1230	BLACKPOOL	1300	ISLE OF MAN	EMB-110	1234567
204	1330	ISLE OF MAN	1400	BLACKPOOL	EMB-110	1234567
205	1730	BLACKPOOL	1800	ISLE OF MAN	EMB-110	12345
206	1830	ISLE OF MAN	1900	BLACKPOOL	EMB-110	12345
401	1200	BLACKPOOL	1250	BELFAST CITY	PA31	12345
402	1330	BELFAST CITY	1420	BLACKPOOL	PA31	12345

CONDOR   *CONDOR FLUGDIENST GMBH   DE/CFG   GERMANY*

1050	1015	FRANKFURT		MIAMI	B.767	1	
1051		MIAMI	0735	FRANKFURT	B.767	2	
1082	1125	COLOGNE		LAS VEGAS	B.767	1	
1083		LAS VEGAS	1110	COLOGNE	B.767	2	
1084	1050	MUNICH		LAS VEGAS	B.767	1	
1085		LAS VEGAS	1140	MUNICH	B.767	2	
1112	0925	FRANKFURT		PUNTA CANA	B.767	1	
1113		PUNTA CANA	0550	FRANKFURT	B.767	2	
1114	0915	FRANKFURT		PUERTO PLATO	B.767	1	
1115		PUERTO PLATO	0605	FRANKFURT	B.767	2	
1156	1125	COLOGNE		CANCUN	B.767	1	
1157		CANCUN	1025	COLOGNE	B.767	2	
1158	1055	MUNICH		CANCUN	B.767	1	
1159		CANCUN	1045	FRANKFURT	B.767	2	
1196	0930	FRANKFURT		HAVANA	B.767	1	
1197		HAVANA	0940	FRANKFURT	B.767	2	
1236	0900	BERLIN		PUERTO PLATT	B.767	1	
1237		PUERTO PLATT	0710	BERLIN	B.767		7
2130	1130	FRANKFURT		SANTO DOMINGO	B.767	2	
2131		SANTO DOMINGO	0825	FRANKFURT	B.767	3	
2156	0840	FRANKFURT		CANCUN	B.767	2	
2157		CANCUN	0810	FRANKFURT	B.767	3	
2176	0925	FRANKFURT		ACAPULCO	B.767	2	
2177		ACAPULCO	1715	FRANKFURT	B.767	3	
2178	0925	FRANKFURT		TAMPA	B.767	2	
2179		PUERTO VALLARTA	1715	FRANKFURT	B.767	3	
2182	1010	FRANKFURT		BARBADOS	B.767	2	
2183		BARBADOS	0820	FRANKFURT	B.767	3	
2196	1205	COLOGNE		VARADERO	B.767	2	
2197		VARADERO	0935	COLOGNE	B.767	3	
2198	1230	MUNICH		VARADERO	B.767	2	
2199		VARADERO	1110	FRANKFURT	B.767	3	
2236	0755	MUNICH		PUERTO PLATT	B.767	2	
2237		PUERTO PLATT	0615	MUNICH	B.767	2	
2238	0815	STUTTGART		PUERTO PLATO	B.767	2	
2239		PUERTO PLATO	0550	STUTTGART	B.767	2	
3066	1045	FRANKFURT		ANCHORAGE	B.767	3	VIA WHITEHORSE
3067		ANCHORAGE	0950	FRANKFURT	B.767	4	

3106	1005	FRANKFURT		PORLAMAR	B.767	3
3107		PORLAMAR	0735	FRANKFURT	B.757	4
3112	1105	COLOGNE		PUNTA CANA	B.767	3
3113		PUNTA CANA	0720	COLOGNE	B.767	4
3130	1105	COLOGNE		SANTO DOMINGO	B.767	3
3131		SANTO DOMINGO	0725	COLOGNE	B.767	4
3196	1045	FRANKFURT		VARADERO	B.767	3
3197		VARADERO	0820	FRANKFURT	B.767	4
3232	0830	STUTTGART		PUNTA CANA	B.767	3
3233		PUNTA CANA	0635	STUTTGART	B.767	3
3234	0830	FRANKFURT		PUNTA CANA	B.767	3
4164	1010	FRANKFURT		MONTEGO BAY	B.767	4
4165		MONTEGO BAY	0950	FRANKFURT	B.767	5
4178	1320	FRANKFURT		TAMPA	B.767	4
4179		TAMPA	1135	FRANKFURT	B.767	5
4196	1025	FRANKFURT		VARADERO	B.767	4
4197		VARADERO	0705	FRANKFURT	B.767	5
4232	0815	HAMBURG		PUNTO CANA	B.767	4
4233		PUNTO CANA	0640	HAMBURG	B.767	4
5082	0935	FRANKFURT		LAS VEGAS	B.767	5
5083		LAS VEGAS	1110	FRANKFURT	B.767	6
5196	1120	FRANKFURT		HOLGUIN	B.767	5
5197		HOLGUIN	0855	FRANKFURT	B.767	6
5232	1050	BERLIN		PUNTO CANA	B.767	5
5233		PUNTA CANA	0905	BERLIN	B.767	5
6050	0840	FRANKFURT		FT.LAUDERDALE	B.767	6
6051		FT.LAUDERDALE	0600	FRANKFURT	B.767	7
6066	1650	FRANKFURT		ANCHORAGE	B.767	6
6067		ANCHORAGE	1525	FRANKFURT	B.767	7
6112	0830	MUNICH		PUNTO CANA	B.767	6
6113		PUNTO CANA	0545	MUNICH	B.767	7
6144	1040	FRANKFURT		SAN JUAN	B.767	6
6145		SANTO DOMINGO	0910	FRANKFURT	B.767	7
6232	0945	DUSSELDORF		PUNTA CANA	B.767	6
6233		PUNTA CANA	0800	DUSSELDORF	B.767	6
6436	1650	FRANKFURT	1900	SHANNON	A.320	6
6437	2000	SHANNON	2200	FRANKFURT	A.320	6
6754	1650	NURNEBERG	1925	SHANNON	B.737	6
6755	1340	SHANNON	1550	NUREMBERG	B.737	6
6908	1030	STUTTGART	1250	SHANNON	B.737	6
6909	1340	SHANNON	1545	STUTTGART	B.737	6
7178	0925	FRANKFURT		TAMPA	B.767	7
7179		TAMPA	0640	FRANKFURT	B.767	1
7232	0815	LEIPZIG		PUNTO CANA	B.767	7
7233		PUNTO CANA	0605	LEIPZIG	B.767	6

CONTINENTAL   *CONTINENTAL AIRLINES INC.*   *CO/COA*   *U.S.A.*

004		HOUSTON	0955	GATWICK	B.777	1234567
005	1200	GATWICK		HOUSTON	B.777	1234567
010		HOUSTON	1015	PARIS CDG	DC-10	1234567
011	1200	PARIS CDG		HOUSTON	DC-10	1234567
016		NEW YORK	0950	GLASGOW	DC-10	1234567
017	1225	GLASGOW		NEW YORK	DC-10	1234567
018		NEW YORK	2155	GATWICK	DC-10	1234567
019	1500	GATWICK		NEW YORK	DC-10	1234567
020		NEW YORK	0750	MANCHESTER	DC-10	1234567
021	1155	MANCHESTER		NEW YORK	DC-10	1234567
028		NEW YORK	0755	GATWICK	B.777	1234567
029	1115	GATWICK		NEW YORK	B.777	1234567
034		HOUSTON	0645	GATWICK	B.777	1234567
035	0940	GATWICK		HOUSTON	B.777	1234567
036		NEW YORK	0550	DUSSELDORF	DC-10	1234567
037	1010	DUSSELDORF		NEW YORK	DC-10	1234567
040		NEW YORK	0635	ROME	DC-10	1234567
041	0845	ROME		NEW YORK	DC-10	1234567
042		NEW YORK	1045	ROME	DC-10	1234567
043	1355	ROME		NEW YORK	DC-10	1234567

CONTINENTAL (Cont.)

Flight	Dep	From	Arr	To	Aircraft	Days	Remarks
044		NEW YORK	0655	MILAN	DC-10	1234567	
045	1005	MILAN		NEW YORK	DC-10	1234567	
050		NEW YORK	0825	FRANKFURT	DC-10	1234567	
051	1035	FRANKFURT		NEW YORK	DC-10	1234567	
054		NEW YORK	0955	PARIS CDG	DC-10	1234567	
055	1455	PARIS CDG		NEW YORK	DC-10	1234567	
056		NEW YORK	0810	PARIS CDG	DC-10	1234567	
057	1220	PARIS CDG		NEW YORK	DC-10	1234567	
066		CLEVELAND	0545	GATWICK	B.757	1234567	ARR 0635 7
067	1100	GATWICK		CLEVELAND	B.757	1234567	
072		HOUSTON	1255	GATWICK	DC-10	1234567	(SHOWN IN LHR &
		HOUSTON	1255	HEATHROW	B.777	1234567	LGW T/TABLES)
073	1500	GATWICK		HOUSTON	DC-10	1234567	(SHOWN IN LHR &
	1500	HEATHROW		HOUSTON	B.777	1234567	LGW T/TABLES)
074		CLEVELAND	0905	HEATHROW	B.777	1234567	
077	1115	HEATHROW		CLEVELAND	B.777	1234567	
080		NEW YORK	0520	PARIS CDG	B.747	1234567	
081	0925	PARIS CDG		NEW YORK	B.747	1234567	
082		HOUSTON	0750	PARIS CDG	B.777	1234567	
083	0930	PARIS CDG		HOUSTON	B.777	1234567	
084		NEW YORK	2140	HEATHROW	B.777	1234567	
085	0815	HEATHROW		NEW YORK	B.777	1234567	
086		NEW YORK	0555	HEATHROW	B.777	1234567	
087	0915	HEATHROW		NEW YORK	B.777	1234567	
088		NEW YORK	0655	HEATHROW	B.777	1234567	
089	1030	HEATHROW		NEW YORK	B.777	1234567	
090		NEW YORK	0755	HEATHROW	B.777	1234567	
091	1215	HEATHROW		NEW YORK	B.777	1234567	
092		NEW YORK	0825	HEATHROW	B.777	1234567	
093	1600	HEATHROW		NEW YORK	B.777	1234567	
094		NEW YORK	0955	HEATHROW	B.777	1234567	
095	1730	HEATHROW		NEW YORK	B.777	1234567	
096		HOUSTON	0645	HEATHROW	B.777	1234567	
097	0930	HEATHROW		HOUSTON	B.777	1234567	
098		NEW YORK	0520	GATWICK	DC-10	34	
099	2100	GATWICK		NEW YORK	DC-10	34	DEP 2000 4

CROATIA

CROATIA AIRLINES   OU/CTN   CROATIA

Flight	Dep	From	Arr	To	Aircraft	Days	Remarks
490		ZAGREB	1100	HEATHROW	B737/A320	1234 67	ARR 1825 1
		ZAGREB	1915	HEATHROW	B.737	5	
491	1150	HEATHROW		ZAGREB	B737/A320	1234 67	DEP 1910 1
	2000	HEATHROW		ZAGREB	B.737	5	
492		SPLIT	1550	HEATHROW	A.320	6	
493	1640	HEATHROW		SPLIT	A.320	6	
494		SPLIT	1615	GATWICK	A.320	45	ARR 1530 5
495	1700	GATWICK		SPLIT	A.320	45	DEP 1625 5
498		DUBROVNIK	1030	GATWICK	B.737	2 7	ARR 1630 2
499	1145	GATWICK		DUBROVNIK	B.737	2 7	DEP 1725 2
506		DUBROVNIK	1635	MANCHESTER	A.320	1	
507	1725	MANCHESTER		DUBROVNIK	A.320	1	

CRONUS AIR

CRONUS AIRLINES   X5/CUS   GREECE

Flight	Dep	From	Arr	To	Aircraft	Days	Remarks
600		ATHENS	2130	HEATHROW	B.737	1 345 7	
601	2230	HEATHROW		ATHENS	B.737	1 345 7	

CROSS AIR

CROSS AIR A.G.   LX/CRX   SWITZERLAND

Flight	Dep	From	Arr	To	Aircraft	Days	Remarks
820	0610	BASLE	0750	HEATHROW	BAE146/SAAB	1234567	
821	0835	HEATHROW	1015	BASLE	BAE146/SAAB	1234567	
824	1125	BASLE	1300	HEATHROW	BAE-146	1234567	1145/1320 7
825	1415	HEATHROW	1555	BASLE	BAE-146	1234567	
826	1720	BASLE	1900	HEATHROW	MD83/BAE146	1234567	
827	2100	HEATHROW	2235	BASLE	MD83/BAE146	1234567	
830		BASLE	0755	BIRMINGHAM	SAAB-2000	123456	
831	0830	BIRMINGHAM		BASLE	SAAB-2000	123456	
836		BASLE	1810	BIRMINGHAM	SAAB-2000	12345 7	
837	1840	BIRMINGHAM		BASLE	SAAB-2000	12345 7	

Flight	Dep	From	Arr	To	Aircraft	Days	Notes
840	0725	GENEVA	0900	LONDON CITY	BAE-146	123456	0700/0835 6
841	0855	LONDON CITY	1025	GENEVA	BAE-146	123456	
842	0900	ZURICH	1135	JERSEY	SAAB-340	1234567	
	1205	GUERNSEY	1655	ZURICH	SAAB-340	1234567	VIA GUERNSEY
844	1120	GENEVA	1255	LONDON CITY	BAE-146	12345 7	
845	1340	LONDON CITY	1515	GENEVA	BAE-146	12345 7	
848	1610	GENEVA	1740	LONDON CITY	BAE-146	12345 7	
849	1815	LONDON CITY	1945	GENEVA	BAE-146	12345 7	
858	1050	ZURICH	1315	EDINBURGH	SAAB-340	1234567	
859	1350	EDINBURGH	1620	ZURICH	SAAB-340	1234567	
860	0615	BASLE	0800	BIRMINGHAM	BAE-146	123456	
861	0840	BIRMINGHAM	1040	ZURICH	BAE-146	123456	
864	1025	ZURICH	1220	BIRMINGHAM	SAAB-2000	12345 7	
865	1310	BIRMINGHAM	1505	ZURICH	SAAB-2000	12345 7	
868	1710	ZURICH	1900	BIRMINGHAM	VARIES	12345 7	
869	1940	BIRMINGHAM	2140	BASLE	VARIES	12345 7	
870	0640	ZURICH	0810	LONDON CITY	BAE-146	123456	
871	0940	LONDON CITY	1110	ZURICH	BAE-146	123456	0910/1110 6
872	1025	GENEVA	1200	LONDON CITY	BAE-146	1234567	0945/1120 7
873	1255	LONDON CITY	1430	GENEVA	BAE-146	1234567	1155/1330 6
874	1940	ZURICH	2120	LONDON CITY	BAE-146	12345 7	
875	0715	LONDON CITY	0845	ZURICH	BAE-146	123456	
876	1515	ZURICH	1650	LONDON CITY	BAE-146	12345 7	
877	1725	LONDON CITY	1855	ZURICH	BAE-146	12345 7	
878	1715	GENEVA	1850	LONDON CITY	BAE-146	12345 7	
879	1835	LONDON CITY	2000	GENEVA	BAE-146	12345 7	
880	0605	BASLE	0810	MANCHESTER	SAAB-2000	123456	
881	0840	MANCHESTER	1040	BASLE	SAAB-2000	123456	
884	1100	BASLE	1305	MANCHESTER	SAAB-2000	12345 7	
885	1335	MANCHESTER	1525	BASLE	SAAB-2000	12345 7	
886	1625	BASLE	1830	MANCHESTER	SAAB-2000	12345 7	
887	1900	MANCHESTER	2055	BASLE	SAAB-2000	12345 7	
890	0610	BASLE	0755	LONDON CITY	SAAB-2000	123456	
891	0820	LONDON CITY	1015	BASLE	SAAB-2000	123456	
894	1100	BASLE	1250	LONDON CITY	SAAB-2000	12345 7	
895	1340	LONDON CITY	1525	BASLE	SAAB-2000	12345 7	
898	1615	BASLE	1805	LONDON CITY	SAAB-2000	12345 7	
899	1835	LONDON CITY	2015	BASLE	SAAB-2000	12345	
2857	0855	EDINBURGH	1000	ZURICH	SAAB-2000	7	
4826	1835	BASLE	2000	HEATHROW	MD-83	7	
4827	2105	HEATHROW	2240	BASLE	MD-83	7	
8580		ZURICH	0920	CORK	BAE-146	5	
8581	1010	CORK		ZURICH	BAE-146	5	
9150		BASLE	1835	SHANNON	SAAB-2000	6	27.05-01.09
9191	1910	SHANNON		BASLE	SAAB-2000	6	27.05-01.09

CSA-LINES   *CSA CZECH AIRLINES.*   *OK/CSA*   *CZECH REPUBLIC*

Flight	Dep	From	Arr	To	Aircraft	Days	Notes
052	1130	PRAGUE		NEW YORK	A.310	1234567	
053		NEW YORK	0650	PRAGUE	A.310	1234567	
108	1115	PRAGUE		MONTREAL	A.310	4 6	
109		MONTREAL	0850	PRAGUE	A.310	5 7	
650	1150	PRAGUE	1350	HEATHROW	B.737	1234567	
651	1450	HEATHROW	1645	PRAGUE	B.737	1234567	
652	1805	PRAGUE	2005	HEATHROW	B.737	1234567	
653	0740	HEATHROW	0935	PRAGUE	B.737	1234567	
654	0600	PRAGUE	0800	HEATHROW	B.737	1234567	
655	0855	HEATHROW	1100	PRAGUE	B.737	1234567	
656		PRAGUE	0820	STANSTED	B.737	12345 7	ARR 1145 7
657	0915	STANSTED		PRAGUE	B.737	12345 7	DEP 1225 7
662		PRAGUE	2015	MANCHESTER	B.737	12345 7	
663	0730	MANCHESTER		PRAGUE	B.737	123456	

CUBANA   *EMPRESA CUBANA DE AVIACION*   *CU/CUB*   *CUBA*

Flight	Dep	From	Arr	To	Aircraft	Days	Notes
333	2335	MOSCOW		HAVANA	IL-96	1 6	DEP 2255 1
334		HAVANA	0425	MOSCOW	IL-96	1 3	ARR 1510 1
335	2300	MOSCOW		HAVANA	IL-96	3 6	

Flt	Dep	From	Arr	To	Type	Days	Notes
336		HAVANA	1535	MOSCOW	IL-96	5	
400		HAVANA	1015	GATWICK	DC-10	2 4	ARR 1140 4
		HAVANA	1325	GATWICK	DC-10	6	
401	1215	GATWICK		HAVANA	DC-10	2 4	DEP 1440 4
	1530	GATWICK		HAVANA	DC-10	6	
406		HAVANA	0900	MANCHESTER	DC-10	3	
407	1020	MANCHESTER	1115	GATWICK	DC-10	3	
	1245	GATWICK		HAVANA	DC-10	3	
420		HAVANA	0710	ROME	DC-10	1 3	ARR 1120 1
421	1320	ROME		HAVANA	DC-10	1	
430		HAVANA	1040	BERLIN	DC-10	7	
431	1430	FRANKFURT		HAVANA	DC-10	7	
440		HAVANA	0800	PARIS ORLY	DC-10	5 7	ARR 1040 5
441	1120	PARIS ORLY		HAVANA	DC-10	5 7	DEP 1240 5
442		HAVANA	0655	PARIS ORLY	DC-10	6	
		HAVANA	0950	LYON	DC-10	2	
443	1015	PARIS ORLY		HAVANA	DC-10	4 6	
	1250	LYON		HAVANA	DC-10	2	
1421	0910	ROME		HAVANA	DC-10	3	
2420		HAVANA	1250	ROME	DC-10	5	
2421	1320	ROME		HAVANA	DC-10	5	

CYPRUS   *CYPRUS AIRWAYS LTD.*   *CY/CYP*   *CYPRUS*

Flt	Dep	From	Arr	To	Type	Days	Notes
206		LARNACA	1205	GATWICK	A.310	1234567	
207	1305	GATWICK		LARNACA	A.310	1234567	
314	1620	LARNACA	2110	GATWICK	A310/A320	5 7	1700/2150 7
315	2215	GATWICK	0230	LARNACA	A.310	5 7	2250/0305 7
326	1600	LARNACA	2050	HEATHROW	A.310	1234567	
327	0945	HEATHROW	1410	LARNACA	A.310	1234567	
332	0200	LARNACA	0655	HEATHROW	A.310	1234567	0235/0725 3567
333	2200	HEATHROW	0225	LARNACA	A.310	1234567	
358	0920	PAPHOS	1420	MANCHESTER	A.310	6	
359	1520	MANCHESTER	1950	PAPHOS	A.310	6	
362	0830	LARNACA	1320	STANSTED	A.310	2 5 7	
363	1420	STANSTED	1840	LARNACA	A.310	2 5 7	
456	1700	LARNACA	2210	MANCHESTER	A.310	3	
457	2310	MANCHESTER	0350	LARNACA	A.310	3	
466	1850	LARNACA	2345	BIRMINGHAM	A.310	4	
	0115	LARNACA	0615	BIRMINGHAM	A.310	3	21.07-
467	0045	BIRMINGHAM	0525	LARNACA	A.310	5	
	0715	BIRMINGHAM	1155	LARNACA	A.310	3	21.07-
504	1145	PAPHOS	1630	HEATHROW	A.310	2	
505	1730	HEATHROW	2145	PAPHOS	A.310	2	
542	0745	PAPHOS	1230	GATWICK	A.310	3	
543	1345	GATWICK	1800	PAPHOS	A.310	3	

DAGOBERT   *QUICK AIR SERVICE*   *QAJ*   *GERMANY*

Flt	Dep	From	Arr	To	Type	Days	Notes
6191	2100	STANSTED	2130	EAST MIDLANDS	LEARJET	1234	
	2230	EAST MIDLANDS		COLOGNE	LEARJET	1234	
6192		COLOGNE	2005	STANSTED	LEARJET	1234	

DAHL   *DHL AIRWAYS INC.*   *ER/DHL*   *U.S.A.*

Flt	Dep	From	Arr	To	Type	Days	Notes
011	0230	BRUSSELS		NEW YORK	DC-8	23456	
012	2100	SHANNON	2225	BRUSSELS	DC-8	6	
017	0345	BRUSSELS		NEW YORK	DC-8	234567	DEP 1720 7
018		NEW YORK	0825	BRUSSELS	DC-8	7	
020		CINCINNATI	1925	EAST MIDLANDS	DC-8	2345	
024		NEW YORK	2155	HEATHROW	DC-8	6	EX. LHR. BCS412

DEBONAIR   *DEBONAIR AIRWAYS*   *2G/DEB*   *U.K.*

Flt	Dep	From	Arr	To	Type	Days	Notes
200	0630	PARIS PONTOISE	0730	LUTON	BAE-146	12345	
201	0755	LUTON	0855	PARIS PONTOISE	BAE-146	12345	
206	1500	PARIS PONTOISE	1600	LUTON	BAE-146	12345	
207	1630	LUTON	1730	PARIS PONTOISE	BAE-146	12345	
208	1800	PARIS PONTOISE	1900	LUTON	BAE-146	12345	

209	1925	LUTON	2025	PARIS PONTOISE	BAE-146	12345	
210	0655	PARIS PONTOISE	0755	LUTON	BAE-146	6	
211	0820	LUTON	0920	PARIS PONTOISE	BAE-146	6	
212	0945	PARIS PONTOISE	1045	LUTON	BAE-146	6	
217	1730	LUTON	1830	PARIS PONTOISE	BAE-146	7	
218	1900	PARIS PONTOISE	2000	LUTON	BAE-146	7	
219	2025	LUTON	2125	PARIS PONTOISE	BAE-146	7	
300	0620	DUSSELDORF	0730	LUTON	BAE-146	12345	
302	0700	DUSSELDORF	0815	LUTON	BAE-146	6	
305	1530	LUTON	1645	DUSSELDORF	BAE-146	7	
307	1900	LUTON	2015	DUSSELDORF	BAE-146	12345 7	
308	1715	DUSSELDORF	1830	LUTON	BAE-146	12345 7	
331	1845	LUTON	2040	MUNICH	BAE-146	12345 7	1530/1725 7
341	0755	LUTON	0905	DUSSELDORF	BAE-146	12345	
350	0645	MUNICH	0840	LUTON	BAE-146	123456	
360	1630	MUNICH	1825	LUTON	BAE-146	12345 7	1800/1955 7
361	0745	LUTON	0945	MUNICH	BAE-146	123456	1130/1330 6
363	2025	LUTON	2220	MUNICH	BAE-146	7	
364	1920	MUNICH	2115	LUTON	BAE-146	7	
501	0930	LUTON	1215	ROME	BAE-146	12345 7	0845/1130 7
502	1245	ROME	1530	LUTON	BAE-146	12345 7	1200/1445 7
701	0900	LUTON	1110	BARCELONA	BAE-146	1234567	
702	1730	BARCELONA	1950	LUTON	BAE-146	1234567	
715	1640	GATWICK		MUNICH	BAE-146	1234567	
716		MUNICH	1600	GATWICK	BAE-146	1234567	
717	1550	GATWICK		BARCELONA	BAE-146	1234567	
718		BARCELONA	1400	GATWICK	BAE-146	1234567	
800	1430	MADRID	1700	LUTON	BAE-146	12345 7	1230/1500 7
	1850	MADRID	2120	LUTON	BAE-146	6	
801	1110	LUTON	1330	MADRID	BAE-146	12345 7	0910/1130 7
	1600	LUTON	1820	MADRID	BAE-146	6	
817	1440	GATWICK		MADRID	BAE-146	1234567	
818		MADRID	1500	GATWICK	BAE-146	1234567	

		DELTA		*DELTA AIRLINES*	*DL/DAL*	*U.S.A.*	
010		ATLANTA	1115	GATWICK	MD-11	1234567	
011	1000	GATWICK		ATLANTA	B.777	1234567	
012		ATLANTA	0655	GATWICK	B.777	1234567	
014		ATLANTA	0950	FRANKFURT	MD11/B767	12345567	
015	1025	FRANKFURT		ATLANTA	MD11/B767	1234567	
019 \	1335	GATWICK		ATLANTA	MD-11	1234567	
020		ATLANTA	0750	FRANKFURT	B.767	1234567	
021	0920	PARIS		ATLANTA	B.767	1234567	
022		ATLANTA	0720	PARIS	B.767	1234567	
030		NEW YORK	0825	MOSCOW	B.767	1234567	
031	1030	MOSCOW		NEW YORK	B.767	1234567	
036		CINCINNATI	0800	GATWICK	B.777	1234567	
037	1105	GATWICK		CINCINNATI	B.777	1234567	
038		ATLANTA	0630	AMSTERDAM	B.767	1234567	
039	0925	AMSTERDAM		ATLANTA	B.767	1234567	
043	0950	PARIS		CINCINNATI	B.767	1234567	
044	0920	PARIS CDG		ATLANTA	B.767	1234567	
045		ATLANTA	0720	PARIS CDG	B.767	1234567	
046		NEW YORK	0710	STOCKHOLM	B.767	1234567	
047	1150	STOCKHOLM		NEW YORK	B.767	1234567	
060		ATLANTA	0930	HAMBURG	B.767	234567	
061	1115	HAMBURG		ATLANTA	B.767	234567	
064		ATLANTA	0900	MANCHESTER	MD-11	1234567	
065	1150	MANCHESTER		ATLANTA	MD-11	1234567	
066		ATLANTA	0945	ZURICH	B.767	1234567	
067	1240	ZURICH		ATLANTA	B.767	1234567	
072		NEW YORK	0825	ISTANBUL	B.767	1234567	
073	1010	ISTANBUL		NEW YORK	B.767	1234567	
076		NEW YORK	0920	MUNICH	B.767	1234567	
077	0945	MUNICH		NEW YORK	B.767	1234567	
080		NEW YORK	0640	AMSTERDAM	B.767	1234567	
081	1255	AMSTERDAM		NEW YORK	B.767	1234567	

082		NEW YORK	0915	NICE	B.767	1234567	
083	1105	NICE		NEW YORK	B.767	1234567	
084		NEW YORK	0720	MILAN	B.767	1234567	
085	1125	MILAN		NEW YORK	B.767	1234567	
090	1040	BUDAPEST		NEW YORK	B.767	1234567	
091		NEW YORK	0750	BUDAPEST	B.767	1234567	
096		NEW YORK	0635	STUTTGART	B.767	1234567	
097	1230	STUTTGART		NEW YORK	B.767	1234567	
100	1130	ZURICH		NEW YORK	MD-11	1234567	
101		NEW YORK	0700	ZURICH	MD-11	1234567	
106		NEW YORK	0855	FRANKFURT	B.767	1234567	
107	0835	FRANKFURT		NEW YORK	B.767	1234567	
117	1020	STUTTGART		ATLANTA	B.767	1234567	
118		NEW YORK	0735	PARIS	B.767	1234567	
119	0940	PARIS		NEW YORK	B.767	1234567	
120	0900	ZURICH		ATLANTA	B.747	1234567	OP. BY SWISSAIR
121		ATLANTA	0715	ZURICH	B.747	1234567	OP. BY SWISSAIR
122		CINCINNATI	0830	ZURICH	B.767	1234567	
123	1025	ZURICH		CINCINNATI	B.767	1234567	
124		ATLANTA	0715	BRUSSELS	B.767	1234567	
125	0935	BRUSSELS		ATLANTA	B.767	1234567	
128		ATLANTA	0735	SHANNON	B.767	3 5 7	
	0945	SHANNON	1035	DUBLIN	B.767	3 5 7	
	1210	DUBLIN		ATLANTA	B.767	3 5 7	
129		ATLANTA	0850	DUBLIN	B.767	12 4 6	
	1010	DUBLIN	1100	SHANNON	B.767	12 4 6	
	1225	SHANNON		ATLANTA	B.767	12 4 6	
130		ATLANTA	0755	MUNICH	B.767	1234567	
131	1215	MUNICH		ATLANTA	B.767	1234567	
132		NEW YORK	0820	ATHENS	B.767	1 3 567	
133	1005	ATHENS		NEW YORK	B.767	1 3 567	
138		NEW YORK	0810	MANCHESTER	B.767	1234567	
139	1030	MANCHESTER		NEW YORK	B.767	1234567	
140		NEW YORK	0725	BRUSSELS	B.767	1234567	
141	1015	BRUSSELS		NEW YORK	B.767	1234567	
146		ATLANTA	0810	VIENNA	B.767	1234567	
147	1010	VIENNA		ATLANTA	B.767	1234567	
148		NEW YORK	0730	ROME	B.767	1234567	
149	1110	ROME		NEW YORK	B.767	1234567	

DIRGANTARA

DIRGANTARA AIR SERVICE   AW/DIR   INDONESIA

9005	0220	AMSTERDAM	0340	MANCHESTER	HERCULES	23456
9006	0440	MANCHESTER	0600	AMSTERDAM	HERCULES	23456

DREAM BIRD

CITY BIRD S.A.   H2/CTB   BELGIUM

701	1230	BRUSSELS		ORLANDO	B.767	3	
702		MIAMI	1040	BRUSSELS	B.767	4	
703	1230	BRUSSELS		MIAMI	B.767	1 6	
704		MIAMI	0900	BRUSSELS	B.767	2 7	
715	1215	BRUSSELS		MEXICO CITY	MD-11	4	
716		MEXICO CITY	1235	BRUSSELS	MD-11	5	
723	1045	BRUSSELS		LOS ANGELES	B.767	2 7	
724		LOS ANGELES	1100	BRUSSELS	B.767	1 3	
725	0900	BRUSSELS		OAKLAND	B.767	5	
726		LOS ANGELES	1100	BRUSSELS	B.767	6	

EASYJET

EASYJET AIRLINES CO. LTD.   U2/EZY   U.K.

012	0640	EDINBURGH	0755	LUTON	B.737	12345
013	1145	LUTON	1300	EDINBURGH	B.737	12345
014	1320	EDINBURGH	1435	LUTON	B.737	12345
016	1000	EDINBURGH	1115	LUTON	B.737	12345
017	0825	LUTON	0940	EDINBURGH	B.737	12345
021	1600	LUTON	1715	EDINBURGH	B.737	12345
023	1920	LUTON	2035	EDINBURGH	B.737	12345
024	1735	EDINBURGH	1850	LUTON	B.737	12345
026	2055	EDINBURGH	2210	LUTON	B.737	12345

027	2100	LUTON	2215	EDINBURGH	B.737	12345	
028	0740	EDINBURGH	0855	LUTON	B.737	6	
029	0925	LUTON	1040	EDINBURGH	B.737	6	
031	1245	LUTON	1400	EDINBURGH	B.737	6	
032	1100	EDINBURGH	1215	LUTON	B.737	6	
034	1420	EDINBURGH	1535	LUTON	B.737	6	
036	0740	EDINBURGH	0855	LUTON	B.737	7	
037	2100	LUTON	2215	EDINBURGH	B.737	6	
038	1515	EDINBURGH	1630	LUTON	B.737	7	
039	1340	LUTON	1455	EDINBURGH	B.737	7	
041	1950	LUTON	2105	EDINBURGH	B.737	7	
042	2125	EDINBURGH	2240	LUTON	B.737	7	
043	2100	LUTON	2215	EDINBURGH	B.737	7	
053	1950	LUTON	2205	GLASGOW	B.737	12345	
071	1035	LUTON	1150	GLASGOW	B.737	1234567	01.09-
072	0630	GLASGOW	0745	LUTON	B.737	12345	
073	0815	LUTON	0930	GLASGOW	B.737	12345	
074	1210	GLASGOW	1325	LUTON	B.737	1234567	01.09-
076	0950	GLASGOW	1105	LUTON	B.737	12345	
078	1725	GLASGOW	1840	LUTON	B.737	12345	
079	1550	LUTON	1705	GLASGOW	B.737	12345	
081	1910	LUTON	2025	GLASGOW	B.737	12345	
082	2045	GLASGOW	2200	LUTON	B.737	12345	
083	2050	LUTON	2205	GLASGOW	B.737	12345	
084	0730	GLASGOW	0845	LUTON	B.737	12345	
086	1050	GLASGOW	1205	LUTON	B.737	6	
087	0915	LUTON	1030	GLASGOW	B.737	67	1900/2015 7
088	1050	GLASGOW	1205	LUTON	B.737	6	
091	2050	LUTON	2205	GLASGOW	B.737	6	
093	1125	LUTON	1240	GLASGOW	B.737	7	
094	0940	GLASGOW	1055	LUTON	B.737	7	
096	1300	GLASGOW	1415	LUTON	B.737	7	
097	1900	LUTON	2015	GLASGOW	B.737	6	
098	2035	GLASGOW	2150	LUTON	B.737	7	
101	2050	LUTON	2205	GLASGOW	B.737	7	
141	0650	LUTON	0820	ABERDEEN	B.737	12345	
142	0850	ABERDEEN	1015	LUTON	B.737	12345	
143	0650	LUTON	0820	ABERDEEN	B.737	6	
146	0850	ABERDEEN	1015	LUTON	B.737	6	
147	0905	LUTON	1035	ABERDEEN	B.737	7	
148	1105	ABERDEEN	1230	LUTON	B.737	7	
149	1655	LUTON	1825	ABERDEEN	B.737	12345	
151	1655	LUTON	1825	ABERDEEN	B.737	6	
152	1855	ABERDEEN	2020	LUTON	B.737	12345	
153	1655	LUTON	1825	ABERDEEN	B.737	7	
154	1855	ABERDEEN	2020	LUTON	B.737	6	
156	1855	ABERDEEN	2020	LUTON	B.737	7	
171	1135	LUTON	1310	INVERNESS	B.737	12345	
172	1330	INVERNESS	1500	LUTON	B.737	12345	
173	1235	LUTON	1410	INVERNESS	B.737	6	
174	1430	INVERNESS	1600	LUTON	B.737	6	
176	1640	INVERNESS	1810	LUTON	B.737	7	
179	1445	LUTON	1620	INVERNESS	B.737	7	
201	0640	LUTON	0750	AMSTERDAM	B.737	12345	
202	0830	AMSTERDAM	0940	LUTON	B.737	12345	
206	1615	AMSTERDAM	1725	LUTON	B.737	12345	
207	1425	LUTON	1535	AMSTERDAM	B.737	12345	
208	2015	AMSTERDAM	2125	LUTON	B.737	12345	
209	1825	LUTON	1935	AMSTERDAM	B.737	12345	
212	0830	AMSTERDAM	0940	LUTON	B.737	6	
213	0640	LUTON	0750	AMSTERDAM	B.737	6	
214	1555	AMSTERDAM	1705	LUTON	B.737	6	
217	1405	LUTON	1515	AMSTERDAM	B.737	6	
218	1730	AMSTERDAM	1840	LUTON	B.737	7	
231	1540	LUTON	1650	AMSTERDAM	B.737	7	
232	2120	AMSTERDAM	2230	LUTON	B.737	7	
237	1925	LUTON	2035	AMSTERDAM	B.737	7	
251	0630	LUTON	0835	NICE	B.737	12345	

252	0600	NICE	0815	LUTON	B.737	12 45		
253	0845	LUTON	1050	NICE	B.737	12345		
254	0915	NICE	1130	LUTON	B.737	12345		
256	1130	NICE	1345	LUTON	B.737	12345		
257	1200	LUTON	1405	NICE	B.737	12345		
258	1445	NICE	1700	LUTON	B.737	12345		
259	1935	LUTON	2140	NICE	B.737	1 345		
261	0630	LUTON	0835	NICE	B.737	67	1200/1505 7
262	0600	NICE	0815	LUTON	B.737	67	1130/1345 7
263	0845	LUTON	1050	NICE	B.737	67	1935/2140 7
264	0915	NICE	1130	LUTON	B.737	67	1445/1700 7
267	1200	LUTON	1405	NICE	B.737	6	
268	1130	LUTON	1345	LUTON	B.737	6	
271	1935	LUTON	2140	NICE	B.737	6	
272	1445	NICE	1700	LUTON	B.737	6	
273	0630	LUTON	0835	NICE	B.737	7	
276	0600	NICE	0815	LUTON	B.737	7	
278	0915	LUTON	1130	LUTON	B.737	7	
279	0845	LUTON	1050	NICE	B.737	7	
281	1200	LUTON	1405	NICE	B.737	7	
282	1945	NICE	2300	LUTON	B.737	7	
283	1935	LUTON	2140	NICE	B.737	7	
284	1445	LUTON	1700	LUTON	B.737	7	
286	2045	NICE	2300	LUTON	B.737	12345	
287	1800	LUTON	2005	NICE	B.737	12345	
289	1800	LUTON	2005	NICE	B.737	6	
291	1800	LUTON	2005	NICE	B.737	7	
292	2045	NICE	2300	LUTON	B.737	6	
294	2045	NICE	2300	LUTON	B.737	7	
301	0715	LUTON	0925	BARCELONA	B.737	12345	
302	0955	BARCELONA	1220	LUTON	B.737	12345	
303	1320	LUTON	1530	BARCELONA	B.737	12345	
304	1610	BARCELONA	1835	LUTON	B.737	12345	
306	2040	BARCELONA	2305	LUTON	B.737	12345	
307	1750	LUTON	2000	BARCELONA	B.737	12345	
308	0955	BARCELONA	1220	LUTON	B.737	6	
309	0705	LUTON	0915	BARCELONA	B.737	6	
312	2055	BARCELONA	2320	LUTON	B.737	6	
313	1805	LUTON	2015	BARCELONA	B.737	6	
314	1605	BARCELONA	1830	LUTON	B.737	6	
316	1840	BARCELONA	2105	LUTON	B.737	6	
317	1315	LUTON	1525	BARCELONA	B.737	6	
318	0955	BARCELONA	1220	LUTON	B.737	7	
319	1550	LUTON	1800	BARCELONA	B.737	6	
321	0705	LUTON	0915	BARCELONA	B.737	7	
323	0925	LUTON	1135	BARCELONA	B.737	7	
324	1215	BARCELONA	1440	LUTON	B.737	7	
326	1610	BARCELONA	1835	LUTON	B.737	7	
327	1320	LUTON	1530	BARCELONA	B.737	7	
328	2040	BARCELONA	2305	LUTON	B.737	7	
329	1750	LUTON	2000	BARCELONA	B.737	7	
351	0700	LUTON	0810	BELFAST	B.737	12345	
352	0840	BELFAST	0955	LUTON	B.737	12345	
353	1040	LUTON	1150	BELFAST	B.737	12345	
354	1220	BELFAST	1335	LUTON	B.737	12345	
356	1605	BELFAST	1720	LUTON	B.737	12345	
357	1435	LUTON	1545	BELFAST	B.737	12345	
358	1915	BELFAST	2030	LUTON	B.737	12345	
359	1735	LUTON	1845	BELFAST	B.737	12345	
361	0700	LUTON	0810	BELFAST	B.737	6	
363	1735	LUTON	1845	BELFAST	B.737	6	
364	1915	BELFAST	2030	LUTON	B.737	6	
367	0700	LUTON	0810	BELFAST	B.737	7	
369	1735	LUTON	1845	BELFAST	B.737	7	
371	1040	LUTON	1150	BELFAST	B.737	6	
372	1915	BELFAST	2030	LUTON	B.737	7	
373	1435	LUTON	1545	BELFAST	B.737	7	
374	1220	BELFAST	1335	LUTON	B.737	6	

376	1605	BELFAST	1720	LUTON	B.737	7		
382	0840	BELFAST	0955	LUTON	B.737	6		
388	0840	BELFAST	0955	LUTON	B.737	7		
401	1045	LUTON	1315	PALMA	B.737	12345		
402	1355	PALMA	1635	LUTON	B.737	12345		
403	1045	LUTON	1320	PALMA	B.737	6		
404	1400	PALMA	1640	LUTON	B.737	6		
406	1940	PALMA	2220	LUTON	B.737	6		
407	1630	LUTON	1900	PALMA	B.737	6		
408	1000	PALMA	1240	LUTON	B.737	7		
409	0650	LUTON	1020	PALMA	B.737	7		
412	1625	PALMA	1905	LUTON	B.737	7		
413	1315	LUTON	1545	PALMA	B.737	7		
451	1220	LUTON	1620	ATHENS	B.737	1234567		
452	0450	ATHENS	0900	LUTON	B.737	1234567		
453	2255	LUTON	0255	ATHENS	B.737	1234567		
454	1720	ATHENS	2130	LUTON	B.737	1234567		
501	1025	LUTON	1250	MADRID	B.737	12345		
502	1330	MADRID	1555	LUTON	B.737	12345		
506	1330	MADRID	1555	LUTON	B.737	6		
507	1025	LUTON	1250	MADRID	B.737	6		
508	2005	MADRID	2230	LUTON	B.737	6		
509	1700	LUTON	1925	MADRID	B.737	6		
512	1330	MADRID	1555	LUTON	B.737	7		
513	1025	LUTON	1250	MADRID	B.737	7		
601	0630	LIVERPOOL	0745	AMSTERDAM	B.737	123456		
602	0835	AMSTERDAM	1000	LIVERPOOL	B.737	123456		
603	1925	LIVERPOOL	2040	AMSTERDAM	B.737	7		
604	2115	AMSTERDAM	2240	LIVERPOOL	B.737	7		
621	1715	LIVERPOOL	1930	NICE	B.737	123456	1100/1315 6	
623	0630	LIVERPOOL	0845	NICE	B.737	7		
624	2010	NICE	2240	LIVERPOOL	B.737	123456	1355/1625 6	
626	0930	NICE	1200	LIVERPOOL	B.737	7		
631	0715	LIVERPOOL	0805	BELFAST	B.737	12345		
631	0715	LIVERPOOL	0805	BELFAST	B.737	1234567		
632	0845	BELFAST	0935	LIVERPOOL	B.737	12345		
632	0845	BELFAST	0935	LIVERPOOL	B.737	6		
634	1535	BELFAST	1535	LIVERPOOL	B.737	1234567	01.09	
636	2130	BELFAST	2220	LIVERPOOL	B.737	1234567		
637	1335	LIVERPOOL	1425	BELFAST	B.737	1234567	01.09	
638	1900	BELFAST	1950	LIVERPOOL	B.737	1234567		
639	2020	LIVERPOOL	2110	BELFAST	B.737	1234567		
641	1750	LIVERPOOL	1840	BELFAST	B.737	1234567		
653	1030	LIVERPOOL	1255	BARCELONA	B.737	123456	1655/1920 6	
654	1345	BARCELONA	1625	LIVERPOOL	B.737	123456	2000/2240 6	
656	1615	BARCELONA	1855	LIVERPOOL	B.737	7		
657	1310	LIVERPOOL	1535	BARCELONA	B.737	7		
671	1010	LIVERPOOL	1310	MALAGA	B.737	1234567		
672	1350	MALAGA	1700	LIVERPOOL	B.737	1234567		
901	0545	GENEVA	0730	LUTON	B.737	1234567		
902	0815	LUTON	1000	GENEVA	B.737	1234567		
903	1100	GENEVA	1255	LIVERPOOL	B.737	1234567		
904	1350	LIVERPOOL	1550	GENEVA	B.737	1234567		
908	1915	LUTON	2100	GENEVA	B.737	1234567		
909	1620	GENEVA	1805	LUTON	B.737	1234567		
912	0850	LUTON	1040	ZURICH	B.737	123456		
913	0530	ZURICH	0725	LUTON	B.737	123456		
914	1420	LUTON	1320	ZURICH	B.737	1234567		
916	1930	LUTON	2120	ZURICH	B.737	1234567		
917	1200	ZURICH	1350	LUTON	B.737	1234567		
919	1650	ZURICH	1845	LUTON	B.737	1234567		

		EGYPTAIR		*EGYPT AIR MS/MSR EGYPT*			
552		CAIRO	1130	STANSTED	A.300	7	
553	1500	STANSTED		CAIRO	A.300	7	
677	0705	LUXOR	1305	HEATHROW	B.747	1	
678	1425	HEATHROW	2105	LUXOR	B.747	1	

Flight	Dep	From	Arr	To	Aircraft	Days	Notes
679		CAIRO	1315	MANCHESTER	A.320	7	04.07-
680	1415	MANCHESTER		CAIRO	A.320	7	04.07-
777	0730	CAIRO	1335	HEATHROW	A.340	234 67	
778	1500	HEATHROW	2140	CAIRO	A.340	234 67	
779	1100	CAIRO	1705	HEATHROW	A.340	1 5	
780	1825	HEATHROW	0105	CAIRO	A.340	1 5	
985	0600	CAIRO		NEW YORK	B.777	5 7	NONSTOP
986		NEW YORK	1230	CAIRO	B.777	1 6	NONSTOP
987	2230	CAIRO		NEW YORK	B.777	1	NONSTOP
988		NEW YORK	1230	CAIRO	B.777	3	NONSTOP
989	2230	CAIRO		NEW YORK	B.767	3 5	
990		NEW YORK	1230	CAIRO	B.767	5 7	
3777		SHARM EL SHEIKH	1815	HEATHROW	A.320	6	
3778	1905	HEATHROW		SHARM EL SHEIKH	A.320	6	

ELAL   *EL AL ISRAELI AIRLINES LTD.   LY/ELY   ISRAEL*

Flight	Dep	From	Arr	To	Aircraft	Days	Notes
001	2200	TEL AVIV		NEW YORK	B.747	1234567	
003	2230	TEL AVIV		NEW YORK	B.747	3	
008		NEW YORK	1415	TEL AVIV	B.747	1234567	
009	2240	TEL AVIV		MONTREAL	B.767	2 7	
010		MONTREAL	0500	TEL AVIV	B.747	2 4	
014		NEW YORK	0505	TEL AVIV	B.747	12 5	
017	0800	TEL AVIV		NEW YORK	B.747	1 34 7	
018		NEW YORK	0955	TEL AVIV	B.747	12 45	ARR 1255 5
027	2130	TEL AVIV		NEW YORK	B747/767	1 4	
028		NEW YORK	0340	TEL AVIV	B747/767	3 7	ARR 1355 7
029	2245	TEL AVIV		TORONTO	B.767	3 6	
030		TORONTO	0455	TEL AVIV	B.767	1 5	
103	0700	TEL AVIV		CHICAGO	B.767	1 3	
213		TEL AVIV	1040	STANSTED	B.767	7	20.06-29.08
214	1215	STANSTED		TEL AVIV	B.767	7	20.06-29.08
215		TEL AVIV	0855	STANSTED	B.757	7	20.06-05.09
216	0930	STANSTED		TEL AVIV	B.757	5	04.06-
	1025	STANSTED		TEL AVIV	B.757	7	20.06-05.09
217		TEL AVIV	0530	STANSTED	B757	5	04.06-
		TEL AVIV	0030	STANSTED	B.767	7	20.06-05.09
218	0205	STANSTED		TEL AVIV	B.757	7	
227		TEL AVIV	2150	STANSTED	B.767	1234 7	
228	2320	STANSTED		TEL AVIV	B.767	1234 7	
302	0825	HEATHROW		OVDA	B.757	1 4	
311		TEL AVIV	1200	MANCHESTER	B.757	1 4	
312	1330	MANCHESTER		TEL AVIV	B.757	1 4	
313		TEL AVIV	1035	HEATHROW	B.757	7	20.06-29.08
314	1200	HEATHROW		TEL AVIV	B.757	7	20.06-29.08
315		TEL AVIV	1350	HEATHROW	B.747	12345 7	ARR 1505 5
316	1630	HEATHROW		TEL AVIV	B.747	12345 7	DEP 0730 5
317		TEL AVIV	2105	HEATHROW	B747/767	34	7
318	2230	HEATHROW		TEL AVIV	B747/757	1234 6	DEP 2030 3
319		OVDA	2100	HEATHROW	B.747	1 4	
385		TEL AVIV	1820	HEATHROW	B.747	23	VIA ROME
812		LOS ANGELES	0615	AMSTERDAM	B.747	1	
831	2040	AMSTERDAM		NEW YORK	B.747	3 6	
832		LOS ANGELES	0605	AMSTERDAM	B.747	5	
841	0920	AMSTERDAM		NEW YORK	B.747	4	
842		CHICAGO	0445	BRUSSELS	B.747	5	
851	1405	LUXEMBOURG		NEW YORK	B.747	4	
852		NEW YORK	1710	LUXEMBOURG	B.747	5	
861	1805	LUXEMBURG		NEW YORK	B.747	6	
908	0900	DUBLIN		FORT MYERS	B767/MD11	4 6	
1821		TEL AVIV	1650	HEATHROW	B.747	3	
	2115	HEATHROW	2230	AMSTERDAM	B.747	3	
1831	0900	AMSTERDAM		NEW YORK	B.747	2	
1832		LOS ANGELES	1730	AMSTERDAM	B.747	3	
1841	0600	BRUSSELS		NEW YORK	B.747	4	
1842		MIAMI	0700	AMSTERDAM	B.747	5	
1852	1320	AMSTERDAM	1425	HEATHROW	B.747	1	
	1725	HEATHROW		TEL AVIV	B.747	1	

Flight	Dep	From	Arr	To	Aircraft	Days	Notes
1871	0920	AMSTERDAM		NEW YORK	B.747	1	
1872		CHICAGO	0915	AMSTERDAM	B.747	2	
1875	2150	AMSTERDAM		CHICAGO	B.747	6	
1876		CHICAGO	1720	AMSTERDAM	B.747	7	
1877	0005	LUXEMBOURG		NEW YORK	B.747	7	
1878		NEW YORK	0300	AMSTERDAM	B.747	1	
2812		NEW YORK	1245	FRANKFURT	B.747	7	
5317		TEL AVIV	2030	GATWICK	B.757	23	ARR 1800 3
5318	2150	GATWICK		TEL AVIV	B.757	23 DEP 1930 3	

ELITE

CANADA 3000 AIRLINES LTD.   2T/CMM   CANADA

Flight	Dep	From	Arr	To	Aircraft	Days	Notes
217		MONTREAL	0840	PARIS CDG	B.757	1 3 7	ARR 0640 1
		MONTREAL	1005	PARIS CDG	B.757	2 6	ARR 1130 2 5
218	0755	PARIS CDG		MONTREAL	B.757	12	DEP 1300 2
	1125	PARIS CDG		MONTREAL	B.757	3 67	DEP 11010 3
309		HALIFAX	0525	HAMBURG	B.757	5	
310	0645	HAMBURG		HALIFAX	B.757	5	
311		OTTAWA	1145	GATWICK	A.330	1	
		TORONTO	1145	GATWICK	A.330	2 56	
		MONTREAL	1125	GATWICK	A.330	3 7	
		HALIFAX	1010	GATWICK	A.330	4	
312	1315	GATWICK		OTTAWA	A.330	1	
	1315	GATWICK		TORONTO	A.330	2 56	
	1255	GATWICK		MONTREAL	A.330	3 7	
	1635	GATWICK		HALIFAX	B.757	4	
319		HALIFAX	0805	VIENNA	A.330	2	
320	1200	STUTTGART		TORONTO	A.330	2	
323		HALIFAX	0700	GLASGOW	B.757	3	
		TORONTO	0700	GLASGOW	B.757	5 7	
324	0820	GLASGOW		HALIFAX	B.757	3	
	0830	GLASGOW		TORONTO	B.757	5 7	DEP 0930 7
327		TORONTO	0555	BIRMINGHAM	B.757	5	
328	0715	BIRMINGHAM		TORONTO	B.757	5	
331		TORONTO	0900	MANCHESTER	A.330	4 67	ARR 1145 6
332	1045	MANCHESTER		TORONTO	A.330	4 67	1305 7 /1650 6
335		TORONTO	1220	BELFAST	B.757	6	-16.10
336	1340	BELFAST		TORONTO	B.757	6	-16.10
339		TORONTO	0835	AMSTERDAM	A.330	7	
		HALIFAX	0910	AMSTERDAM	B.757	2	
340	1110	AMSTERDAM		TORONTO	A.330	7	
	1040	AMSTERDAM		HALIFAX	B.757	2	
341		MONTREAL	0530	BRUSSELS	B.757	4	
342	0655	BRUSSELS		MONTREAL	B.757	4	
345		HALIFAX	0735	DUSSELDORF	B.757	4	03.06-30.09
346	0905	DUSSELDORF		HALIFAX	B.757	4	03.06-30.09
363		TORONTO	0825	DUBLIN	B.757	1	-27.09
364	0910	DUBLIN		TORONTO	B.757	1	VIA SHANNON
365		HALIFAX	0850	MUNICH	A.330	5	
366	1100	MUNICH		HALIFAX	A.330	5	
713		CALGARY	1350	DUSSELDORF	A.330	3	
714	1520	DUSSELDORF		CALGARY	A.330	3	
725		CALGARY	0940	AMSTERDAM	A.330	7	
726	1110	AMSTERDAM		CALGARY	A.330	7	
731		REYKJAVIK	0755	STUTTGART	B.757	1	-27.09
732	0915	STUTTGART		REYKJAVIK	B.757	1	-27.09
737		CALGARY	1055	MANCHESTER	A.330	3 6	ARR 1520 6
738	1115	MANCHESTER		CALGARY	A.330	3 6	DEP 1015 6
753		CALGARY	0845	GLASGOW	B.757	5 7	ARR 1630 7
754	1015	GLASGOW	1305	REYKJAVIK	B.757	5 7	DEP 1800 7
759		REYKJAVIK	1230	MUNICH	A.330	5	
760	1400	MUNICH		REYKJAVIK	A.330	5	
769		CALGARY	1425	HAMBURG	B.757	2	ARR 0925 21.06-
770	1045	HAMBURG		CALGARY	B.757	2	
775		CALGARY	1200	GATWICK	A.330	2 4	ARR 1505 4
		REYKJAVIK	1100	GATWICK	B.757	1 6	ARR 1250 6
776	1230	GATWICK		REYKJAVIK	A.330	1 6	DEP 1430 6
	1150	GATWICK		CALGARY	A.330	2 4	DEP 1330 2

EMERY — EMERY WORLDWIDE   EWW   U.S.A.

173	2145	BRUSSELS		DAYTON	MD-11	12345	
174		DAYTON	1900	BRUSSELS	MD-11	23456	

EMIRATES — EMIRATES AIRLINES   EK/UAE   UNITED ARAB EMIRATES

001		DUBAI	1215	HEATHROW	B.777	1234567	
002	1345	HEATHROW		DUBAI	B.777	1234567	
003		DUBAI	1915	HEATHROW	B.777	1234567	
004	2045	HEATHROW		DUBAI	B.777	1234567	
005		DUBAI	2145	HEATHROW	A310/A330	1234567	01.07-
006	2300	HEATHROW		DUBAI	A310/A330	1234567	01.07-
007		DUBAI	0710	GATWICK	A310/B777	1234567	
008	1015	GATWICK		DUBAI	A310/B777	1234567	
035		DUBAI	1230	MANCHESTER	A.330	1234566	
036	1355	MANCHESTER		DUBAI	A.330	1234567	

ENGIADINA — AIR ENGIADINA   RQ/RQX   SWITZERLAND

844	0605	BERNE	0745	LONDON CITY	DO-328	123456	0700/0845 6
845	0805	LONDON CITY	0955	BERNE	DO-328	123456	0915/1100 6
846	1200	BERNE	1345	LONDON CITY	DO-328	1 45 7	
847	1415	LONDON CITY	1605	BERNE	DO-328	1 45 7	
848	1650	BERNE	1835	LONDON CITY	DO-328	12345 7	
849	1900	LONDON CITY	2050	BERNE	DO-328	12345 7	
860	0700	GENEVA	0945	DUBLIN	DO-328	12345 7	1000/1245 5
861	1030	DUBLIN	1305	GENEVA	DO-328	12345 7	1330/1615 5

ERA — EUROPEAN REGIONS AIRLINES   EA/EUA   SPAIN

130		VITORIA	1550	GATWICK	EMB-145	12345	
131	1635	GATWICK		VITORIA	EMB-145	12345	

ESTONIAN — ESTONIAN AIR   OV/ELL   ESTONIA

101		TALLINN	1715	GATWICK	B.737	12345 7	
102	1800	GATWICK		TALLINN	B.737	12345 7	
103		TALLINN	0945	GATWICK	B.737	1 3 6	
104	1030	GATWICK		TALLINN	B.737	1 3 6	

ETHIOPIAN — ETHIOPIAN AIRLINES   ET/ETH   ETHIOPIA

711	2125	HEATHROW		ADDIS ABBA	B.767	1	VIA ROME
730		ADDIS ABBA	2115	HEATHROW	B.767	3	VIA ROME
731	2230	HEATHROW		ADDIS ABBA	B.767	3	VIA ROME
750		ADDIS ABBA	1635	HEATHROW	B.767	5	VIA ROME
751	2130	HEATHROW		ADDIS ABBA	B.767	5	VIA ROME
770		ADDIS ABBA	2105	HEATHROW	B.767	7	VIA ROME

EURALAIR — EURALAIR INTERNATIONAL   RN/EUL   FRANCE

1500		PARIS	0640	CORK	B.737	5	
1501	1315	CORK		PARIS	B.737	5	
1502		LYON	1225	CORK	B.737	5	
1503	0730	CORK		LYON	B.737	5	

EUROCYPRIA — EUROCYPRIA AIRLINES LTD.   UI/ECA   CYPRUS

EVEN NUMBERS - FLIGHTS INTO THE U.K.   UNEVEN NUMBERS - FLIGHTS LEAVING THE U.K.

???	1910	NORWICH	1825	PAPHOS	A.320	2	29.06-31.08
???	1115	NORWICH	1030	PAPHOS	A.320	2	31.08-
800/1	1100	GLASGOW	1000	PAPHOS	A.320	3	
812/3	1100	BOURNEMOUTH	1000	LARNACA	A.320	3	
814/5	1130	GATWICK	1015	PAPHOS	A.320	6	
822/3	1330	BELFAST	1230	LARNACA	A.320	2	22.06-
824/5	1130	BELFAST	1030	LARNACA	A.320	3	
836/7	2305	BELFAST	2205	LARNACA	A.320	3	02.06-
84/99	2325	BRISTOL	2225	LARNACA	A.320	3	
844/5	2105	BIRMINGHAM	2105	LARNACA	A.320	4	
846/7	2210	GATWICK	2110	LARNACA	A.320	5	

Flight	Dep	From	Arr	To	Type	Days	Notes
???	1015	CARDIFF	0915	PALMA	/	5	
???	2325	CARDIFF	2255	LANZAROTE	/	6	
242	1520	SOUTHAMPTON	0815	PALMA	737	1	
247	0905	SOUTHAMPTON	1430	MAHON	737	1	
282	2150	SOUTHAMPTON	1510	PALMA	737	5	
283	1600	SOUTHAMPTON	2100	IBIZA	737	5	
166/7	1625	CORK	1525	MALAGA	B.737	6	
171/2	1115	EDINBURGH	1015	TENERIFE	737	2	
171/2	2355	BRISTOL	2300	PALMA	B.737	6	
173/4	1445	EDINBURGH	2125	IBIZA	737	1	
173/4	1530	BELFAST	2110	REUS	B.737	3	
173/4	??	LIVERPOOL	??	MAHON	B.737	6	
175/6	2200	BELFAST	1440	PALMA	B.737	3	
175/6	2225	EDINBURGH	1345	PALMA	737	1	
175/6	??	LIVERPOOL	??	PALMA	B.737	6	
177/8	1655	PRESTWICK	1605	PALMA	737	6	
179/0	1625	PRESTWICK	1540	IBIZA	737	6	
194/5	2010	TEESSIDE	1300	PALMA	737	6	
196/7	1350	TEESSIDE	1920	GERONA	737	6	
201/2	2345	EAST MIDLANDS	2255	TENERIFE	737	5	
203/4	1010	NORWICH	0920	MALAGA	737	4	
205/6	??	LIVERPOOL	??	ALICANTE	B.737	6	
207/8	0950	NORWICH	0900	PALMA	737	6	
207/8	1305	ABERDEEN	1115	TENERIFE	737	5	
209/0	0930	NORWICH	0840	IBIZA	737	6	
212/3	0850	EDINBURGH	1525	PALMA	737	6	
212/3	1155	BRISTOL	1105	TENERIFE	B.737	7	
214/5	2315	LEEDS	2225	PALMA	B.737	5	
216/7	2140	CARDIFF	1505	PALMA	737	4	
218/9	1555	CARDIFF	2050	GERONA	737	4	
218/9	1600	PALMA	1510	NORWICH	737	7	-20.06 / 01.08-
221/2	2350	BOURNEMOUTH	2300	TENERIFE	B.737	7	
225/6	1205	NORWICH	1115	TENERIFE	737	2	-22.06 / 27.07-
227/8	2155	MANCHESTER	2105	PALMA	B.737	6	
229/0	2325	PALMA	2240	EAST MIDLANDS	737	5	
234/5	1620	MANCHESTER	1530	PALMA	B.737	1	
236/7	0940	EAST MIDLANDS	0850	PALMA	737	1	
237/8	?	LIVERPOOL	?	PALMA	B.737	6	
239/0	0925	BRISTOL	0835	MALAGA	B.737	7	
241/2	0935	BIRMINGHAM	0835	PALMA	B.757	6	
245/6	1415	CARDIFF	1325	PALMA	737	5	
246/7	??	LIVERPOOL	??	LAS PALMAS	B.737	6	
249/0	1525	PALMA	0835	NORWICH	737	2	
254/5	2355	GATWICK	2310	LAS PALMAS	B.737	7	25.07-
256/7	1615	EDINBURGH	0800	PALMA	737	6	
258/9	0925	NORWICH	1435	GERONA	737	2	
258/9	1630	EDINBURGH	1450	PALMA	757	6	
261/2	0115	EAST MIDLANDS	0025	LAS PALMAS	737	7	
261/2	1355	BOURNEMOUTH	1305	PALMA	B.737	4	
263/4	2355	CARDIFF	2245	TENERIFE	/	5	
272/3	1735	BELFAST	1645	MALAGA	B.737	4	-30.09
278/9	1525	GLASGOW	1435	LANZAROTE	B.737	4	
279/01	0035	EAST MIDLANDS	2345	LAS PALMAS	737	1	
281/2	1135	NORWICH	1045	LAS PALMAS	737	1	
285/6	1410	TEESSIDE	1329	LANZAROTE	737	4	
287/8	2320	PRESTWICK	2230	TENERIFE	737	2	
288/9	1615	IBIZA	1525	TEESSIDE	737	5	
294/5	0940	LEEDS	0850	PALMA	B.737	2	
296/7	1140	TENERIFE	1025	ABERDEEN	737	2	
611/2	2035	EAST MIDLANDS	1945	PALMA	737	6	
1011		MADRID	1315	GATWICK	B.737	12345 7	ARR 2045 7
1012	1415	GATWICK		MADRID	B.737	12345 7	DEP 2130 7

EUROTRANS   *EUROPEAN AIR TRANSPORT   QY/BCS   BELGIUM*

Flight	Dep	From	Arr	To	Type	Days
020	2245	EAST MIDLANDS	2355	BRUSSELS	DC-8	2345
034	1920	REYKJAVIK	2120	EDINBURGH	B.737	1234
	2200	EDINBURGH	2330	BRUSSELS	B.727	1234

Flight	Dep	From	Arr	To	Aircraft	Days	
037	0250	BRUSSELS	0420	EDINBURGH	B.737	2345	
	0500	EDINBURGH	0700	REYKJAVIK	B.737	2345	
111P	1515	STANSTED	1655	COPENHAGEN	A.300	7	
411	0255	BRUSSELS	0355	LUTON	A.300	23456	
412	2050	LUTON	2120	HEATHROW	A.300	23 5	
	2230	HEATHROW	2330	BRUSSELS	A.300	123 5	
414	2330	LUTON	0030	BRUSSELS	B.727	7	
417	2230	BRUSSELS	2330	LUTON	B.727	1234	2250/2350 1
421	0115	BRUSSELS	0225	EAST MIDLANDS	B.727	2345	
422	0105	EAST MIDLANDS	0205	BRUSSELS	B.727	2345	
423	2300	BRUSSELS	0010	EAST MIDLANDS	B.727	234	
424	2245	EAST MIDLANDS	2345	BRUSSELS	B.727	1	
436	2030	BELFAST	2125	EAST MIDLANDS	B.727	5	
473	1800	EDINBURGH	1840	ABERDEEN	B.727	1	
	1610	BRUSSELS	1710	LUTON	B.727	7	
	1930	LUTON	2040	EDINBURGH	B.727	7	
476		EDINBURGH	2315	EAST MIDLANDS	B.727	1234	
	0105	EAST MIDLANDS		BRUSSELS	B.727	2345	
480	2030	DUBLIN	2145	COVENTRY	HERCULES	12345	
	2345	COVENTRY	0100	BRUSSELS	HERCULES	12345	
481	0315	BRUSSELS	0415	EAST MIDLANDS	B.727	6	
	0515	EAST MIDLANDS	0610	DUBLIN	B.727	6	
482	2100	DUBLIN	2155	EAST MIDLANDS	A.300	5	
	2320	EAST MIDLANDS	0030	BRUSSELS	A.300	5	
483	1915	BRUSSELS	2100	DUBLIN	A.300	7	
484	2045	CORK	2200	EAST MIDLANDS	B.727	5	
486	2120	DUBLIN	2225	LUTON	B.727	12345	
	2330	LUTON	0030	BRUSSELS	B.727	12345	
487	0200	BRUSSELS	0300	LUTON	B.727	2345	
	0400	LUTON	0500	DUBLIN	B.727	2345	
488	0800	DUBLIN	0855	EAST MIDLANDS	B.727	2345	
	1045	EAST MIDLANDS	1155	BRUSSELS	B.727	2345	
489	1505	BRUSSELS	1615	EAST MIDLANDS	B.727	2345	
	1715	EAST MIDLANDS	1810	DUBLIN	B.727	2345	
492	2040	SHANNON	2140	EAST MIDLANDS	B.727	12345	
	2250	EAST MIDLANDS	2350	BRUSSELS	B.727	12345	2220/2320 5
	1830	SHANNON	1915	DUBLIN	B.727	6	
	2000	DUBLIN	2100	LUTON	B.727	6	
	2330	LUTON	0030	BRUSSELS	B.727	6	
493	0125	BRUSSELS	0225	EAST MIDLANDS	B.727	6	
	0520	EAST MIDLANDS	0615	SHANNON	B.727	6	
495	0245	BRUSSELS	0345	EAST MIDLANDS	B.727	2345	
	0510	EAST MIDLANDS	0610	DUBLIN	B.727	2345	
	0650	DUBLIN	0735	SHANNON	B.727	2345	
499	0125	BRUSSELS	0225	LUTON	B.727	6	
	0315	LUTON	0405	DUBLIN	B.727	6	
	0730	DUBLIN	0815	CORK	B.727	6	
511P	0100	EAST MIDLANDS	0135	STANSTED	A.300	6	
665	0030	COLOGNE	0140	EAST MIDLANDS	A.300	2345	
	0410	EAST MIDLANDS	0510	DUBLIN	A.300	2345	
666	2100	DUBLIN	2200	EAST MIDLANDS	A.300	1234	
	0001	EAST MIDLANDS	0120	COLOGNE	A.300	2345	
669	0015	COLOGNE	0135	EAST MIDLANDS	B.727	6	
692	2200	COLOGNE	2345	LUTON	F-27	12345	
693	0100	LUTON	0215	PARIS CDG	F-27	2345	
695	0120	LUTON	0235	PARIS CDG	F-27	6	
781	0030	EAST MIDLANDS	0145	PARIS CDG	B.727	2345	
782	0010	PARIS CDG	0125	EAST MIDLANDS	B.727	2 6	
904	2000	ABERDEEN	2045	EDINBURGH	B.727	5	
	2230	EDINBURGH	2335	EAST MIDLANDS	B.727	5	
905	0315	EAST MIDLANDS	0415	EDINBURGH	B.727	2345	
	0545	EDINBURGH	0630	ABERDEEN	B.727	2345	
906	0005	DUBLIN	0045	SHANNON	B.727	7	
907	0200	EAST MIDLANDS	0255	DUBLIN	B.727	6	
911	0245	EAST MIDLANDS	0425	COPENHAGEN	A.300	2345	
912	2220	COPENHAGEN	0110	EAST MIDLANDS	A.300	12345	
915	0030	EAST MIDLANDS	0210	COPENHAGEN	B.727	2345	
916	2150	COPENHAGEN	2330	EAST MIDLANDS	B.727	1234	

930	0125	EAST MIDLANDS	0245	COLOGNE	B.727	345	
932	0015	LUTON	0125	COLOGNE	B.727	2345	
946	2145	BERGAMO	2345	EAST MIDLANDS	B.727	1234	
948	0010	PARIS CDG	0125	EAST MIDLANDS	B.727	345	
949	0210	EAST MIDLANDS	0410	BERGAMO	B.727	2345	
957	0140	EAST MIDLANDS	0350	LYON	B.727	2345	
958	2140	LYON	2350	EAST MIDLANDS	B.727	1234	
962	1600	EAST MIDLANDS	1630	LUTON	B.727	7	
964	2045	CORK	2200	EAST MIDLANDS	B.727	1234	
965	0115	EAST MIDLANDS	0215	DUBLIN	B.727	2345	
	0700	DUBLIN	0745	CORK	B.727	2345	
982	2030	BELFAST	2125	EAST MIDLANDS	B.727	12345	
983	0450	EAST MIDLANDS	0545	BELFAST	B.727	2345	
988	2245	VITORIA	0035	EAST MIDLANDS	B.727	1	
990	2245	VITORIA	0035	EAST MIDLANDS	B.727	234	
991	2330	EAST MIDLANDS	0040	PARIS CDG	B.727	1234	
994	2245	VITORIA	0045	LUTON	B.727	5	
995	0130	EAST MIDLANDS	0310	VITORIA	B.727	2345	
997	0230	LUTON	0445	MADRID	B.727	6	
6513	1840	HELSINKI	2120	HEATHROW	B.727	4	
6515	1300	HELSINKI	1545	EAST MIDLANDS	B.727	7	

EUROWINGS   *EUROWINGS AG NURNBERG   NS/EWG   GERMANY*

210	0550	NUREMBERG	0800	STANSTED	ATR-42	123456	0620/0830 6
211	0840	STANSTED	1035	NUREMBERG	ATR-42	123456	0910/1105 6
216	1700	NUREMBERG	1910	STANSTED	ATR-42	12345 7	
217	1935	STANSTED	2230	NUREMBERG	ATR-42	12345 7	
219		NUREMBERG	0800	STANSTED	ATR-42	12345	28.06
220	0630	DORTMUND	0940	JERSEY	ATR-42	7	VIA GUERNSEY
221	1015	JERSEY	1335	DORTMUND	ATR-42	7	
260	0555	DORTMUND	0730	STANSTED	ATR-42	123456	0650/0825 6
261	0800	STANSTED	0930	DORTMUND	ATR-42	123456	0900/1030 6
266	1555	DORTMUND	1730	STANSTED	ATR-42	12345 7	
267	1800	STANSTED	1930	DORTMUND	ATR-42	12345 7	
284	1520	DUSSELDORF	1720	NEWCASTLE	ATR-42	12345	
286	1810	DUSSELDORF	2010	NEWCASTLE	ATR-42	7	
1680		HANOVER	1245	SHANNON	BAE-146	6	-29.09
1681	2035	SHANNON		HANOVER	BAE-146	6	-25.09
1682		BERLIN	1945	SHANNON	BAE-146	6	-25.09
1683	1335	SHANNON		BERLIN	BAE-146	6	-25.09

EVA   *EVA AIRWAYS CORP.   BR/EVA   TAIWAN*

67		TAIPEI	1905	HEATHROW	B.747	2 4 6	VIA BANGKOK
68	2130	HEATHROW		TAIPEI	B.747	2 4 6	VIA BANGKOK
1067		TAIPEI	1115	HEATHROW	MD-11	5 7	ARR 1740 7
1068	1345	HEATHROW		TAIPEI	MD-11	5 7	DEP 2135 7

EXEL COMMUTER   *AIR EXEL NETHERLANDS   XT/AXL   NETHERLANDS*

3923	0605	EINDHOVEN	0730	HEATHROW	ATR-72	12345	
3924	0805	HEATHROW	0930	EINDHOVEN	ATR-72	12345	
3925	1205	EINDHOVEN	1335	HEATHROW	ATR-72	12345	
3926	1415	HEATHROW	1440	EINDHOVEN	ATR-72	12345	
3927	1635	EINDHOVEN	1800	HEATHROW	ATR-72	7	
3928	1830	HEATHROW	1955	EINDHOVEN	ATR-72	7	
3929	0615	EINDHOVEN	0725	STANSTED	EMB-120	45	
3930	0755	STANSTED	0905	EINDHOVEN	EMB-120	12345	
3931	1350	EINDHOVEN	1500	STANSTED	EMB-120	12345	
3932	1530	STANSTED	1640	EINDHOVEN	EMB-120	23 5	
3933	1710	EINDHOVEN	1820	STANSTED	EMB-120	12345 7	
3934	1915	STANSTED	2025	EINDHOVEN	EMB-120	1	
3937	0615	MAASTRICT	0735	STANSTED	EMB-120	23456	
3938	0805	STANSTED	0915	MAASTRICT	EMB-120	23456	
3939	1345	MAASTRICT	1455	STANSTED	EMB-120	12345	
3940	1525	STANSTED	1635	MAASTRICT	EMB-120	12345	
3941	1705	MAASTRICT	1815	STANSTED	EMB-120	12345 7	
3942	1920	STANSTED	2030	MAASTRICT	EMB-120	12345 7	

EXPRESS FARNER — EXPRESS AIRWAYS EPA GERMANY

423	2140	MANCHESTER	2245	STANSTED	SH-360	1234	01.06-
823	0605	BIRMINGHAM	0640	MANCHESTER	SH-360	2345	01.06-
7081	2140	MANCHESTER	2245	STANSTED	SH-360	1234	
7081	2310	STANSTED		PARIS CDG	SH-360	1234	
8081		PARIS CDG	0410	STANSTED	SH-360	2345	01.06-
	0450	STANSTED	0540	BIRMINGHAM	SH-360	2345	01.06-
	0605	BIRMINGHAM		MANCHESTER	SH-360	2345	01.06-

FAROELINE — ATLANTIC AIRWAYS RC/FLI DENMARK

360		FAROE IS.	1715	GLASGOW	BAE-146	1 4	21.06-12.08
	1800	GLASGOW	1840	ABERDEEN	BAE-146	1 4	21.06-12.08
361	1900	ABERDEEN		FAROE IS.	BAE-146	1 4	21.06-12.08
452		FAROE IS.	1840	ABERDEEN	BAE-146	4	
	1925	ABERDEEN		FAROE IS.	BAE-146	4	

FEDEX — FEDERAL EXPRESS FM/FDX U.S.A.

1X	1740	FRANKFURT	1940	STANSTED	B.727	1234	
1	2055	STANSTED		MEMPHIS	MD-11	12345	
2		MEMPHIS	1730	STANSTED	MD-11	23456	ARR 1755 6
	2005	STANSTED	2125	PARIS CDG	MD-11	1234	
2X	2025	STANSTED	2145	PARIS CDG	B.727	1234	
3	1940	PARIS CDG		MEMPHIS	MD-11	123456	DEP 2255 6
4		NEW YORK	1505	PRESTWICK	MD-11	1	
	1610	PRESTWICK		PARIS CDG	MD-11	1	
		MEMPHIS	1845	PARIS CDG	MD-11	234567	
5	2050	PARIS CDG	2200	STANSTED	MD-11	23456	
	2300	STANSTED		NEW YORK	MD-11	23456	DEP 2215 6
6		NEW YORK	1435	PRESTWICK	MD-11	234567	ARR 1500 6
	1535	PRESTWICK	1720	PARIS CDG	MD-11	234567	1600/1745 6
8		MEMPHIS	1845	PARIS CDG	MD-11	234567	
9	2010	PARIS CDG		MEMPHIS	DC-10	6	
10		MEMPHIS	1835	PARIS CDG	DC-10	6	

FINNAIR — FINNAIR AY/FIN FINLAND

006		NEW YORK	0650	HELSINKI	MD-11	1234567	
005	1215	HELSINKI		NEW YORK	MD-11	1234567	
073	1520	HELSINKI		TOKYO	MD-11	2 6	
085	1535	HELSINKI		TOKYO	MD-11	3 5	
831	0610	HELSINKI	0915	HEATHROW	MD80/A320	1234567	
832	1020	HEATHROW	1310	HELSINKI	MD80/A320	1234567	
833	1405	HELSINKI	1710	HEATHROW	MD80/A320	1234567	
834	1800	HEATHROW	2050	HELSINKI	MD80/A320	1234567	
835	1725	HELSINKI	2030	HEATHROW	MD-80	12345 7	
836	0725	HEATHROW	1015	HELSINKI	MD-80	123456	
837	0925	HELSINKI	1235	HEATHROW	MD-80	7	
838	1335	HEATHROW	1630	HELSINKI	MD-80	7	
885	1305	STOCKHOLM	1545	DUBLIN	MD-80	12 4 7	
886	1635	DUBLIN	1905	STOCKHOLM	MD-80	12 4 7	
921		HELSINKI	0755	GATWICK	MD-82	1234567	
922	0930	GATWICK		HELSINKI	MD-82	1234567	
925		HELSINKI	1725	GATWICK	MD-82	1234567	
926	1810	GATWICK		HELSINKI	MD-82	1234567	
933		STOCKHOLM	0950	MANCHESTER	MD-82	123456	
934	1025	MANCHESTER		STOCKHOLM	MD-82	123456	
937		STOCKHOLM	1730	MANCHESTER	MD-82	12345 7	
938	1815	MANCHESTER		STOCKHOLM	MD-82	12345 7	
1307		HELSINKI	1845	STANSTED	B.757	7	
1308	1950	STANSTED		HELSINKI	B.757	7	
6512	0830	LUTON	1100	HELSINKI	B.727	4	
6513	1840	HELSINKI	2120	HEATHROW	B.727	4	
6514	2345	STANSTED	0215	HELSINKI	B.727	6	
6515	1300	HELSINKI	1545	EAST MIDLANDS	B.727	7	
6582	0715	STANSTED	1150	HELSINKI	A.300	7	
6583	1450	HELSINKI	1740	STANSTED	A.300	7	

181	0900	BOURNEMOUTH	1120	PALMA	BAE-146	1	
182	1220	PALMA	1440	BOURNEMOUTH	BAE-146	1	-05.07
	1220	PALMA	1435	JERSEY	BAE-146	1	13.09-18.10
183	1540	BOURNEMOUTH	1800	MAHON	BAE-146	1	-05.07
	1535	JERSEY	1750	PALMA	BAE-146	1	13.09-18.10
184	1900	MAHON	2120	BOURNEMOUTH	BAE-146	1	05.07-06.09
	1850	PALMA	2110	BOURNEMOUTH	BAE-146	1	13.09-18.10
281	0800	BOURNEMOUTH	0840	JERSEY	BAE-146	2	-13.07
282	0925	JERSEY	1140	PALMA	BAE-146	2	-13.07
283	1240	PALMA	1455	JERSEY	BAE-146	2	-13.07
284	1540	JERSEY	1620	BOURNEMOUTH	BAE-146	2	-13.07
285	1720	BOURNEMOUTH	1930	SALZBURG	BAE-146	2	-13.07
286	2030	SALZBURG	2240	BOURNEMOUTH	BAE-146	2	-13.07
287/8	0730	BOURNEMOUTH	DAY TRIPS TO VARIOUS DESTINATIONS			2	07.09-26.10
381	0900	BOURNEMOUTH	1115	VENICE	BAE-146	3	-07.07
382	1700	VENICE	1915	BOURNEMOUTH	BAE-146	3	-08.07
388	1845	VENICE	2100	BOURNEMOUTH	BAE-146	3	08.09
388	1850	MADRID	2100	BOURNEMOUTH	BAE-146	3	13.10
481	0800	BOURNEMOUTH	1050	FARO	BAE-146	4	-28.10
482	1135	FARO	1405	GUERNSEY	BAE-146	4	01.07-26.08
	1135	FARO	1425	BOURNEMOUTH	BAE-146	4	-24.06/ 02.09-
483	1450	GUERNSEY	1510	JERSEY	BAE-146	4	01.07-26.08
	1510	BOURNEMOUTH	1550	JERSEY	BAE-146	4	-24.06
	1540	JERSEY	1825	FARO	BAE-146	4	01.07-26.08
	1635	JERSEY	1920	FARO	BAE-146	4	-24.06/ 02.09-
484	1920	FARO	2210	BOURNEMOUTH	BAE-146	4	
581	1000	BOURNEMOUTH	1220	MAHON	BAE-146	5	-15.10
582	1320	MAHON	1540	BOURNEMOUTH	BAE-146	5	-15.10
583	1630	BOURNEMOUTH	1850	PALMA	BAE-146	5	-15.19
584	1950	PALMA	2210	BOURNEMOUTH	BAE-146	5	-15.10
681	0850	BOURNEMOUTH	1010	PALMA	BAE-146	6	-30.10
682	1210	PALMA	1430	BOURNEMOUTH	BAE-146	6	-30.10
683	1600	BOURNEMOUTH	1830	ALICANTE	BAE-146	6	-30.10
684	1930	ALICANTE	2200	BOURNEMOUTH	BAE-146	6	-30.10
781	0800	BOURNEMOUTH	1015	CALVI	BAE-146	7	-11.07
782	1115	CALVI	1330	BOURNEMOUTH	BAE-146	7	-11.07
783	1430	BOURNEMOUTH	1715	MALAGA	BAE-146	7	-11.07
	0800	BOURNEMOUTH	1045	MALAGA	BAE-146	7	18.07-
784	1815	MALAGA	2100	BOURNEMOUTH	BAE-146	7	-11.07
	1145	MALAGA	1430	BOURNEMOUTH	BAE-146	7	18.07-29.08
785	1530	BOURNEMOUTH	1840	DUBROVNIK	BAE-146	7	12.09-
786	1925	DUBROVNIK	2235	BOURNEMOUTH	BAE-146	7	12.-09-

	FLY CARGO			*AFRICAN INTERNATIONAL AIRWAYS AIN SWAZILAND*				
101	1100	STANSTED		MAASTRICT	DC-8	2	
102		MAASTRICT	1000	STANSTED	DC-8		5
201	1100	STANSTED		CHR??	DC-8	3	
301	1110	STANSTED		MAASTRICT	DC-8		4
302		MAASTRICT	1855	STANSTED	DC-8		5
357	1600	STANSTED		CAIRO	DC-8		7
506	0915	STANSTED		MAASTRICT	DC-8		7
817		ASWAN	0930	STANSTED	DC-8	3	
951		ASWAN	0745	STANSTED	DC-8		7
953		ASWAN	0910	STANSTED	DC-8		7
955		ASWAN	0930	STANSTED	DC-8	4	
956	2100	STANSTED		CAIRO	DC-8		5
957		ASWAN	0910	STANSTED	DC-8	2	

	FLYER			*CITYFLYER EXPRESS FD/CFE U.K.*			

A BA FRANCHISEE COMPANY. ALL THEIR SCHEDULED SERVICES (I.E. THOSE WITH 4 - DIGIT FLIGHT NUMBERS IN THE BA 8000-8199 RANGE ARE OPERATED UNDER THE BRITISH AIRWAYS EXPRESS BRAND NAME.

11HK	1555	JERSEY	1700	GATWICK	ATR-72		67	BA8044
13GR	1515	GATWICK	1615	GUERNSEY	ATR42/72	12345		BA8025
	1600	GATWICK	1700	GATWICK	ATR42/72		67	BA8025

16HM	1650	GUERNSEY	1755	GATWICK	ATR-42	12345	BA8026
	1735	GUERNSEY	1835	GATWICK	ATR42/72	67	BA8026
17FH	1735	JERSEY	1840	GATWICK	ATR-42	12345	BA8046
	1755	JERSEY	1855	GATWICK	ATR-42	6	BA8046
	1835	JERSEY	1935	GATWICK	ATR-72	7	BA8046
18GH	0710	NEWCASTLE	0855	GATWICK	ATR-42	12345	BA8066
19JB	1755	GATWICK	1900	GUERNSEY	ATR-42	12345	BA8027
	1115	GATWICK	1220	GUERNSEY	ATR-42	6	BA8027
21HC	1830	GATWICK	2015	NEWCASTLE	ATR-42	123456	BA8067
	2035	GATWICK	2215	NEWCASTLE	ATR-42	7	BA8067
22KG	1930	GUERNSEY	2030	GATWICK	ATR-42	12345	BA8028
	1315	GUERNSEY	1415	GATWICK	ATR-42	6	BA8028
23BF	1955	JERSEY	2055	GATWICK	ATR42/72	1234567	BA8048
26AC	1955	GATWICK	2055	JERSEY	ATR-42	5	BA8049
28MH	0910	GUERNSEY	1020	GATWICK	ATR-42	6	BA8030
29LF	0910	ROTTERDAM	1025	GATWICK	ATR-72	12345	BA8050
33MR	0630	DUBLIN	0755	GATWICK	BAE-146	1234567	BA8081
36RV	0710	GATWICK	0855	NEWCASTLE	ATR-42	12345	BA8071
37WC	0945	GATWICK	1055	JERSEY	ATR-72	6	BA8033
38HA	1445	GATWICK	1605	ROTTERDAM	ATR-72	12345 7	BA8053
39VW	0930	NEWCASTLE	1115	GATWICK	ATR-42	1234567	BA8072
41RE	1640	ROTTERDAM	1755	GATWICK	ATR-72	12345 7	BA8054
42WX	0810	GATWICK	1000	NEWCASTLE	ATR42/72	1234567	BA8073
43YM	0755	GATWICK	0915	JERSEY	ATR-72	1234567	BA8035
44YC	1915	GATWICK	2025	ROTTERDAM	ATR42/72	12345	BA8055
	2015	GATWICK	2125	ROTTERDAM	ATR42/72	7	BA8055
45XY	1030	NEWCASTLE	1220	GATWICK	ATR-72	1234567	BA8074
46XH	0950	JERSEY	1100	GATWICK	ATR-72	123456	BA8036
47VB	2055	ROTTERDAM	2205	GATWICK	ATR-42	5	BA8056
48YA	1400	GATWICK	1535	NEWCASTLE	ATR-42	1234567	BA8075
	1400	GATWICK	1535	NEWCASTLE	ATR-42	1234567	BA8075
49WY	1030	GATWICK	1140	JERSEY	ATR-42	12345	BA8037
	1515	GATWICK	1615	JERSEY	ATR-72	6	BA8037
	0925	GATWICK	1035	JERSEY	ATR-72	7	BA8036
51AB	1605	NEWCASTLE	1740	GATWICK	ATR-42	12345 7	BA8076
52VX	1650	JERSEY	1755	GATWICK	ATR42/72	6	BA8038
53WP	0545	ROTTERDAM	0655	GATWICK	ATR42/72	12345	BA8058
54VE	1620	GATWICK	1755	NEWCASTLE	ATR42/72	12345 7	BA8077
55RW	1445	GATWICK	1550	JERSEY	ATR-42	12345	BA8039
	1050	GATWICK	1300	JERSEY	ATR-42	6	BA8039
56CK	0715	GATWICK	0835	ROTTERDAM	ATR-72	12345	BA8059
57BT	1830	NEWCASTLE	2010	GATWICK	ATR42/72	12345 7	BA8078
58MV	1620	JERSEY	1720	GATWICK	ATR-42	12345	BA8040
	1830	JERSEY	1930	GATWICK	ATR-42	6	BA8040
	1500	JERSEY	1600	GATWICK	ATR-72	7	BA8040
61FV	1230	GUERNSEY	1435	GATWICK	ATR42/72	1234567	BA8024
62MF	1720	DUSSELDORF	1905	GATWICK	ATR-72	12345 7	BA8079
66KV	0710	GATWICK	0830	DUBLIN	BAE-146	123456	BA8080
69GB	1940	GATWICK	2125	NEWCASTLE	ATR-72	12345 7	BA8079
72BG	1330	NEWCASTLE	1515	GATWICK	ATR-42	12345	BA8045
	1625	GATWICK	1730	JERSEY	ATR-72	6	BA8045
	1700	GATWICK	1800	JERSEY	ATR-72	7	BA8045
81AY	0755	GATWICK	0905	GUERNSEY	ATR-42	1234567	BA8021
82LR	1220	GATWICK	1330	JERSEY	ATR-42	6	BA8041
83BV	1335	NEWCASTLE	1525	JERSEY	ATR-72	6	BA8061
84BX	0940	GUERNSEY	1045	GATWICK	ATR42/72	123456	BA8022
	1420	GUERNSEY	1525	GATWICK	ATR-42	7	BA8022
85KM	1635	JERSEY	1740	GATWICK	ATR-42	6	BA8042
86YL	1805	JERSEY	1955	NEWCASTLE	ATR-72	6	BA8062
87CW	1115	GATWICK	1255	GUERNSEY	ATR42/72	1234567	BA8023
89AR	1120	GATWICK	1300	NEWCASTLE	ATR42/72	123456	BA8063
214F	1905	GATWICK	2050	DUSSELDORF	ATR42/72	1234567	BA8195
217J	0900	CORK	1020	GATWICK	BAE-146	6	07.08- BA8153
	1145	CORK	1330	GATWICK	ATR-72	7	-25.07 BA8153
231	1115	GATWICK	1320	NICE	BAE-146	123456	BA8131
243M	0655	GATWICK	0820	CORK	BAE-146	6	07.08- BA8152
	0915	GATWICK	1100	CORK	ATR-72	7	-25.07 BA8152

253A	1830	CORK	2015	GATWICK	ATR-72	6	BA8157
	1850	CORK	2015	GATWICK	BAE-146	12345 7	01.08- BA8157
262Y	1930	GATWICK	2110	CORK	BAE146/AT7	6	BA8158
271B	1955	CORK	2140	GATWICK	ATR-72	7	BA8159
287W	0550	BREMEN	0750	GATWICK	ATR42/72	1234567	BA8160
289C	0810	GATWICK	1010	BREMEN	ATR-72	1234567	BA8161
298Y	1050	BREMEN	1250	GATWICK	ATR-72	1234567	BA8162
301	0850	HEATHROW	0950	GUERNSEY	ATR-72	1234567	
313Y	0620	ZURICH	0810	GATWICK	BAE-146	1234567	BA8102
315	1100	GATWICK	1225	AMSTERDAM	ATR-72	12345	02.08- BA8115
319	0545	LUXEMBOURG	0720	GATWICK	ATR-42	123456	BA8141
326	1440	GATWICK	1620	LUXEMBOURG	ATR-42	7	-25.07 BA8144
328	1015	LUXEMBOURG	1200	GATWICK	ATR42/72	12345	BA8143
337	1300	DUBLIN	1420	GATWICK	BAE-146	1234567	01.08 BA8144
	1500	GATWICK	1620	LUXEMBOURG	BAE-146	12345 7	BA8144
346	1700	LUXEMBOURG	1835	GATWICK	ATR-72	12345 7	-30.07 BA8145
	1855	GATWICK	2015	DUBLIN	BAE-146	12345 7	01.08- BA8145
349B	1445	CORK	1610	GATWICK	BAE-146	1234567	BA8119
354	1915	GATWICK	2050	LUXEMBOURG	ATR42/72	12345 7	BA8146
364	1545	LUXEMBOURG	1720	GATWICK	ATR-42	12345	-30.07 BA8147
386	1555	GATWICK	1700	JERSEY	ATR-42	12345	BA8045
387	1700	LUXEMBOURG	1815	GATWICK	BAE-146	12345 7	01.08- BA8145
392	1640	GATWICK	1800	DUBLIN	BAE-146	1234567	01.08- BA8132
395R	1140	ZURICH	1330	GATWICK	BAE-146	12345 7	BA8104
	1115	ZURICH	1300	GATWICK	BAE-146	6	BA8104
413	1405	DUSSELDORF	1545	GATWICK	ATR42/72	1234567	BA8192
415	0855	GATWICK	1020	DUBLIN	BAE-146	1234567	BA8102
418	0840	GATWICK	1035	ZURICH	BAE-146	1234567	BA8081
426	0835	GATWICK	1005	DUBLIN	BAE-146	1234567	BA8082
429	1040	DUBLIN	1225	GATWICK	BAE-146	1234567	BA8083
432	1240	GATWICK	1405	CORK	BAE-146	1234567	BA8114
438	1240	GATWICK	1400	DUBLIN	BAE-146	1234567	BA8084
442	1410	GATWICK	1600	ZURICH	BAE-146	1234567	BA8105
447	1440	DUBLIN	1600	GATWICK	BAE-146	1234567	BA8085
451	1700	ZURICH	1850	GATWICK	BAE-146	12345 7	BA8106
	1615	ZURICH	1800	GATWICK	BAE-146	6	BA8106
456	1440	GATWICK	1620	COLOGNE	ATR42/72	12345	BA8125
	1600	GATWICK	1745	COLOGNE	ATR-42	7	BA8125
464	1700	COLOGNE	1840	GATWICK	ATR42/72	12345	BA8126
	1820	COLOGNE	2000	GATWICK	ATR-42	7	BA8126
465	1840	DUBLIN	2000	GATWICK	BAE-146	1234567	BA8087
473	0755	GATWICK	0935	LUXEMBOURG	ATR42/72	12345	BA8142
474	2040	GATWICK	2200	DUBLIN	BAE-146	1234567	BA8088
483	1100	DUBLIN	1220	GATWICK	BAE-146	1234567	BA8089
487	0600	AMSTERDAM	0720	GATWICK	ATR-72	1234567	BA8110
514	1300	AMSTERDAM	1425	GATWICK	ATR-72	12345	02.08- BA8116
515	2030	GATWICK	2155	CORK	BAE-146	12345 7	BA8120
521	1840	GATWICK	2000	AMSTERDAM	ATR-72	1234567	BA8121
525	1650	GATWICK	1800	AMSTERDAM	BAE-146	12345 7	BA8119
528	1400	GATWICK	1520	DUBLIN	BAE-146	6	BA8094
528	2230	GATWICK	0100	ALICANTE	BAE-146	5	28.05-24.09
529	0150	ALICANTE	0425	GATWICK	BAE-146	6	29.05-25.09
532	0910	DUBLIN	1035	GATWICK	BAE-146	123456	BA8131
537	0725	GATWICK	0905	COLOGNE	ATR-42	123456	BA8123
545	1300	DUBLIN	1420	GATWICK	BAE-146	12345	BA8117
	1500	GATWICK	1610	AMSTERDAM	BAE-146	12345 7	BA8117
548	0940	COLOGNE	1125	GATWICK	ATR-42	123456	BA8124
553	1640	GATWICK	1800	DUBLIN	BAE-146	1234567	BA8086
556	08409	AMSTERDAM	0955	GATWICK	BAE-146	1234567	BA8113
561	1100	GATWICK	1225	DUBLIN	BAE-146	1234567	BA8092
562	0920	GATWICK	1130	NICE	BAE-146	7	01.08- BA8133
568	1100	GATWICK	1225	DUBLIN	BAE-146	12345	-30.07 BA8112
571L	1645	GATWICK	1810	CORK	BAE-146	12345 7	01.08- BA8157
	1500	GATWICK	1645	CORK	ATR-72	6	BA8156
576	1215	JERSEY	1315	GATWICK	ATR-42	12345	BA8075
579	0630	CORK	0755	GATWICK	BAE-146	123456	02.08- BA8113
	0855	GATWICK	1015	AMSTERDAM	ATR-72	1234567	-25.07 BA8113
585	1840	GATWICK	2030	ZURICH	BAE-146	1234567	BA8107

Flight	Dep	From	Arr	To	Aircraft	Days	Notes
596	0710	GATWICK	0830	AMSTERDAM	BAE-146	12345	BA8111
602	1445	SOUTHEND	1600	JERSEY	ATR-42	6	-25.09
603	1255	JERSEY	1410	SOUTHEND	ATR-42	6	-25.09
616	1620	MANCHESTER	1755	JERSEY	ATR-42	6	
617	1410	JERSEY	1545	MANCHESTER	ATR-42	6	
620	1720	CORK	1905	JERSEY	ATR-72	6	05.06-28.08
621	1605	JERSEY	1750	CORK	ATR-72	6	05.06-28.08
630	2345	GATWICK	0215	PALMA	BAE-146	6	24.07-09.10
631	0305	PALMA	0535	GATWICK	BAE-146	6	25.07-10.10
640	1510	GATWICK	1740	PALMA	BAE-146	6	
641	1850	PALMA	2120	GATWICK	BAE-146	6	
644	2225	GATWICK	0055	IBIZA	BAE-146	6	29.05-25.09
645	0155	IBIZA	0425	GATWICK	BAE-146	7	30.05-26.09
647		JERSEY	1100	BOURNEMOUTH	ATR-42	6	-25.09
648	1135	BOURNEMOUTH		JERSEY	ATR-42	6	-25.09
648	1015	JERSEY	1100	BOURNEMIOUTH	ATR-42	6	-25.09
649	1135	BOURNEMOUTH	1220	JERSEY	ATR-42	6	-25.09
658	1545	MANCHESTER	1720	JERSEY	ATR-42	6	
659	1335	JERSEY	1510	MANCHESTER	ATR-42	6	
664	1340	BIRMINGHAM	1510	JERSEY	ATR-72	6	
665	1130	JERSEY	1300	BIRMINGHAM	ATR-72	6	
692	1700	GATWICK	1930	MAHON	BAE-146	6	
693	2020	MAHON	2250	GATWICK	BAE-146	6	
712	0910	AMSTERDAM	1020	GATWICK	BAE-146	12345	BA8112
717	2055	DUBLIN	2215	GATWICK	BAE-146	12345 7	BA8091
723	1045	AMSTERDAM	1200	GATWICK	BAE-146	1234567	BA8114
726	0600	GATWICK	0820	MAHON	BAE-146	7	18.07-03.10
727	0905	MAHON	1125	GATWICK	BAE-146	7	18.07-03.10
731	1225	SHANNON	1420	JERSEY	ATR-72	7	06.06-29.08
732	0955	JERSEY	1150	SHANNON	ATR-72	7	06.06-29.08
734	1840	AMSTERDAM	1950	GATWICK	BAE-146	12345 7	BA8120
736	1215	NICE	1415	GATWICK	BAE-146	7	01.08- BA8134
739	0900	DUBLIN	1020	GATWICK	BAE-146	6	-31.07 BA8095
	1610	DUBLIN	1730	GATWICK	BAE-146	6	07.08- BA8095
745	1650	GATWICK	1855	NICE	BAE-146	1234567	12.08- BA8135
756	1200	MANCHESTER	1330	GUERNSEY	ATR-42	7	-03.10
757	0945	GUERNSEY	1115	MANCHESTER	ATR-42	7	-03.10
768	1300	DUBLIN	1420	GATWICK	BAE-146	6	-31.07 BA8117
776	1935	NICE	2135	GATWICK	BAE-146	1234567	12.07- BA8136
778	1335	BLACKPOOL	1520	JERSEY	ATR-72	7	-03.10
779	1115	JERSEY	1300	BLACKPOOL	ATR-72	7	
797	1150	GATWICK	1325	LUXEMBOURG	ATR-42	12345	-30.07 BA8140
813G	1400	GATWICK	1555	BREMEN	ATR-72	1234567	BA8163
818	1400	NICE	1600	GATWICK	BAE-146	123456	02.08- BA8132
827L	1630	BREMEN	1825	GATWICK	ATR-72	1234567	BA8164
831F	1920	GATWICK	2115	BREMEN	BAE146/AT7	12345 7	BA8165
	1830	GATWICK	2030	BREMEN	ATR42/72	6	BA8165
848W	0650	NEWCASTLE	0815	GATWICK	ATR-72	1234567	BA8070
	0850	GATWICK	1030	DUSSELDORF	ATR-72	1234567	BA8070
851L	1105	DUSSELDORF	1300	GATWICK	ATR-72	1234567	BA8188
872C	1500	GATWICK	1645	DUSSELDORF	ATR-72	12345 7	BA8193
875H	0630	CORK	0800	GATWICK	BAE146/AT7	1234567	BA8151
878B	1140	GATWICK	1325	DUSSELDORF	ATR42/72	1234567	BA8191
883Y	0545	DUSSELDORF	0725	GATWICK	ATR42/72	1234567	BA8190
892	1650	AMSTERDAM	1755	GATWICK	BAE-146	12345 7	BA8118
896K	1755	GATWICK	1925	CORK	ATR-72	7	BA8150
8300	0715	GUERNSEY	0815	HEATHROW	ATR-72	1234567	
8302	1055	GUERNSEY	1155	HEATHROW	ATR-72	1234567	
8304	1230	HEATHROW	1330	GUERNSEY	ATR-72	1234567	
8304	1440	GUERNSEY	1540	HEATHROW	ATR-72	1234567	
8305	1615	HEATHROW	1715	GUERNSEY	ATR-72	1234567	
306	1820	GUERNSEY	1920	HEATHROW	ATR-72	1234567	
8307	1955	HEATHROW	2055	GUERNSEY	ATR-72	1234567	
8330	0630	NANTES	0745	HEATHROW	ATR-42	1234567	
8331	0820	HEATHROW	0940	NANTES	ATR-42	1234567	
8332	1030	NANTES	1145	HEATHROW	ATR-42	1234567	
8333	1520	HEATHROW	1640	NANTES	ATR-42	1234567	
8334	1730	NANTES	1845	HEATHROW	ATR-42	1234567	

8335	1800	NANTES	1920	HEATHROW	ATR-42	1234567
8346	1700	LUXEMBURG	1820	HEATHROW	BAE-146	1234567
8347	1910	HEATHROW	2030	LUXEMBURG	BAE-146	1234567

FRENCH LINES — AOM MINERVE S.A.   IW/AOM   FRANCE

301	1100	PARIS ORLY		FORT DE FRANCE	DC-10	1 34 67
302		FORT DE FRANCE	0610	PARIS ORLY	DC-10	12 45 7
313	1115	PARIS ORLY		POINTE-A-PITRE	DC-10	345 7
314		POINTE-A-PITRE	0555	PARIS ORLY	DC-10	1 456
317	1430	PARIS ORLY		POINTE-A-PITRE	DC-10	6
318		POINTE-A-PITRE	0845	PARIS ORLY	DC-10	7
331	1010	PARIS ORLY		POINTE A PITRE	DC-10	2
		FORT DE FRANCE	0555	PARIS ORLY	DC-10	3
341	1020	PARIS ORLY		ST. MAARTEN	DC-10	5
		FORT DE FRANCE	0555	PARIS ORLY	DC-10	6
343	1015	PARIS ORLY		ST. MAARTEN	DC-10	1 6
		POINTE-A-PITRE	0555	PARIS ORLY	DC-10	2 7
349	1145	PARIS ORLY		ST. MAARTEN	DC-10	2
		PUNTA CANA	0830	PARIS ORLY	DC-10	3
355	1310	PARIS ORLY		PUNTA CANA	DC-10	6
356		PUNTA CANA	0830	PARIS ORLY	DC-10	7
357	1135	PARIS ORLY		PUERTO PLATO	DC-10	4
		PUNTA CANA	0830	PARIS ORLY	DC-10	5
440		VARADERO	0800	PARIS ORLY	DC-10	7
		HAVANA	1040	PARIS ORLY	DC-10	5
441	1120	PARIS ORLY		HAVANA	DC-10	7
	1240	PARIS ORLY		HOLGUIN	DC-10	5
623	1010	PARIS ORLY		NASSAU	DC-10	5
		HAVANA	0845	PARIS ORLY	DC-10	6
629	1020	PARIS ORLY		HAVANA	DC-10	1
		NASSAU	0925	PARIS ORLY	DC-10	2
645	1325	PARIS ORLY		VARADERO	DC-10	7
646		VARADERO	0955	PARIS ORLY	DC-10	1
655	1105	PARIS ORLY		HAVANA	DC-10	4
		VARADERO	0945	PARIS ORLY	DC-10	5
901	1840	PARIS ORLY		LOS ANGELES	A.340	2 5 7
902		LOS ANGELES	1635	PARIS ORLY	A.340	1 3 6
925	1105	PARIS CDG		NEW YORK	B.767	1234567

FUTURA — COMPANIA HISPANO IRLANDESA DE AVIACION   FH/FUA   SPAIN

EVEN NUMBERS - FLIGHTS INTO THE U.K. & EIRE						UNEVEN NUMBERS - FLIGHTS FROM THE U.K. & EIRE	
118/9	1640	TEESSIDE	1540	PALMA	B.737	5	
122/3	1340	EDINBURGH	1240	TENERIFE	B.737	5	
128/9	1620	CORK	1520	PALMA	B.737	6	
136/7	1720	CORK	1630	MALAGA	B.737	5	
148/9	1810	GLASGOW	1710	MALAGA	B.737	7	
152/3	1540	SHANNON	1440	PALMA	B.737	2	-26.09
152/3	1600	CARDIFF	1500	PALMA	B.737	2	
154/5	1120	GLASGOW	1025	MAHON	B.737	5	
156/7	??	LIVERPOOL	??	MAHON	B.737	5	
162/3	1455	EDINBURGH	1355	LANZAROTE	B.737	4	
164/5	0115	GATWICK	0015	PALMA	B.737	7	
166/7	1735	BELFAST	1635	PALMA	B.737	4	-07.10
168/9	1420	CORK	1320	LANZAROTE	B.737	4	
170/1	1620	EDINBURGH	1520	PALMA	B.737	6	
174/5	0335	BELFAST	0130	FUERTVENTURA	B.737	4	
174/5	2330	GATWICK	2230	PALMA	B.737	5	
176/7	0210	GATWICK	0110	TENERIFE	B.737	5	
178/9	??	LIVERPOOL	??	PALMA	B.737	6	
184/5	1910	EDINBURGH	1810	MAHON	B.737	5	
186/7	0055	BELFAST	0010	LAS PALMAS	B.737	1	07.06-27.09
192/3	1750	GLASGOW	1650	MALAGA	B.737	5	-23.07
198/9	1800	GLASGOW	1700	PALMA	B.737	6	
214/5	1745	SHANNON	1655	PALMA	B.737	7	
216/7	1445	BIRMINGHAM	1345		B.737	3	
228/9	2345	GATWICK	2245	PALMA	B.737	2	

242/3	1040	BIRMINGHAM	0940	MALAGA	B.737		6	
244/5	0135	MANCHESTER	0035	MALAGA	B.737		7	
248/9	1010	LEEDS	0920	MALAGA	B.737		7	
254/5	0905	BELFAST	0805	PALMA	B.737		6	
256/7	1715	CORK	1625	MAHON	B.737	1		
256/7	1835	SHANNON	1745	MAHON	B.737	1		VIA CORK
258/9	1130	GLASGOW	1035	MAHON	B.737	1		
260/1	1345	GLASGOW	1245	LANZAROTE	B.737		4	
262/3	1255	MANCHESTER	1155	MALAGA	B.737	2		
268/9	1620	BELFAST	1520	PALMA	B.737	2		25.05-21.09
272/3	0135	GATWICK	0035	MALAGA	B.737		6	
272/3	0920	STANSTED	0820	PALMA	B.737		6	
278/9	0215	GATWICK	0125	TENERIFE	B.737		5	
280/1	2030	CORK	0930	PALMA	B.737		4	
282/3	1030	CORK	1930	LANZAROTE	B.737		4	
284/5	1205	CORK	1115	TENERIFE	B.737		7	VIA DUBLIN
292/3	1855	CORK	1010	PALMA	B.737		7	
294/5	1110	CORK	1755	MALAGA	B.737		7	
296/7	1400	CORK	1300	LANZAROTE	B.737		7	
1101		PALMA	1615	GATWICK	B.737		12 45 7	
1102	1715	GATWICK		PALMA	B.737		12 45 7	

GEEBEE   *G.B. AIRWAYS LTD.   GT/GBL   U.K.*

A BRITISH AIRWAYS SUBSIDIARY. THE FIRST TWO NUMBERS ARE OMITTED FROM THEIR TRANSMISSIONS. A LETTER IS ADDED TO SIGNIFY THE ROUTE - A = PALMA/ TUNIS; B = GIBRALTAR; C = CASABLANCA/MURCIA/VALENCIA; D = AGADIR; G = MALAGA; L = MALTA; R=FARO/OPORTO/JEREZ; T = LISBON/TANGIER; X = MARAKECH E.G. CALL SIGN 861R REFERS TO FLIGHT NO. 6861 OPORTO - GATWICK.

6856	1430	GATWICK		LISBON	B.737	1234567	
6857		LISBON	2230	GATWICK	B.737	1234567	
6859	1930	GATWICK		LISBON	B.737	12345 7	
6861		OPORTO	0920	GATWICK	B.737	123456	
6864	1115	GATWICK		OPORTO	B.737	1234567	DEP 1445 7
6865		OPORTO	1635	GATWICK	B.737	1234567	ARR 2015 7
6868	2000	GATWICK		OPORTO	B.737	12345 7	DEP 2100 57
6872	0730	GATWICK		FUNCHAL	B.734	2 6	DEP 0930 2
	1130	GATWICK		FANTAIL	B.737	5	
6873		FUNCHAL	1600	GATWICK	B.737	2 6	ARR 1855 2
		FANTAIL	2045	GATWICK	B.737	5	
6880	0940	GATWICK		FARO	B.737	7	
6881		FARO	1620	GATWICK	B.737	7	
6882	0825	GATWICK		FARO	B.737	123 567	DEP 0915 7
	0955	GATWICK		FARO	B.737	4	
6883		FARO	1500	GATWICK	B.737	2	
6884	1710	HEATHROW	1905	FARO	B.737	1234567	2105/2300 2
6885		FARO	1925	HEATHROW	B.737	6	
6886	1200	GATWICK		FARO	B.737	6	
6887		FARO	2335	GATWICK	B.737	1 34567	
6888	1440	GATWICK		FARO	B.737	4	
6889		FARO	2120	GATWICK	B.737	4	
6902	0740	GATWICK	1000	GIBRALTAR	B.737	1234567	DEP 0710 157
6903		GIBRALTAR	1255	GATWICK	B.737	1 3 7	ARR 1355 17
		GIBRALTAR	1415	GATWICK	B.737	2 456	ARR 1515 4
6906	1535	GATWICK		GIBRALTAR	B.737	1 3 567	DEP 1715 67
6907		GIBRALTAR	2200	GATWICK	B.737	1 3 567	ARR 2345 67
6912	1515	GATWICK		MARRAKECH	B.737	5	
6913		MARRAKECH	2320	GATWICK	B.737	5	
6914	1445	GATWICK		TANGIERS	B.737	3 6	
6915		TANGIERS	1330	GATWICK	B.737	3 6	
6916	1355	GATWICK		MARRAKECH	B.737	2	
		AGADIR	2345	GATWICK	B.737	2	
6920	1445	GATWICK		SEVILLE	B.737	12 45 7	DEP 1515 15
6921		SEVILLE	1330	GATWICK	B.737	12 45 7	ARR 1500 4
6934	2000	GATWICK		MALTA	B.737	6	
6935		MALTA	0525	GATWICK	B.737	7	
6938	0545	GATWICK		MALTA	B.737	2 45 7	DEP 0825 7
	1500	GATWICK		MALTA	B.737	1 3	

Flight	Dep	From	Arr	To	Aircraft	Days	Notes
6939		MALTA	1355	GATWICK	B.737	2 45 7	ARR 1605 7
		MALTA	2230	GATWICK	B.737	1 3	
6944	1045	GATWICK		TUNIS	B.737	1 34 7	DEP 1145 1
6945		TUNIS	1725	GATWICK	B.737	1 34 7	ARR 1755 1
6952	1325	GATWICK		VALENCIA	B.737	12345 7	DEP 1630 7
6953		VALENCIA	1755	GATWICK	B.737	12345 7	ARR 2200 7
6966	0545	GATWICK		ALICANTE	B.737	12 45	DEP 0625 4
	1730	GATWICK		ALICANTE	B.737	67	
6967		ALICANTE	1140	GATWICK	B.737	12 5	ARR 1155 12
		ALICANTE	1230	GATWICK	B.737	4 67	ARR 2305 67
6968	1530	GATWICK		MURCIA	B.737	2 4 6	DEP 1640 46
6969		MURCIA	2125	GATWICK	B.737	2 4 6	ARR 2235 46
6978	0815	GATWICK		PALMA	B.737	67	DEP 0915 7
	1730	GATWICK		PALMA	B.737	12345	
6979		PALMA	2345	GATWICK	B.737	1234567	ARR 1510 67
6980	0545	GATWICK	1010	MALAGA	B.737	1 3 7	DEP 0715 7
6981		MALAGA	1335	GATWICK	B.737	1 3 7	
6982	0800	GATWICK		MALAGA	B.737	1234567	
6983	1135	MALAGA	1425	HEATHROW	B.737	1234567	
6984	1530	HEATHROW	1815	MALAGA	B.737	1234567	1605/1850 2
6986	1345	GATWICK		MALAGA	B.737	6	
6987		MALAGA	2145	GATWICK	B.737	1234567	
6988	1515	GATWICK		MALAGA	B.737	5	02.07-03.09
6989		MALAGA	2025	GATWICK	B.737	56	ARR 2140 5
6992	0825	MANCHESTER	1145	GIBRALTAR	BAE-146	7	
6993	1235	GIBRALTAR	1555	MANCHESTER	BAE-146	7	
6994	2300	GATWICK		GIBRALTAR	B.737	2	
6995		GIBRALTAR	2300	GATWICK	B.737	3	
6996	2300	GATWICK		GIBRALTAR	B.737	2	
6998		GIBRALTAR	0615	GATWICK	B.737	2	

		GEMINI		*GEMINI AIR CARGO*	*GR/GCO*	*U.S.A.*	
016		NEW YORK	0915	BRUSSELS	DC-10	2345 7	ARR 0915 7
017	0230	BRUSSELS		NEW YORK	DC-10	23456	DEP 0300 6

		GEMSTONE		*EMERALD AIRWAYS*	*G3/JEM*	*U.K.*	
01M	2240	CARDIFF	2255	BRISTOL	BAE-748	1235	
	2320	BRISTOL	0010	LIVERPOOL	BAE-748	1345	
06M	0050	LIVERPOOL	0140	BRISTOL	BAE-748	23456	
	0210	BRISTOL	0230	CARDIFF	BAE-748	23456	
10M	1950	NEWCASTLE	2035	EAST MIDLANDS	BAE-748	7	
11M	1945	NEWCASTLE	2030	EAST MIDLANDS	BAE-748	7	
	2145	EAST MIDLANDS	2230	NEWCASTLE	BAE-748	7	
22M	2215	BOURNEMOUTH	2315	EAST MIDLANDS	BAE-748	12345	
22N	0005	EAST MIDLANDS	0105	BOURNEMOUTH	BAE-748	23456	
41M	2140	LIVERPOOL	2220	BELFAST	BAE-748	12345	
42M	2310	BELFAST	2350	LIVERPOOL	BAE-748	12345	
250	2045	BELFAST INT.	2145	COVENTRY	BAE-748	12345	
251	0130	COVENTRY	0230	BELFAST INTL.	BAE-748	23456	
301	2020	BELFAST	2120	GLASGOW	BAE-748	6	
302	2210	GLASGOW	2310	BELFAST	BAE-748	6	
405	0550	LIVERPOOL	0630	BELFAST INTL.	BAE-748	2345	
406	0710	BELFAST INTL.	0745	DUBLIN	BAE-748	2345	
530	0110	LIVERPOOL	0150	BELFAST INTL.	BAE-748	123456	
531	0225	BELFAST	0305	LIVERPOOL	BAE-748	123456	
531P	0515	BELFAST INTL.	0555	LIVERPOOL	BAE-748	5	
620	0140	LIVERPOOL	0225	BELFAST INTL.	BAE-748	6	
621	0255	BELFAST INTL.	0335	LIVERPOOL	BAE-748	6	
621P	0400	BELFAST INTL.	0500	LIVERPOOL	BAE-748	6	
710	2245	LIVERPOOL	2325	BELFAST INTL.	BAE-748	6	
711	2355	BELFAST INTL	0035	LIVERPOOL	BAE-748	6	
771	2115	BELFAST INTL.	2215	COVENTRY	BAE-748	12345	
772	0225	COVENTRY	0325	BELFAST INTL.	BAE-748	23456	
811	0300	BELFAST	0340	LIVERPOOL	BAE-748	2345	
812	0525	COVENTRY	0625	BELFAST INTL.	BAE-748	2345	
814	2030	BELFAST INTL.	2130	COVENTRY	BAE-748	1234	
815	0345	COVENTRY	0425	BELFAST INTL.	BAE-748	2345	

GEMSTONE (Cont.)

915	0400	LIVERPOOL	0445	BELFAST INTL.	BAE-748	12345
916	2020	BELFAST INTL.	2105	LIVERPOOL	BAE-748	12345

GHANA   *GHANA AIRWAYS CORPORATION   GH/GHA   GHANA*

710		ACCRA	0700	HEATHROW	DC-10	2
711	0940	HEATHROW		ACCRA	DC-10	2
730		ACCRA	0700	HEATHROW	DC-10	4
731	1330	HEATHROW		ACCRA	DC-10	4
750		ACCRA	0700	HEATHROW	DC-10	6
751	1505	HEATHROW		ACCRA	DC-10	6
770		ACCRA	1900	HEATHROW	DC-10	7
771	2230	HEATHROW		ACCRA	DC-10	7

GILLAIR   *GILL AVIATION LTD.   9C/GIL   U.K.*

FLIGHTS BETWEEN PRESTWICK/BELFAST & VV, AND NEWCASTLE/BELFAST AND VV OMIT THE FIRST '7' FROM THE FLIGHT NUMBER AND ADD A SUFFIX LETTER AS FOLLOWS:- PRESTWICK - BELFAST 'KB'; BELFAST - PRESTWICK 'BK; NEWCASTLE - BELFAST 'NB'; BELFAST - NEWCASTLE 'BN'

31A	0001	STANSTED	0130	BELFAST INTL.	ATR-72	23456
41L	2225	BELFAST INTL.	2359	STANSTED	ATR-72	12345
42	0030	STANSTED	0055	GATWICK	ATR-72	23456
43P	0125	GATWICK	0155	STANSTED	ATR-72	23456
61	2150	EDINBURGH	2300	STANSTED	ATR-42	23456
62	0015	STANSTED	0140	EDINBURGH	ATR-42	23456
171P	2155	NEWCASTLE	2255	EDINBURGH	ATR-42	12345
172	2300	EDINBURGH	0015	BRISTOL	ATR-42	12345
173H	0100	BRISTOL	0130	BOURNEMOUTH	ATR-42	23456
174P	0300	BOURNEMOUTH	0430	NEWCASTLE	ATR-42	23456
181G	2225	BOURNEMOUTH	2155	BRISTOL	ATR-72	12345
182	0100	BRISTOL	0215	EDINBURGH	ATR-42	23456
183P	0300	EDINBURGH	0430	BOURNEMOUTH	ATR-72	23456
241	0630	STANSTED	0815	HAMBURG	ATR-42	12345
273A	0010	LIVERPOOL	0055	BELFAST	SH-360	23456
274P	0130	BELFAST	0235	NEWCASTLE	SH-360	23456
284	1520	DUSSELDORF	1720	NEWCASTLE	ATR-42	12345
285	1250	NEWCASTLE	1450	DUSSELDORF	ATR-72	12345
286	1810	DUSSELDORF	2010	NEWCASTLE	ATR-72	7
287	1545	NEWCASTLE	1745	DUSSELDORF	ATR-72	7
370	1845	HUMBERSIDE	1945	STANSTED	ATR-72	123345
371B	2100	STANSTED	2240	BELFAST	ATR-42	12345
372B	2340	BELFAST	0130	STANSTED	ATR-42	12345
501	0800	MANCHESTER	0835	TEESSIDE	ATR-42	2 4
502	0855	TEESSIDE	0930	MANCHESTER	ATR-42	2 4
505	1715	MANCHESTER	1750	TEESSIDE	ATR-42	2 4
506	1810	TEESSIDE	1845	MANCHESTER	ATR-42	2 4
622	0725	LEEDS	0830	EDINBURGH	SH-360	12345
623	0855	EDINBURGH	0955	LEEDS	SH-360	12345
628	1610	LEEDS	1710	EDINBURGH	SH-360	12345
629	1735	EDINBURGH	1835	LEEDS	SH-360	12345
640B	0650	NEWCASTLE	0750	BELFAST CITY	SH-360	12345
642B	0700	NEWCASTLE	0855	BELFAST CITY	ATR-42	12345
643B	0920	BELFAST CITY	1015	NEWCASTLE	ATR-72	12345
644B	0725	NEWCASTLE	0825	BELFAST CITY	SH-360	6
646B	0955	NEWCASTLE	1055	BELFAST CITY	SH-360	7
647B	1340	BELFAST CITY	1445	NEWCASTLE	SH-360	6
648B	1245	NEWCASTLE	1345	BELFAST CITY	ATR-42	7
649B	1410	BELFAST CITY	1505	NEWCASTLE	ATR-42	7
650B	1755	NEWCASTLE	1855	BELFAST CITY	ATR-42	12345
651B	1920	BELFAST CITY	2020	NEWCASTLE	ATR-42	12345
651	1920	BELFAST CITY	2015	NEWCASTLE	ATR-42	12345
653	2045	BELFAST CITY	2150	NEWCASTLE	SH-360	7
655B	1945	BELFAST CITY	2050	NEWCASTLE	SH-360	12345
680	0950	PRESTWICK	1050	CARRICKFINN	SH-360	6
681	1115	CARRICKFINN	1215	PRESTWICK	SH-360	6
682	1305	PRESTWICK	1405	CARRICKFINN	SH-360	1 3
683	1430	CARRICKFINN	1530	PRESTWICK	SH-360	1 3
684	1440	PRESTWICK	1540	CARRICKFINN	SH-360	7

685	1600	CARRICKFINN	1700	PRESTWICK	SH-360	7	
701	0700	BELFAST	0800	NEWCASTLE	ATR-72	123456	
	0840	NEWCASTLE	0900	TEESSIDE	ATR-72	123456	
	0920	TEESSIDE	1020	BELFAST	ATR-72	123456	
705A	1210	BELFAST	1230	BELFAST CITY	ATR-72	12345	
	1250	BELFAST CITY	1345	NEWCASTLE	ATR-72	12345	
706A	1540	BELFAST CITY	1600	BELFAST	ATR-72	12345	
706B	1420	NEWCASTLE	1520	BELFAST CITY	ATR-72	12345	
707	1415	BELFAST	1515	NEWCASTLE	ATR-72	7	
	1545	NEWCASTLE	1605	TEESSIDE	ATR-72	7	
	1625	TEESSIDE	1740	BELFAST	ATR-72	7	
709	1635	BELFAST	1735	NEWCASTLE	ATR-72	12345	
	1805	NEWCASTLE	1825	TEESSIDE	ATR-72	12345	
710	1805	NEWCASTLE	1825	TEESSIDE	ATR-72	12345	
	1845	TEESSIDE	1950	BELFAST	ATR-72	12345	
711	1815	BELFAST	1920	TEESSIDE	ATR-72	7	
	1940	TEESSIDE	2000	NEWCASTLE	ATR-72	7	
	2030	NEWCASTLE	2130	BELFAST	ATR-72	7	
713	1635	BELFAST	1740	TEESSIDE	ATR-72	6	
	1900	TEESSIDE	2000	BELFAST	ATR-72	6	
761	0800	NEWCASTLE	0900	ABERDEEN	SH-360	12345	
	0925	ABERDEEN	1005	WICK	SH-360	12345	
762	1020	WICK	1100	ABERDEEN	SH-360	12345	
767	1630	ABERDEEN	1710	WICK	SH-360	12345	
768	1730	WICK	1810	ABERDEEN	SH-360	12345	
781	0700	TEESSIDE	0810	ABERDEEN	SH-360	12345	
782	0830	ABERDEEN	0940	TEESSIDE	SH-360	12	
783	1000	TEESSIDE	1110	ABERDEEN	SH-360	12	
784	1300	ABERDEEN	1410	TEESSIDE	SH-360	12345	
787	1430	TEESSIDE	1540	ABERDEEN	SH-360	12345	
788	1830	ABERDEEN	1930	TEESSIDE	SH-360	12345	
789	1800	TEESSIDE	1820	NEWCASTLE	SH-360	7	
	1840	NEWCASTLE	1940	ABERDEEN	SH-360	7	
790	1945	ABERDEEN	2040	TEESSIDE	SH-360	12345	
791	1800	TEESSIDE	1910	ABERDEEN	SH-360	12345	
792	2000	ABERDEEN	2100	NEWCASTLE	SH-360	7	
	2120	NEWCASTLE	2140	TEESSIDE	SH-360	7	
793	1800	TEESSIDE	1910	ABERDEEN	SH-360	7	
794	1930	ABERDEEN	2040	TEESSIDE	SH-360	12345 7	
800K	0815	BELFAST CITY	0900	PRESTWICK	SH-360	12345	
801K	0920	PRESTWICK	1005	BELFAST CITY	SH-360	12345	
802K	0850	BELFAST CITY	0930	PRESTWICK	ATR-42	6	
804K	1126	BELFAST CITY	1205	PRESTWICK	ATR-42	7	
806K	1200	BELFAST CITY	1245	PRESTWICK	SH-360	1 3	
808K	1235	BELFAST CITY	1320	PRESTWICK	SH-360	45	
809K	1235	PRESTWICK	1320	BELFAST CITY	SH-360	67	
810	1315	BELFAST CITY	1420	PRESTWICK	SH-360	7	
813	1555	PRESTWICK	1700	BELFAST CITY	SH-360	1 345	
819	1335	BELFAST CITY	1420	PRESTWICK	SH-360	7	
811K	1340	PRESTWICK	1425	BELFAST CITY	SH-360	5	
812K	1450	BELFAST CITY	1535	PRESTWICK	SH-360	45	
813K	1555	PRESTWICK	1640	BELFAST CITY	SH-360	1 345	
818K	1705	BELFAST CITY	1750	PRESTWICK	SH-360	12345	
819K	1720	PRESTWICK	1805	BELFAST CITY	SH-360	7	
821K	1810	PRESTWICK	1855	BELFAST CITY	SH-360	12345	
822K	1830	BELFAST CITY	1915	PRESTWICK	ATR-42	7	
825K	1935	PRESTWICK	2020	BELFAST CITY	SH-360	7	

GO-FLIGHT   *BRITISH AIRWAYS*   *OG/GOE*   *U.K.*

BRITISH AIRWAYS CUT PRICE AIRLINE

110	0630	MILAN	0845	STANSTED	B.737	123456	
111	0740	STANSTED	0940	MILAN	B.737	123456	
112	1015	MILAN	1220	STANSTED	B.737	1234567	
117	1715	STANSTED	1915	MILAN	B.737	12345 7	
118	1915	MILAN	2155	STANSTED	B.737	12345 7	
119	2025	STANSTED	2225	MILAN	B.737	123456	1940/2140 6
120	0630	BOLOGNA	0900	STANSTED	B.737	123456	

GO-FLIGHT (Cont.)

121	0855	STANSTED	1105	BOLOGNA	B.737	1234567	
124	1135	BOLOGNA	1400	STANSTED	B.737	1234567	
129	2000	STANSTED	2210	BOLOGNA	B.737	12345 7	
150	0630	ROME	0915	STANSTED	B.737	123456	
151	0825	STANSTED	1100	ROME	B.737	1234567	
152	1130	ROME	1415	STANSTED	B.737	1234567	
153	1250	STANSTED	1525	ROME	B.737	1234567	
154	1555	ROME	1840	STANSTED	B.737	1234567	
156	0840	ROME	1125	STANSTED	B.737	7	
157	1620	STANSTED	1855	ROME	B.737	1234567	
158	1925	ROME	2210	STANSTED	B.737	12345 7	
159	1930	STANSTED	2210	ROME	B.737	12345 7	09.06-
181	0655	STANSTED	0910	VENICE	B.737	123456	
182	0940	VENICE	1200	STANSTED	B.737	123456	
183	1035	STANSTED	1245	VENICE	B.737	1234567	
184	1325	VENICE	1545	STANSTED	B.737	1234567	
185	1435	STANSTED	1640	VENICE	B.737	1234567	
186	1710	VENICE	1930	STANSTED	B.737	1234567	
250	0630	MUNICH	0830	STANSTED	B.737	123456	
251	0900	STANSTED	1055	MUNICH	B.737	123456	
252	1125	MUNICH	1325	STANSTED	B.737	1234567	
257	1650	STANSTED	1845	MUNICH	B.737	1234567	
258	1915	MUNICH	2115	STANSTED	B.737	12345 7	
259	2030	STANSTED	2225	MUNICH	B.737	1234567	
281	0730	STANSTED		PRAGUE	B.737	1234567	12.06-
284		PRAGUE	1210	STANSTED	B.737	1234567	12.07-
285	1705	STANSTED		PRAGUE	B.737	1234567	12.07-
299		PRAGUE	2145	STANSTED	B.737	1234567	12.07-
301	0925	STANSTED	1115	LISBON	B.737	1234567	
304	1355	LISBON	1550	STANSTED	B.737	1234567	
305	1355	STANSTED	1445	LISBON	B.737	1234567	
306	1815	LISBON	2005	STANSTED	B.737	1234567	
321	0945	STANSTED	1210	MADRID	B.737	1234567	10.06-
324	1245	MADRID	1515	STANSTED	B.737	1234567	10.06-
325	1500	STANSTED	1725	MADRID	B.737	1234567	10.06-
328	1800	MADRID	2025	STANSTED	B.737	1234567	
333	1220	STANSTED	1420	BILBAO	B.737	1234567	1445/1645 6
336	1450	BILBAO	1650	STANSTED	B.737	1234567	1715/1915 6
373	1225	STANSTED	1535	MALAGA	B.737	1 3 56	
374	1605	MALAGA	1905	STANSTED	B.737	1 3 56	
375	1430	STANSTED	1740	MALAGA	B.737	6	
376	1835	MALAGA	2135	STANSTED	B.737	6	
383	1225	STANSTED	1435	FARO	B.737	2 4 67	1710/1920 6
384	1705	FARO	1905	STANSTED	B.737	2 4 67	2100/2355 6
400	0600	COPENHAGEN	0755	STANSTED	B.737	123456	
401	0715	STANSTED	0905	COPENHAGEN	B.737	123456	
402	1000	COPENHAGEN	1155	STANSTED	B.737	1234567	
407	1505	STANSTED	1655	COPENHAGEN	B.737	12345 7	
408	1755	COPENHAGEN	1950	STANSTED	B.737	12345 7	
409	1940	STANSTED	2130	COPENHAGEN	B.737	1234567	
501	0655	STANSTED	0815	EDINBURGH	B.737	12345	
502	0740	EDINBURGH	0900	STANSTED	B.737	123456	
503	0915	STANSTED	1030	EDINBURGH	B.737	1234567	
504	1055	EDINBURGH	1215	STANSTED	B.737	1234567	
505	1245	STANSTED	1400	EDINBURGH	B.737	1234567	
506	1335	EDINBURGH	1555	STANSTED	B.737	1234567	
507	1610	STANSTED	1725	EDINBURGH	B.737	1234567	
508	1750	EDINBURGH	1910	STANSTED	B.737	1234567	
509	1910	STANSTED	2025	EDINBURGH	B.737	12345 7	
510	2050	EDINBURGH	2205	STANSTED	B.737	12345 7	
511	2055	STANSTED	2210	EDINBURGH	B.737	12345 7	
512	0710	EDINBURGH	0830	STANSTED	B.737	12345	
700		COLOGNE	0725	STANSTED	B.737	1234567	12.08-
701	0850	STANSTED		COLOGNE	B.737	1234567	12.08-
702		COLOGNE	1315	STANSTED	B.737	1234567	
703	1155	STANSTED		COLOGNE	B.737	1234567	12.08-
704		COLOGNE	1530	STANSTED	B.737	1234567	
705	1430	STANSTED		COLOGNE	B.737	1234567	12.08-

Flight	Dep	From	Arr	To	Aircraft	Days	Dates
706		COLOGNE	1535	STANSTED	B.737	1234567	12.08-
707	1545	STANSTED		COLOGNE	B.737	1234567	12.08-
708		COLOGNE	1730	STANSTED	B.737	1234567	
709	1555	STANSTED		COLOGNE	B.737	1234567	
710		COLOGNE	1755	STANSTED	B.737	1234567	12,08-
711	1830	STANSTED		COLOGNE	B.737	1234567	
712		COLOGNE	1855	STANSTED	B.737	1234567	
713	1945	STANSTED		COLOGNE	B.737	1234567	12,08-
714		COLOGNE	2040	STANSTED	B.737	1234567	12.08-
715	1945	STANSTED		COLOGNE	B.737	1234567	12.08-
912	1945	STANSTED		MALAGA	B.737	6	17.07-
913		MALAGA	0245	STANSTED	B.737	7	18.07-
930	1455	EDINBURGH		PISA	B.737	6	
931		PISA	2255	EDINBURGH	B.737	6	
932	1555	EDINBURGH		ALICANTE	B.737	6	
933		ALICANTE	2335	EDINBURGH	B.737	6	
934	1845	EDINBURGH		PALMA	B.737	6	29.05-25.09
935		PALMA	0145	EDINBURGH	B.737	7	30.05-25.09
936	0600	EDINBURGH		FARO	B.737	7	
937		FARO	1540	EDINBURGH	B.737	7	
941	1700	STANSTED		SALZBURG	B.737	6	
942		SALZBURG	2230	STANSTED	B.737	6	

GOLF NOVEMBER   *AIR GABON   GN/AGN   GABON*

Flight	Dep	From	Arr	To	Aircraft	Days	Dates
610		LIBREVILLE	0455	GATWICK	B.747	1	
	0555	GATWICK	0700	PARIS	B.747	1	
611	1610	PARIS CDG	1715	GATWICK	B.747	6	
	1910	GATWICK	2015	PARIS CDG	B.747	6	

GRANITE   *BUSINESS AIR   II/GNT   U.K.*

Flight	Dep	From	Arr	To	Aircraft	Days
387P	2015	EDINBURGH	2055	ABERDEEN	SAAB-340	12345
722	2120	ABERDEEN	2200	EDINBURGH	SAAB-340	12345
723	2235	EDINBURGH	2335	EAST MIDLANDS	SAAB-340	12345
724	0015	EAST MIDLANDS	0120	EDINBURGH	SAAB-340	23456
725	2130	ABERDEEN	2210	EDINBURGH	SAAB-340	12345
726	2250	EDINBURGH	2355	EAST MIDLANDS	SAAB-340	12345
727	0035	EAST MIDLANDS	0140	EDINBURGH	SAAB-340	23456
728	0210	EAST MIDLANDS	0250	FSS???	SAAB-340	23456
728P	0610	FSS ???	0630	ABERDEEN	SAAB-340	2345
800	2210	NORWICH	2245	STANSTED	SAAB-340	12345
800P	2055	EAST MIDLANDS	2125	NORWICH	SAAB-340	12345
801	2310	STANSTED	2355	BRISTOL	SAAB-340	12345
802	0025	BRISTOL	0110	STANSTED	SAAB-340	23456
803	0130	STANSTED	0205	NORWICH	SAAB-340	23456
803P	0230	NORWICH	0300	EAST MIDLANDS	SAAB-340	23456

GREENISLE   *VIRGIN EXPRESS (IRELAND) LTD.   VK/VEI   EIRE*

EVEN NUMBERS - FLIGHTS LEAVING THE U.K.   UNEVEN NUMBERS - FLIGHTS INTO THE U.K.

Flight	Dep	From	Arr	To	Aircraft	Days	Dates
152/3	2130	STANSTED	0430	CORFU	B.737	5	16.07-02.10
1682/3	1355	STANSTED	1935	ALICANTE	B.737	6	29.05-
1704/5	0630	STANSTED	1245	MALAGA	B.737	7	30.05-

SCHEDULE SERVICES

Flight	Dep	From	Arr	To	Aircraft	Days	Dates
900	0715	SHANNON	0845	STANSTED	B.737	123456	
901	0915	STANSTED	1045	SHANNON	B.737	123456	
902	1555	SHANNON	1725	STANSTED	B.737	1234 7	
903	1825	STANSTED	1955	SHANNON	B.737	1234 7	
904	1125	SHANNON	1255	STANSTED	B.737	1 456	29.05-13.09
905	1340	STANSTED	1510	SHANNON	B.737	1 45 7	29.05-13.09
906	2035	SHANNON	2205	STANSTED	B.737	5 7	18.06-12.09
907	2240	STANSTED	0010	SHANNON	B.737	5 7	18.06-12.09

GULF AIR   *GULF AIR   GF/GFA   BAHRAIN /OMAN/QATAR/UAE*

Flight	Dep	From	Arr	To	Aircraft	Days
002	1000	HEATHROW		BAHRAIN	A.340	1234567
003		BAHRAIN	1750	HEATHROW	A.330	1234567

004	1130	HEATHROW			DOHA	A.330	123 567	
005		DOHA	1710	HEATHROW		A340/B767	1234567	
006	2030	HEATHROW			MUSCAT	A340/B767	1234567	
007		BAHRAIN	0555	HEATHROW		A.330	1234567	ARR 0620 4
008	2200	HEATHROW			BAHRAIN	A330/340	1234567	
009		ABU DHABI	0640	HEATHROW		A.330	123 567	

HAPAG LLOYD   *HAPAG LLOYD   HF/HLF   GERMANY*

1606		PUNTA CANA	1305	FRANKFURT	A.310	1
2601	1445	HANOVER		PUNTA CANA	A.310	2
2602		PUERTO PLATO	1305	HANOVER	A.310	3

HEAVYLIFT   *HEAVYLIFT CARGO AIRLINES   HLA   U.K.*

9019	2000	STANSTED	2110	AMSTERDAM	BELFAST	1
9020	1900	DUBLIN	2030	STANSTED	BELFAST	7
9063	0045	STANSTED		BOLOGNA	BELFAST	2 4
9064		BOLOGNA	0515	STANSTED	BELFAST	2 4

HUNTING   *HUNTING AIR CARGO   AG/ABR   U.K.*

431	0240	BRUSSELS	0355	COVENTRY	HERCULES	2345
	0155	BRUSSELS	0310	EAST MIDLAND	HERCULES	6
	0500	COVENTRY	0605	BELFAST	HERCULES	2345
	0445	EAST MIDLANDS	0550	BELFAST	HERCULES	6
432	1935	BELFAST	2045	COVENTRY	HERCULES	12345
	2325	COVENTRY	0045	BRUSSELS	HERCULES	12345
607	2330	LIVERPOOL	0015	BELFAST	B.727	6
607P	1930	BASLE	2100	LIVERPOOL	B.727	6

IBERIA   *IBERIA   IB/IBE   SPAIN*

3161	0730	HEATHROW	0940	MADRID	A.320	1234567
3162	0815	MADRID	1030	HEATHROW	A.300	1234567
3163	1135	HEATHROW	1345	MADRID	A.300	1234567
3164	1205	MADRID	1420	HEATHROW	A.320	1234567
3166	1600	MADRID	1815	HEATHROW	B757/A320	1234567
3167	1915	HEATHROW	2125	MADRID	B757/A320	1234567
3174	1340	MADRID	1555	HEATHROW	A320/MD87	1234567
3175	1700	HEATHROW	1910	MADRID	A320/MD87	1234567
3178	1855	MADRID	2110	HEATHROW	A.320	1234567
3179	1530	HEATHROW	1740	MADRID	A.320	1234567
3184	1600	MADRID	1815	GATWICK	MD-87	12345 7
3185	1900	GATWICK	2115	MADRID	MD-87	12345 7
4120	0845	BILBAO	1035	HEATHROW	MD-88	1234567
4121	1805	HEATHROW	1955	BILBAO	MD-88	1234567
4128	1320	SANTIAGO	1515	HEATHROW	MD-88	1234567
4129	1615	HEATHROW	1810	SANTIAGO	MD-88	1234567
4138		MALAGA	1555	HEATHROW	B.757	1234567
4139	1615	HEATHROW		MALAGA	B.757	1234567
4142		ALICANTE	1715	HEATHROW	MD-88	1234567
4143	1635	HEATHROW		SEVILLE	MD-88	1234567
4144		SEVILLE	1545	HEATHROW	MD-88	1234567
4147	1135	HEATHROW	1335	ALICANTE	MD-88	1234567
4150		VALENCIA	1640	HEATHROW	A.320	1234567
4151	1740	HEATHROW		VALENCIA	A.320	1234567
4182	1610	BARCELONA	1810	HEATHROW	A.320	1234567
4184	1045	BARCELONA	1245	HEATHROW	A.320	1234567
4185	1145	HEATHROW	1345	BARCELONA	A.320	1234567
4187	1540	HEATHROW	1740	BARCELONA	MD87/A320	1234567
4188	1240	BARCELONA	1440	HEATHROW	MD87/A320	1234567
4189	1930	HEATHROW	2130	BARCELONA	A.320	1234567
6911	1215	MANCHESTER		BARCELONA	A.320	1234567
6912		BARCELONA	1130	MANCHESTER	A.320	1234567

IBERWORLD — *IBERWORLD TY//IWD SPAIN*

EVEN NUMBERS - FLIGHTS LEAVING THE UK			UNEVEN NUMBERS - FLIGHTS INTO THE UK				
3215/6	1640	EAST MIDLANDS	1540	PALMA	A.320	2	
3217/8	2330	GLASGOW	2230	LAS PALMAS	A.320	6	
3321/2	1340	EAST MIDLANDS	1240	LANZAROTE	A.320	4	
3333/4	1305	EAST MIDLANDS	1205	TENERIFE	A.320	5	
3335/6	2325	LEEDS	2225	TENERIFE	A.320	5	
3555/6	1540	MANCHESTER	1440	PALMA	A.320	6	

ICEAIR — *ICELANDAIR FI/ICE ICELAND*

430		REYKJAVIK	1030	GLASGOW	B737/757	1234567	
431	1400	GLASGOW		REYKJAVIK	B737/757	1234567	
450	0850	REYKJAVIK	1145	HEATHROW	B.757	1234567	
451	1300	HEATHROW	1605	REYKJAVIK	B.757	1234567	
452	1600	REYKJAVIK	1955	HEATHROW	B.737	45 7	1705/2100 5
453	2100	HEATHROW	2359	REYKJAVIK	B.737	45 7	2200/0155 5

ICEBIRD — *ICEBIRD AIRLINE CO. HH/ICB ICELAND*

100		REYKJAVIK	1415	GATWICK	B.737	123456	
101	1500	GATWICK		REYKJAVIK	B.737	123456	
102		REYKJAVIK	2130	GATWICK	B.737	5	
103	1030	GATWICK		REYKJAVIK	B.737	7	
104	1630	REYKJAVIK	1630	GATWICK	B.737	7	
105	1800	GATWICK		REYKJAVIK	B.737	7	

IMPEX — *AVIOIMPEX M4/AXX MACEDONIA*

| 20 | | SKOPJE | 1050 | GATWICK | MD-83 | 4 6 | |
| 21 | 1200 | GATWICK | | SKOPJE | MD-83 | 4 6 | |

INDONESIA — *GARUDA GA/GIA INDONESIA*

970		FRANKFURT	0655	GATWICK	B.747	1 3	ARR 0755 1
		FRANKFURT	1015	GATWICK	B.747	6	
971	1600	GATWICK		FRANKFURT	B.747	1 3 6	

IRANAIR — *IRAN NATIONAL AIRLINES CORP. IR/IRA IRAN*

| 711 | | TEHRAN | 1145 | HEATHROW | B.747 | 2 4 7 | IRAN NATIONAL |
| 710 | 1700 | HEATHROW | | TEHRAN | B.747 | 2 4 7 | |

ISRAIR — *ISRAIR 6H/ISR ISRAEL*

101		TEL AVIV	1855	STANSTED	B.737	1	
		TEL AVIV	1740	STANSTED	B.737	3	07.07-
102	2015	STANSTED		TEL AVIV	B.737	1	
	1900	STANSTED		TEL AVIV	B.737	3	07.07-

ISTANBUL — *ISTANBUL AIRLINES IL/IST TURKEY*

701		ISTANBUL	0600	GATWICK	B.737	3 5	
702	0655	GATWICK		ISTANBUL	B.737	3 5	
703		ISTANBUL	0640	HEATHROW	B.737	3 7	
704	0740	HEATHROW		ISTANBUL	B.737	3 7	
707		ISTANBUL	0740	STANSTED	B.737	1 4	ARR 1115 4
	1215	STANSTED	1305	MANCHESTER	B.737	4	
708	1425	STANSTED		ISTANBUL	B.737	1	
711		ISTANBUL	1135	MANCHESTER	B.727	1	
	1235	MANCHESTER	1325	STANSTED	B.727	1	
712	1235	MANCHESTER		ISTANBUL	B.737	1 4	DEP 1405 4
751		ANTALYA	2200	HEATHROW	B.737	4	22.07-30.09
737		DALAMAN	1000	GATWICK	B.737	45	ARR 2230 4
		DALAMAN	2010	GATWICK	B.737	1 6	ARR 2045 1
738	1100	GATWICK		DALAMAN	B.737	45	DEP 2330 4
	2110	GATWICK		DALAMAN	B.737	1 6	DEP 2145 1
752	2250	HEATHROW		ANTALYA	B.737	4	22.07-30.09
763		DALAMAN	0930	MANCHESTER	B.737	56	ARR 2030 5
764	1030	MANCHESTER		DALAMAN	B.737	56	DEP 2145 5
767		BODRUM	0900	GATWICK	B.757	1	

768	1030	GATWICK		BODRUM	B.757	1	
769		BODRUM	2045	MANCHESTER	B.737	1	19.07-04.10
770	2145	MANCHESTER		BODRUM	B.737	1	19.07-04.10
817		BODRUM	1950	CORK	B.757	7	
818	2120	CORK		BODRUM	B.757	7	
825		IZMIR	0800	CORK	B.757	7	
826	0930	CORK		IZMIR	B.757	7	
7011		ISTANBUL	2000	GATWICK	B.737	3 5	07.07-24.09
7021	2100	GATWICK		ISTANBUL	B.737	3 5	07.07-24.09
7031		ISTANBUL	2100	HEATHROW	B.737	3 7	ARR 2035 7
7041	2155	HEATHROW		ISTANBUL	B.737	3 7	
7071		ISTANBUL	2120	STANSTED	B.737	1 4	19.07-23.09
7081	2220	STANSTED		ISTANBUL	B.737	1 4	19.07-23.09
7671		BODRUM	0930	GATWICK	B.757	1	-04.10
7681	1030	GATWICK		BODRUM .	B.757	1	-04.10

JAMBO   *ALLIANCE   AIRLINES   Y2/AFJ   UGANDA*

1	2105	HEATHROW		ENTEBBE	B.767	4 6	
2		ENTEBBE	0630	HEATHROW	B.767	4 67	
3	2105	HEATHROW		KILMANJARO	B.767	7	

JAPANAIR   *JAPAN   AIRLINES   JL/JAL   JAPAN*

401		TOKYO	1625	HEATHROW	B.747	1234567	
402	1945	HEATHROW		TOKYO	B.747	1234567	
403		TOKYO	1550	HEATHROW	B747/MD11	56	ARR 1705 5
		TOKYO	1920	HEATHROW	B.747	7	
404	1750	HEATHROW		TOKYO	B747/MD11	5 7	DEP 2125 57
405		TOKYO	1525	PARIS	B.747	1234567	ARR 1435 7
406	1800	PARIS		TOKYO	B.747	1234567	DEP 1910 7
407		TOKYO	1700	FRANKFURT	B.747	1234567	
408	1950	FRANKFURT		TOKYO	B.747	1234567	
410	1310	MILAN		TOKYO	B.747	12 67	
411		TOKYO	1555	AMSTERDAM	B.747	1234567	
412	1820	AMSTERDAM		TOKYO	B.747	1234567	
415		TOKYO	1810	PARIS	B.747	4 6	ARR 1945 4
416	1330	PARIS		TOKYO	B.747	56	DEP 1925 6
419		TOKYO	1620	MILAN	B.747	1 567	
421		OSAKA	1615	HEATHROW	B747/MD11	1234567	
422	1855	HEATHROW		OSAKA	B747/MD11	123 567	DEP 2000 1
	2100	HEATHROW		OSAKA	B.747	4	
423		NAGOYA	1430	HEATHROW	MD-11	2 5	
424	2030	HEATHROW		NAGOYA	MD-11	2 5	DEP 2100 2
425		OSAKA	1605	PARIS	B.747	2 56	
426	1855	PARIS		OSAKA	B.747	2 56	
427		OSAKA	1625	FRANKFURT	MD-11	1 4 7	
435		OSAKA	1600	PARIS	A.340	1 34 7	
436	1215	PARIS		OSAKA	A.340	34 7	AFRANCE A/C
451	1100	ZURICH		TOKYO	B.747	34	
452	1130	ZURICH		TOKYO	B.747	3 5	DEP 2030 3
453		TOKYO	1635	ZURICH	MD-11	12 567	
454	1150	ZURICH		TOKYO	MD-11	1 4 67	
455		OSAKA	1630	ZURICH	MD-11	1234567	
456	1210	ZURICH		OSAKA	MD-11	1234567	
6401		ANCHORAGE	0605	HEATHROW	B.747	3 5 7	
6402	0925	HEATHROW		ANCHORAGE	B.747	3 7	DEP 1605 3
	2000	HEATHROW		ANCHORAGE	B.747	5	

JAT   *JUGOSLOVENSKI AEROTRANSPORT   JU/JAT   YUGOSLAVIA*

210		BELGRADE	1240	HEATHROW	B.737	3 5	
211	1340	HEATHROW		BELGRADE	B.737	3 5	

JERSEY   *JERSEY EUROPEAN AIRWAYS   JY/JEA   U.K.*

031P	1845	BRISTOL FILTON	1915	BIRMINGHAM	BAE-146	5	
	1645	BIRMINGHAM	1715	BRISTOL FILTON	BAE-146	7	

101	0710	BELFAST CITY	0745	ISLE OF MAN	SH-360	123456	
	0800	ISLE OF MAN	0835	BLACKPOOL	SH-360	123456	
102	0900	BLACKPOOL	0935	ISLE OF MAN	SH-360	123456	
	0950	ISLE OF MAN	1025	BELFAST CITY	SH-360	123456	
106	1345	BELFAST CITY	1420	ISLE OF MAN	SH-360	6	
	1435	ISLE OF MAN	1510	BLACKPOOL	SH-360	6	
106	1535	BLACKPOOL	1610	ISLE OF MAN	SH-360	6	
	1625	ISLE OF MAN	1700	BELFAST CITY	SH-360	6	
109	1750	BELFAST CITY	1825	ISLE OF MAN	SH-360	12345 7	
	1840	ISLE OF MAN	1915	BLACKPOOL	SH-360	12345 7	
110	1940	BLACKPOOL	2015	ISLE OF MAN	SH-360	12345 7	
	2030	ISLE OF MAN	2105	BELFAST CITY	SH-360	12345 7	
123	0935	BELFAST CITY	1025	BLACKPOOL	F-27	6	19.06-25.09
124	1100	BLACKPOOL	1150	BELFAST CITY	F-27	6	19.06-25.09
125	1040	BELFAST CITY	1135	BLACKPOOL	F-27	67	
126	1205	BLACKPOOL	1305	BELFAST CITY	F-27	67	
129	1220	BELFAST CITY	1310	BLACKPOOL	F-27	6	10.07-18.09
130	1340	BLACKPOOL	1430	BELFAST CITY	F-27	6	10.07-18.09
131	1455	BELFAST CITY	1550	BLACKPOOL	SH-360	12345	
132	1615	BLACKPOOL	1715	BELFAST CITY	SH-360	12345	
133	1455	BELFAST CITY	1535	BLACKPOOL	BAE-146	6	10.07-18.09
134	1615	BLACKPOOL	1655	BELFAST CITY	F-27	6	10.07-18.09
135	1540	BELFAST CITY	1630	BLACKPOOL	F-27	6	29.05-02.10
136	1705	BLACKPOOL	1755	BELFAST CITY	F-27	6	29.05-02.10
137	1900	BLACKPOOL	2000	BELFAST CITY	SH-360	6	10.07-18.09
138	1810	BLACKPOOL	1910	BELFAST CITY	SH-360	6	20.06-26.09
273	0800	CARDIFF	0855	JERSEY	??	6	
301	0730	EXETER	0815	JERSEY	SH-360	123456	
302	0835	JERSEY	0900	GUERNSEY	SH-360	123456	
	0910	GUERNSEY	1000	EXETER	SH-360	123456	
	1020	EXETER	1145	DUBLIN	SH-360	123456	
303	1015	EXETER	1100	JERSEY	F-27	1234567	
	1125	JERSEY	1150	GUERNSEY	F-27	1234567	
	1205	GUERNSEY	1320	LUTON	F-27	1234567	
305	1035	EXETER	1120	JERSEY	SH-360	7	
306	1145	JERSEY	1210	GUERNSEY	SH-360	7	
	1220	GUERNSEY	1305	EXETER	SH-360	7	
	1325	EXETER	1450	DUBLIN	SH-360	7	
307	1230	DUBLIN	1355	EXETER	SH-360	1 5	
	1425	EXETER	1515	JERSEY	SH-360	1 5	
308	1535	JERSEY	1600	GUERNSEY	SH-360	1 5	
	1610	GUERNSEY	1655	EXETER	SH-360	1 5	
310	1435	LUTON	1545	GUERNSEY	F-27	1234567	
	1600	GUERNSEY	1620	JERSEY	F-27	1234567	
	1645	JERSEY	1735	EXETER	F-27	1234567	
311	1535	DUBLIN	1700	EXETER	SH-360	234 7	
	1725	EXETER	1805	GUERNSEY	SH-360	12345 7	
312	1815	GUERNSEY	1835	JERSEY	SH-360	12345 7	
	1855	JERSEY	1950	EXETER	SH-360	12345 7	
333	1430	EXETER	1515	GUERNSEY	SH-360	6	
334	1545	GUERNSEY	1635	EXETER	SH-360	6	
367	1055	EXETER	1145	JERSEY	SH-360	6	
368	1135	JERSEY	1210	EXETER	BAE-146	7	
371	1255	EXETER	1330	JERSEY	BAE-146	7	
372	1210	JERSEY	1305	EXETER	SH-360	6	
375	1225	DUBLIN	1350	EXETER	SH-360	6	
	1425	EXETER	1350	JERSEY	SH-360	6	
376	1545	JERSEY	1640	EXETER	SH-360	6	
379	1710	EXETER	1800	JERSEY	SH-360	6	
380	1830	JERSEY	1925	EXETER	SH-360	6	
386	1430	BELFAST CITY	1540	EXETER	BAE-146	6	10.07-18.09
387	1615	EXETER	1725	BELFAST CITY	BAE-146	6	10.07-18.09
400	0700	BIRMINGHAM	0800	BELFAST CITY	BAE-146	12345	
401	0720	BELFAST CITY	0820	BIRMINGHAM	BAE-146	123456	
404	0900	BIRMINGHAM	1000	BELFAST CITY	BAE-146	123456	
407	1045	BELFAST CITY	1145	BIRMINGHAM	BAE-146	1234567	
408	1250	BIRMINGHAM	1350	BELFAST CITY	BAE-146	6	10.07-18.09
411	1435	BELFAST CITY	1535	BIRMINGHAM	BAE-146	12345 7	

414	1630	BIRMINGHAM	1730	BELFAST CITY	BAE-146	1234567	
415	1810	BELFAST CITY	1910	BIRMINGHAM	BAE-146	6	
418	2005	BIRMINGHAM	2105	BELFAST CITY	BAE-146	12345 7	
419	1955	BELFAST CITY	2050	BIRMINGHAM	BAE-146	12345 7	
	2115	BIRMINGHAM	2155	GATWICK	BAE-146	5	
442	0700	EXETER	0755	BIRMINGHAM	SH-360	123456	
443	0900	BIRMINGHAM	1000	EXETER	SH-360	123456	
	1025	EXETER	1200	CORK	SH-360	1 5	
446	1040	EXETER	1135	BIRMINGHAM	SH-360	12345 7	
447	1225	BIRMINGHAM	1325	EXETER	SH-360	12345 7	
	1345	EXETER	1525	CORK	SH-360	7	
450	1220	CORK	1355	EXETER	SH-360	1 5	
	1415	EXETER	1515	BIRMINGHAM	SH-360	12345	
451	1630	BIRMINGHAM	1730	EXETER	SH-360	12345	
454	1600	CORK	1730	EXETER	SH-360	7	
	1820	EXETER	1915	BIRMINGHAM	SH-360	12345 7	
455	1945	BIRMINGHAM	2045	EXETER	SH-360	12345 7	
483P	2115	EXETER	2145	BRISTOL	SH-360	12345	
503	0840	BIRMINGHAM	0945	JERSEY	BAE-146	123456	
504	1010	JERSEY	1035	GUERNSEY	BAE-146	123456	
	1105	GUERNSEY	1210	BIRMINGHAM	BAE-146	123456	
	1250	BIRMINGHAM	1400	GLASGOW	BAE-146	12345	
511	1610	BIRMINGHAM	1710	GUERNSEY	BAE-146	12345 7	
512	1740	GUERNSEY	1800	JERSEY	BAE-146	12345 7	
	1825	JERSEY	1930	BIRMINGHAM	BAE-146	12345 7	
523	0910	BIRMINGHAM	1010	GUERNSEY	BAE-146	6	
524	1050	GUERNSEY	1155	BIRMINGHAM	BAE-146	6	
561	0855	BIRMINGHAM	1000	JERSEY	BAE-146	6	
563	0950	BIRMINGHAM	1055	JERSEY	BAE-146	7	
564	1045	JERSEY	1155	BIRMINGHAM	BAE-146	6	
565	1210	BIRMINGHAM	1315	JERSEY	BAE-146	6	
568	1400	JERSEY	1505	BIRMINGHAM	BAE-146	6	
569	1240	BIRMINGHAM	1345	JERSEY	BAE-146	6	
570	1410	JERSEY	1520	BIRMINGHAM	BAE-146	7	
572	1435	JERSEY	1545	BIRMINGHAM	BAE-146	6	
573	1600	BIRMINGHAM	1705	JERSEY	BAE-146	6	
575	1630	BIRMINGHAM	1735	JERSEY	BAE-146	6	
576	1750	JERSEY	1900	BIRMINGHAM	BAE-146	6	
578	1820	JERSEY	1930	BIRMINGHAM	BAE-146	6	10.07-25.09
616	0700	GUERNSEY	0750	SOUTHAMPTON	VARIES	123456	
617	0815	SOUTHAMPTON	0905	GUERNSEY	VARIES	123456	
620	0940	GUERNSEY	1025	SOUTHAMPTON	VARIES	1234567	
621	1055	SOUTHAMPTON	1145	GUERNSEY	VARIES	1234567	
624	1255	GUERNSEY	1340	SOUTHAMPTON	VARIES	1234567	
625	1410	SOUTHAMPTON	1500	GUERNSEY	VARIES	1234567	
628	1555	GUERNSEY	1640	SOUTHAMPTON	VARIES	1234567	
629	1710	SOUTHAMPTON	1800	GUERNSEY	VARIES	1234567	
632	1835	GUERNSEY	1920	SOUTHAMPTON	VARIES	6	
633	1950	SOUTHAMPTON	2040	GUERNSEY	VARIES	1234567	
675	0655	BELFAST CITY	0810	STANSTED	BAE-146	123456	
676	0845	STANSTED	1000	BELFAST CITY	BAE-146	123456	
679	1040	BELFAST CITY	1155	STANSTED	BAE-146	1234567	
680	1230	STANSTED	1345	BELFAST CITY	BAE-146	1234567	
683	1430	BELFAST CITY	1545	STANSTED	BAE-146	12345 7	
684	1620	STANSTED	1735	BELFAST CITY	BAE-146	12345 7	
687	1815	BELFAST CITY	1930	STANSTED	BAE-146	1234567	
688	2005	STANSTED	2120	BELFAST CITY	BAE-146	1234567	
702	0850	JERSEY	0950	LUTON	BAE-146	6	
705	1030	LUTON	1130	JERSEY	BAE-146	6	
730	0700	LEEDS	0805	BELFAST CITY	F-27	12345	
732	0800	LEEDS	0905	BELFAST CITY	F-27	6	
733	0835	BELFAST CITY	0940	LEEDS	F-27	12345	
734	1020	LEEDS	1125	BELFAST CITY	F-27	12345	
736	1200	LEEDS	1305	BELFAST CITY	F-27	7	
737	1155	BELFAST CITY	1300	LEEDS	F-27	12345	
738	1405	LEEDS	1510	BELFAST CITY	F-27	6	
739	1220	BELFAST CITY	1325	LEEDS	F-27	6	
740	1530	LEEDS	1635	BELFAST CITY	F-27	12345 7	

741	1335	BELFAST CITY	1440	LEEDS	F-27		7	
743	1720	BELFAST CITY	1825	LEEDS	F-27	12345	7	
744	1905	LEEDS	2010	BELFAST CITY	F-27	12345	7	
745	1825	BELFAST CITY	1930	LEEDS	F-27		6	
747	2035	BELFAST CITY	2140	LEEDS	F-27	12345	7	
773	0650	BELFAST CITY	0815	CORK	SH-360		6	
774	0845	CORK	1005	BELFAST CITY	SH-360		6	
777	1100	BELFAST CITY	1225	CORK	SH-360	12345		
778	1255	CORK	1415	BELFAST CITY	SH-360	12345		
779	1350	BELFAST CITY	1505	CORK	SH-360		7	
780	1535	CORK	1655	BELFAST CITY	SH-360		7	
805	1220	BELFAST CITY	1355	EXETER	F-27		6	
806	1425	EXETER	1455	BRISTOL	F-27		6	
	1525	BRISTOL	1650	BELFAST CITY	F-27		6	
817	0700	GLASGOW	0805	BIRMINGHAM	BAE-146	123456		
818	0845	BIRMINGHAM	1010	GLASGOW	F-27	1234567		
821	1035	GLASGOW	1200	BIRMINGHAM	F-27	1234567		
822	1245	BIRMINGHAM	1355	GLASGOW	BAE146/F27	1234567		ARR 1410 67
825	1430	GLASGOW	1535	BIRMINGHAM	BAE-146	12345		07.06-
826	1555	BIRMINGHAM	1720	GLASGOW	F-27	12345		
829	1745	GLASGOW	1910	BIRMINGHAM	F-27	1234567		
830	2010	BIRMINGHAM	2125	GLASGOW	BAE-146	12345	7	
839	0650	BELFAST CITY	0820	BRISTOL	F-27	12345		
840	0850	BRISTOL	1015	BELFAST CITY	F-27	12345		
843	0710	BELFAST CITY	0745	ISLE OF MAN	F-27		6	
	0800	ISLE OF MAN	0915	BRISTOL	F-27		6	
844	0940	BRISTOL	1055	ISLE OF MAN	F-27		6	
	1110	ISLE OF MAN	1145	BELFAST CITY	F-27		6	
845	1145	BELFAST CITY	1220	ISLE OF MAN	F-27	12345	7	
	1235	ISLE OF MAN	1350	BRISTOL	F-27	12345	7	
846	1450	BRISTOL	1605	ISLE OF MAN	F-27	12345	7	
	1620	ISLE OF MAN	1655	BELFAST CITY	F-27	12345	7	
847	1510	BELFAST CITY	1640	ISLE OF MAN	F-27		6	10.07-18.09
848	1710	BRISTOL	1835	BELFAST CITY	F-27		6	10.07-18.09
849	1735	BELFAST CITY	1905	BRISTOL	F-27	12345	7	
850	1935	BRISTOL	2100	BELFAST CITY	F-27	12345	7	
900	0715	GUERNSEY	0810	GATWICK	BAE-146	123456		
903	0855	GATWICK	0950	GUERNSEY	BAE-146	1234567		
904	1045	GUERNSEY	1140	GATWICK	BAE-146	1234567		
905	1055	GATWICK	1150	GUERNSEY	BAE-146	12345		
907	1225	GATWICK	1320	GUERNSEY	BAE-146		67	
908	1245	GUERNSEY	1340	GATWICK	BAE-146	12345		
909	1255	GATWICK	1350	GUERNSEY	BAE-146	12345		
910	1420	GUERNSEY	1515	GATWICK	BAE-146		6	
911	1555	GATWICK	1645	GUERNSEY	BAE-146		6	
912	1445	GUERNSEY	1540	GATWICK	BAE-146	12345	7	
913	1620	GATWICK	1710	GUERNSEY	BAE-146	12345	7	
918	1800	GUERNSEY	1855	GATWICK	BAE-146	1234567		
919	1935	GATWICK	2030	GUERNSEY	BAE-146	1234567		
930	0705	JERSEY	0810	GATWICK	BAE-146	123456		
931	0710	GATWICK	0810	JERSEY	BAE-146		6	
932	0725	JERSEY	0830	GATWICK	BAE-146		7	
933	0910	GATWICK	1010	JERSEY	BAE-146	1234567		
935	1015	GATWICK	1110	JERSEY	BAE-146		7	
936	1055	JERSEY	1155	GATWICK	BAE-146	1234567		
938	1150	JERSEY	1245	GATWICK	BAE-146		7	
939	1235	GATWICK	1335	JERSEY	BAE-146	1234567		
940	1215	JERSEY	1315	GATWICK	BAE-146		6	
942	1420	JERSEY	1520	GATWICK	BAE-146		6	
943	1425	GATWICK	1525	JERSEY	BAE-146		6	
944	1450	JERSEY	1550	GATWICK	BAE-146	12345	7	
945	1600	GATWICK	1655	JERSEY	BAE-146		6	
946	1620	JERSEY	1720	GATWICK	BAE-146		6	
947	1630	GATWICK	1725	JERSEY	BAE-146	12345	7	
948	1740	JERSEY	1840	GATWICK	BAE-146		6	
949	1800	GATWICK	1855	JERSEY	BAE-146		6	
950	1805	JERSEY	1900	GATWICK	BAE-146	12345	7	
952	1935	JERSEY	2035	GATWICK	BAE-146		6	

953	1950	GATWICK	2050	JERSEY	BAE-146	1234567	
961	0700	BELFAST CITY	0830	GATWICK	BAE-146	123456	
962	0915	GATWICK	1040	BELFAST CITY	BAE-146	123456	
963	0840	BELFAST CITY	1005	GATWICK	BAE-146	12345 7	
964	1045	GATWICK	1210	BELFAST CITY	BAE-146	7	
967	1125	BELFAST CITY	1250	GATWICK	BAE-146	123456	
968	1330	GATWICK	1500	BELFAST CITY	BAE-146	1234567	
969	1320	BELFAST CITY	1445	GATWICK	BAE-146	7	
970	1530	GATWICK	1655	BELFAST CITY	BAE-146	12345 7	
971	1540	BELFAST CITY	1700	GATWICK	BAE-146	1234567	
972	1740	GATWICK	1905	BELFAST CITY	BAE-146	1234567	
973	1740	BELFAST CITY	1905	GATWICK	BAE-146	1234567	
974	1940	GATWICK	2110	BELFAST CITY	BAE-146	1234567	
1388	1950	PARIS CDG	2130	EDINBURGH	BAE-146	1234567	
2200	0640	PARIS CDG	0805	BIRMINGHAM	BAE-146	1234567	AIR FRANCE
2201	0640	BIRMINGHAM	0755	PARIS CDG	BAE-146	1234567	AIR FRANCE
2202	0845	PARIS CDG	1010	BIRMINGHAM	BAE-146	1234567	AIR FRANCE
2203	0900	BIRMINGHAM	1015	PARIS CDG	BAE-146	123456	AIR FRANCE
2204	1300	PARIS CDG	1425	BIRMINGHAM	BAE-146	123456	AIR FRANCE
2205	1220	BIRMINGHAM	1335	PARIS CDG	BAE-146	1234567	AIR FRANCE
2206	1525	PARIS CDG	1545	BIRMINGHAM	BAE-146	1234567	AIR FRANCE
2207	1525	BIRMINGHAM	1640	PARIS CDG	BAE-146	12345 7	AIR FRANCE
2208	1755	PARIS CDG	1915	BIRMINGHAM	BAE-146	12345 7	AIR FRANCE
2209	1820	BIRMINGHAM	1935	PARIS CDG	BAE-146	1234567	AIR FRANCE
2210	2020	PARIS CDG	2145	BIRMINGHAM	BAE-146	12345 7	AIR FRANCE
2211	1955	BIRMINGHAM	2110	PARIS CDG	BAE-146	12345 7	AIR FRANCE
8830	0600	LYONS	0755	HEATHROW	BAE-146	123456	
8831	0850	HEATHROW	1030	LYONS	BAE-146	123456	
8832	1130	LYONS	1315	HEATHROW	BAE-146	1234567	
8833	1405	HEATHROW	1550	LYONS	BAE-146	1234567	
8834	1645	LYONS	1835	HEATHROW	BAE-146	12345 7	
8835	1915	HEATHROW	2100	LYONS	BAE-146	12345 7	
8836	0630	TOULOUSE	0840	HEATHROW	BAE-146	1234567	
8837	0920	HEATHROW	1110	TOULOUSE	BAE-146	1234567	
8838	1210	TOULOUSE	1405	HEATHROW	BAE-146	1234567	
8839	1505	HEATHROW	1655	TOULOUSE	BAE-146	1234567	
8840	1740	TOULOUSE	1935	HEATHROW	BAE-146	1234567	
8841	2010	HEATHROW	2200	TOULOUSE	BAE-146	1234567	
8931	0650	BIRMINGHAM	0810	PARIS CDG	BAE-146	1234567	
8932	0640	PARIS CDG	0805	BIRMINGHAM	BAE-146	1234567	
8933	1205	BIRMINGHAM	1320	PARIS CDG	BAE-146	1234567	
8934	1010	PARIS CDG	1130	BIRMINGHAM	BAE-146	1234567	0930/1050 7
8935	1355	BIRMINGHAM	1510	PARIS CDG	BAE-146	12345 7	
8936	1420	PARIS CDG	1540	BIRMINGHAM	BAE-146	12345 7	
8937	1740	BIRMINGHAM	1855	PARIS CDG	BAE-146	1234567	
8938	1545	PARIS CDG	1705	BIRMINGHAM	BAE-146	1234567	
8939	1940	BIRMINGHAM	2055	PARIS CDG	BAE-146	12345 7	
8940	1945	PARIS CDG	2105	BIRMINGHAM	BAE-146	12345 7	

JET SET   *AIR 2000 LTD.   DP/AMM   U.K.*

EVEN NUMBERS - FLIGHTS LEAVING THE UK				UNEVEN NUMBERS - FLIGHTS INTO THE UK			
'C'		FLIGHTS LEAVING THE UK		'D' FLIGHTS INTO THE UK			
4	0700	GATWICK		LARNACA	B.757	4	
5		LARNACA	1730	GATWICK	B.757	4	
6	1810	GATWICK		LARNACA	B.757	5	
7		LARNACA	0430	GATWICK	B.757	6	
8/9	1655	GATWICK	0315	LARNACA	B.757	1	
10	0725	BIRMINGHAM	0815	CANCUN	767	1	VIA SHANNON
11	1100	MANCHESTER	0655	PUERTO PLATO	B.767	2	
11P	0930	BIRMINGHAM	1000	MANCHESTER	B.767	2	POSITIONING
12/3	1700	GATWICK	0320	LARNACA	B.757	3	
14/5	0915	GATWICK	1935	LARNACA	B.757	3	
16/7	1345	GATWICK	2355	LARNACA	A.320	3	
20/1	0655	GATWICK	1710	PAPHOS	B.757	3	
24/5	0940	GATWICK	1950	PAPHOS	B.757	7	
26/7	1940	GATWICK	0545	PAPHOS	A.320	7	

28/9	1645	GATWICK	0240	PAPHOS	B.757	3	
30	1025	GATWICK	0630	BRIDGETOWN	B.767	7	
32	1020	MANCHESTER	0530	ORLANDO	B.767	1	
34	1100	MANCHESTER	0835	ORLANDO	B.767	2	
35	0945	GATWICK	0710	ORLANDO	B.767	5	
36	1125	MANCHESTER	0625	ORLANDO	B.767	5	
37	1100	MANCHESTER	0845	CANCUN	B.767	7	
38	0920	MANCHESTER	0620	ST.KITTS	B.767	3	
39	0730	MANCHESTER		NEWCASTLE	B.767	4	POSITIONING
40/1	0935	BIRMINGHAM	2005	LARNACA	B.757	3	
42	1150	GLASGOW	0555	ORLANDO	B.767	5	
42P		NEWCASTLE	1050	GLASGOW	B.767	5	POSITIONING
43	0930	GLASGOW	0545	PUERTO PLATO	B.767	6	EX/TO B/HAM
44	1000	BIRMINGHAM	0440	ORLANDO	B.767	7	
48	0800	GATWICK	1240	ORLANDO	B.767	1	
49	1440	GATWICK	1210	CANCUN	B.767	2	
50/1	1010	BIRMINGHAM	2030	PAPHOS	A.320	3	
52/3	1520	BIRMINGHAM	0135	PAPHOS	B.757	7	
54	1530	GATWICK	1115	PORLAMAR	B.767	3	
55	1315	GATWICK	0710	ORLANDO	B.767	4	
56	1035	MANCHESTER	0905	ORLANDO	B.767	5	VIA NEWCASTLE
57	1000	GATWICK	0700	ORLANDO	B.767	6	
58	0805	MANCHESTER	1230	ORLANDO	B.767	2	
65	0930	NEWCASTLE	0820	ORLANDO	767	3	VIA SHANNON
59	0715	BIRMINGHAM	0740	CANCUN	B.767	1	VIA DUB
60/1	1755	MANCHESTER	0445	LARNACA	B.757	3	
62/3	1845	MANCHESTER	0530	LARNACA	B.757	7	
65	0730	MANCHESTER	1405	ORLANDO	B.767	4	VIA NEWCASTLE
66/7	1610	MANCHESTER	0305	LARNACA	B.757	7	
70/1	0835	MANCHESTER	1920	PAPHOS	B.757	3	
72/3	1450	MANCHESTER	0130	PAPHOS	A.320	3	
74/5	1845	MANCHESTER	0535	PAPHOS	B.757	3	
80/1	0850	GLASGOW	1815	PAPHOS	B.757	3	
101	1325	BELFAST	2005	MAHON	A.320	5	
102	0705	BELFAST	2135	PALMA	A.320	2	
103	2230	BELFAST	0810	TENERIFE	A.320	2	
104	1600	BELFAST	2155	PALMA	A.320	6	
105	1505	BELFAST	2130	PALMA	A.320	2	
106	0730	BELFAST	1650	LANZAROTE	A.320	4	
107	1750	BELFAST	0040	FARO	A.320	4	
108	0620	BELFAST	1225	REUS	A.320	5	
109	1935	BELFAST	0555	BODRUM	A.320	1	
111	0800	BELFAST	1500	ALMERIA	A.320	6	-25.09
112	0915	BELFAST	0620	RHODES	A.320	3	
113	2305	BELFAST	0545	IBIZA	A.320	6	
114	0655	BELFAST	2110	MALAGA	A.320	7	
116	0915	BELFAST	1830	LANZAROTE	A.320	1	
117	2115	BELFAST	0700	TENERIFE	A.320	5	
118	2240	BELFAST	0815	LAS PALMAS	A.320	7	
151	1910	GLASGOW	0505	BODRUM	B.757	1	
152	0710	GLASGOW	1710	HERAKLION	B.757	2	
153	1810	GLASGOW	0015	REUS	B.757	2	
154	0115	GLASGOW	0750	PALMA	B.757	3	-04.08
156	1925	GLASGOW	0530	RHODES	B.757	3	
157	0635	GLASGOW	1345	FARO	B.757	4	
159	0115	GLASGOW	0715	GERONA	B.757	5	
161	1915	GLASGOW	0325	CORFU	B.757	5	
162	1700	GLASGOW	1430	FARO	B.757	6	
164	2340	GLASGOW	0630	IBIZA	B.757	6	
165	0910	GLASGOW	1755	ZAKYNTHOS	B.757	7	
167	0730	GLASGOW	1440	MALAGA	B.757	6	
168	1830	GLASGOW	1725	FARO	B.757	7	-18.07
169	1525	GLASGOW	1425	PALMA	B.757	2	
172	0710	GLASGOW	1725	DALAMAN	B.757	1	
173	0825	GLASGOW	1815	TENERIFE	B.757	5	
174	1300	GLASGOW	1150	MALAGA	B.757	5	
175	1540	GLASGOW	2230	ALICANTE	B.757	6	
179	1440	GLASGOW	0015	LANZAROTE	B.757	4	

181	2000	GLASGOW	0555	LAS PALMAS	B.757	7	
202	1740	GATWICK	0035	CORFU	A.320	1	19.07-
203	1230	GATWICK	2025	ZAKYNTHOS	B.757	2	
204	2140	GATWICK	0555	ATHENS	B.757	2	
205	1745	GATWICK	1645	FARO	B.757	7	25.07-
206	1815	GATWICK	2350	IBIZA	B.757	3	
207	0700	GATWICK	1555	LANZAROTE	B.757	3	
208	1705	GATWICK	0035	THESSALONIKI	B.757	4	
209	0620	GATWICK	1540	TENERIFE	B.757	5	
212	1410	GATWICK	1930	PALMA	B.757	6	
213	2150	GATWICK	0655	KOS	B.757	6	
215	1655	GATWICK	0200	DALAMAN	B.757	7	12.07-
216	0735	GATWICK	1720	DALAMAN	B.757	1	
217	2015	GATWICK	0230	CORFU	B.757	1	
218	1615	GATWICK	2135	PALMA	B.757	2	
219	0710	GATWICK	1515	ZAKYNTHOS	B.757	2	
221	1640	GATWICK	2225	ALICANTE	A.321	5	16.07-
222	2035	GATWICK	0600	RHODES	B.757	3	
224	0655	GATWICK	1615	DALAMAN	A.300	7	
225	0625	GATWICK	1505	MAHON	A.321	5	
226	1405	GATWICK	2020	NAPLES	B.757	5	
227	2125	GATWICK	0625	HERAKLION	B.757	5	
228	0720	GATWICK	1335	FARO	B.757	6	
229	1435	GATWICK	2045	MALAGA	B.757	6	
234	2115	GATWICK	0620	LAS PALMAS	B.757	7	
235	0845	GATWICK	1600	CORFU	B.757	1	
236	1705	GATWICK		MAHON	B.757	1	
237	1020	GATWICK	1930	CHANIA	B.757	2	
238	2320	GATWICK	0630	CORFU	B.757	1	
239	2030	GATWICK	0530	HERAKLION	B.757	2	
242	0645	GATWICK	1435	THESSALONIKI	B.757	4	
243	1545	GATWICK	2110	PALMA	A.320	4	
244	1410	GATWICK	2310	HERAKLION	A.320	2	
245	0020	GATWICK	0540	PALMA	A.320	5	
246	2045	GATWICK	0555	TENERIFE	B.757	5	
248	1305	BIRMINGHAM	1205	SALZBURG	B.757	6	
251	1415	GATWICK	2200	ZAKYNTHOS	A.321	7	
252	2340	GATWICK	0550	FARO	B.757	7	18.07-
254	2030	GATWICK	0535	BODRUM	B.757	1	
255	0645	GATWICK	1605	TENERIFE	B.757	2	
256	1715	GATWICK	2255	ALICANTE	A.321	2	
257	0005	GATWICK	0545	ALICANTE	B.757	3	
258	0745	GATWICK	1525	PREVEZZA	B.757	3	
262	2135	GATWICK	0545	ATHENS	B.757	4	
263	0745	GATWICK	2115	MAHON	B.757	5	
265	2330	GATWICK	0650	ATHENS	B.757	5	
266	0835	GATWICK	1400	PALMA	B.757	6	
267	1530	GATWICK	2145	FARO	B.757	6	
268	2315	GATWICK	0455	IBIZA	B.757	6	
269	0615	GATWICK	1130	CALVI	B.757	7	
271	2300	GATWICK	0715	ATHENS	B.757	7	
272	0700	GATWICK	1515	FUNCHAL	A.320	1	
273	0630	GATWICK	1545	BODRUM	B.757	1	
275	0730	GATWICK	1340	FARO	A.320	4	
275	2045	GATWICK	0610	FARO	A.321	4	22.07-14.10
277	0610	GATWICK	1145	MAHON	A.320	3	
282	0715	GATWICK	1615	HERAKLION	A.321	2	
284	0640	GATWICK	1600	SKIATHOS	A.320	5	
285	1720	GATWICK	2240	MAHON	A.320	5	
286	2340	GATWICK	0640	CORFU	A.320	5	
287	0740	GATWICK	1330	PALMA	A.320	6	
288	1515	GATWICK	2055	ALICANTE	A.320	6	
292	0555	GATWICK	1510	BODRUM	A.320	1	
293	1610	GATWICK	0055	LANZAROTE	A.320	1	
294	0610	GATWICK	1520	HERAKLION	A.320	2	
295	1625	GATWICK	2355	MALTA	A.320	2	
296	0035	GATWICK	0540	PALMA	A.320	2	
297	0650	GATWICK	1600	MIKONOS	A.320	3	

No	Dep	From	Arr	To	Aircraft	Day	Notes
298	1710	GATWICK	2255	IBIZA	A.320	3	
299	2355	GATWICK	0530	IBIZA	A.320	3	
300	0655	GATWICK	1535	MURCIA	A.320	4	
301	1640	GATWICK	2145	VENICE	A.320	4	
302	2310	GATWICK	0400	GERONA	A.320	4	
303	0700	GATWICK	1150	GERONA	A.320	5	
304	1315	GATWICK	1915	MALAGA	A.320	5	
305	2325	GATWICK	0540	MALAGA	A.321	5	02.07-
306	0725	GATWICK	1255	PALMA	A.320	6	
307	1415	GATWICK	2000	ALICANTE	A.320	6	
308	2230	GATWICK	0420	PALMA	A.320	6	
309	0630	GATWICK	1255	MALAGA	A.320	7	
311	0610	GATWICK	1325	CORFU	A.321	1	
312	1500	GATWICK	0010	LAS PALMAS	A.321	1	
313	0600	GATWICK	1200	ALICANTE	A.321	2	
314	1255	GATWICK	2210	SKIATHOS	A.321	2	
315	0615	GATWICK	1800	VERONA	A.321	3	
316	1910	GATWICK	0415	KOS	A.321	3	
318	0610	GATWICK	1230	FARO	A.321	4	
319	1340	GATWICK	2220	MURCIA	A.321	4	
322	2135	GATWICK	0440	CORFU	A.321	5	
323	0730	GATWICK	1350	FARO	A.321	6	
324	1500	GATWICK	2040	PALMA	A.321	6	
325	2230	GATWICK	0450	MALAGA	A.321	6	
326	0740	GATWICK	1400	FARO	A.321	7	
327	1505	GATWICK	2030	IBIZA	B.757	7	
328	2145	GATWICK	0305	IBIZA	B.757	7	
329	0640	GATWICK	1415	CORFU	A.321	1	
331	2315	GATWICK	0615	CORFU	A.321	1	
332	2145	GATWICK	0710	RHODES	B.757	6	
333	1725	GATWICK	2345	MALAGA	A.321	2	
335	1155	GATWICK	2105	SKIATHOS	A.321	3	
337	0645	GATWICK	1600	LANZAROTE	A.321	4	
338	1730	GATWICK	2350	MALAGA	A.321	4	
338	2350	GATWICK	0625	MALAGA	A.321	4	
339	0625	GATWICK	1545	SKIATHOS	A.321	5	
340	2030	GATWICK	0600	TENERIFE	A.320	5	
341	0635	GATWICK	0635	QBS	A.321	6	
341	1915	GATWICK	1915	VERONA	A.321	6	05.06-02.10
342	1400	GLASGOW	1210	QBS	A.321	6	-02.10
343	2025	GATWICK	0600	RHODES	A.321	6	
344	0705	GATWICK	1455	KEFALLINIA	A.321	7	
345	1600	GATWICK	2135	IBIZA	A.321	7	
346	2250	GATWICK	0430	ALICANTE	A.321	7	
347	1515	GATWICK	1415	INN	A.321	6	-25.09
352	2235	GATWICK	0740	TENERIFE	B.757	2	
356	0550	GATWICK	1935	FARO	B.757	4	
359	0755	GATWICK	1745	ANTALYA	B.757	7	
360	1400	GATWICK	2150	ZAKYNTHOS	A.320	7	
361	2320	GATWICK	0455	ALICANTE	A.321	4	
362	0630	GATWICK	2215	MALAGA	A.321	5	
363	1620	GATWICK	2205	ALICANTE	A.321	1	
364	0730	GATWICK	1300	PALMA	A.320	2	
365	0930	GATWICK	1905	DALAMAN	B.757	1	
367	0630	GATWICK	1135	REUS	B.757	2	
368	0615	GATWICK	1055	SALZBURG	A.321	3	-29.09
369	0745	GATWICK	1710	TENERIFE	B.757	5	
371	0625	GATWICK	1210	ALICANTE	B.757	6	
372	0700	GATWICK	1755	SALZBURG	B.757	6	
373	1530	GATWICK	1430	MALAGA	B.757	6	
374	0635	GATWICK	1550	KOS	B.757	3	
381	2140	GATWICK	0625	KOS	A.321	6	
382	0800	GATWICK	1555	KEFALLINIA	B.757	7	
383	0630	GATWICK	1315	TEL AVIV	B.757	7	
384	1230	GATWICK	2030	KALAMATA	B.757	7	
400	1405	MANCHESTER	1305	MALAGA	A.321	5	
401	0835	MANCHESTER	1825	BODRUM	B.757	1	
402	1930	MANCHESTER	0535	DALAMAN	B.757	1	

Flight	Dep	From	Arr	To	Aircraft	Day	Date
403	0645	MANCHESTER	1505	ZAKYNTHOS	B.757	2	
404	1500	MANCHESTER	2300	PREVEZZA	A.321	7	
405	0650	MANCHESTER	1655	RHODES	B.757	3	
407	0605	MANCHESTER	1520	LANZAROTE	B.757	4	
408	0950	MANCHESTER	1950	TENERIFE	B.757	5	
409	0915	MANCHESTER	1725	KEFALLINIA	B.757	7	
411	1515	MANCHESTER	2155	MALAGA	B.757	6	
412	0720	MANCHESTER	2350	FARO	B.757	6	
412/3	2335	GATWICK	0635	CORFU	A.320	1	05.07-
413	0650	MANCHESTER	1510	ZAKYNTHOS	B.757	7	
415	0650	MANCHESTER	1255	MAHON	B.757	1	
416	1415	MANCHESTER	0005	DALAMAN	B.757	1	
417	0725	MANCHESTER	1335	PALMA	B.757	2	
418	1535	MANCHESTER	2155	ALICANTE	B.757	2	
419	0040	MANCHESTER	0640	PALMA	B.757	2	
420	0945	MANCHESTER	1745	PREVEZZA	B.757	3	
421	0650	MANCHESTER	1630	HERAKLION	B.757	2	
422	0625	MANCHESTER	2100	FARO	A.321	4	
423	1555	MANCHESTER	1455	PALMA	B.757	2	
424	2145	MANCHESTER	0345	PALMA	B.757	6	
425	0935	MANCHESTER	1935	TENERIFE	B.757	5	
426	2035	MANCHESTER	0605	HERAKLION	B.757	5	
427	0720	MANCHESTER	1345	ALICANTE	B.757	6	
428	1445	MANCHESTER	2045	PALMA	B.757	6	
432	0645	MANCHESTER	1605	LANZAROTE	B.757	1	
433	1710	MANCHESTER	2305	MAHON	B.757	1	
433		TENERIFE	1255	GATWICK	A.320	5	16.07-
434	0005	MANCHESTER	0750	CORFU	B.757	2	
435	0850	MANCHESTER	1815	CHANIA	B.757	2	
436	2015	MANCHESTER	0605	TENERIFE	B.757	2	
438	2050	MANCHESTER	0625	RHODES	B.757	3	
439	0725	MANCHESTER	1530	THESSALONIKI	B.757	4	
440	1640	MANCHESTER	2245	PALMA	B.757	4	
441	2345	MANCHESTER	0515	GERONA	B.757	4	
442	0640	MANCHESTER	1315	MALAGA	B.757	5	
443	1425	MANCHESTER	2120	NAPLES	B.757	5	
444	2230	MANCHESTER	0615	CORFU	B.757	5	
445	0730	MANCHESTER	1405	MALAGA	B.757	6	
446	2330	MANCHESTER	0900	RHODES	B.757	6	
447	1015	MANCHESTER	0110	FARO	B.757	7	
448	1005	MANCHESTER	1800	CORFU	B.757	1	
449	2010	MANCHESTER	0550	BODRUM	B.757	1	
451	1725	MANCHESTER	2300	REUS	B.757	2	
452	0030	MANCHESTER	0610	REUS	B.757	3	
453	0730	MANCHESTER	1705	KOS	B.757	3	
454	1010	MANCHESTER	1650	FARO	B.757	4	
455	1750	MANCHESTER	0300	LANZAROTE	B.757	4	
456	0735	MANCHESTER	1340	MAHON	B.757	5	
457	1450	MANCHESTER	2020	GERONA	B.757	5	
458	2130	MANCHESTER	0715	TENERIFE	B.757	5	
459	0815	MANCHESTER	1500	FARO	B.757	6	
460	1645	MANCHESTER	2310	ALICANTE	B.757	6	
461	0010	MANCHESTER	0615	IBIZA	757	7	
462	0830	MANCHESTER	1835	ANTALYA	B.757	7	
463	1935	MANCHESTER	0210	MALAGA	B.757	7	
464	0600	MANCHESTER	1345	CORFU	A.321	7	
465	1445	MANCHESTER	2045	MAHON	A.321	1	
466	2150	MANCHESTER	0525	CORFU	A.321	1	
467	2120	MANCHESTER	0610	ATHENS	B.757	5	
468	2120	MANCHESTER	0340	ALICANTE	A.321	2	
469	0530	MANCHESTER	1135	IBIZA	A.321	3	
470	1240	MANCHESTER	2220	SKIATHOS	A.321	3	
471	2320	MANCHESTER	0525	IBIZA	A.321	3	
472	0735	MANCHESTER	1630	MURCIA	A.321	4	
473	1725	MANCHESTER	0125	THESSALONIKI	A.321	4	
474	0605	MANCHESTER	1350	CORFU	B.757	5	
475	1845	MANCHESTER	0410	BODRUM	A.321	1	
476	0910	MANCHESTER	1900	SKIATHOS	A.321	2	

477	0900	MANCHESTER	2000	INN	A.321	6	-25.09
478	0600	MANCHESTER	1915	IBIZA	A.321	7	
479	2200	MANCHESTER	0735	RHODES	B.757	6	
480	0650	MANCHESTER	1330	MALAGA	A.321	7	
482	1715	GATWICK		TEL AVIV	B.757	6	
483	0720	MANCHESTER	1725	DALAMAN	A.321	1	
484	1510	MANCHESTER	2115	MAHON	A.321	5	
485	0640	MANCHESTER	1315	ALICANTE	A.321	2	
487	2255	MANCHESTER	0515	ALICANTE	B.757	2	
488	0640	MANCHESTER	1305	IBIZA	A.321	3	
490	0615	MANCHESTER	1305	FARO	A.321	4	
491	1420	MANCHESTER	2330	LANZAROTE	A.321	4	
492	0755	MANCHESTER	1800	SKIATHOS	.321	5	
493	2005	MANCHESTER	0555	TENERIFE	A.321	5	
494	0700	MANCHESTER	2025	ALICANTE	A.321	6	
495	2030	MANCHESTER	0615	LAS PALMAS	A.321	7	
496	1605	MANCHESTER	2340	MALTA	B.757	2	
497	2220	MANCHESTER	0815	DALAMAN	B.757	4	
498	1420	MANCHESTER	0050	FUERTVENTURA	B.767	3	
519	??	LIVERPOOL	?	ALICANTE	A.320	2	
550	0650	BRISTOL	1225	MAHON	B.757	1	
551	1330	BRISTOL	2055	CORFU	B.757	1	
552	2200	BRISTOL	0725	BODRUM	B.757	1	
553	0915	BRISTOL	3245	PALMA	B.757	2	
555	0700	BRISTOL	1730	LARNACA	B.757	3	
556	1855	BRISTOL	0415	RHODES	B.757	3	
558	1300	BRISTOL	2125	LANZAROTE	B.757	4	
560	0900	BRISTOL	2235	MALAGA	B.757	5	
561	2335	BRISTOL	0840	HERAKLION	B.757	5	
562	1100	BRISTOL	1630	PALMA	B.757	6	
562/3	2030	GATWICK	0605	DALAMAN	B.757	1	19.07-
563	1730	BRISTOL	2345	FARO	B.757	6	
564	0655	BRISTOL	0535	IBIZA	B.757	7	
565	0755	BRISTOL	1825	PAPHOS	B.757	7	
566	2005	BRISTOL	0445	LAS PALMAS	B.757	7	
568	0530	BRISTOL	1140	FARO	B.757	4	
590	??	LIVERPOOL	??	IBIZA	A.320	3	
592/3	1700	GATWICK	0355	TEL AVIV	B.757	4	
595	0840	FARO	1320	LEEDS	B.757	4	
600	0700	CORFU	1430	EAST MIDLANDS	321	1	
601	1550	EAST MIDLANDS	2130	MAHON	321	1	
602	2240	EAST MIDLANDS	0825	DALAMAN	321	1	
603	0925	EAST MIDLANDS	1600	ALICANTE	321	1	
604	1735	EAST MIDLANDS	0055	MALTA	321	2	
605	0200	EAST MIDLANDS	0740	PALMA	321	2	
606	0840	EAST MIDLANDS	1750	FUERTVENTURA	321	3	
607C	1915	EAST MIDLANDS	0530	PAPHOS	321	3	
608C	0850	EAST MIDLANDS	1500	FARO	321	4	
610	0825	EAST MIDLANDS	1415	MAHON	321	5	
611	1510	EAST MIDLANDS	2145	NAPLES	321	5	
612	2245	EAST MIDLANDS	0800	HERAKLION	321	5	
613	0915	EAST MIDLANDS	1455	PALMA	321	6	
614	1550	EAST MIDLANDS	2230	FARO	321	6	
615	0005	EAST MIDLANDS	0550	IBIZA	321	1	
616	0705	EAST MIDLANDS	1500	ZAKYNTHOS	321	7	
617	1600	EAST MIDLANDS	0235	LARNACA	321	7	
618	2025	EAST MIDLANDS	1925	RHODES	320	3	
619	1705	EAST MIDLANDS	1545	FARO	757	4	
620	1320	EAST MIDLANDS	1210	IBIZA	321	7	
621	1415	EAST MIDLANDS	1315	ALICANTE	321	6	
623	1700	EAST MIDLANDS	0205	LANZAROTE	321	4	
700	0715	STANSTED	1255	PALMA	320	1	
701	1400	STANSTED	2300	DALAMAN	320	1	
704	0730	STANSTED	1200	SALZBURG	320	3	-22.09
706	0715	STANSTED	1345	FARO	320	4	
707	1455	STANSTED	2345	LANZAROTE	320	4	
708	0600	STANSTED	1220	MALAGA	320	5	
709	1320	STANSTED	1900	MAHON	320	5	

JET SET   (Cont.)

710	2010	STANSTED	0535	TENERIFE	320	5	
711	0755	STANSTED	1340	PALMA	320	6	
712	1455	STANSTED	2125	FARO	320	6	
713	2230	STANSTED	0410	PALMA	320	6	
714	0600	STANSTED	1230	FARO	320	7	
715	1330	STANSTED	1950	MALAGA	320	7	
716	2055	STANSTED	0620	ANTALYA	320	7	
717	1350	STANSTED	1250	PALMA	757	2	
718	1420	STANSTED	1305	MAHON	320	1	
719	0905	STANSTED	2210	ALICANTE	320	2	
720	1315	STANSTED	1215	FARO	757	4	
750	0920	BIRMINGHAM	1825	IZMIR	B.757	1	
751	1930	BIRMINGHAM	0455	BODRUM	B.757	1	
752	1445	BIRMINGHAM	2240	ZAKYNTHOS	B.757	2	
753	0750	BIRMINGHAM	1335	PALMA	B.757	2	
754	1450	BIRMINGHAM	2030	MAHON	B.757		5
756/7	2300	MANCHESTER	0515	IBIZA	B.757		6
758	2340	BIRMINGHAM	0835	HERAKLION	B.757	2	
761	0835	BIRMINGHAM	1435	ALICANTE	B.757		6
765		ALICANTE	1525	EAST MIDLANDS	320	2	
766	0730	BIRMINGHAM	2000	MAHON	A.320	1	
768	0825	BIRMINGHAM	1615	KEFALLINIA	A.320	2	
769	1810	BIRMINGHAM	2335	REUS	A.320	2	
771	2130	BIRMINGHAM	0700	RHODES	A.320	3	
772	0925	BIRMINGHAM	1815	LANZAROTE	A.320		4
773	1955	BIRMINGHAM	0545	DALAMAN	A.320		4
773	2050	BRISTOL	0615	DALAMAN	A.320		4
774	0900	BIRMINGHAM	1820	TENERIFE	A.320		5
775	1945	BIRMINGHAM	0500	TENERIFE	A.320		5
776	0805	BIRMINGHAM	1425	FARO	A.320		6
777	1545	BIRMINGHAM	2200	PALMA	A.320		6
779	0600	BIRMINGHAM	2030	FARO	A.320		7
780	2115	BIRMINGHAM	0615	LAS PALMAS	A.320		7
781	0810	BIRMINGHAM	2230	FARO	B.757		4
782	0705	BIRMINGHAM	1315	MALAGA	B.757		5
783	2345	BIRMINGHAM	0520	PALMA	B.757		4
784	2130	BIRMINGHAM	0645	BODRUM	A.320	1	
785	2145	BIRMINGHAM	0650	KOS	B.757		3
786	2340	BIRMINGHAM	0705	CORFU	B.757		5
787	1605	BIRMINGHAM	2145	PALMA	B.757		6
789	2310	BIRMINGHAM	0450	PALMA	B.757		6
790	0645	BIRMINGHAM	1355	MONASTIR	B.757		7
791	2300	BIRMINGHAM	0450	IBIZA	A.320		6
792	0015	STANSTED	0730	CORFU	320	2	
805	1315	STANSTED	1805	VENICE	320	3	26.05-13.10

JORDANIAN   *ROYAL JORDANIAN AIRLINES*   *RJ/RJA*   *JORDAN*

051		AMMAN	1600	GATWICK	B.707	1	
052	1800	GATWICK		AMMAN	B.707	1	
091	0400	AMMAN		NEW YORK	B.707	6	
092		NEW YORK	0600	MAASTRICT	B.707	7	
111		AMMAN	1645	HEATHROW	A.310	234 67	ARR 1725 26
112	1025	HEATHROW		AMMAN	A.310	1 345 7	DEP 1145 57
113		FRANKFURT	1645	HEATHROW	A.310	1	
114	1025	HEATHROW		FRANKFURT	A.310	2	
117	1455	BERLIN	1645	HEATHROW	A.310		5
118	1025	HEATHROW	1215	BERLIN	A.310		6
261	1225	AMSTERDAM		NEW YORK	A.310	23 567	DEP 1530 67
262		NEW YORK	0730	AMSTERDAM	A.310	1 34 67	ARR 0915 17
263		AMMAN	1620	SHANNON	A.310	1 4	
	1720	SHANNON		CHICAGO	A.310	1 4	
264		CHICAGO	1045	SHANNON	A.310	2 5	
	1145	SHANNON		AMMAN	A.310	2 5	
267		AMMAN	1700	SHANNON	A.310	2	01.06-22.09
	1800	SHANNON		DETROIT	A.310	2	01.06-22.09
268		DETROIT	1015	SHANNON	A.310	3	01.06-22.09
	1115	SHANNON		AMMAN	A.310	3	01.06-22.09

1		MONTEGO BAY	1035	HEATHROW	A.310	34 6		ARR 1335 4
		MONTEGO BAY	1430	HEATHROW	A.310	1 7		ARR 1505 1
2	1250	HEATHROW		MONTEGO BAY	A.310	34 6		DEP 1605 46
	1705	HEATHROW		MONTEGO BAY	A.310	1 7		

KENYA   *KENYA AIRWAYS LTD.   KQ/KQA   KENYA*

101	2000	HEATHROW		NAIROBI	A.310	123 6	DEP 2115 ON 5
102		NAIROBI	0645	HEATHROW	A.310	12 5 7	
104		NAIROBI	1800	HEATHROW	A.310	6	
115	2115	HEATHROW	2225	AMSTERDAM	A.310	4	
116	1650	AMSTERDAM	1800	HEATHROW	A.310	3 7	1850/1900 5
117	2000	HEATHROW	2110	AMSTERDAM	A.310	5 7	

KESTREL   *AIRTOURS INTERNATIONAL   AIH   UK*

6P	0530	BIRMINGHAM	0615	MANCHESTER	B.767	7	
11/2	1115	MANCHESTER	0650	BRIDGETOWN	A.330	1	
15/6	1025	MANCHESTER	0555	ORLANDO	B.767	1	
17/8	1045	GATWICK	0555	ORLANDO	B.767	1	
19/0	1015	GATWICK	0725	MONTEGO BAY	A.330	1	
21/2	1015	MANCHESTER	0600	ORLANDO	A.330	2	
23/4	1030	NEWCASTLE	0635	ORLANDO	B.767	2	
24P	0745	NEWCASTLE	0845	MANCHESTER	B.767	3	POSITIONING
27/8	1130	GATWICK	0640	ORLANDO	A.330	2	
31/2	0930	MANCHESTER	0940	ORLANDO	B.767	3	VIA BELFAST
33/4	1030	MANCHESTER	0555	PUERTO PLATT	B.767	3	
35/6	0830	MANCHESTER	1505	PALMA	A.330	3	
37/8	0930	GATWICK	0800	CANCUN	A.330	3	
41/2	0930	MANCHESTER	0655	CANCUN	B.767	4	
43P	0900	MANCHESTER	0950	TEESSIDE	B.767	4	
43/4	1050	TEESSIDE	0855	ORLANDO	B.767	4	VIS PRESTWICK
44P	0955	TEESSIDE	1045	GLASGOW	B.767	5	POSITIONING
45/6	1150	CARDIFF	0545	ORLANDO	B.767	4	
45P	0855	MANCHESTER	0950	CARDIFF	B.767	4	POSITIONING
46P	0700	CARDIFF	0745	BIRMINGHAM	B.767	5	POSITIONING
47/8	1030	GATWICK	0600	ORLANDO	A.330	4	
51/2	1010	CARDIFF	0600	ORLANDO	A.330	5	
53/4	1100	GLASGOW	0710	ORLANDO	B.767	5	
54P	0710	GLASGOW	0800	BELFAST	B.767	6	POSITIONING
55/6	1020	BIRMINGHAM	0545	ORLANDO	B.767	5	
57/8	1030	GATWICK	0600	ORLANDO	A.330	5	
61/2	1015	MANCHESTER	0600	ORLANDO	A.330	6	
63/4	1100	BELFAST	0545	ORLANDO	B.767	6	
64P	0645	BELFAST	0735	MANCHESTER	B.767	7	POSITIONING
67/8	1030	GATWICK	0555	ORLANDO	A.330	6	
69/0	1030	GATWICK	0825	MONTEGO BAY	B.767	7	
71/2	1010	MANCHESTER	0640	MONTEGO BAY	A.330	7	
73/4	1030	MANCHESTER	0650	VARADERO	B.767	7	
77/8	1030	GATWICK	0610	BRIDGETOWN	A.330	7	
101/2	0850	MANCHESTER	1845	TENERIFE	B.767	2	
105/6	1335	MANCHESTER	2235	LANZAROTE	B.757	5	
107/8	2350	MANCHESTER	0600	IBIZA	B.757	5	
109/0	0700	MANCHESTER	2020	PALMA	B.757	6	
111/2	1420	MANCHESTER	2320	FUERTVENTURA	A.320	6	
113/4	0030	MANCHESTER	0640	PALMA	A.320	7	
115/6	0755	MANCHESTER	1535	MONASTIR	B.757	7	
117/8	1735	MANCHESTER	0355	PAPHOS	B.757	7	
121/2	0700	MANCHESTER	1235	REUS	B.757	3	
123/4	2000	MANCHESTER	0530	BODRUM	B.757	1	
125/6	0915	MANCHESTER	1745	KEFALLINIA	B.757	2	
127/8	0800	MANCHESTER	1735	DALAMAN	A.320	2	
129/0	0855	MANCHESTER	1720	ZAKINTHOS	B.757	3	
131/2	0715	MANCHESTER	1650	LAS PALMAS	A.320	4	
133/4	0830	MANCHESTER	0450	DALAMAN	B.757	5	
135/6	0725	MANCHESTER	1325	MAHON	B.757	6	
137/8	1435	MANCHESTER	2035	PALMA	B.757	6	
139/0	2200	MANCHESTER	0545	CORFU	B.757	6	
141/2	0830	MANCHESTER	1440	IBIZA	B.757	7	

KESTREL (Cont.)

Flight	Dep	Origin	Arr	Destination	Aircraft	Day
151/2	0715	MANCHESTER	1335	ALICANTE	B.757	2
153/4	2340	MANCHESTER	0600	ALICANTE	B.757	2
157/8	1845	MANCHESTER	0415	RHODES	B.757	3
161/2	1530	MANCHESTER	2150	MALAGA	B.757	4
163/4	2155	MANCHESTER	0715	LAS PALMAS	B.757	4
165/6	0730	MANCHESTER	1325	PALMA	B.757	5
167/8	1140	MANCHESTER	0040	MAHON	A.320	5
169/0	2330	MANCHESTER	2200	PALMA	A.320	5
171/2	0630	MANCHESTER	1250	ALICANTE	A.320	6
173/4	1420	LIVERPOOL	1305	PALMA	B.757	6
175/6	2145	MANCHESTER	0725	LAS PALMAS	B.757	6
177/8	0810	MANCHESTER	1420	PALMA	A.320	7
179/0	1555	MANCHESTER	0240	LARNACA	B.757	1
181/2	0810	MANCHESTER	1415	PALMA	B.757	1
187/8	1450	MANCHESTER	2225	MALTA	B.757	2
189/0	1900	MANCHESTER	0430	DALAMAN	B.757	2
191/2	1355	MANCHESTER	2130	MONASTIR	B.757	3
193/4	1435	MANCHESTER	2035	MAHON	B.757	4
195/6	0700	MANCHESTER	1320	MALAGA	B.757	4
197/8	2305	MANCHESTER	0430	GERONA	B.757	4
201/2	1400	MANCHESTER	2040	NAPLES	A.320	5
205/6	0745	MANCHESTER	2135	ALICANTE	A.320	6
207/8	2250	MANCHESTER	0825	KOS	A.320	6
209/0	0945	MANCHESTER	1730	MONASTIR	A.320	7
211/2	1535	MANCHESTER	2205	MALAGA	A.320	7
213/4	1345	MANCHESTER	2045	FARO	A.320	1
219/0	1900	MANCHESTER	0435	TENERIFE	A.320	2
221/2	1805	MANCHESTER	2350	RIMINI	A.320	2
223/4	1900	MANCHESTER	0440	BODRUM	A.320	3
225/6	2330	MANCHESTER	0540	PALMA	A.320	7
229/0	1555	MANCHESTER	0125	DALAMAN	B.757	7
233/4	0715	MANCHESTER	1650	HERAKLION	A.320	2
235/6	0800	MANCHESTER	1725	FUERTVENTURA	A.320	3
237/8	1900	MANCHESTER	0225	THESSALONIKI	A.320	3
239/0	1745	MANCHESTER	0330	KOS	A.320	4
241/2	1820	MANCHESTER	0030	PALMA	A.320	4
243/4	1455	MANCHESTER	1330	FARO	A.320	7
251/2	0730	MANCHESTER	1820	LARNACA	B.757	1
263/4	2210	MANCHESTER	0420	PALMA	A.320	5
265/6	1845	MANCHESTER	0035	PALMA	A.320	1
269/0	0700	MANCHESTER	1230	REUS	A.320	1
287/8	0800	MANCHESTER	1630	ZAKINTHOS	A.320	4
291/2	1955	MANCHESTER	0530	LAS PALMAS	A.320	1
293/4	0615	MANCHESTER	1220	IBIZA	B.757	5
359/0	2130	LEEDS	0345	PALMA	A.320	1
363/4	2100	LEEDS	0240	GERONA	A.320	4
365/6	1000	LEEDS	1935	LANZAROTE	A.320	4
367/8	1845	LEEDS	0425	BODRUM	A.320	3
369/0	0800	LEEDS	1720	FUERTVENTURA	A.320	3
371/2	0900	LEEDS	1955	LARNACA	A.320	1
373/4	0750	LEEDS	2140	ALICANTE	A.320	2
377/8	1955	LEEDS	1835	GERONA	A.320	2
379/0	1645	LEEDS	2320	FARO	A.320	7
381/2	0910	LEEDS	1530	MALAGA	A.320	7
383/4	2230	LEEDS	0800	LAS PALMAS	A.320	6
385/6	1445	LEEDS	2105	PALMA	A.320	6
387/8	0700	LEEDS	1335	ALICANTE`	A.320	6
389/0	2230	LEEDS	0525	LAS PALMAS	A.320	5
391/2	0625	LEEDS	2105	MAHON	A.320	5
393/4	1445	HUMBERSIDE	1305	MAHON	A.320	5
395/6	0035	LEEDS	0650	PALMA	A.320	1
397/8	1510	HUMBERSIDE	1405	ALICANTE	A.320	6
399/0	1905	HUMBERSIDE	1800	DALAMAN	B.757	5
401/2	0800	GATWICK	1715	LANZAROTE	B.767	5
403/4	1915	GATWICK	0530	TENERIFE	B.767	5
405/6	0655	GATWICK	1250	PALMA	B.767	6
407/8	1420	GATWICK	2010	PALMA	B.767	6
409/0	2210	GATWICK	0400	PALMA	B.767	6

Flight	Dep	From	Arr	To	Aircraft	Day
411/2	0700	GATWICK	1415	MONASTIR	B.767	7
413/4	1540	GATWICK	2205	MALAGA	B.767	7
415/6	2335	GATWICK	0525	IBIZA	B.767	7
417/8	0700	GATWICK	1200	REUS	B.757	1
419/0	1400	GATWICK	2315	LAS PALMAS	B.757	1
421/2	0810	GATWICK	1735	DALAMAN	B.767	2
423/4	1905	GATWICK	0445	TENERIFE	B.767	2
425/6	1030	GATWICK	1740	MONASTIR	B.767	3
427/8	1940	GATWICK	0515	RHODES	B.767	3
429/0	0715	GATWICK	1305	MAHON	B.767	4
431/2	1505	GATWICK	0045	LAS PALMAS	B.767	4
433/4	0700	GATWICK	1230	PALMA	B.757	5
435/6	1345	GATWICK	1930	IBIZA	B.757	5
437/8	2100	GATWICK	0600	HERAKLION	B.757	5
439/0	0710	GATWICK	1630	FUERTVENTURA	B.757	6
441/2	1755	GATWICK	0315	LAS PALMAS	B.757	6
443/4	0810	GATWICK	1830	PAPHOS	B.757	7
445/6	2000	GATWICK	0500	DALAMAN	B.757	7
447/8	0730	GATWICK	1755	LARNACA	B.767	1
449/0	1925	GATWICK	0450	BODRUM	B.767	1
451/2	0710	GATWICK	1440	KEFALLINIA	B.757	2
453/4	1615	GATWICK	0110	TENERIFE	B.757	2
455/6	0810	GATWICK	1535	ZAKINTHOS	B.757	3
457/8	1655	GATWICK	0200	FUERTVENTURA	B.757	3
459/0	0615	GATWICK	1515	LANZAROTE	B.757	4
461/2	1645	GATWICK	2130	GERONA	B.757	4
463/4	2300	GATWICK	0455	MALAGA	B.757	4
465/6	0600	GATWICK	2045	NAPLES	A.320	5
467/8	2230	GATWICK	0415	PALMA	A.320	5
469/0	0725	GATWICK	1920	MAHON	A.320	6
471/2	2135	GATWICK	0435	CORFU	A.320	6
473/4	0700	GATWICK	1210	VERONA	A.320	7
475/6	1325	GATWICK	1835	VENICE	A.320	7
477/8	2100	GATWICK	0245	PALMA	A.320	7
479/0	0700	GATWICK	1440	CORFU	A.320	1
481/2	1530	GATWICK	2130	FARO	A.320	1
483/4	2245	GATWICK	0455	PALMA	A.320	1
485/6	0640	GATWICK	1400	MALTA	A.320	2
487/8	155	GATWICK	2120	RIMINI	A.320	2
489/0	2245	GATWICK	0440	ALICANTE	A.320	2
491/2	0715	GATWICK	1620	BODRUM	A.320	3
493/4	1855	GATWICK	0320	THESSALONIKI	A.320	3
495/6	0700	GATWICK	1615	KOS	A.320	4
497/8	1730	GATWICK	0250	LAS PALMAS	A.320	4
501/2	0700	EAST MIDLANDS	1255	PALMA	A.320	5
503/4	1515	EAST MIDLANDS	2110	MAHON	A.320	5
505/6	2230	EAST MIDLANDS	0430	IBIZA	A.320	5
507/8	0630	EAST MIDLANDS	1225	PALMA	A.320	6
509/0	1340	EAST MIDLANDS	1955	ALICANTE	A.320	6
511/2	0850	EAST MIDLANDS	1935	LARNACA	A.320	1
513/4	2100	EAST MIDLANDS	0300	PALMA	A.320	1
515/6	1410	EAST MIDLANDS	2055	FARO	A.320	7
517/8	0700	EAST MIDLANDS	1255	IBIZA	A.320	7
519/0	2110	EAST MIDLANDS	0455	CORFU	A.320	6
521/2	2150	EAST MIDLANDS	0730	DALAMAN	A.320	7
523/4	0730	EAST MIDLANDS	1710	TENERIFE	A.320	2
525/6	1825	EAST MIDLANDS	0355	HERAKLION	A.320	2
527/8	0715	EAST MIDLANDS	1535	ZAKINTHOS	A.320	3
529/0	1700	EAST MIDLANDS	0235	BODRUM	A.320	3
531/2	0610	EAST MIDLANDS	1230	MALAGA	A.320	4
533/4	1850	EAST MIDLANDS	0220	LANZAROTE	A.320	4
535/6	0010	EAST MIDLANDS	0540	GERONA	A.320	5
537/8	1440	EAST MIDLANDS	1325	MAHON	A.320	6
539/0	1530	EAST MIDLANDS	1415	ALICANTE	A.320	2
541/2	1450	EAST MIDLANDS	1250	ALICANTE	B.757	6
545/6	2230	BIRMINGHAM	0430	PALMA	B.757	1
547/8	1855	EAST MIDLANDS	1725	PALMA	B.757	4
549/0	0800	BIRMINGHAM	0425	LAS PALMAS	B.757	4

Flight	Dep	From	Arr	To	Aircraft	Day	
551/2	1920	BIRMINGHAM	0500	BODRUM	B.757	3	
555/6	0900	BIRMINGHAM	1635	MALTA	B.757	2	
557/8	1640	BIRMINGHAM	0220	DALAMAN	B.757	2	
559/0	0810	BIRMINGHAM	1720	FUERTVENTURA	B.757	3	
561/2	0900	BIRMINGHAM	1620	MONASTIR	B.757		7
563/4	0900	BIRMINGHAM	1835	KOS	A.320		4
567/8	0730	BIRMINGHAM	2115	IBIZA	B.757	1	
569/0	1850	BIRMINGHAM	0420	TENERIFE	B.757		5
571/2	0835	BIRMINGHAM	1435	MAHON	B.767		6
573/4	1600	BIRMINGHAM	2205	PALMA	B.757		6
575/6	2215	BIRMINGHAM	0740	LAS PALMAS	B.757		6
579/0	1735	BIRMINGHAM	2340	MALAGA	B.757		7
583/4	0800	BIRMINGHAM	1315	REUS	B.757	1	
585/6	1430	BIRMINGHAM	2055	FARO	B.757	1	
587/8	2245	BIRMINGHAM	0515	CORFU	B.757	1	
589/0	0800	BIRMINGHAM	1400	ALICANTE	B.757	2	
591/2	1800	BIRMINGHAM	0325	TENERIFE	B.757	2	
593/4	0855	BIRMINGHAM	1705	ZAKINTHOS	B.757	3	
595/6	1830	BIRMINGHAM	0410	RHODES	B.757	3	
597/8	2005	BIRMINGHAM	0610	PALMA	B.757		4
599/0	0800	BIRMINGHAM	1720	LANZAROTE	B.757		5
631/2	1325	LUTON	2230	LANZAROTE	A.320		4
633/4	0700	LUTON	1210	GERONA	A.320		4
635/6	2345	LUTON	0600	PALMA	A.320		7
637/8	1530	LUTON	0055	FUERTVENTURA	A.320		3
639/0	0900	LUTON	0520	DALAMAN	A.320		2
643/4	2030	LUTON	0215	PALMA	A.320	1	
645/6	0850	LUTON	1910	LARNACA	A.320	1	
647/8	0600	LUTON	1145	IBIZA	A.320		5
649/0	0700	LUTON	1415	MONASTIR	A.320		3
651/2	0745	LUTON	2230	MALAGA	A.320		7
653/4	2100	LUTON	0630	LAS PALMAS	A.320		6
655/6	0725	LUTON	1935	PALMA	A.320		6
657/8	1410	BOURNEMOUTH	1255	PALMA	A.320		6
659/0	2030	LUTON	0600	TENERIFE	A.320		5
661/2	1330	LUTON	1915	MAHON	A.320		5
663/4	1350	MANCHESTER	1235	NAPLES	A.320		5
665/6	1625	STANSTED	0155	LANZAROTE	A.320		4
667/8	0720	STANSTED	1515	ZAKINTHOS	A.320		4
669/0	1735	STANSTED	0240	RHODES	A.320		3
671/2	0700	STANSTED	1620	FUERTVENTURA	A.320		3
673/4	1600	STANSTED	0115	HERAKLION	A.320	2	
675/6	0700	STANSTED	1430	MALTA	A.320	2	
677/8	2255	STANSTED	0820	DALAMAN	A.320		7
679/0	1705	STANSTED	2215	REUS	A.320	1	
681/2	0955	STANSTED	1450	PALMA	A.320	1	
683/4	2330	STANSTED	0510	PALMA	A.320	1	
685/6	1445	STANSTED	2110	MALAGA	A.320		7
687/8	0655	STANSTED	1330	FARO	A.320		7
689/0	1930	STANSTED	0505	LAS PALMAS	A.320		6
691/2	1230	STANSTED	1805	MAHON	A.320		6
693/4	0600	STANSTED	1135	PALMA	A.320		6
695/6	1930	STANSTED	0345	TENERIFE	A.320		5
697/8	1245	STANSTED	1815	MAHON	A.320		5
699/0	0600	STANSTED	1145	IBIZA	A.320		5
701/2	0620	BRISTOL	1155	MAHON	A.320		5
703/4	2245	BRISTOL	0425	PALMA`	A.320		7
705/6	1700	BRISTOL	2210	REUS	A.320	1	
707/8	1425	BRISTOL	2015	ALICANTE	A.320		6
709/0	0800	BRISTOL	1325	PALMA	A.320		6
711/2	1315	BRISTOL	1900	IBIZA	A.320		5
713/4	1520	BRISTOL	2125	FARO	A.320		7
715/6	0800	BRISTOL	1405	MALAGA	A.320		7
717/8	0815	BRISTOL	1600	CORFU	A.320	1	
719/0	1855	BRISTOL	0420	HERAKLION	A.320	2	
721/2	2145	BRISTOL	0640	LAS PALMAS	A.320		6
723/4	0800	BRISTOL	1730	DALAMAN	A.320	2	
725/6	0700	BRISTOL	0540	LARNACA	A.320	3	

598 RET. 0610 1

Flight	Dep	Origin	Arr	Dest	Aircraft	Day
727/8	1750	BRISTOL	2330	PALMA	A.320	4
729/0	0800	BRISTOL	1620	ZAKINTHOS	A.320	4
731/2	2100	BRISTOL	0610	TENERIFE	A.320	5
751/2	0830	CARDIFF	1415	IBIZA	A.320	5
753/4	1840	CARDIFF	1725	MAHON	A.320	5
755/6	1600	CARDIFF	0525	PALMA	A.320	5
757/8	0710	CARDIFF	1245	ALICANTE	A.320	6
759/0	1350	CARDIFF	1925	PALMA	A.320	6
761/2	2040	CARDIFF	0615	KOS	A.320	6
763/4	2225	CARDIFF	0405	PALMA	A.320	7
765/6	1455	CARDIFF	2105	MALAGA	A.320	7
767/8	1345	CARDIFF	1930	IBIZA	A.320	1
769/0	0730	CARDIFF	1230	REUS	A.320	1
771/2	0735	CARDIFF	1340	FARO	A.320	7
773/4	2110	CARDIFF	0445	CORFU	A.320	1
775/6	0730	CARDIFF	1655	HERAKLION	A.320	2
777/8	1810	CARDIFF	0345	DALAMAN	A.320	2
779/0	0800	CARDIFF	1730	RHODES	A.320	3
781/2	1910	CARDIFF	0445	BODRUM	A.320	3
783/4	0600	CARDIFF	1410	ZAKINTHOS	A.320	4
785/6	1620	CARDIFF	0110	LANZAROTE	A.320	4
799/0	1845	CARDIFF	1740	LARNACA	A.320	3
801/2	0735	TEESSIDE	1405	ALICANTE	A.320	6
805/6	1855	NEWCASTLE	0135	PALMA	A.320	7
807/8	1545	NEWCASTLE	0125	DALAMAN	A.320	2
809/0	1845	NEWCASTLE	0050	GERONA	A.320	4
811/2	0600	NEWCASTLE	1230	MAHON	A.320	5
813/4	1330	TEESSIDE	1950	MAHON	A.320	5
817/8	0730	NEWCASTLE	1355	PALMA	A.320	6
819/0	1505	NEWCASTLE	2140	ALICANTE	A.320	6
821/2	2255	NEWCASTLE	0840	LAS PALMAS	A.320	6
823/4	2255	TEESSIDE	0525	PALMA	A.320	7
825/6	2105	TEESSIDE	0630	TENERIFE	A.320	5
827/8	1520	TEESSIDE	2145	PALMA	A.320	6
829/0	2255	TEESSIDE	0525	PALMA	A.320	6
831/2	0700	TEESSIDE	2140	FARO	A.320	7
837/8	2230	NEWCASTLE	0455	PALMA	A.320	3
841/2	0800	NEWCASTLE	1730	KOS	A.320	4
843/4	0645	TEESSIDE	1935	REUS	A.320	1
845/6	1355	NEWCASTLE	1240	REUS	A.320	1
847/8	0600	TEESSIDE	1240	IBIZA	A.320	5
849/0	2100	NEWCASTLE	0630	TENERIFE	A.320	5
851/2	2055	TEESSIDE	0640	LAS PALMAS	A.320	1
853/4	0700	TEESSIDE	1630	BODRUM	A.320	3
855/6	1730	NEWCASTLE	0310	BODRUM	A.320	1
857/8	0700	TEESSIDE	2140	MALAGA	A.320	4
861/2	1745	TEESSIDE	0325	RHODES	A.320	3
865/6	0800	NEWCASTLE	1615	CORFU	A.320	1
867/8	0935	NEWCASTLE	2040	LARNACA	A.320	3
877/8	0900	TEESSIDE	0540	TENERIFE	A.320	2
879/0	1030	NEWCASTLE	1735	MALAGA	A.320	7
881/2	1355	NEWCASTLE	2000	IBIZA	A.320	5
883/4	0730	NEWCASTLE	1420	ALICANTE	A.320	2
899/0	1530	NEWCASTLE	1425	FARO	B.757	7
901/2	0810	BELFAST INTL.	1800	TENERIFE	A.320	5
903/4	1810	BELFAST INTL.	0535	LARNACA	A.320	3
905/6	2245	BELFAST INTL.	0530	GERONA	A.320	6
907/8	0900	GLASGOW	1605	ALICANTE	B.757	2
909/0	1930	BELFAST INTL.	0215	PALMA	A.320	5
911/2	0705	BELFAST INTL.	1340	PALMA	A.320	6
913/4	1515	BELFAST INTL.	2150	ALICANTE	A.320	6
917/8	0730	BELFAST INTL.	1435	MALAGA	A.320	7
919/0	1545	BELFAST INTL.	2245	FARO	A.320	7
921/2	0805	BELFAST INTL.	1450	IBIZA	A.320	1
923/4	0005	BELFAST INTL.	0640	PALMA	A.320	1
925/6	1630	BELFAST INTL.	0240	BODRUM	A..320	1
929/0	0730	BELFAST INTL.	1740	DALAMAN	A.320	2
931/2	1855	BELFAST INTL.	0500	HERAKLION	A.320	2

933/4	0700	BELFAST INTL.	1650	FUERTVENTURA	A.320	3	
937/8	0755	BELFAST INTL.	1730	LANZAROTE	A.320	4	
939/0	1845	BELFAST INTL.	0100	GERONA	A.320	4	
951/2	2200	GLASGOW	0400	GERONA	B.757	4	
953/4	1055	GLASGOW	2040	LANZAROTE	B.757	4	
955/6	0910	GLASGOW	2040	LARNACA	B.757	1	
957/8	1855	GLASGOW	0540	DALAMAN	B.757	2	
959/0	0920	GLASGOW	1750	MALTA	B.757	2	
961/2	2155	GLASGOW	0740	LAS PALMAS	B.757	1	
963/4	0800	GLASGOW	2120	REUS	B.757	3	
965/6	2340	GLASGOW	0605	PALMA	B.757	7	
967/8	0700	GLASGOW	2255	MALAGA	B.757	7	
969/0	1525	ABERDEEN	1425	MALAGA	B.757	7	
971/2	1845	GLASGOW	0435	LAS PALMAS	B.757	6	
973/4	0955	GLASGOW	1705	ALICANTE	B.757	6	
975/6	2235	GLASGOW	0825	TENERIFE	B.757	5	
977/8	0620	GLASGOW	2140	PALMA	B.757	5	
979/0	1445	ABERDEEN	1320	PALMA	B.757	5	
981/2	0010	GLASGOW	0210	PALMA	B.757	1	982 RET. 0210 5
985/6	0725	GLASGOW	2225	FARO	B.757	7	
987/8	2245	GLASGOW	0510	PALMA	B.757	6	
989/0	1450	PRESTWICK	1335	PALMA	B.757	6	
991/2	0700	GLASGOW	2120	PALMA	B.757	6	
993/4	2255	GLASGOW	0535	PALMA	B.757	5	
995/6	0645	GLASGOW	2130	MAHON	B.757	5	
997/8	1450	EDINBURGH	1330	MAHON	B.757	5	
3122/3	1525	PRESTWICK	1355	REUS	B.757	3	
3299/0	1530	PRESTWICK	1415	IBIZA	B.757	1	
3375/6	1500	PRESTWICK	1350	MALAGA	A.320	4	
3641/2	1955	PRESTWICK	1830	DALAMAN	A.320	2	
5001/2	1540	GLASGOW	1425	MALAGA	A.320	7	
	0715	MANCHESTER	1810	LARNACA	A.320	1	
5003/4	0635	MANCHESTER	1140	THESSALONIKI	A.320	5	
5567/8	0700	BIRMINGHAM	2045	PALMA	B.757	6	
5569/0	2345	BIRMINGHAM	0545	PALMA	B.767	6	

KILRO   *AIR KILROE LTD.,   AKL   UK*

501	0800	MANCHESTER		TEESSIDE	J'STREAM 31	12345
502		TEESSIDE	0930	MANCHESTER	J'STREAM 31	12345
505	1715	MANCHESTER		TEESSIDE	J'STREAM 31	12345
506		TEESSIDE	1845	MANCHESTER	J'STREAM 31	12345

KLM   *K.L.M. ROYAL DUTCH A/LINES   KL/KLM   NETHERLANDS*

FLIGHTS TO/FROM BRISTOL, CARDIFF, CORK & ROTTERDAM ARE OPERATED BY K.L.M. CITY HOPPER -CALL SIGN 'CITY'

601	1040	AMSTERDAM		LOS ANGELES	B.747	1234567	
602		LOS ANGELES	1035	AMSTERDAM	B.747	1234567	
603	1340	AMSTERDAM		LOS ANGELES	B.737	23 6	26.06-28.08
604		LOS ANGELES	1315	AMSTERDAM	B.747	34 7	26.06-28.08
605	1050	AMSTERDAM		SAN FRANCISCO	MD-11	1234567	
606		SAN FRANCISCO	1035	AMSTERDAM	MD-11	1234567	
611	1310	AMSTERDAM		CHICAGO	B.747	1234567	
612		CHICAGO	0740	AMSTERDAM	B.747	1234567	
617	1315	AMSTERDAM		DETROIT	B.747	1234567	
618		DETROIT	0735	AMSTERDAM	B.747	1234567	
621	1000	AMSTERDAM		ATLANTA	B.767	1234567	
622		ATLANTA	0650	AMSTERDAM	B.767	1234567	
625	1500	AMSTERDAM		MEMPHIS	MD-11	1234567	
626		MEMPHIS	1110	AMSTERDAM	MD-11	1234567	
641	1300	AMSTERDAM		NEW YORK	B.747	1234567	
642		NEW YORK	0555	AMSTERDAM	B.747	1234567	
642		NEW YORK	0640	AMSTERDAM	B.747	1234567	
643	1820	AMSTERDAM		NEW YORK	B.747	1234567	
644		NEW YORK	1115	AMSTERDAM	B.747	1234567	
661	0945	AMSTERDAM		HOUSTON	B.747	1234567	
662		HOUSTON	0655	AMSTERDAM	B.747	1234567	
664		MINNEAPOLIS	0510	AMSTERDAM	B.747	1234567	

665	1015	AMSTERDAM		MINNEAPOLIS	B.747	1234567	
671	1510	AMSTERDAM		MONTREAL	B747/MD11	1234567	
672		MONTREAL	0700	AMSTERDAM	B747/MD11	1234567	
678		MEXICO	1605	AMSTERDAM	B.747	123 67	
681	1515	AMSTERDAM		VANCOUVER	MD-11	1234567	
682		VANCOUVER	1235	AMSTERDAM	MD-11	1234567	
687	1000	AMSTERDAM		MEXICO	B.747	12 567	
688		MEXICO	1605	AMSTERDAM	B.747	123 67	
691	1255	AMSTERDAM		TORONTO	B.747	1234567	
692		TORONTO	0555	AMSTERDAM	B.747	1234567	
713	1235	AMSTERDAM		PARAMARIBO	B.747	12345 7	
714		PARAMARIBO	0955	AMSTERDAM	B.747	123456	
741	0925	AMSTERDAM		ARUBA	MD-11	1 34 7	
742		ARUBA	1610	AMSTERDAM	MD-11	12 456	
743	2240	AMSTERDAM		CARACAS	MD-11	6	
744		CURACAO	0505	AMSTERDAM	MD-11	1	
749	2245	AMSTERDAM		ARUBA	MD-11	2	
750		CURACAO	0500	AMSTERDAM	MD-11	4	
753	2245	AMSTERDAM		CURACAO	MD-11	1 5 7	
754		CURACAO	0505	AMSTERDAM	MD-11	23 7	
775	0945	AMSTERDAM		CARACAS	MD-11	1 34567	
776		CARACAS	0650	AMSTERDAM	MD-11	12 4567	
781	1205	AMSTERDAM		ARUBA	B.747	5	
		CURACAO	1000	AMSTERDAM	MD-11	1 4 6	
783	1205	AMSTERDAM		ARUBA	MD-11	2 4 6	DEP 1005 4
		ARUBA	0800	AMSTERDAM	MD-11	3 5 7	ARR 1000 3 7
785	1205	AMSTERDAM		ST.MAARTEN	B.747	1 4	
		ST.MAARTEN	1015	AMSTERDAM	B.747	2 5	
789		CURACAO	1000	AMSTERDAM	B.747	1	
861	1325	AMSTERDAM		TOKYO	B.747	1 345 7	
862		TOKYO	1410	AMSTERDAM	B.747	12 456	
867	1335	AMSTERDAM		OSAKA	B.747	1234567	
868		OSAKA	1415	AMSTERDAM	B.747	1234567	
869	1130	AMSTERDAM		SAPPORO	B.747	2 6	
879		SAPPORO	1645	AMSTERDAM	B.747	3 7	
1000	0650	HEATHROW	0805	AMSTERDAM	B.737	1234567	
1001	0625	AMSTERDAM	0740	HEATHROW	B.767	1234567	
1002	0835	HEATHROW	0940	AMSTERDAM	B.767	1234567	
1007	0745	AMSTERDAM	0900	HEATHROW	B.767	1234567	
1008	0955	HEATHROW	1110	AMSTERDAM	B.767	1234567	
1009	0930	AMSTERDAM	1045	HEATHROW	B.737	12345 7	
1010	1135	HEATHROW	1250	AMSTERDAM	B.737	12345 7	
1014	1300	HEATHROW	1415	AMSTERDAM	B.737	6	
1017	1215	AMSTERDAM	1330	HEATHROW	B.767	1234567	
1018	1420	HEATHROW	1535	AMSTERDAM	B.767	1234567	
1019	1300	AMSTERDAM	1415	HEATHROW	B.737	12345	
1020	1505	HEATHROW	1620	AMSTERDAM	B.737	12345	
1021	1500	AMSTERDAM	1615	HEATHROW	B.737	1234567	
1022	1705	HEATHROW	1820	AMSTERDAM	B.737	1234567	
1023	1600	AMSTERDAM	1715	HEATHROW	B.737	1234567	
1024	1805	HEATHROW	1920	AMSTERDAM	B.737	1234567	
1027	1805	AMSTERDAM	1920	HEATHROW	B.737	1234567	
1028	2020	HEATHROW	2135	AMSTERDAM	B.737	1234567	
1033	1855	AMSTERDAM	2010	HEATHROW	B.737	1234567	
1046	0630	BRISTOL	0805	AMSTERDAM	F50	1234567	
1047	0715	AMSTERDAM	0855	BRISTOL	F50	12345	
1048	0945	BRISTOL	1120	AMSTERDAM	F50	12345	
1049	0915	AMSTERDAM	1055	BRISTOL	F50	1234567	
1050	1135	BRISTOL	1310	AMSTERDAM	F50	1234567	
1053	1510	AMSTERDAM	1645	BRISTOL	F70	1234567	
1054	1720	BRISTOL	1850	AMSTERDAM	F-70	1234567	
1057	1820	AMSTERDAM	2000	BRISTOL	F50	1234567	
1058	0615	CARDIFF	0755	AMSTERDAM	F50	1234567	
1059	0745	AMSTERDAM	0930	CARDIFF	F50	1234567	
1060	1000	CARDIFF	1140	AMSTERDAM	F50	1234567	
1061	0915	AMSTERDAM	1100	CARDIFF	F50	12345 7	
1062	1150	CARDIFF	1330	AMSTERDAM	F50	12345 7	
1063	1505	AMSTERDAM	1650	CARDIFF	F-50	1234567	

1064	1720	CARDIFF	1900	AMSTERDAM	F-50	1234567	
1069	1800	AMSTERDAM	1945	CARDIFF	F50	1234567	
1331	0610	ROTTERDAM	0715	HEATHROW	F-50	123456	
1332	0750	HEATHROW	0850	ROTTERDAM	F-50	123456	
1333	1100	ROTTERDAM	1205	HEATHROW	F-50	12345 7	
1334	1300	HEATHROW	1400	ROTTERDAM	F-50	12345 7	
1337	1550	ROTTERDAM	1655	HEATHROW	F-50	12345	
1338	1735	HEATHROW	1835	ROTTERDAM	F-50	12345	
1339	1920	ROTTERDAM	2025	HEATHROW	F-50	1234567	
1340	2100	HEATHROW	2200	ROTTERDAM	F-50	1234567	
9101	1130	AMSTERDAM		NEW YORK	B.747	1 3	DEP 2100 3
9102		NEW YORK	0535	AMSTERDAM	B.747	2 4	ARR 1505 4
9107	1045	AMSTERDAM		CHICAGO	B.747	2	
9108		CHICAGO	0645	AMSTERDAM	B.747	2	
9111	1300	AMSTERDAM		CHICAGO	B.747	6	
9112		CHICAGO	2040	AMSTERDAM	B.747	7	
9195	1915	AMSTERDAM		ANCHORAGE	B.747	2 4	
9196		ANCHORAGE	0840	AMSTERDAM	B.747	3 5	

KOREANAIR   *KOREAN AIRLINES CO. LTD.   KE/KAL   KOREA*

507		TASHKENT	1520	HEATHROW	B.747	1	
508	2140	HEATHROW		TASHKENT	B.747	1	
907		SEOUL	1655	HEATHROW	B.747	1 3 567	
908	2200	HEATHROW		SEOUL	B.747	1 3 567	

KUWAITI   *KUWAIT AIRWAYS CORP.   KU/KAC   KUWAIT*

101		KUWAIT	1400	HEATHROW	B.777	2 4 6	
	1600	HEATHROW		NEW YORK	B.777	2 4 6	DEP 1515 4
102		NEW YORK	1000	HEATHROW	B.777	3 5 7	
	1130	HEATHROW		KUWAIT	B.777	3 5 7	
103		KUWAIT	1700	HEATHROW	B.777	1 3 5 7	
104	1035	HEATHROW		KUWAIT	B.777	12 4 6	
105		KUWAIT	0640	HEATHROW	B.777	1 4	24.06-09.09
106	2140	HEATHROW		KUWAIT	B.777	3	23.06-09.09
107		KUWAIT	1430	HEATHROW	A.310	6	26.06-11.09
108	1815	HEATHROW		KUWAIT	A.310	6	26.06-11.09
115	1440	AMSTERDAM		CHICAGO	A.340	1 4	
116		CHICAGO	1045	AMSTERDAM	A.340	2 5	
175	1425	FRANKFURT		NEW YORK	A.340	7	
176		NEW YORK	0930	FRANKFURT	A.340	1	
2103		KUWAIT	1650	HEATHROW	DC-8	4	
2104	2115	HEATHROW		KUWAIT	DC-8	4	
2105		KUWAIT	0800	HEATHROW	DC-8	7	
2106	1005	HEATHROW		KUWAIT	DC-8	7	

LAUDA AIR   *LAUDA AIR   NG/LDA   AUSTRIA*

106	0915	GATWICK	1130	VIENNA	B.737	2 5	
107	0605	VIENNA	0825	GATWICK	B.737	2 5	
108	1755	GATWICK	2015	VIENNA	B.737	5 7	1920/2135 7
109	1435	VIENNA	1655	GATWICK	B.737	5 7	1605/1830 7
4961		VIENNA	0930	SHANNON	B.737	3	-01.09
4962	1020	SHANNON		VIENNA	B.737	3	-01.09
4967		VIENNA	1700	SHANNON	B.737	3	-30.06
4968	1750	SHANNON		VIENNA	B.737	3	-30.06
9220	1040	MUNICH		MIAMI	B.767	2 4567	
9221		MIAMI	0900	MUNICH	B.767	1 3 567	
9226	0605	VIENNA	0835	MANCHESTER	CANADAIR	12345	
9227	0915	MANCHESTER	1140	VIENNA	CANADAIR	12345	
9228	1605	VIENNA	1835	MANCHESTER	CANADAIR	12345 7	
9229	1905	MANCHESTER	2135	VIENNA	CANADAIR	12345 7	
9290	0840	SALZBURG	1030	GATWICK	CANADAIR	2 4 67	
9291	1100	GATWICK	1255	SALZBURG	CANADAIR	2 4 67	
9292	1300	SALZBURG	1455	GATWICK	CANADAIR	1234567	
9293	1530	GATWICK	1725	SALZBURG	CANADAIR	1234567	

LITHUANIA AIR *LITHUANIAN AIRLINES   TE/LIL   LITHUANIA*

452		VILNIUS	1515	HEATHROW	B.737	1234567
453	1615	HEATHROW		VILNIUS	B.737	1234567

LOGAN *LOGANAIR LTD.   LC/LOG   U.K.*

A BRITISH AIRWAYS FRANCHISEE. SCHEDULED SERVICES OPERATE IN THE RANGE BA8840 -BA8899
ATC CALLSIGNS DROP THE FIRST 8, E.G. BA8841 USES CALL SIGN 'LOGAN 841'

664	0650	GLASGOW		BENBECULA	SH-360	123456	
665		STORNOWAY	1815	GLASGOW	SH-360	123456	ARR 1615 6
8841	0720	GLASGOW	0755	CAMBELTOWN	DHC-6	12345	
8842	0815	CAMBELTOWN	0850	GLASGOW	DHC-6	12345	
8843	0920	GLASGOW	0955	CAMBELTOWN	DHC-6	12345	
8844	1015	CAMBELTOWN	1050	GLASGOW	DHC-6	12345	
8847	1545	GLASGOW	1620	CAMPBELTOWN	DHC-6	12345	
8848	1640	CAMPBELTOWN	1715	GLASGOW	DHC-6	12345	
8851	0910	GLASGOW	1015	BARRA	DHC-6	12345	
8852	1155	BARRA	1300	GLASGOW	DHC-6	12345	
8853	1115	GLASGOW	1200	TIREE	DHC-6	12345	FORTNIGHTLY
	1330	GLASGOW	1415	TIREE	DHC-6	123456	FORTNIGHTLY
8854	1215	TIREE	1300	GLASGOW	DHC-6	12345	FORTNIGHTLY
	1430	TIREE	1515	GLASGOW	DHC-6	123456	FORTNIGHTLY
8855	1330	GLASGOW	1435	TIREE	DHC-6	12345	
8860	0845	LERWICK	0910	FAIR ISLE	BN.ISLAN	12 4	1140/1205 2 4
8861	0920	FAIR ISLE	0945	LERWICK	BN.ISLAN	1 3 5	1015/1040 3
8862	1430	SUMBURGH	1445	FAIR ISLE	BN.ISLAN.	2 4 6	
8863	1115	FAIR ISLE	1130	SUMBURGH	BN.ISLAN.	2 4 6	
8868	1515	LERWICK	1540	FAIR ISLE	BN.ISLAN	3 5	1705/1730 1
8864	1215	LERWICK	1240	SUMBURGH	BN.ISLAN	1 3 5	05.07-
8865	1340	SUMBURGH	1415	UNST	BN.ISLAN.	12345	-02.07
	1255	SUMBURGH	1330	UNST	BN.ISLAN.	12345	05.07-
8866	1235	UNST	1310	SUMBURGH	BN.ISLAN	12345	-02.07
	1340	UNST	1415	SUMBURGH	BN.ISLAN	12345	05.07-
8867	1430	SUMBURGH	1455	LERWICK	BN.ISLAN.	1 3 5	
8869	1500	FAIR ISLE	1525	LERWICK	BN.ISLAN.	2 45	1540/1605 5
	1605	FAIR ISLE	1630	LERWICK	BN.ISLAN.	1 3	1740/1805 1
8890	0735	KIRKWALL	0825	INVERNESS	SH6/SF3	123456	0845/0920 6
8892	0935	KIRKWALL	1055	EDINBURGH	SH-360	6	
8894	1150	SUMBURGH	1310	EDINBURGH	SAAB-340	12345	30.08-
8895	1050	EDINBURGH	1145	WICK	SH6/SF3	123456	
8896	1245	WICK	1340	EDINBURGH	SH6/SF3	123456	
8897	1350	EDINBURGH	1510	SUMBURGH	SAAB-340	12345	30.08-
	1450	EDINBURGH	1535	INVERNESS	SAAB-340	6	
	1555	INVERNESS	1635	KIRKWALL	SH-360	6	14.08-
8899	1625	EDINBURGH	1720	INVERNESS	SH-360	12345	
	1740	INVERNESS	1835	KIRKWALL	SH-360	12345	
8890	0845	INVERNESS	0925	EDINBURGH	SAAB-340	12345	
8895	1200	WICK	1240	SUMBURGH	SAAB-340	123456	
8896	1430	SUMBURGH	1510	WICK	SAAB-340	123456	1150/1230 6
8901	0950	STORNOWAY	1025	BENBECULA	SH-360	12345	
8902	1105	BENBECULA	1140	STORNOWAY	SH-360	12345	
8907	1440	STORNOWAY	1515	BENBECULA	SH-360	12345	
8908	1530	BENBECULA	1605	STORNOWAY	SH-360	12345	
8910	0705	INVERNESS	0800	GLASGOW	SH-360	12345	
8911	0835	GLASGOW	0920	INVERNESS	SAAB-340	123456	
	0940	INVERNESS	1020	KIRKWALL	SAAB-340	123456	
8911	1045	KIRKWALL	1120	SUMBURGH	SAAB-340	123456	
8912	1310	SUMBURGH	1345	KIRKWALL	SAAB-340	1 3 5	
8913	0920	GLASGOW	1040	KIRKWALL	SH-360	6	-26.06
8914	1525	KIRKWALL	1645	GLASGOW	SH-360	6	-26.06
8915	1415	GLASGOW	1510	INVERNESS	SH-360	2345	
8916	1540	INVERNESS	1635	GLASGOW	SH-360	2345	
8917	1410	KIRKWALL	1445	SUMBURGH	SAAB-340	1 3 5	
8918	1540	SUMBURGH	1620	KIRKWALL	SH6/SF3	123456	1330/1405 6
8918	1630	KIRKWALL	1720	INVERNESS	SH6/SF3	12345	
	1740	INVERNESS	1835	GLASGOW	SH-360	123456	1530/1610 6
8919	1915	GLASGOW	2010	INVERNESS	SH-360	12345 7	
8920	2040	INVERNESS	2135	GLASGOW	SH-360	5	
8921	0910	GLASGOW	0950	ISLAY	SH-360	123456	1010/1050 6

8922	1010	ISLAY	1050	GLASGOW	SH-360	123456	1110/1150 6
8927	1710	GLASGOW	1750	ISLAY	SH-360	12345	
8928	1810	ISLAY	1850	GLASGOW	SH-360	12345	
8935	1115	GLASGOW	1210	LONDONDERRY	SH-360	123456	1215/1310 6
8936	1240	LONDONDERRY	1335	GLASGOW	SH-360	123456	1340/1435 6
8937	1515	GLASGOW	1610	LONDONDERRY	SH-360	67	1615/1710 7
8938	1640	LONDONDERRY	1735	GLASGOW	SH-360	67	1740/1835 7
8939	1915	GLASGOW	2010	LONDONDERRY	SH-360	567	04.07-22.08
8940	2040	LONDONDERRY	2135	GLASGOW	SH-360	567	04.07-22.08
8957	1305	EDINBURGH	1400	INVERNESS	SAAB-340	12345	
8958	1430	INVERNESS	1525	EDINBURGH	SAAB-340	12345	

LTU   *LTU LUFTTRANS. UNTER. GMBH   LT/LTU GERMANY*

400	0810	DUSSELDORF		MONTEGO BAY	B.767	1	
401		MONTEGO BAY	0600	DUSSELDORF	B.767	2	
416	0830	DUSSELDORF		CANCUN	B.767	2	
417		CANCUN	0715	DUSSELDORF	B.767	3	
430	0550	MUNICH		VARADERO	B.767	1	
431		VARADERO	0405	MUNICH	B.767	1	
432	0810	DUSSELDORF		VARADERO	B.767	2	
433		VARADERO	0620	DUSSELDORF	B.767	2	
434	0940	DUSSELDORF		HOLGUIN	B.767	4	
435		HOLGUIN	0715	DUSSELDORF	B.767	5	
440	1055	DUSSELDORF		PUERTO PLATA	B.767	34	DEP 0925 4
441		PUERTO PLATA	0925	DUSSELDORF	B.767	34	ARR 0725 4
446	0815	DUSSELDORF		PUNTA CANA	B.767	2 4 6	DEP 0705 6
447		PUNTA CANA	0655	DUSSELDORF	B.767	2 4 6	ARR 0505 6
474	0900	DUSSELDORF		ISLA MARGARITA	B.767	3	
475		ISLA MARGARITA	0555	DUSSELDORF	B.767	4	
516	0630	FRANKFURT		CANCUN	B.767	5	
517		CANCUN	0550	FRANKFURT	B.767	6	
532	0540	FRANKFURT		VARADERO	B.767	7	
533		VARADERO	0720	FRANKFURT	B.767	7	
540	0815	MUNICH		PUNTA PLATO	B.767	5	
541		PUNTA PLATO	0615	MUNICH	B.767	5	
542	0955	MUNICH		PUNTA CANA	B.767	1	
543		PUNTA CANA	0745	MUNICH	B.767	1	
564	0905	FRANKFURT		PUNTA CANA	B.767	5	
565		PUNTA CANA	0600	FRANKFURT	B.767	6	
566	0735	FRANKFURT		PUERTO PLATA	B.767	3	
567		PUERTO PLATA	0540	FRANKFURT	B.767	3	
900	0930	DUSSELDORF		MIAMI	B.767	3 56	
901		MIAMI	0630	DUSSELDORF	B.767	4 67	
908	0935	DUSSELDORF		FORT MYERS	B.767	4 6	
909		FORT MYERS	0700	DUSSELDORF	B.767	5 7	
910	0915	DUSSELDORF		ORLANDO	B.767	5 7	
911		ORLANDO	0605	DUSSELDORF	B.767	1 6	
918	0715	MUNICH		CANCUN	B.767	3	
918		CANCUN	0705	MUNICH	B.767	4	
1020		PUERTO PLATA	0630	ZURICH	B.767	7	
1021		PUERTO PLATA	0630	ZURICH	B.767	7	
1436	0820	BERLIN		VARADERO	B.767	1	
1437		VARADERO	0655	BERLIN	B.767	1	
1530	0815	DUSSELDORF		LOS ANGELES	B.767	1 4	
1531		LOS ANGELES	0900	DUSSELDORF	B.767	2 5	
3432	0820	HANOVER		VARADERO	B.767	1	

LUFTHANSA   *LUFTHANSA   LH/DLH   GERMANY*

400	0900	FRANKFURT		NEW YORK	B.747	1234567
401		NEW YORK	0500	FRANKFURT	B.747	1234567
402	1230	FRANKFURT		NEW YORK	B.747	1234567
403		NEW YORK	0630	FRANKFURT	B.747	1234567
404	1620	FRANKFURT		NEW YORK	B.747	1234567
405		NEW YORK	0940	FRANKFURT	B.747	1234567
408	0920	DUSSELDORF		NEW YORK	A.340	1234567
409		NEW YORK	0525	DUSSELDORF	A.340	1234567

410	1030	MUNICH		NEW YORK	A.340	1234567	
411		NEW YORK	0510	MUNICH	A.340	1234567	
418	1220	FRANKFURT		WASHINGTON	B.747	1234567	
419		WASHINGTON	0630	FRANKFURT	B.747	1234567	
420	1640	FRANKFURT		BOSTON	A.340	1234567	
421		BOSTON	0940	FRANKFURT	A.340	1234567	
422	0950	FRANKFURT		BOSTON	B.747	1234567	
423		BOSTON	0510	FRANKFURT	B.747	1234567	
427		PHILADELPHIA	0705	FRANKFURT	A.340	1234567	
431		CHICAGO	0700	FRANKFURT	B.747	1234567	
432	1630	FRANKFURT		CHICAGO	A.340	1234567	
433		CHICAGO	1250	FRANKFURT	A.340	1234567	
434	1030	MUNICH		CHICAGO	A.340	1234567	
435		CHICAGO	0800	MUNICH	A.340	1234567	
440	0920	FRANKFURT		HOUSTON	A.340	1234567	
441		HOUSTON	0815	FRANKFURT	A.340	1234567	
444	0935	FRANKFURT		ATLANTA	A.340	1234567	
445		ATLANTA	0610	FRANKFURT	A.340	1234567	
450	0950	FRANKFURT		LOS ANGELES	B.747	1234567	
451		LOS ANGELES	1005	FRANKFURT	B.747	1234567	
452	1300	FRANKFURT		LOS ANGELES	A.747	1234567	
453		LOS ANGELES	1620	FRANKFURT	A.747	1234567	
454	0940	FRANKFURT		SAN FRANCISCO	B.747	1234567	
455		SAN FRANCISCO	1105	FRANKFURT	B.747	1234567	
458	1140	MUNICH		SAN FRANCISCO	B.747	1234567	
459		SAN FRANCISCO	0825	MUNICH	B.747	1234567	
462	0920	FRANKFURT		MIAMI	B.747	1234567	
463		MIAMI	0550	FRANKFURT	B.747	1234567	
474	1600	FRANKFURT		TORONTO	B.747	1234567	
475		TORONTO	0940	FRANKFURT	B.747	1234567	
492	1220	FRANKFURT		VANCOUVER	B.747	34567	
493		VANCOUVER	0935	FRANKFURT	B.747	1 4567	
498	1220	FRANKFURT		MEXICO CITY	B.747	1234567	
499		MEXICO CITY	1325	FRANKFURT	B.747	1234567	
531		BOGOTA	1720	FRANKFURT	B.747	3 5 7	
535		CARACAS	0950	FRANKFURT	A.340	1 4 6	
710	1250	FRANKFURT		TOKYO	B.747	1234567	
711		TOKYO	1350	FRANKFURT	B.747	1234567	
714	1610	FRANKFURT		TOKYO	B.747	2 5 7	
715		TOKYO	1750	FRANKFURT	B.747	1 3 6	
736	1255	FRANKFURT		NAGOYA	A.340	4 6	
737		NAGOYA	1430	FRANKFURT	A.340	5 7	
740	1215	FRANKFURT		OSAKA	B.747	1234567	
741		OSAKA	1335	FRANKFURT	B.747	1234567	
2750	1110	FRANKFURT	1300	LONDON CITY	BAE146/CRJ	12345	
2751	1340	LONDON CITY	1535	FRANKFURT	BAE146/CRJ	12345	
4502	0729	HAMBURG	0855	HEATHROW	A.320	1234567	
4503	1810	HEATHROW	1940	FRANKFURT	A.320	1234567	
4505	0900	STANSTED	1030	FRANKFURT	B.737	1234567	
4507	1320	STANSTED	1450	FRANKFURT	B.737	1234567	
4508	1310	FRANKFURT	1555	JERSEY	B.737	6	VIA GUERNSEY
4509	2005	HEATHROW	2140	NUREMBERG	B.737	1234567	
4510	1235	HAMBURG	1405	HEATHROW	A.320	1234567	
4511	1440	HEATHROW	1555	DUSSELDORF	B.737	1234567	
4512	1540	FRANKFURT	1710	STANSTED	B.737	12345 7	
4513	2100	HEATHROW	2225	FRANKFURT	A320/B737	1234567	
4514	1835	FRANKFURT	2010	HEATHROW	A320/B737	1234567	
4515	1755	STANSTED	1925	FRANKFURT	B.737	1234567	
4516	1110	FRANKFURT	1240	STANSTED	B.737	1234567	
4517	0700	HEATHROW	0830	FRANKFURT	A.320	1234567	
4518	0930	MUNICH	1130	HEATHROW	A.320	1234567	
4519	0700	HEATHROW	0825	FRANKFURT	A.320	1234567	
4520	0615	FRANKFURT	0745	STANSTED	B.737	1234567	
4521	1905	HEATHROW	2020	DUSSELDORF	A.320	1234567	
4522		FRANKFURT	1100	BIRMINGHAM	B.737	1234567	
4524	1140	DUSSELDORF	1415	JERSEY	B.737	7	VIA GUERNSEY
4525	0750	HEATHROW	0955	MUNICH	B.737	1234567	
4529	1805	MANCHESTER	1955	FRANKFURT	B.737	1234567	

Flight	Dep	From	Arr	To	Aircraft	Days	Notes
4530	2030	FRANKFURT	2205	HEATHROW	A.320	1234567	
4532	1710	HAMBURG	1845	HEATHROW	A.320	1234567	
4533	0700	BIRMINGHAM		MUNICH	AVRO RJ-85	1234567	
4537	0620	FRANKFURT	0810	MANCHESTER	B.737	1234567	
4540	1520	FRANKFURT	1655	HEATHROW	A.320	1234567	
4543	0815	HEATHROW	0930	DUSSELDORF	B737/A320	1234567	
4544	2050	FRANKFURT	2235	MANCHESTER	B.737	1234567	
4545	0925	HEATHROW	1105	MUNICH	B.737	1234567	
4547	1155	JERSEY	1315	DUSSELDORF	B.737	7	-26.09
4551	0840	BIRMINGHAM	1015	DUSSELDORF	BAE-146	123456	FLIGHTLINE A/C
4552	0615	DUSSELDORF	0755	BIRMINGHAM	BAE-146	123456	FLIGHTLINE A/C
4554	1640	DUSSELDORF	1800	HEATHROW	A.320	1234567	
4555	1515	HEATHROW	1655	MUNICH	A320/B737	1234567	
4556	1210	DUSSELDORF	1330	HEATHROW	A320/B737	1234567	
4557	1900	HEATHROW	2030	FRANKFURT	A.320	1234567	
4564	1210	MUNICH	1410	HEATHROW	A320/B737	1234567	
4565	2005	HEATHROW	2145	MUNICH	A.320	1234567	
4566	0630	MUNICH	0830	HEATHROW	B.737	1234567	
4568	1705	MUNICH	1905	HEATHROW	A.320	1234567	
4569	1505	HEATHROW	1640	HAMBURG	A.320	1234567	
4576		FRANKFURT	1720	BIRMINGHAM	A.320	1234567	
4579	1135	HEATHROW	1305	FRANKFURT	B.737	1234567	
4580	0600	DUSSELDORF	0720	HEATHROW	B737/A320	1234567	
4581	1230	MANCHESTER	1420	FRANKFURT	B.737	1234567	
4583	2000	HEATHROW	2125	HAMBURG	A.320	1234567	
4585	1805	BIRMINGHAM	1940	FRANKFURT	A.320	1234567	
4588	0830	FRANKFURT	10005	HEATHROW	A.300	1234567	
4590		MUNICH	1245	BIRMINGHAM	BAE-146	1234567	
4591	1420	BIRMINGHAM		MUNICH	BAE-146	1234567	
4595	1225	HEATHROW	1405	MUNICH	A.320	1234567	
4596		MUNICH	2000	BIRMINGHAM	BAE-146	1234567	
4598	1535	FRANKFURT	1725	MANCHESTER	B.737	12345 7	
4601	1710	HEATHROW	1845	FRANKFURT	A.300	1234567	
4602		FRANKFURT	1435	EDINBURGH	B737/F100	1234567	ARR 1525 3
4603	1630	EDINBURGH		FRANKFURT	B737/F100	1234567	
4605	1155	BIRMINGHAM	1330	FRANKFURT	B.737	12345 7	
4606	1830	MUNICH	2030	HEATHROW	B.737	1234567	
4607	1305	HEATHROW	1440	FRANKFURT	A.300	1234567	
4608		FRANKFURT	2315	EDINBURGH	F-100	1234567	
4609	0745	EDINBURGH		FRANKFURT	F-100	1234567	
4611	0900	HEATHROW	1030	FRANKFURT	A.300	1234567	
4612	1225	FRANKFURT	1400	HEATHROW	A.300	1234567	
4615	1000	HEATHROW	1125	FRANKFURT	A.320	1234567	
4619	1655	JERSEY	1825	FRANKFURT	B.737	6	
4620		MUNICH	1250	MANCHESTER	BAE-146	1234567	
4621	1435	MANCHESTER		MUNICH	BAE-146	1234567	
4622		MUNICH	2005	MANCHESTER	BAE-146	1234567	
4623	0705	MANCHESTER		MUNICH	BAE-146	1234567	
4624		MUNICH	1655	MANCHESTER	BAE-146	12345 7	
4625	1815	MANCHESTER		MUNICH	BAE-146	12345 7	
4634	1720	FRANKFURT	1855	HEATHROW	B.737	1234567	
4640	1620	FRANKFURT	1750	HEATHROW	A.300	1234567	
4644	0625	FRANKFURT	0800	HEATHROW	A.300	1234567	
4646	0905	FRANKFURT	1050	MANCHESTER	B.737	1234567	
4780		DUSSELDORF	0740	STANSTED	B.737	1234567	
4781	0845	STANSTED		DUSSELDORF	B.737	1234567	
4782		DUSSELDORF	1255	STANSTED	B.737	1234567	
4783	1330	STANSTED		DUSSELDORF	B.737	1234567	
4784		DUSSELDORF	1830	STANSTED	B.737	1234567	
4785	1915	STANSTED		DUSSELDORF	B.737	1234567	
5932		MUNICH	1005	BIRMINGHAM	CANADAIR	12345	
5933	1335	BIRMINGHAM	1500	DUSSELDORF	CANADAIR	12345	
5934		MUNICH	1615	BIRMINGHAM	CANADAIR	12345	
5938		DUSSELDORF	1835	BIRMINGHAM	BAE-146	12345	
5939	1050	BIRMINGHAM		MUNICH	CANADAIR	12345	
5942	0555	HAMBURG	0740	MANCHESTER	CANADAIR	123456	
5945	1915	MANCHESTER	2100	HAMBURG	CANADAIR	12345 7	
5946	0645	FRANKFURT	0830	HEATHROW	AVRO RJ-85	12345	

Flight	Dep	From	Arr	To	Aircraft	Days	Notes
5948		DUSSELDORF	1300	BIRMINGHAM	CANADAIR	12345	
5949	0850	LONDON CITY	1010	FRANKFURT	AVRO RJ-85	12345	
5950		STUTTGART	1735	MANCHESTER	CANADAIR	12345	
5957	1645	BIRMINGHAM		MUNICH	CANADAIR	12345	
5962	1635	FRANKFURT	1815	LONDON CITY	AVRO RJ-85	12345 7	1650/1825 7
5965	1845	LONDON CITY	2005	FRANKFURT	AVRO RJ-85	12345 7	1905/2020 7
5967	0810	MANCHESTER	0955	HAMBURG	CANADAIR	123456	
5970	1655	HAMBURG	1845	MANCHESTER	CANADAIR	12345 7	
5971	1855	BIRMINGHAM		DUSSELDORF	CANADAIR	12345 7	
5989	1805	MANCHESTER		STUTTGART	CANADAIR	12345	
5990	1100	DUSSELDORF	1310	KNOCK	BAE-146	6	FLIGHTLINE A/C
5991	1345	KNOCK		DUSSELDORF	BAE-146	6	FLIGHTLINE A/C
6371		NEW YORK	1015	FRANKFURT	B.747	1234567	
6400	1135	FRANKFURT		WASHINGTON	B.747	1234567	
6401		WASHINGTON	0610	FRANKFURT	B.747	1234567	
6500	1255	FRANKFURT		CHICAGO	B.777	1234567	
6501		CHICAGO	1110	FRANKFURT	B.777	1234567	
6502	0740	FRANKFURT		CHICAGO	B.777	1234567	
6503		CHICAGO	0500	FRANKFURT	B.777	1234567	
6600	1445	DUSSELDORF		CHICAGO	B.767	1234567	
6601		CHICAGO	1105	DUSSELDORF	B.767	1234567	
6602	1610	FRANKFURT		WASHINGTON	B.747	1234567	
6603		WASHINGTON	1025	FRANKFURT	B.777	1234567	
6630	1110	MUNICH		WASHINGTON	B.767	1234567	
6631		WASHINGTON	0655	MUNICH	B.767	1234567	
6840	1210	FRANKFURT		TORONTO	A.340	1234567	
6841		TORONTO	0620	FRANKFURT	A.340	1234567	
6850	1300	FRANKFURT	1535	CALGARY	B.767	1234567	
6851	1800	CALGARY	1010	FRANKFURT	B.767	1234567	
6857		MONTREAL	0650	FRANKFURT	B.767	1234567	
8005	2110	DUBLIN	2315	COLOGNE	ELECTRA	12345	
8023		ATLANTA	2010	FRANKFURT	B.747	7	
8161		NEW YORK	2255	FRANKFURT	B.747	2 4 6	
8162	1600	FRANKFURT		NEW YORK	B.747	6	
8163		NEW YORK	0945	BRUSSELS	B.747	7	
8182	0230	COLOGNE		NEW YORK	B.747	23456	
8183		NEW YORK	2105	COLOGNE	B.747	2345	
		NEW YORK	1815	BRUSSELS	B.747	7	
8189		CHICAGO	1840	PRESTWICK	B.747	1	
8189	2010	PRESTWICK	2200	FRANKFURT	B.747	1	
8189	2015	SHANNON	2215	FRANKFURT	B.747	5	
8189		CHICAGO	2000	FRANKFURT	B.747	3467	
8200	0905	FRANKFURT		NEW YORK	B.747	1 4 7	DEP 1010 47
8201		ATLANTA	1400	PRESTWICK	B.747	2	
	1530	PRESTWICK	1740	FRANKFURT	B.747	2	
8201		NEW YORK	1150	FRANKFURT	B.747	1 5	
8203		NEW YORK	2010	FRANKFURT	B.747	7	
8241		MEXICO CITY	0505	FRANKFURT	MD-11	1 3 5	DEP 1700 1 5
8243		MEXICO CITY	2010	FRANKFURT	MD-11	5	
8253		LOS ANGELES	1250	PRESTWICK	MD-11	4	
	1420	PRESTWICK	1640	FRANKFURT	MD-11	4	
8255		SAN FRANCISCO	1725	FRANKFURT	MD-11	3	
8382	1730	GOTHENBURG		FAIRBANKS	B.747	1 3 5	DEP 0005 1
8670	0500	COLOGNE	0620	HEATHROW	B.737	23456	
8672		FRANKFURT	2105	HEATHROW	B.737	6	
8674	0005	FRANKFURT	0140	EAST MIDLANDS	B.737	23456	
8677	2215	HEATHROW		FRANKFURT	B.737	6	
8693	0245	EAST MIDLANDS	0405	FRANKFURT	B.737	23456	
8695	2235	HEATHROW	2345	COLOGNE	B.737	12345	

LUXAIR   *LUXAIR   LG/LGL   LUXEMBOURG*

Flight	Dep	From	Arr	To	Aircraft	Days
401	0610	LUXEMBOURG	0725	HEATHROW	B737EMB4	1234567
402	0810	HEATHROW	0915	LUXEMBOURG	B737/EM4	1234567
403	1150	LUXEMBOURG	1300	HEATHROW	B.737	1234567
404	1345	HEATHROW	1450	LUXEMBOURG	B.737	1234567
423	0610	LUXEMBOURG	0725	STANSTED	EMB-145	12345
424	0815	STANSTED	0930	LUXEMBOURG	EMB-145	12345

LUXAIR   (Cont.)

Flight	Dep	From	Arr	To	Aircraft	Days
427	1715	LUXEMBOURG	1830	STANSTED	B.737	12345 7
428	1930	STANSTED	2045	LUXEMBOURG	B.737	12345 7
489	0955	LUXEMBOURG	1150	MANCHESTER	EMB-145	12345
	1210	MANCHESTER	1320	DUBLIN	EMB-145	12345
490	1355	DUBLIN	1505	MANCHESTER	EMB-145	12345
	1525	MANCHESTER	1720	LUXEMBOURG	EMB-145	12345
491	0605	LUXEMBOURG	0730	LONDON CITY	EMB-145	12345
492	0800	LONDON CITY	0925	LUXEMBOURG	EMB-145	12345
493	0800	LUXEMBOURG	0925	LONDON CITY	EMB-145	6
494	1000	LONDON CITY	1125	LUXEMBOURG	EMB-145	6
495	1000	LUXEMBOURG	1125	LONDON CITY	EMB-145	12345
496	1500	LONDON CITY	1620	LUXEMBOURG	EMB-145	12345
497	1655	LUXEMBOURG	1825	LONDON CITY	EMB-145	12345 7
498	1855	LONDON CITY	2015	LUXEMBOURG	EMB-145	12345 7

MAERSKAIR   *MAERSK AIR I/S   DM/DAN   DENMARK*

Flight	Dep	From	Arr	To	Aircraft	Days
113	0725	COPENHAGEN	0925	GATWICK	B.737	123456
114	1020	GATWICK	1225	COPENHAGEN	B.737	123456
115	1240	COPENHAGEN	1440	GATWICK	B.737	7
116	1520	GATWICK	1720	COPENHAGEN	B.737	7
117	1550	COPENHAGEN	1750	GATWICK	B.737	12345 7
118	1830	GATWICK	2035	COPENHAGEN	B.737	12345 7
201	0625	BILLUND	0820	GATWICK	B.737	1234567
202	0900	GATWICK	1055	BILLUND	B.737	1234567
205	1055	BILLUND	1250	GATWICK	B.737	1234567
206	1345	GATWICK	1540	BILLUND	B.737	1234567
209	1600	BILLUND	1755	GATWICK	B.737	12345 7
210	1835	GATWICK	2030	BILLUND	B.737	12345 7

MAKAVIO   *MACEDONIAN AIRLINES   IN/MAK   MACEDONIA*

Flight	Dep	From	Arr	To	Aircraft	Days	
520		SKOPJE	1540	HEATHROW	B.737	3 6	ARR 1650 6
521	2205	HEATHROW		SKOPJE	B.737	3 6	DEP 1815 6

MALAWI   *AIR MALAWI   QM/AML   MALAWI*

Flight	Dep	From	Arr	To	Aircraft	Days
718		LILONGWE	1930	GATWICK	B.767	2
719	2100	GATWICK		LILONGWE	B.767	2

MALAYSIAN   *MALAYSIAN AIRLINE SYSTEM   MH/MAS   MALAYSIA*

Flight	Dep	From	Arr	To	Aircraft	Days	
01	2200	HEATHROW		KUALA LUMPA	B.747	234 67	
02		KUALA LUMPA	0605	HEATHROW	B.747	23 567	
03	1055	HEATHROW		KUALA LUMPUR	B.747	123 567	DEP 1200 1
04		KUALA LUMPUR	1710	HEATHROW	B.747	1234 67	
11	0950	MANCHESTER		MUNICH	B.777	4	
12		MUNICH	0830	MANCHESTER	B.777	4	
20		MUNICH	0825	MANCHESTER	B.777	2 7	
21	0950	MANCHESTER		MUNICH	B.777	2 7	
90	2230	DUBAI		NEW YORK	B.777	1 4 6	
91		NEW YORK	0400	DUBAI	B.777	1 3 6	

MALEV   *MALEV   MA/MAH   HUNGARY*

Flight	Dep	From	Arr	To	Aircraft	Days	
090	1040	BUDAPEST		NEW YORK	B.767	1234567	
091		NEW YORK	0750	BUDAPEST	B.767	1234567	
094	1010	BUDAPEST		TORONTO	B.767	2	
095		TORONTO	0955	BUDAPEST	B.767	3	
610	0910	BUDAPEST	1140	HEATHROW	B.737	1234567	
611	1245	HEATHROW	1515	BUDAPEST	B.737	1234567	
614		BUDAPEST	1600	GATWICK	F-70	123 567	
615	1655	GATWICK		BUDAPEST	F-70	123 567	
616	1810	BUDAPEST	2015	HEATHROW	B.737	1234567	
617	0825	HEATHROW	0905	BUDAPEST	B.737	1234567	DEP 0755 24

WITH BRITISH REGIONAL AIRLINES, THESE TWO AIRLINES COMPRISE THE BRITISH REGIONAL AIRLINES GROUP

001	0940	ISLE OF MAN	1015	LIVERPOOL	BAE-ATP	12345	
002	1045	LIVERPOOL	1120	ISLE OF MAN	BAE-ATP	12345	
003	1515	ISLE OF MAN	1550	LIVERPOOL	BAE-ATP	12345	
004	1620	LIVERPOOL	1655	ISLE OF MAN	BAE-ATP	12345	
007	1630	ISLE OF MAN	1705	LIVERPOOL	BAE-ATP	5	
008	1740	LIVERPOOL	1815	ISLE OF MAN	BAE-ATP	5	
011	0730	ISLE OF MAN	0805	LIVERPOOL	BAE-ATP	6	
012	0835	LIVERPOOL	0910	ISLE OF MAN	BAE-ATP	6	
013	1310	ISLE OF MAN	1345	LIVERPOOL	BAE-ATP	6	29.05-25.09
014	1420	LIVERPOOL	1455	ISLE OF MAN	BAE-ATP	6	29.05-25.09
015	0940	ISLE OF MAN	1015	LIVERPOOL	BAE-ATP	6	
016	1045	LIVERPOOL	1120	ISLE OF MAN	BAE-ATP	6	
017	1600	ISLE OF MAN	1635	LIVERPOOL	BAE-ATP	6	
018	1710	LIVERPOOL	1745	ISLE OF MAN	BAE-ATP	6	
019	1850	ISLE OF MAN	1925	LIVERPOOL	BAE-ATP	6	
020	1955	LIVERPOOL	2030	ISLE OF MAN	BAE-ATP	6	
021	0815	ISLE OF MAN	0850	LIVERPOOL	BAE-ATP	6	
022	0930	LIVERPOOL	1005	ISLE OF MAN	BAE-ATP	6	
023	1115	ISLE OF MAN	1150	LIVERPOOL	BAE-ATP	6	
024	1230	LIVERPOOL	1305	ISLE OF MAN	BAE-ATP	6	
025	1400	ISLE OF MAN	1435	LIVERPOOL	BAE-ATP	6	29.05-25.09
026	1510	LIVERPOOL	1545	ISLE OF MAN	BAE-ATP	6	29.05-25.09
031	0830	ISLE OF MAN	0905	LIVERPOOL	BAE-ATP	7	
032	0940	LIVERPOOL	1015	ISLE OF MAN	BAE-ATP	7	
033	1015	ISLE OF MAN	1050	LIVERPOOL	BAE-ATP	7	
034	1130	LIVERPOOL	1205	ISLE OF MAN	BAE-ATP	7	
035	1300	ISLE OF MAN	1335	LIVERPOOL	BAE-ATP	7	
036	1405	LIVERPOOL	1440	ISLE OF MAN	BAE-ATP	7	
037	1600	ISLE OF MAN	1635	LIVERPOOL	BAE-ATP	7	
038	1710	LIVERPOOL	1745	ISLE OF MAN	BAE-ATP	7	
039	1850	ISLE OF MAN	1925	LIVERPOOL	BAE-ATP	7	
040	1955	LIVERPOOL	2030	ISLE OF MAN	BAE-ATP	7	
041	1510	ISLE OF MAN	1545	LIVERPOOL	BAE146/ATP	7	
042	1620	LIVERPOOL	1655	ISLE OF MAN	BAE146/ATP	7	
043	1430	ISLE OF MAN	1505	LIVERPOOL	BAE-ATP	7	
044	1545	LIVERPOOL	1620	ISLE OF MAN	BAE-ATP	7	
045	1720	ISLE OF MAN	1755	LIVERPOOL	BAE-ATP	7	
046	1830	LIVERPOOL	1905	ISLE OF MAN	BAE-ATP	7	
051	1200	ISLE OF MAN	1235	LIVERPOOL	BAE-ATP	12345	
052	1305	LIVERPOOL	1340	ISLE OF MAN	BAE-ATP	12345	
203	0820	ISLE OF MAN	0900	DUBLIN	SH-460	12345	
204	0930	DUBLIN	1010	ISLE OF MAN	SH-360	12345	
207	1640	ISLE OF MAN	1720	DUBLIN	SH-360	12345	
208	1750	DUBLIN	1830	ISLE OF MAN	SH-360	12345	
213	0750	ISLE OF MAN	0825	DUBLIN	BAE-ATP	6	
214	0855	DUBLIN	0930	ISLE OF MAN	BAE-ATP	6	
223	1250	ISLE OF MAN	1325	DUBLIN	J'STREAM41	7	30.05-29.08
224	1355	DUBLIN	1430	ISLE OF MAN	J'STREAM41	7	30.05-29.08
225	1510	ISLE OF MAN	1545	DUBLIN	BAE-ATP	7	-23.05 / 05.09-
226	1620	DUBLIN	1655	ISLE OF MAN	BAE-ATP	7	23.05- / 05.09
265	1045	CARDIFF	1140	JERSEY	BAE-ATP	12345	
266	1205	JERSEY	1300	CARDIFF	BAE-ATP	12345	
269	1220	CARDIFF	1315	JERSEY	BAE-ATP	6	-02.10
270	1045	JERSEY	1140	CARDIFF	BAE-ATP	6	-02.10
271	0950	ISLE OF MAN	1030	DUBLIN	BAE-ATP	12345	
	1100	DUBLIN	1205	CARDIFF	BAE-ATP	12345	
	1235	CARDIFF	1330	JERSEY	BAE-ATP	12345	
272	1405	JERSEY	1500	CARDIFF	BAE-ATP	12345	
	1530	CARDIFF	1635	DUBLIN	BAE-ATP	12345	
	1705	DUBLIN	1745	ISLE OF MAN	BAE-ATP	12345	
273	0800	CARDIFF	0855	JERSEY	BAE-ATP	6	
274	1330	JERSEY	1435	CARDIFF	BAE-ATP	6	
275	1215	CARDIFF	1310	JERSEY	BAE-ATP	6	
276	1745	JERSEY	1840	CARDIFF	BAE-ATP	6	29.05-25.09

277	1515	CARDIFF	1610	JERSEY	BAE-ATP	6	29.05-25.09
	0955	CARDIFF	1050	JERSEY	J'STREAM41	7	05.09-26.09
	1400	CARDIFF	1455	JERSEY	J'STREAM41	7	30.05-29.08
278	1640	JERSEY	1735	CARDIFF	BAE-ATP	6	29.05-25.09
	1530	JERSEY	1625	CARDIFF	J'STREAM41	7	05.09-26.09
	1530	JERSEY	1625	CARDIFF	J'STREAM41	7	30.05-29.08
279	1100	CARDIFF	1155	JERSEY	J'STREAM41	7	30.05-29.08
280	1235	JERSEY	1330	CARDIFF	J'STREAM41	7	30.05-29.08
281	0750	ISLE OF MAN	0820	DUBLIN	BAE-146	7	30.05-29.08
	0900	DUBLIN	1015	JERSEY	BAE-146	7	30.05-29.08
282	1445	JERSEY	1600	DUBLIN	BAE-146	7	30.05-29.08
	1640	DUBLIN	1710	ISLE OF MAN	BAE-146	7	30.05-29.08
283	1100	ISLE OF MAN	1130	DUBLIN	BAE-146	6	29.05-25.09
	1210	DUBLIN	1325	JERSEY	BAE-146	6	29.05-25.09
284	1410	JERSEY	1525	DUBLIN	BAE-146	6	29.05-25.09
	1600	DUBLIN	1630	ISLE OF MAN	BAE-146	6	29.05-25.09
286	1340	JERSEY	1510	DUBLIN	BAE-ATP	6	29.05-25.09
287	1540	DUBLIN	1710	JERSEY	BAE-ATP	6	29.05-25.09
301	0700	ISLE OF MAN	0815	HEATHROW	BAE-146	123456	
302	0900	HEATHROW	1010	ISLE OF MAN	BAE-146	123456	
305	1440	ISLE OF MAN	1540	HEATHROW	BAE-146	12345	
306	1610	HEATHROW	1720	ISLE OF MAN	BAE-146	12345	
307	1755	ISLE OF MAN	1900	HEATHROW	BAE-146	12345 7	
308	1930	HEATHROW	2040	ISLE OF MAN	BAE-146	12345 7	
309	0740	ISLE OF MAN	0845	HEATHROW	BAE-ATP	7	
310	0930	HEATHROW	1035	ISLE OF MAN	BAE-ATP	7	
311	1755	ISLE OF MAN	1855	HEATHROW	BAE-146	6	22.05-25.09
312	1925	HEATHROW	2035	ISLE OF MAN	BAE-146	6	22.05-25.09
321	0720	ISLE OF MAN	0805	MANCHESTER	BAE-ATP	1234567	
322	0845	MANCHESTER	0930	ISLE OF MAN	BAE-ATP	1234567	
325	1240	ISLE OF MAN	1325	MANCHESTER	BAE-ATP	123456	1300/1345 6
326	1400	MANCHESTER	1445	ISLE OF MAN	BAE-ATP	123456	1415/1500 6
329	1820	ISLE OF MAN	1905	MANCHESTER	BAE-ATP	1234567	
330	1940	MANCHESTER	2020	ISLE OF MAN	BAE-ATP	1234567	
375	0745	BELFAST	0845	EDINBURGH	SH-360	12345	
376	0910	EDINBURGH	1010	BELFAST	SH-360	12345	
377	1550	BELFAST	1650	EDINBURGH	SH-360	12345	
378	1720	EDINBURGH	1820	BELFAST	SH-360	12345	
410	1015	LEEDS	1055	ISLE OF MAN	J'STREAM41	12345	
411	1325	ISLE OF MAN	1405	LEEDS	J'STREAM41	12345	
413	0930	ISLE OF MAN	1010	LEEDS	BAE-ATP	6	29.05-25.09
414	1040	LEEDS	1120	ISLE OF MAN	BAE-ATP	6	29.05-25.09
418	1530	LEEDS	1610	ISLE OF MAN	J'STREAM41	7	
419	1635	ISLE OF MAN	1715	LEEDS	J'STREAM41	7	
490	1055	JERSEY	1210	CORK	BAE146/J'ST41	7	
491	1250	CORK	1405	JERSEY	BAE146/J'ST41	7	
492	0925	JERSEY	1055	CORK	BAE-ATP	6	29.05-25.09
493	1125	CORK	1255	JERSEY	BAE-ATP	6	29.05-25.09
501	0730	ISLE OF MAN	0805	LIVERPOOL	BAE-ATP	12345	
502	0835	LIVERPOOL	0910	ISLE OF MAN	BAE-ATP	12345	
509	1810	ISLE OF MAN	1845	LIVERPOOL	BAE-ATP	12345	1850/1925 5
510	1915	LIVERPOOL	1950	ISLE OF MAN	BAE-ATP	12345	1955/2030 5
552	0750	EDINBURGH	1000	JERSEY	BAE-ATP	6	-25.09
553	1040	JERSEY	1215	MANCHESTER	BAE-ATP	6	-25.09
556	1250	MANCHESTER	1425	JERSEY	BAE-ATP	6	-25.09
557	1800	JERSEY	2010	EDINBURGH	BAE-ATP	6	-25.09
558	0815	MANCHESTER	0950	JERSEY	BAE-ATP	6	-25.09
559	1025	JERSEY	1155	NORWICH	BAE-ATP	6	-25.09
560	1235	NORWICH	1405	JERSEY	BAE-ATP	6	-25.09
562	0830	MANCHESTER	0945	JERSEY	EMB-145	6	-25.09
563	1020	JERSEY	1135	NEWCASTLE	EMB-145	6	-25.09
564	1225	NEWCASTLE	1340	JERSEY	EMB-145	6	-25.09
565	1420	JERSEY	1535	MANCHESTER	EMB-145	6	-25.09
566	1625	MANCHESTER	1740	JERSEY	EMB-145	6	-25.09
567	1815	JERSEY	1930	MANCHESTER	EMB-145	6	-25.09
568	0810	SOUTHAMPTON	0850	JERSEY	EMB-145	6	-25.09
569	0930	JERSEY	1025	BIRMINGHAM	EMB-145	6	-25.09
570	1100	BIRMINGHAM	1155	JERSEY	EMB-145	6	-25.09

571	1245	JERSEY	1345	EAST MIDLANDS	EMB-145	6	-25.09
572	1430	EAST MIDLANDS	1530	JERSEY	EMB-145	6	-25.09
573	1800	JERSEY	1840	SOUTHAMPTON	EMB-145	6	-25.09
574	0950	MANCHESTER	1025	JERSEY	BAE-ATP	7	-26.09
575	1105	JERSEY	1240	MANCHESTER	BAE-ATP	7	-26.09
600	0940	GLASGOW	1030	ISLE OF MAN	J'STREAM41	12345	
601	1100	ISLE OF MAN	1150	GLASGOW	BAE-ATP	12345	
602	1230	GLASGOW	1320	ISLE OF MAN	J'STREAM41	12345	
603	1400	ISLE OF MAN	1450	GLASGOW	J'STREAM41	12345	
605	1010	ISLE OF MAN	1100	GLASGOW	BAE-ATP	12345	
606	1140	GLASGOW	1230	ISLE OF MAN	BAE-ATP	12345	
611	1000	ISLE OF MAN	1050	GLASGOW	BAE-ATP	6	29.05-25.09
612	1140	GLASGOW	1230	ISLE OF MAN	BAE-ATP	6	29.05-25.09
613	1200	ISLE OF MAN	1250	GLASGOW	BAE-ATP	7	
614	1330	GLASGOW	1420	ISLE OF MAN	BAE-ATP	7	
739	1200	GLASGOW	1250	BELFAST	SH-360	12345	
740	1040	BELFAST	1130	GLASGOW	SH-360	12345	
811	0700	ISLE OF MAN	0755	BIRMINGHAM	BAE-ATP	12345	
812	0825	BIRMINGHAM	0920	ISLE OF MAN	BAE-ATP	12345	
813	1010	ISLE OF MAN	1105	BIRMINGHAM	BAE-ATP	6	
814	1135	BIRMINGHAM	1230	ISLE OF MAN	BAE-ATP	6	
817	1730	ISLE OF MAN	1825	BIRMINGHAM	BAE-ATP	12345 7	
818	1855	BIRMINGHAM	1950	ISLE OF MAN	BAE-ATP	12345 7	
840	2030	SOUTHAMPTON	2130	ISLE OF MAN	EMB-145	5	
847	1150	ISLE OF MAN	1310	SOUTHAMPTON	BAE-ATP	6	29.05-25.09
848	1340	SOUTHAMPTON	1510	ISLE OF MAN	BAE-ATP	6	29.05-25.09
849	1900	ISLE OF MAN	2000	SOUTHAMPTON	EMB-145	7	
850	0800	CARDIFF	0900	ISLE OF MAN	BAE-ATP	6	
851	1530	ISLE OF MAN	1630	CARDIFF	J'STREAM41	7	
881	1100	ISLE OF MAN	1215	LUTON	BAE146/ATP	12345	
882	1250	LUTON	1410	ISLE OF MAN	BAE146/ATP	12345	
883	1200	ISLE OF MAN	1315	LUTON	BAE-ATP	6	
884	1355	LUTON	1515	ISLE OF MAN	BAE-ATP	6	
885	1500	ISLE OF MAN	1615	LUTON	BAE-ATP	7	
886	1650	LUTON	1810	ISLE OF MAN	BAE-ATP	7	

		MAROCAIR		*ROYAL AIR MAROC*	*AT/RAM*	*MOROCCO*	
800		CASABLANCA	1645	HEATHROW	B.737	1 34567	
801	1740	HEATHROW		CASABLANCA	B.737	1 34567	DEP 1715 3
802		TANGIERS	1500	HEATHROW	B.737	2	
803	1715	HEATHROW		TANGIERS	B.737	2	
806		TANGIERS	2130	HEATHROW	B.737	3456	ARR 1900 6
807	2220	HEATHROW		TANGIERS	B.737	3456	DEP 1950 6
808		MARRAKECH	1805	HEATHROW	B.737	4	
809	1855	HEATHROW		MARRAKECH	B.737	4	

		MARTINAIR		*MARTINAIR HOLLAND BV*	*MP/MPH*	*HOLLAND*	
62		BRIDGETOWN	0600	STANSTED	MD-11	1	
	0730	STANSTED	0840	AMSTERDAM	MD-11	1	
		BOGATA	0355	STANSTED	MD-11	7	
	0525	STANSTED	0635	AMSTERDAM	MD-11	7	
601	0945	AMSTERDAM		PUNTA CANA	B.767	6	
		SAN JUAN	0745	AMSTERDAM	B.767	7	
605	1350	AMSTERDAM		PUERTO PLATO	B.767	1 5	DEP 0945 5
		PUERTO PLATA	1105	AMSTERDAM	B.767	2 6	ARR 0745 6
627	0925	AMSTERDAM		HOLGUIN	B.767	4	
		VARADERO	0905	AMSTERDAM	B.767	5	
629	0925	AMSTERDAM		VARADERO	B.767	2 4	
		MONTEGO BAY	0945	AMSTERDAM	B.767	3	
631	0930	AMSTERDAM		ORLANDO	B.767	1 4	DEP 1130 4
	1045	AMSTERDAM	0515	ORLANDO	B.767	56	DEP 1245 6
632		ORLANDO	0515	AMSTERDAM	B.767	2 6	ARR 0720 6
		ORLANDO	0750	AMSTERDAM	B.767	5 7	ARR 0905 7
643	0945	AMSTERDAM		MIAMI	B747/B767	345 7	DEP 1100 4
	1400	AMSTERDAM		MIAMI	B747/767	6	
645		MIAMI	1600	AMSTERDAM	B767/MD11	1 4	

MARTINAIR (Cont.)

Flight	Dep	From	Time	To	Aircraft	Days	Notes
646		MIAMI	1440	AMSTERDAM	B.767	1 4 6	ARR 0645 6
		MIAMI	1015	AMSTERDAM	B.767	5 7	ARR 0800 5
801	1315	AMSTERDAM		OAKLAND	B767/MD11	1 5	DEP 1400 5
802		OAKLAND	1330	AMSTERDAM	B767/MD11	2 6	ARR 1355 6
805	1550	AMSTERDAM		NEW YORK	B.767	3 7	
806		NEW YORK	0910	AMSTERDAM	B.767	1 4	
807	1335	AMSTERDAM		LOS ANGELES	B767/MD11	1 4 6	
808		LOS ANGELES	1245	AMSTERDAM	B767/MD11	2 5 7	
811	1445	AMSTERDAM		TORONTO	B.767	1 4	DEP 1400 4
812		TORONTO	0745	AMSTERDAM	B.767	2 5	ARR 0700 5
815	1100	AMSTERDAM		EDMONTON	B.767	1	-20.09
		EDMONTON	1105	AMSTERDAM	B.767	6	-25.09
	1135	AMSTERDAM		CALGARY	B.767	3	-22.09
		CALGARY	0830	AMSTERDAM	B.767	2	-21.09
	1210	AMSTERDAM		VANCOUVER	B.767	5	-24.09
		VANCOUVER	1105	AMSTERDAM	B.767	4	-23.09
829	1300	AMSTERDAM		CANCUN	B.747	3 5	DEP 1330 3
830		CANCUN	1200	AMSTERDAM	B.747	4 6	

MERAIR
MERIDIANA SPA   IG/ISS   ITALY

Flight	Dep	From	Time	To	Aircraft	Days	Notes
543		OLBIA	1225	GATWICK	MD-82	2 56	ARR 1350 26
544	1255	GATWICK		OLBIA	MD-82	2 56	DEP 1445 26
3531		FLORENCE	0900	GATWICK	BAE-146	1234567	
3534	1925	GATWICK		FLORENCE	BAE-146	1234567	
3535		FLORENCE	1845	GATWICK	BAE-146	1234567	
3536	0955	GATWICK		FLORENCE	BAE-146	1234567	
3537		FLORENCE	1330	GATWICK	BAE-146	1 34567	
3538	1415	GATWICK		FLORENCE	BAE-146	1 34567	

MIDLAND
BRITISH MIDLAND AIRWAYS   BD/BMA   U.K.

Flight	Dep	From	Arr	To	Aircraft	Days	Code
1AX	0850	AMSTERDAM	1000	HEATHROW	A.320	1234567	BD102
1EH	0845	EDINBURGH	1005	HEATHROW	B.737	1234567	BD53
1HY	2040	HEATHROW	2155	EDINBURGH	A320/B737	1234567	BD64
1KE	0850	DUBLIN	1000	HEATHROW	A.320	1234567	BD122
1LJ	0655	LEEDS	0755	HEATHROW	B737/F100	1234567	BD411
1MR	2015	BRUSSELS	2125	BIRMINGHAM	EMB-145	12345 7	BD660
1NL	0650	GLASGOW	0810	HEATHROW	B.737	1234567	BD1
1NZ	1440	HEATHROW	1540	BRUSSELS	B.737	12345	BD151
1RM	0650	BIRMINGHAM	0800	BRUSSELS	EMB-145	12345	BD651
1RN	0845	BRUSSELS	0955	HEATHROW	B.737	12345	BD142
1TW	0645	TEESSIDE	0750	HEATHROW	B737/F100	1234567	BD331
1VX	0840	GLASGOW	0940	LEEDS	SAAB-340	12345	BD291
1WC	1700	GLASGOW	1815	HEATHROW	B.737	12345 7	BD011
1XF	0910	BELFAST	1020	HEATHROW	B.737	1234567	BD083
1XV	0710	LEEDS	0810	GLASGOW	SAAB-340	12345	BD292
2AB	0730	HEATHROW	0905	FRANKFURT	B.737	12345	BD831
	0825	HEATHROW	1220	FRANKFURT	B.737	67	
2AX	1025	AMSTERDAM	1135	HEATHROW	B.737	1234567	BD104
2EH	1040	EDINBURGH	1155	HEATHROW	A320/B737	1234567	BD55
2EV	1925	HEATHROW	2035	DUBLIN	A.320	1234567	BD133
2FP	0905	HEATHROW	1020	BELFAST	A.320	1234567	BD82
2KE	1110	DUBLIN	1225	HEATHROW	A.320	1234567	BD124
2LJ	1010	LEEDS	1110	HEATHROW	B.737	1234567	BD413
2LN	1900	HEATHROW	2015	GLASGOW	B.737	12345 7	BD12
2NZ	1630	HEATHROW	1735	BRUSSELS	B.737	1234567	BD153
2RN	1030	BRUSSELS	1135	HEATHROW	B.737	12345	BD146
2TW	1020	TEESSIDE	1130	HEATHROW	B737/F100	1234567	BD333
2XF	1115	BELFAST	1230	HEATHROW	A.320	1234567	BD085
2XV	1500	LEEDS	1600	GLASGOW	SAAB-340	12345	BD294
2CW	0900	HEATHROW	1015	GLASGOW	B.737	1234567	BD2
3XC	0640	HEATHROW	0750	AMSTERDAM	A.320	123456	BD101
3AB	1120	HEATHROW	1310	FRANKFURT	B.737	12345	BD833
3AX	1240	AMSTERDAM	1350	HEATHROW	A.320	1234567	BD106
3EH	1240	EDINBURGH	1355	HEATHROW	B.737	1234567	BD57
3EV	2135	HEATHROW	2250	DUBLIN	A.320	1234567	BD135
3FP	1110	HEATHROW	1225	BELFAST	A.320	1234567	BD84

3HY	0645	HEATHROW	0800	EDINBURGH	B.737	123456	BD50
3KE	1300	DUBLIN	1415	HEATHROW	A.320	1234567	BD126
3LJ	1335	LEEDS	1430	HEATHROW	B.737	12345 7	BD415
3LN	1700	HEATHROW	1815	GLASGOW	B.737	1234567	BD10
3NL	0900	GLASGOW	1020	HEATHROW	B.737	1234567	BD3
3NZ	1820	HEATHROW	1920	BRUSSELS	B.737	12345	BD155
3RM	1830	BIRMINGHAM	1945	BRUSSELS	EMB-145	12345	BD659
3RN	1645	BRUSSELS	1745	HEATHROW	B.737	12345	BD152
3TW	1355	TEESSIDE	1500	HEATHROW	F100/B.737	12345 7	BD335
3VX	1630	GLASGOW	1730	LEEDS	SAAB-340	12345	BD295
3WC	1900	GLASGOW	2015	HEATHROW	B.737	1234567	BD013
3XC	0825	HEATHROW	0930	AMSTERDAM	A320/B737	1234567	BD103
3XF	1320	BELFAST	1430	HEATHROW	A.320	1234567	BD087
3XV	1800	LEEDS	1900	GLASGOW	SAAB-340	12345	BD296
4AX	1425	AMSTERDAM	1535	HEATHROW	B737/A320	1234567	BD108
4CW	1100	HEATHROW	1215	GLASGOW	B.737	1234567	BD4
4EH	1440	EDINBURGH	1555	HEATHROW	A320/B737	1234567	BD59
4EV	0650	HEATHROW	0800	DUBLIN	A.320	123456	BD121
4FA	0625	FRANKFURT	0805	HEATHROW	B.737	1234567	BD830
4FP	1300	HEATHROW	1435	BELFAST	A.320	1234567	BD86
4HY	0645	HEATHROW	0805	EDINBURGH	B.737	123456	BD050
4JL	0835	HEATHROW	0930	LEEDS	B.737	1234567	BD412
4KE	1510	DUBLIN	1635	HEATHROW	A.320	1234567	BD128
4LJ	1555	LEEDS	1655	HEATHROW	B.737	12345	BD417
	1720	LEEDS	1815	HEATHROW	B.737	6	
4LN	2100	HEATHROW	2215	GLASGOW	B.737	1234567	BD14
4MR	0840	BRUSSELS	0950	BIRMINGHAM	EMB-145	12345	BD652
4NZ	2015	HEATHROW	2115	BRUSSELS	B.737	12345 7	BD157
4RM	1835	BIRMINGHAM	1945	BRUSSELS	EMB-145	12345 7	BD659
4RN	1435	BRUSSELS	1540	HEATHROW	B.737	1234567	BD150
4TW	1530	TEESSIDE	1640	HEATHROW	B737/F100	12345	BD337
	1745	TEESSIDE	1845	HEATHROW	F-70	6	
4VX	1930	GLASGOW	2030	LEEDS	SAAB-340	12345	BD297
4XC	1045	HEATHROW	1110	AMSTERDAM	A.320	1234567	BD105
4XF	1530	BELFAST	1640	HEATHROW	A.320	1234567	BD089
4XV	1830	LEEDS	1930	GLASGOW	SAAB-340	7	BD298
5AB	1340	HEATHROW	1515	FRANKFURT	B.737	67	BD835
5AX	1625	AMSTERDAM	1735	HEATHROW	A.320	1234567	BD110
5EH	1640	EDINBURGH	1755	HEATHROW	B.737	12345 7	BD61
5EV	0850	HEATHROW	1005	DUBLIN	A.320	1234567	BD123
5FP	1520	HEATHROW	1635	BELFAST	A.320	1234567	BD88
5HY	1040	HEATHROW	1155	EDINBURGH	B.737	1234567	BD54
5JL	1135	HEATHROW	1230	LEEDS	B.737	1234567	BD414
5KE	1710	DUBLIN	1825	HEATHROW	A.320	1234567	BD130
5LJ	1910	LEEDS	2015	HEATHROW	B.737	12345 7	BD419
5NL	1100	GLASGOW	1215	HEATHROW	B.737	1234567	BD5
5NZ	0655	HEATHROW	0755	BRUSSELS	B.737	12345	BD141
5TW	1915	TEESSIDE	2020	HEATHROW	B.737	12345 7	BD339
5WC	2100	GLASGOW	2215	HEATHROW	B.737	12345 7	BD015
5WT	0825	HEATHROW	0935	TEESSIDE	F100/B737	1234567	BD332
5XC	1225	HEATHROW	1330	AMSTERDAM	B737/A320	1234567	BD107
5XF	1750	BELFAST	1900	HEATHROW	A.320	1234567	BD091
6AB	1600	HEATHROW	1730	FRANKFURT	B.737	1234567	BD837
6AX	1825	AMSTERDAM	1935	HEATHROW	B.737	1234567	BD112
6CW	1300	HEATHROW	1415	GLASGOW	B.737	1234567	BD6
6EH	1840	EDINBURGH	1955	HEATHROW	A320/B737	1234567	BD63
6EV	1050	HEATHROW	1205	DUBLIN	A.320	1234567	BD125
6FA	0955	FRANKFURT	1135	HEATHROW	B.737	12345	BD832
6FP	1730	HEATHROW	1845	BELFAST	/A.320	1234567	BD90
6HY	1240	HEATHROW	1355	EDINBURGH	A320/B737	1234567	BD56
6JL	1405	HEATHROW	1500	LEEDS	B.737	12345	BD416
6KE	1930	DUBLIN	2045	HEATHROW	A.320	1234567	BD132
6NZ	0830	HEATHROW	0935	BRUSSELS	B.737	12345	BD145
6RB	1815	BRUSSELS	1925	HEATHROW	B.737	1234567	BD154
6RM	1505	BIRMINGHAM	1615	BRUSSELS	EMB-145	12345	BD655
6WT	1210	HEATHROW	1315	TEESSIDE	F100/B737	1234567	BD334
6XC	1435	HEATHROW	1540	AMSTERDAM	A.320	1234567	BD109
6XF	1940	BELFAST	2100	HEATHROW	A.320	1234567	BD093

7AB	1830	HEATHROW	2005	FRANKFURT	B.737	1234567	BD839
7AX	2020	AMSTERDAM	2125	HEATHROW	A.320	12345 7	BD114
7EH	2055	EDINBURGH	2210	HEATHROW	B.737	12345 7	BD65
7EV	1300	HEATHROW	1430	DUBLIN	A.320	1234567	BD127
7FA	1050	FRANKFURT	1230	HEATHROW	B.737	67	BD834
7FP	2000	HEATHROW	2110	BELFAST	A.320	1234567	BD92
7HY	1430	HEATHROW	1545	EDINBURGH	B.737	1234567	BD58
7JL	1900	HEATHROW	1950	LEEDS	B.737	6	BD418
	1730	HEATHROW	1825	LEEDS	B.737	12345 7	
7KE	2120	DUBLIN	2235	HEATHROW	A.320	12345 7	BD134
7NL	1300	GLASGOW	1415	HEATHROW	B.737	1234567	BD7
7RN	2020	BRUSSELS	2125	HEATHROW	B.737	12345	BD156
7WT	1345	HEATHROW	1450	TEESSIDE	B.737	12345	BD336
7XC	1630	HEATHROW	1735	AMSTERDAM	A320/B737	1234567	BD111
7XF	2145	BELFAST	2255	HEATHROW	A.320	12345 7	BD095
8AX	0625	AMSTERDAM	0735	HEATHROW	A320/B737	123456	BD100
8CW	1500	HEATHROW	1615	GLASGOW	B.737	1234567	BD8
8EH	1130	EDINBURGH	1250	HEATHROW	B.737	234	BD67
8EV	1506	HEATHROW	1620	DUBLIN	A.320	1234567	BD129
8FA	1600	FRANKFURT	1740	HEATHROW	B.737	1234567	BD836
8FP	2145	HEATHROW	2255	BELFAST	A.320	1234567	BD94
8HY	1640	HEATHROW	1755	EDINBURGH	A320/B737	1234567	BD60
8JL	2100	HEATHROW	2215	GLASGOW	B.737	12345 7	BD420
8KE	0650	DUBLIN	0805	HEATHROW	A.320	1234567	BD120
8NZ	1220	HEATHROW	1325	BRUSSELS	B.737	1234567	BD149
8RN	0640	BRUSSELS	0745	HEATHROW	B.737	123456	BD140
8WT	1725	HEATHROW	1830	TEESSIDE	F100/B737	12345 7	BD338
	1935	HEATHROW	2040	TEESSIDE	F70/F100	6	
8XC	1825	HEATHROW	1930	AMSTERDAM	A.320	1234567	BD113
8XF	0650	BELFAST	0820	HEATHROW	A.320	12345	BD081
9CW	0705	HEATHROW	0820	GLASGOW	B.737	123456	BD16
9EH	0650	EDINBURGH	0810	HEATHROW	B.737	1234567	BD51
9EV	1725	HEATHROW	1840	DUBLIN	A.320	1234567	BD131
9FA	1820	FRANKFURT	2000	HEATHROW	B.737	1234567	BD838
9FP	0700	HEATHROW	0830	BELFAST	A.320	123456	BD80
9HY	1900	HEATHROW	2010	EDINBURGH	B.737	12345 7	BD62
9NL	1500	GLASGOW	1615	HEATHROW	B.737	1234567	BD9
9NZ	0730	HEATHROW	0835	BRUSSELS	B.737	67	BD143
9RN	0925	BRUSSELS	1035	HEATHROW	B.737	67	BD144
9WT	2100	HEATHROW	2155	TEESSIDE	B.737	12345 7	BD340
9XC	2030	HEATHROW	2130	AMSTERDAM	A320/B737	12345 7	BD115
17	1540	GLASGOW	1650	HEATHROW	B.737	7	
52	0900	HEATHROW	1010	EDINBURGH	B.737	1234567	
97	2030	BELFAST	2145	HEATHROW	B.737	7	19.07-30.08
98	0750	HEATHROW	0905	BELFAST	B.737	234	
99	1015	BELFAST	1130	HEATHROW	B.737	234	
157	2015	HEATHROW	2115	BRUSSELS	B.737	12345 7	
163	1045	HEATHROW	1305	PALMA	B.737	1234567	
164	1350	PALMA	1615	HEATHROW	B.737	1234567	
165	1240	HEATHROW	1500	PALMA	B.737	6	
166	1545	NICE	1810	HEATHROW	B.737	6	
170	0640	PARIS CDG	0750	HEATHROW	B.737	123456	
171	0650	HEATHROW	0800	PARIS CDG	B.737	123456	
172	0845	PARIS CDG	0955	HEATHROW	B.737	1234567	
173	0830	HEATHROW	0935	PARIS CDG	B.737	1234567	
174	1025	PARIS CDG	1130	HEATHROW	B.737	1234567	
175	1040	HEATHROW	1145	PARIS CDG	B.737	1234567	
176	1225	PARIS CDG	1330	HEATHROW	B.737	1234567	
177	1300	HEATHROW	1405	PARIS CDG	B.737	1234567	
180	1625	PARIS CDG	1730	HEATHROW	B.737	1234567	
181	1630	HEATHROW	1735	PARIS CDG	B.737	1234567	
182	1825	PARIS CDG	1930	HEATHROW	B.737	1234567	
183	1825	HEATHROW	1930	PARIS CDG	B.737	1234567	
184	2040	PARIS CDG	2145	HEATHROW	B.737	1234567	
185	2015	HEATHROW	2115	PARIS CDG	B.737	1234567	
193	0850	HEATHROW	1040	NICE	B.737	1234567	
194	1130	NICE	1330	HEATHROW	B.737	1234567	

195	1630	HEATHROW	1825	NICE	B.737	1234567	1415/1610 6
196	1910	NICE	2110	HEATHROW	B.737	1234567	1655/1855 6
201	0650	EAST MIDLANDS	0750	AMSTERDAM	F-100	123456	
202	0830	AMSTERDAM	0940	EAST MIDLANDS	F-100	123456	
203	1055	EAST MIDLANDS	1200	AMSTERDAM	SF3/F100	12345 7	1030/1155 7
204	1300	AMSTERDAM	1405	EAST MIDLANDS	SF3/F100	12345 7	1235/1350 7
205	1700	EAST MIDLANDS	1800	AMSTERDAM	F-100	12345 7	
206	1850	AMSTERDAM	1955	EAST MIDLANDS	F-100	12345 7	
207	1445	EAST MIDLANDS	1610	AMSTERDAM	SAAB-340	12345	
208	1640	AMSTERDAM	1810	EAST MIDLANDS	SAAB-340	12345	
213	0700	EAST MIDLANDS	0755	EDINBURGH	F70/F100	12345	
214	0825	EDINBURGH	0920	EAST MIDLANDS	F70/F100	12345	
215	1045	EAST MIDLANDS	1150	EDINBURGH	SAAB-340	12345	
216	1220	EDINBURGH	1315	EAST MIDLANDS	SAAB-340	12345	
217	1525	EAST MIDLANDS	1620	EDINBURGH	VARIES	12345 7	1500/1610 7
218	1700	EDINBURGH	1755	EAST MIDLANDS	VARIES	12345 7	1645/1740 7
219	1825	EAST MIDLANDS	1920	EDINBURGH	VARIES	12345 7	
220	1950	EDINBURGH	2045	EAST MIDLANDS	VARIES	12345 7	2005/2115 7
223	0700	EAST MIDLANDS	0810	EDINBURGH	SAAB-340	6	
224	0840	EDINBURGH	0950	EAST MIDLANDS	SAAB-340	6	
225	0655	EAST MIDLANDS	0820	ABERDEEN	SAAB-340	12345	
226	0845	ABERDEEN	1010	EAST MIDLANDS	SAAB-340	12345	
227	1340	EAST MIDLANDS	1505	ABERDEEN	SAAB-340	12345	
228	1530	ABERDEEN	1655	EAST MIDLANDS	SAAB-340	12345	
229	1755	EAST MIDLANDS	1920	ABERDEEN	SAAB-340	12345 7	1740/1910 7
230	1950	ABERDEEN	2115	EAST MIDLANDS	SAAB-340	12345 7	1935/2100 7
233	0730	EAST MIDLANDS	0900	BRUSSELS	SAAB-340	12345	
234	0930	BRUSSELS	1055	EAST MIDLANDS	SAAB-340	12345	
235	1400	EAST MIDLAND	1525	BRUSSELS	EMB-145	12345	
236	1555	BRUSSELS	1725	EAST MIDLANDS	SAAB-340	12345	
237	1725	EAST MIDLANDS	1850	BRUSSELS	SAAB-340	12345 7	1535/1655 7
238	1920	BRUSSELS	2050	EAST MIDLANDS	EMB-145	12345 7	1735/1855 7
240	0850	GLASGOW	0945	EAST MIDLANDS	F-100	12345	
241	0715	EAST MIDLANDS	0810	GLASGOW	F100/SAAB340	123456	0710/0820 6
242	0850	GLASGOW	1000	EAST MIDLANDS	SAAB-340	6	
243	1125	EAST MIDLANDS	1235	GLASGOW	SAAB-340	12345	
244	1305	GLASGOW	1415	EAST MIDLANDS	SAAB-340	12345	
245	1515	EAST MIDLANDS	1610	GLASGOW	F-100	12345	
246	1650	GLASGOW	1745	EAST MIDLANDS	F-100	12345	
247	1830	EAST MIDLANDS	1925	GLASGOW	F.100	12345 7	
248	1955	GLASGOW	2050	EAST MIDLANDS	F.100	12345 7	
251	0710	EAST MIDLANDS	0830	PARIS CDG	F-100	12345	
252	0900	PARIS CDG	1015	EAST MIDLANDS	F-100	12345	
255	1025	EAST MIDLANDS	1135	PARIS CDG	F-100	12345	
256	1320	PARIS CDG	1430	EAST MIDLANDS	F-100	12345	
257	1450	EAST MIDLANDS	1600	PARIS CDG	F-100	12345 7	
258	1635	PARIS CDG	1745	EAST MIDLANDS	F-100	12345 7	
259	1830	EAST MIDLANDS	1940	PARIS CDG	F-100	12345	
260	2015	PARIS CDG	2125	EAST MIDLANDS	F-100	12345	
263	0950	EAST MIDLANDS	1240	MALAGA	F-100	3	
264	1320	MALAGA	1610	EAST MIDLANDS	F-100	3	
265	1035	EAST MIDLANDS	1145	PARIS CDG	F-100	6	
266	1230	PARIS CDG	1340	EAST MIDLANDS	F-70	6	
267	1430	EAST MIDLANDS	1625	FARO	F-70	7	
268	1910	FARO	2105	EAST MIDLAND	F-70	7	
269	1030	EAST MIDLANDS	1140	BELFAST	SAAB-340	6	
270	1210	BELFAST	1315	EAST MIDLANDS	SAAB-340	6	
271	0645	EAST MIDLANDS	0800	BELFAST	SAAB-340	12345	
272	0830	BELFAST	0940	EAST MIDLANDS	SAAB-340	12345	
273	1350	EAST MIDLANDS	1500	BELFAST	SAAB-340	12345	
274	1530	BELFAST	1640	EAST MIDLANDS	SAAB-340	12345	
275	1715	EAST MIDLANDS	1830	BELFAST	SAAB-340	12345	
276	1855	BELFAST	2005	EAST MIDLANDS	SAAB-340	12345	
277	1835	EAST MIDLANDS	1930	BELFAST	F-100	7	
278	2010	BELFAST	2105	EAST MIDLANDS	F-100	7	
279	1020	EAST MIDLANDS	1130	BELFAST	SAAB-340	12345	
280	1200	BELFAST	1310	EAST MIDLANDS	SAAB-340	12345	
281	0800	EAST MIDLANDS	1015	PALMA	F70/F100	67	

282	1100	PALMA	1330	EAST MIDLANDS	F70/F100		6	
283	1015	EAST MIDLANDS	1230	PALMA	F-100	2		
284	1315	PALMA	1545	EAST MIDLANDS	F-100	2		
285	1430	EAST MIDLANDS	1720	MALAGA	F-100		6	
286	1805	MALAGA	2055	EAST MIDLANDS	F-100		6	
287	0950	EAST MIDLANDS	1145	FARO	F-100	4		
288	1425	FARO	1620	EAST MIDLANDS	F-100	4		
289	1050	EAST MIDLANDS	1255	NICE	F-100	1 5		
290	1340	NICE	1550	EAST MIDLANDS	F-100	1 5		
291	0840	GLASGOW	0940	LEEDS	SAAB-340	12345		
292	0710	LEEDS	0810	GLASGOW	SAAB-340	12345		
294	1500	LEEDS	1600	GLASGOW	SAAB-340	12345		
295	1630	GLASGOW	1730	LEEDS	SAAB-340	12345		
296	1800	LEEDS	1900	GLASGOW	SAAB-340	12345		
297	1930	GLASGOW	2030	LEEDS	SAAB-340	12345		
298	1830	LEEDS	1930	GLASGOW	SAAB-340	7		
299	2000	GLASGOW	2100	LEEDS	SAAB-340	7		
303	0640	EAST MIDLANDS	0750	DUBLIN	SAAB-340	123456	0655/0750 6	
304	0820	DUBLIN	0920	EAST MIDLANDS	SAAB-340	123456		
305	1400	EAST MIDLANDS	1500	DUBLIN	SAAB-340	1234567	1420/1525 7	
306	1535	DUBLIN	1640	EAST MIDLANDS	SAAB-340	1234567	1555/1700 7	
307	1840	EAST MIDLANDS	1950	DUBLIN	SAAB-340	12345		
308	2020	DUBLIN	2125	EAST MIDLANDS	SAAB-340	12345		
309	1915	EAST MIDLANDS	2010	DUBLIN	SAAB-340	7		
310	2040	DUBLIN	2135	EAST MIDLANDS	SAAB-340	7		
361	1055	ABERDEEN	1240	ESBJERG	SAAB-340	12345		
362	1310	ESBJERG	1505	ABERDEEN	SAAB-349	12345		
363	1125	ABERDEEN	1310	ESBJERG	SAAB-340	12345 7		
364	1340	ESBJERG	1535	ABERDEEN	SAAB-340	12345 7		
365	0725	MANCHESTER	0840	ABERDEEN	SAAB-340	1234567		
366	0855	ABERDEEN	1010	MANCHESTER	SAAB-340	12345		
367	1645	MANCHESTER	1800	ABERDEEN	SAAB-340	12345		
368	1840	ABERDEEN	1955	MANCHESTER	SAAB-340	12345		
370	0700	ABERDEEN	0815	MANCHESTER	SAAB-340	12345		
371	0920	MANCHESTER	1045	ABERDEEN	SAAB-340	12345		
373	1155	MANCHESTER	1315	ABERDEEN	SAAB-340	12345		
374	1345	ABERDEEN	1505	MANCHESTER	SAAB-340	12345		
376	1700	ABERDEEN	1815	MANCHESTER	SAAB-340	12345		
377	1845	MANCHESTER	2005	ABERDEEN	SAAB-340	12345		
380	0715	EDINBURGH	0815	MANCHESTER	SAAB-340	12345		
381	0900	MANCHESTER	1000	EDINBURGH	SAAB-340	12345		
382	1025	EDINBURGH	1125	MANCHESTER	SAAB-340	12345		
383	1535	MANCHESTER	1640	EDINBURGH	SAAB-340	12345		
384	0750	ABERDEEN	0830	EDINBURGH	SAAB-340	6		
	0850	EDINBURGH	0955	MANCHESTER	SAAB-340	6		
385	1025	MANCHESTER	1130	EDINBURGH	SAAB-340	6		
	1150	EDINBURGH	1230	ABERDEEN	SAAB-340	6		
386	1715	EDINBURGH	1815	MANCHESTER	SAAB-340	12345		
387	1855	MANCHESTER	2000	EDINBURGH	SAAB-340	12345		
388	1610	ABERDEEN	1650	EDINBURGH	SAAB-340	7		
	1710	EDINBURGH	1815	MANCHESTER	SAAB-340	7		
389	1845	MANCHESTER	1945	EDINBURGH	SAAB-340	7		
	2010	EDINBURGH	2050	ABERDEEN	SAAB-340	7		
390	0700	GLASGOW	0810	MANCHESTER	SAAB-340	12345		
391	0910	MANCHESTER	1015	GLASGOW	SAAB-340	12345		
392	1400	GLASGOW	1500	MANCHESTER	SAAB-340	12345		
393	1530	MANCHESTER	1630	GLASGOW	SAAB-340	12345		
396	1655	GLASGOW	1800	MANCHESTER	SAAB-340	12345 7		
397	1835	MANCHESTER	1940	GLASGOW	SAAB-340	12345 7		
398	1045	GLASGOW	1150	MANCHESTER	SAAB-340	12345		
399	1220	MANCHESTER	1325	GLASGOW	SAAB-340	12345		
466	1425	DUBLIN	1540	HEATHROW	B.737	12345		
493	0720	LEEDS	0845	PARIS	F-70	123456	0805/0930 6	
494	0925	PARIS	1045	LEEDS	F-70	123456	1005/1135 6	
495	1115	LEEDS	1240	PARIS	F-70	12345		
496	1510	PARIS	1640	LEEDS	F-70	12345		
497	1720	LEEDS	1840	PARIS	F-70	12345 7		
498	1915	PARIS	2045	LEEDS	F-70	12345 7		

581	0655	MANCHESTER	0800	HEATHROW	B.737	1234567	
582	0725	HEATHROW	0825	MANCHESTER	B.737	1234567	
584	0840	HEATHROW	0935	MANCHESTER	B.737	1234567	
585	0855	MANCHESTER	1000	HEATHROW	B.737	1234567	
586	1055	HEATHROW	1150	MANCHESTER	B.737	1234567	
587	1055	MANCHESTER	1200	HEATHROW	B.737	1234567	
588	1245	HEATHROW	1340	MANCHESTER	B.737	1234567	
589	1425	MANCHESTER	1520	HEATHROW	B.737	12345	
590	1700	HEATHROW	1755	MANCHESTER	B.737	1234567	
591	1645	MANCHESTER	1740	HEATHROW	B.737	1234567	
592	1820	HEATHROW	1915	MANCHESTER	B.737	1234567	
593	1825	MANCHESTER	1925	HEATHROW	B.737	1234567	
594	2030	HEATHROW	2120	MANCHESTER	B.737	1234567	
595	1955	MANCHESTER	2055	HEATHROW	B.737	1234567	
597	1240	MANCHESTER	1340	HEATHROW	B.737	1234567	
598	1505	HEATHROW	1600	MANCHESTER	B.737	12345	
651	0650	BIRMINGHAM	0810	BRUSSELS	EMB-145	12345	
652	0840	BRUSSELS	0950	BIRMINGHAM	EMB-145	12345	
653	1035	BIRMINGHAM	1145	BRUSSELS	EMB-145	12345	
654	1230	BRUSSELS	1340	BIRMINGHAM	EMB-145	12345	
655	1500	BIRMINGHAM	1610	BRUSSELS	EMB-145	12345	
656	1650	BRUSSELS	1800	BIRMINGHAM	EMB-145	12345	
659	1830	BIRMINGHAM	1940	BRUSSELS	EMB-145	12345 7	
660	2015	BRUSSELS	2125	BIRMINGHAM	EMB-145	12345 7	
713	0700	HEATHROW	0900	PRAGUE	B.737	1 56	
714	0950	PRAGUE	1155	HEATHROW	B.737	1 56	
717	1610	HEATHROW	1805	PRAGUE	B.737	12345 7	
718	1850	PRAGUE	2100	HEATHROW	B.737	12345 7	
733	1355	HEATHROW	1620	BUDAPEST	B.737	12345 7	
734	1710	BUDAPEST	1950	HEATHROW	B.737	12345 7	
735	1505	HEATHROW	1730	BUDAPEST	B.737	6	
736	1815	BUDAPEST	2055	HEATHROW	B.737	6	
740	0625	WARSAW	0915	HEATHROW	B.737	1234567	
741	0855	HEATHROW	1220	WARSAW	B.737	1234567	
742	1215	WARSAW	1155	HEATHROW	B.737	1234567	
747	1915	HEATHROW	2140	WARSAW	B.737	1234567	
749	0900	HEATHROW		MOSCOW	A.320	1234567	
750		MOSCOW	1755	HEATHROW	A.320	1234567	
800	0620	COLOGNE	0745	HEATHROW	B.737	1234567	
801	0740	HEATHROW	0900	COLOGNE	B.737	1234567	
802	1025	COLOGNE	1150	HEATHROW	B.737	6	
804	1700	COLOGNE	1825	HEATHROW	B.737	12345 7	
805	2000	HEATHROW	2120	COLOGNE	B.737	1234567	
808	0655	DUSSELDORF	0835	MANCHESTER	F-70	123456	
809	0910	MANCHESTER	1035	DUSSELDORF	F-70	123456	
810	1130	DUSSELDORF	1305	MANCHESTER	F-70	123456	
811	1425	MANCHESTER	1550	DUSSELDORF	F-70	12345 7	
812	1630	DUSSELDORF	1805	MANCHESTER	F-70	12345 7	
813	1850	MANCHESTER	2015	DUSSELDORF	F-70	12345 7	
815	0710	HEATHROW	0840	HANOVER	B.737	1234567	
816	0925	HANOVER	1105	HEATHROW	B.737	1234567	
817	1150	HEATHROW	1320	HANOVER	B.737	1234567	
818	1405	HANOVER	1545	HEATHROW	B.737	1234567	
819	1800	HEATHROW	1930	HANOVER	B.737	1234567	
820	2010	HANOVER	2145	HEATHROW	B.737	1234567	
821	0655	HEATHROW	0830	STUTTGART	B.737	1234567	
822	0915	STUTTGART	1100	HEATHROW	B.737	1234567	
823	1140	HEATHROW	1315	STUTTGART	B.737	1234567	
824	1405	STUTTGART	1550	HEATHROW	B.737	1234567	
825	1650	HEATHROW	1825	STUTTGART	B.737	1234567	
826	1915	STUTTGART	2105	HEATHROW	B.737	1234567	
830	0625	FRANKFURT	0805	HEATHROW	B.737	1234567	
831	0730	HEATHROW	0905	FRANKFURT	B.737	1234567	0830/1005 67
832	0950	FRANKFURT	1135	HEATHROW	B.737	12345	
833	1120	HEATHROW	1300	FRANKFURT	B.737	12345	
834	1050	FRANKFURT	1220	HEATHROW	B.737	67	
835	1340	HEATHROW	1515	FRANKFURT	B.737	67	
836	1600	FRANKFURT	1740	HEATHROW	B.737	1234567	

Flt	Dep	From	Arr	To	Aircraft	Days	Notes
837	1600	HEATHROW	1735	FRANKFURT	B.737	1234567	
838	1820	FRANKFURT	2000	HEATHROW	B.737	1234567	
839	1830	HEATHROW	2005	FRANKFURT	B.737	1234567	
901	0645	EDINBURGH	0835	PARIS CDG	F-100	123456	
902	0935	PARIS CDG	1125	EDINBURGH	F-100	123456	
	1215	EDINBURGH	1240	GLASGOW	F-100	123456	
903	1515	GLASGOW	1540	EDINBURGH	F-100	12345 7	
	1610	EDINBURGH	1740	PARIS CDG	F-100	12345 7	
904	1820	PARIS CDG	1950	EDINBURGH	F-100	12345 7	
	2025	EDINBURGH	2050	GLASGOW	F-100	12345 7	
1124	0905	JERSEY	1015	LEEDS	F-70	7	
1143	1250	JERSEY	1405	TEESSIDE	SAAB-34	67	1545/1700 6
1153	1440	TEESSIDE	1555	JERSEY	SAAB-340	7	18.07-29.08
1154	1025	LEEDS	1155	JERSEY	SAAB-340	12345	
1175	0720	EAST MIDLANDS	0820	JERSEY	F-100	7	
1184	1255	JERSEY	1425	LEEDS	SAAB-340	12345	
1196	0700	BIRMINGHAM	0755	JERSEY	F-70	67	0715/0815 7
1204	1700	JERSEY	1810	LEEDS	SAAB-340	6	29.05-21.08
1212	1040	LIVERPOOL	1140	JERSEY	F-100	7	-26.09
1214	1210	LEEDS	1320	JERSEY	SAAB-340	6	
1226	0900	JERSEY	1015	BIRMINGHAM	SF3/F70	67	1600/1715 6
1234	0800	LEEDS	0930	JERSEY	SAAB-340	6	05.06-11.09
1235	1030	EAST MIDLANDS	1150	JERSEY	F-70	7	
1236	1750	BIRMINGHAM	1905	JERSEY	F-70	6	28.08-25.09
1239	1430	GLASGOW	1550	JERSEY	F-100	7	-26.09
1245	2000	JERSEY	2105	EAST MIDLANDS	F-100	6	
1255	0720	EAST MIDLANDS	0820	JERSEY	F-100	7	
1256	1405	BIRMINGHAM	1520	JERSEY	SAAB-340	6	05.06-8.08
1265	1630	JERSEY	1730	EAST MIDLANDS	F-100	7	
1266	1200	JERSEY	1335	BIRMINGHAM	SAAB-340	6	05.06-28.08
1274	1050	LEEDS	1200	JERSEY	F-70	7	
1275	1120	EAST MIDLANDS	1220	JERSEY	F-100	12345	
1289	1220	JERSEY	1345	GLASGOW	F-70	6	26.06-25.09
1296	1045	BIRMINGHAM	1205	JERSEY	SAAB-340	7	-15.08
1299	1415	GLASGOW	1540	JERSEY	F-70	6	26.06-25.09
1308	0905	JERSEY	1025	BELFAST	F-70	7	-26.09
1318	1055	BELFAST	1215	JERSEY	SAAB-340	7	-26.09
1335	0700	EAST MIDLANDS	0800	JERSEY	SAAB-340	6	
1342	0900	JERSEY	1005	LIVERPOOL	??	7	
1343	??	JERSEY	??	LIVERPOOL	??	7	
1346	1355	JERSEY	1445	BIRMINGHAM	F-70	6	17.05-21.08
1355	0950	EAST MIDLANDS	1050	JERSEY	F-70	6	
1369	1220	JERSEY	1345	GLASGOW	F-100	7	-26.09
1385	1145	EDINBURGH	1230	ABERDEEN	SAAB-340	6	
1388	1205	JERSEY	1325	BELFAST	F-70	6	-25.09
1413	1350	TEESSIDE	1505	JERSEY	F-70	6	
1415	1420	EAST MIDLANDS	1520	JERSEY	F-70	6	
1443	1545	TEESSIDE	1700	JERSEY	F-100	6	
1445	1250	JERSEY	1345	EAST MIDLANDS	F-100	7	
1464	1600	JERSEY	1730	LEEDS	F-100	7	
1465	2100	JERSEY	2155	EAST MIDLANDS	B.737	6	
1468	1615	JERSEY	1735	BELFAST	F-100	6	-25.09
1478	1810	BELFAST	1930	JERSEY	F-100	6	-25.09
1488	0830	JERSEY	0950	BELFAST	F-70	6	
1493	1740	TEESSIDE	1855	JERSEY	F-70	6	03.07-11.09
1496	1530	BIRMINGHAM	1625	JERSEY	F-70	6	05.06-21.08
1506	1635	JERSEY	1735	BIRMINGHAM	F-70	7	
1519	1340	GLASGOW	1505	JERSEY	F-100	6	
1523	1545	JERSEY	1700	TEESSIDE	F-70	6	03.07-11.09
1533	0645	GLASGOW	0835	COPENHAGEN	F-100	123456	
	0725	EDINBURGH	0915	COPENHAGEN	F-100	6	
1534	0925	COPENHAGEN	1115	EDINBURGH	F-100	123456	1000/1155 6
	1135	EDINBURGH	1200	GLASGOW	F-100	123456	1215/1240 6
1535	1455	GLASGOW	1515	COPENHAGEN	F-100	12345 7	
	1540	EDINBURGH	1730	COPENHAGEN	F-100	12345 7	
1536	1830	COPENHAGEN	2030	EDINBURGH	F-100	12345 7	
	2050	EDINBURGH	2110	GLASGOW	F-100	12345 7	
1555	1100	EAST MIDLANDS	1215	GUERNSEY	SAAB-340	7	

1568	0840	JERSEY	1000	BELFAST	B.737	6	03.07-28.08
1574	0920	LEEDS	1050	JERSEY	SAAB-340	7	06.06-29.08
1595	1255	BELFAST	1415	JERSEY	F-70	6	-25.09
1598	1025	BELFAST	1145	JERSEY	F-70	6	
1604	0840	JERSEY	0950	LEEDS	F-100	6	-18.09
1605	1300	JERSEY	1400	EAST MIDLANDS	F-100	12345	
1606	1950	JERSEY	2055	BIRMINGHAM	F-70	6	
1614	1020	LEEDS	1130	JERSEY	F-100	6	-18.09
1625	2010	JERSEY	2105	EAST MIDLANDS	F-70	6	
1629	1910	JERSEY	2035	GLASGOW	B.737	6	
1631	1805	EDINBURGH	1935	JERSEY	F-100	6	04.07-15.08
1659	1700	GLASGOW	1825	JERSEY	B.737	6	
1661	1600	JERSEY	1725	EDINBURGH	F-100	6	03.07-28.08
1664	1425	JERSEY	1555	LEEDS	SAAB-340	6	05.06-26.06
1671	1750	EDINBURGH	1915	JERSEY	F-100	6	
1681	1540	JERSEY	1705	EDINBURGH	F-100	6	
1684	1545	JERSEY	1715	LEEDS	SAAB-340	7	06.06-
1705	1945	JERSEY	2105	EAST MIDLANDS	SAAB-340	6	
1714	1330	LEEDS	1440	JERSEY	F-70	7	
1724	1520	JERSEY	1630	LEEDS	F-70	6	
1809	1955	JERSEY	2120	GLASGOW	F-100	6	-25.09
1838	1040	BELFAST	1200	JERSEY	B.737	67	1100/1220 7
1849	1240	JERSEY	1405	GLASGOW	B.737	67	1300/1425 7
1859	1445	GLASGOW	1610	JERSEY	B.737	67	1505/1630 7
1868	1650	JERSEY	1810	BELFAST	B.737	67	1710/1830 7
1878	1855	BELFAST	2015	JERSEY	B.737	6	03.07-07.08
1895	0700	EAST MIDLANDS	0800	JERSEY	B.737	6	03.07-07.08
1915	1040	EAST MIDLANDS	1155	GUERNSEY	SAAB-340	6	
1925	1225	GUERNSEY	1340	EAST MIDLANDS	SAAB-340	6	
1935	1410	EAST MIDLANDS	1525	GUERNSEY	SAAB-340	6	
1945	1245	GUERNSEY	1400	EAST MIDLANDS	SAAB-340	67	1555/1710 6
1955	1015	EAST MIDLANDS	1135	GUERNSEY	SAAB-340	12345	
1975	1740	EAST MIDLANDS	1900	GUERNSEY	SAAB-340	6	
1985	1205	GUERNSEY	1320	EAST MIDLANDS	SAAB-340	12345	
8801	2315	EDINBURGH	0025	HEATHROW	A.320	12345	FREIGHT
8802	2315	HEATHROW	0025	EDINBURGH	A.320	12345	FREIGHT
9871	1525	HEATHROW	1620	EAST MIDLANDS	F-100		

UNEVEN NUMBERS - FLIGHTS LEAVING THE UK   EVEN NUMBERS - FLIGHTS INTO THE UK

4037/8	1340	EAST MIDLANDS	1840	REUS	A.320	3	30.06-
4047/8	1435	EAST MIDLANDS	1930	GERONA	A.320	4	01.07-30.09
4951/2	1700	GATWICK	1600	NAPLES	B.737	5	23.07-17.09
7071/2	0725	HEATHROW	1110	GENEVA	B.737	7	
7451/2	2300	GLASGOW	0540	PALMA	B.737	5	
7461/2	0730	GLASGOW	1345	PISA	B.737	6	
7463/4	1445	GLASGOW	2125	ALICANTE	B.737	6	
7465/6	2225	GLASGOW	0530	IBIZA	B.737	6	
7467/8	1355	GLASGOW	2020	PISA	F-100	6	
7471/2	0700	GLASGOW	1315	VENICE	F-100	7	30.05-27.09
7473/4	0715	GLASGOW	1315	GERONA	B.737	7	
7475/6	0730	GLASGOW	1405	RIMINI	F-100	7	06.06-26.09
7563/4	1645	EDINBURGH	2335	PALMA	B.737	6	
7959/0	2300	HEATHROW	0555	PALERMO	B.737	6	17.07-18.09
7963/4	1425	HEATHROW	2025	CAGLIARI	B.737	6	-02.10
7965/6	1715	HEATHROW	2110	NAPLES	A.320	6	
7967/8	1605	HEATHROW	1910	LA CORUNA	B.737	6	29.05-02.10
7969/0	2020	HEATHROW	0055	SANTIAGO	A.320	6	29.05-
7973/4	1205	HEATHROW	1855	BODRUM	B.737	7	-10.10
7975/6	0700	HEATHROW	1220	AJACCIO	B.737	7	-10.10
7991/2	0625	HEATHROW	1135	VENICE	B.737	7	

		MK AIRCARGO		*CALL SIGN NOT KNOWN MKA U.K.*			
102		CAIRO	1000	STANSTED	DC-8	1	
103	2100	STANSTED		ACCRA	DC-8	1	
108		CAIRO	1000	STANSTED	DC-8	2	
109	2030	STANSTED		KANO	DC-8	2	
115	2030	STANSTED		KANO	DC-8		7

MK AIRCARGO (Cont.)

Flight	Dep	From	Arr	To	Aircraft	Days
118		CAIRO	1000	STANSTED	DC-8	3
119	1215	STANSTED		NAIROBI	DC-8	3
122		CAIRO	1000	STANSTED	DC-8	4
123	1200	STANSTED		LUXEMBOURG	DC-8	34 7
124		CAIRO	1000	STANSTED	DC-8	5
126		CAIRO	1000	STANSTED	DC-8	6
128		CAIRO	1000	STANSTED	DC-8	7
218		CAIRO	1030	STANSTED	DC-8	3
222		CAIRO	1030	STANSTED	DC-8	4
228		CAIRO	1030	STANSTED	DC-8	7
801		NAIROBI	0720	STANSTED	DC-8	2
	0930	STANSTED		LUXEMBOURG	DC-8	2
919	1200	STANSTED		NAIROBI	DC-8	6

MONARCH — MONARCH AIRLINES OM/MON U.K.

SCHEDULED FLIGHTS

Flight	Dep	From	Arr	To	Aircraft	Days
012/3	0815	LUTON	1445	MALAGA	A.320	1234567
016/7	1630	LUTON	2250	MALAGA	A.320	6
020/1	0750	LUTON	1335	ALICANTE	A.320	23
024/5	0930	LUTON	1515	ALICANTE	A.320	6
026/7	1615	LUTON	2155	ALICANTE	A.320	4 7
032/3	0645	LUTON	1220	MAHON	A.320	1 3 5
054/5	1345	LUTON	2300	TENERIFE	A.320	5
056/7	1445	LUTON	2359	TENERIFE	A320/B757	2
068/9	1600	LUTON	2225	GIBRALTAR	A.320	123456

UNEVEN NOS. - FLIGHTS LEAVING THE U.K. EVEN NOS. - FLIGHTS INTO THE U.K.

Flight	Dep	From	Arr	To	Aircraft	Days	Notes
19P	2000	LUTON	2030	GATWICK	B.757	3	POSITIONING
	2000	LUTON	2105	GLASGOW	B.757	3	POSITIONING
48/9	1030	GLASGOW	1050	CANCUN	B.757	7	FORTNIGHTLY
	1140	GLASGOW	1250	LUTON	B.757	1	FORTNIGHTLY
63P	0500	GATWICK	0530	LUTON	B.757	3	-16.06
	0500	GATWICK	0555	MANCHESTER	B.757	3	23.06-
69P	2345	LUTON	0015	GATWICK	A.320	3	POSITIONING
78/9	1030	GLASGOW	0755	ORLANDO	B.757	7	
	0845	GLASGOW	0955	LUTON	B.757	1	
88/9	0700	GLASGOW	0440	ORLANDO	B.757	4	
92/3	1455	GATWICK	1525	PUERTO PLATT	B.757	1	
136/7	1130	MANCHESTER	0650	ORLANDO	DC-10	6	
139P	0900	LIVERPOOL	0930	MANCHESTER	A.320	1	POSITIONING
142P	0625	GLASGOW	0725	BIRMINGHAM	DC-10	5	POSITIONING
142/3	1100	GLASGOW	0535	ORLANDO	DC-10	4	
143P	0855	MANCHESTER	1000	GLASGOW	DC-10	4	POSITIONING
158P	0710	BIRMINGHAM	0750	MANCHESTER	DC-10	6	-26.06 / 31.07-
	0650	GLASGOW	0750	MANCHESTER	DC-10	6	03.07-24.07
158/9	1000	BIRMINGHAM	0610	ORLANDO	DC-10	5	
183P	2000	MANCHESTER	2030	LIVERPOOL	A.320	1	POSITIONING
306/7	0915	MANCHESTER	0455	ORLANDO	A.330	4	
314/5	0740	GATWICK	0610	MONTEGO BAY	A.330	7	
316/7	0900	MANCHESTER	0440	ORLANDO	A.330	5	
324/5	0710	GATWICK	0545	VARADERO	A.330	5	
328/9	0945	GATWICK	0450	ORLANDO	A.330	6	
327P	2130	LUTON	2210	MANCHESTER	A.300	6	
346/7	0715	GATWICK	0640	VARADERO	A.330	3	
358/9	1045	MANCHESTER	0725	MONTEGO BAY	A.330	1	
364/5	0900	MANCHESTER	0610	ORLANDO	A.330	6	
374/5	0845	GATWICK	0455	ORLANDO	A.330	4	
378/9	0700	GATWICK	0510	PUERTO PLATT	A.330	2	
384/5	0930	MANCHESTER	0755	LAS VEGAS	A.330	2	
396/7	0900	MANCHESTER	0725	ORLANDO	A.330	7	VIA BELFAST
505P	2310	GATWICK	2340	LUTON	A.320	2	POSITIONING
543P	0540	GATWICK	0625	LUTON	A.320	3	POSITIONING
563P	0500	MANCHESTER	0550	LUTON	A.300	4	POSITIONING
586P	1000	LUTON	1050	MANCHESTER	A.300	3	POSITIONING
623P	2350	GATWICK	0020	LUTON	A.300	1	26.07-
753P	1840	MANCHESTER	1940	GATWICK	A.300	7	POSITIONING
867P	2235	EDINBURGH	2300	GLASGOW	A.320	7	POSITIONING

Flight	Dep	From	Arr	To	Aircraft	Day	Notes
877P	2155	GLASGOW	2225	EDINBURGH	A.320	3	POSITIONING

EVEN NOS. - FLIGHTS LEAVING THE UK   UNEVEN NOS. - FLIGHTS INTO THE U.K.

Flight	Dep	From	Arr	To	Aircraft	Day	Notes
1102/3	0945	GATWICK	1945	RHODES	A.300	3	
1116/7	0800	GATWICK	1550	FUNCHAL	A.320	1	
1138/9	2030	GATWICK	0530	DALAMAN	B.757	6	19.06-
1174/5	1910	GATWICK	0440	TENERIFE	B.757	5	
1200/1	0645	MANCHESTER	1500	ZAKINTHOS	B.757	4	
1208/9	1620	MANCHESTER	2225	MAHON	B.757	5	
1216/7	1025	MANCHESTER	1845	ZAKINTHOS	B.757	7	
1244/5	2310	MANCHESTER	0530	PALMA	A.300	6	
1248/9	0700	MANCHESTER	1330	FARO	B.757	7	
1276/7	1030	MANCHESTER	2020	LAS PALMAS	A.300	1	
1286/7	1800	MANCHESTER	0350	TENERIFE	A.300	5	
1326/7	1515	LUTON	2040	PALMA	A.300	6	
1358/9	0110	LUTON	0655	IBIZA	A.320	7	
1362/3	1420	LUTON	2330	LAS PALMAS	B.757	1	
1414/5	1115	GATWICK	2215	TEL AVIV	B.757	4	
1418/9	0945	GATWICK	2130	HURGHADA	B.757	5	
1420/1	1555	GATWICK	2200	FARO	A.320	6	
1462/3	2200	GATWICK	0515	CORFU	B.757	1	
1484/5	1015	GATWICK	1945	DALAMAN	B.757	1	
1496/7	2315	GATWICK	0505	IBIZA	B.757	3	14.07-29.09
1504/5	2150	GATWICK	0545	ATHENS	B.757	5	
1514/5	1455	GATWICK	1950	VENICE	A.300	7	
1536/7	0730	GATWICK	1535	KALAMATA	B.757	7	
1538/9	0800	GATWICK	1355	PISA	A.300	6	
1542/3	2130	GATWICK	0455	THESSALONIKI	A.320	2	06.07-05.10
1578/9	1015	GATWICK	2155	SHARM EL SHEIKH	B.757	4	
1588/9	0930	GATWICK	1600	MALAGA	A.300	6	
1604/5	0900	BIRMINGHAM	1500	ALICANTE	A.320	6	
1606/7	2345	BIRMINGHAM	0745	ZAKINTHOS	A.320	4	
1608/9	2245	BIRMINGHAM	0425	PALMA	A.320	2	
1618/9	0830	BIRMINGHAM	1800	HERAKLION	A.320	2	
1630/1	0910	BIRMINGHAM	1515	MALAGA	A.320	7	
1634/5	0700	BIRMINGHAM	1145	SALZBURG	A.320	3	19.05-22.09
1642/3	0650	BIRMINGHAM	1605	FUNCHAL	A.320	1	
1648/9	1640	BIRMINGHAM	2320	FARO	A.320	6	
1652/3	1400	BIRMINGHAM	2245	LANZAROTE	A.320	4	
1656/7	1930	BIRMINGHAM	0500	DALAMAN	A.320	5	
1662/3	0620	BIRMINGHAM	1240	FARO	A.320	4	
1672/3	1310	BIRMINGHAM	2350	LARNACA	A.320	3	
1676/7	1930	BIRMINGHAM	0505	TENERIFE	A.320	2	
1678/9	1625	BIRMINGHAM	2250	FARO	A.320	7	
1680/1	0115	BIRMINGHAM	0725	IBIZA	A.320	7	
1694/5	0830	BIRMINGHAM	1800	TENERIFE	A.320	5	
1698/9	1720	BIRMINGHAM	0035	CORFU	A.320	1	
1702/3	0900	GATWICK	1445	ALICANTE	B.757	2	
1734/5	0555	GATWICK	1305	MALAGA	A.300	5	
1738/9	1745	GATWICK	0440	TEL AVIV	A.300	3	21.07-22.09
1744/5	2230	GATWICK	0640	ATHENS	A.320	4	01.07-30.09
1804/5	1630	MANCHESTER	0215	TENERIFE	DC10	2	
1812/3	0715	MANCHESTER	1245	VERONA	A.320	3	
1828/9	0830	MANCHESTER	1605	CORFU	B.757	1	
1832/3	2345	MANCHESTER	0730	MALTA	B.757	6	
1842/3	0915	MANCHESTER	1850	LANZAROTE	A.320	4	
1854/5	1610	MANCHESTER	2240	MALAGA	B.757	4	
1878/9	0815	MANCHESTER	1450	ALICANTE	DC-10	2	
1882/3	0800	MANCHESTER	1345	PISA	B.757	6	-02.10
1892/3	1315	MANCHESTER	1915	PALMA	B.757	3	-30.06
1932/3	0915	GATWICK	1740	SFAX, TUNISIA	A.320	2	
1934/5	2150	GATWICK	0725	DALAMAN	A.300	5	
1960/1	1430	GATWICK	2015	MAHON	A.300	5	
1986/7	1340	GATWICK	2105	CATANIA	B.757	6	
1996/7	1430	GATWICK	2030	FARO	A.320	7	
3004/5	1255	GATWICK	2025	ZAKINTHOS	B.757	4	
3024/5	0630	GATWICK	1415	PREVEZA	B.757	3	
3026/7	2315	GATWICK	0815	ATHENS	B.757	3	07.07-06.10

Flight	Time	UK Airport	Time	Destination	Aircraft	Day	Notes
3038/9	1625	GATWICK	2230	FARO	B.757	7	
3052/3	0545	GATWICK	1055	MAHON	B.757	5	
3062/3	2250	GATWICK	0410	PALMA	B.757	1	
3084/5	0720	GATWICK	1240	BASTIA	A.320	7	
3106/7	0700	MANCHESTER	1640	TENERIFE	A.300	5	
3118/9	0900	MANCHESTER	1550	FARO	A.320	6	
3124/5	0845	MANCHESTER	1445	MAHON	B.757	5	
3134/5	1335	MANCHESTER	2345	TENERIFE	B.757	2	
3144/5	1100	MANCHESTER	2100	DALAMAN	DC-10	1	
3164/5	2130	MANCHESTER	0605	ATHENS	B.757	5	
3182/3	0720	MANCHESTER	1405	FARO	A.300	4	
3284/5	2315	GATWICK	0430	PALMA	B.757	4	
3308/9	1435	BIRMINGHAM	2025	IBIZA	A.320	7	
3314/5	0740	BIRMINGHAM	1405	ALICANTE	A.320	2	
3316/7	2330	BIRMINGHAM	0510	IBIZA	A.320	6	
3342/3	0655	BIRMINGHAM	1310	FARO	A.320	7	
3346/7	1520	BIRMINGHAM	0140	PAPHOS	A.320	3	
3348/9	1550	BIRMINGHAM	2110	MAHON	A.320	5	
3354/5	2050	BIRMINGHAM	0410	CORFU	A.320	1	
3356/7	0735	BIRMINGHAM	1400	FARO	A.320	4	
3362/3	0700	BIRMINGHAM	1235	VERONA	A.320	3	-06.10
3364/5	1530	BIRMINGHAM	2135	MALAGA	A.320	6	
3376/7	0815	BIRMINGHAM	1430	ALICANTE	A.320	6	
3378/9	0905	BIRMINGHAM	1450	MAHON	A.320	5	
3386/7	1520	BIRMINGHAM	0025	LANZAROTE	A.320	4	
3392/3	2210	BIRMINGHAM	0730	TENERIFE	A.320	5	
3396/7	0720	BIRMINGHAM	1300	MAHON	A.320	1	17.05-11.10
3410/1	1455	GATWICK	2015	PALMA	B.757	6	
3418/9	2240	GATWICK	0925	TEL AVIV	B.757	6	
3436/7	1700	GATWICK	2250	MALAGA	B.757	2	
3438/9	1815	GATWICK	2355	ALICANTE	B.757	4	
3468/9	0625	GATWICK	1530	FUERTVENTURA	B.757	3	
3534/5	1045	MANCHESTER	1915	FUNCHAL	A.320	1	
3554/5	2045	MANCHESTER	0655	TENERIFE	B.757	7	-18.07
	2255	MANCHESTER	0900	TENERIFE	A.300	7	25.07-
3560/1	1300	MANCHESTER	1155	PALMA	B.757	6	
3562/3	2120	MANCHESTER	0400	IBIZA	A.300	3	
3586/7	1240	MANCHESTER	2340	LARNACA	A.300	3	
3604/5	1540	GATWICK	0150	LARNACA	B.757	3	-14.07
3606/7	0915	GATWICK	1835	HERAKLION	A.300	2	
3608/9	0705	GATWICK	1600	LANZAROTE	A.300	4	
3612/5	0615	GATWICK	1900	PALMA	B.757	6	
3620/1	1715	GATWICK	2345	MONASTIR	A.300	7	
3622/3	1645	GATWICK	2300	MALAGA	A.300	1	
3654/5	1725	GATWICK	0535	MALE	B.757	1	VIA BAHRAIN
3656/7	0700	GATWICK	1330	FARO	A.300	7	
3662/3	0855	GATWICK	1545	NAPLES	B.757	5	
3670/1	0900	GATWICK	2130	BANJUL	A.300	5	
3690/1	0745	GATWICK	1510	PREVEZA	B.757	7	-03.10
3694/5	1540	GATWICK	0035	RHODES	B.757	3	21.07-
3722/3	1415	MANCHESTER	0050	PAPHOS	A.320	3	
3724/5	0600	MANCHESTER	1215	PALMA	A.300	2	
3752/3	0830	MANCHESTER	1510	MALAGA	A.300	7	
3768/9	0825	MANCHESTER	1930	LARNACA	A.320	7	
3782/3	1500	MANCHESTER	2135	ALMERIA	B.757	4	
3824/5	2355	LUTON	0725	CORFU	A.320	5	16.07-03.10
3904/5	0930	MANCHESTER	1845	FUERTVENTURA	B.757	3	
3924/5	0655	MANCHESTER	1350	FARO	B.757	4	
3968/9	0035	MANCHESTER	0915	ZAKINTHOS	A.320	5	
3972/3	1015	MANCHESTER	2005	TENERIFE	A.320	5	
3974/5	1325	MANCHESTER	2255	HERAKLION	A.300	2	
3978/9	2000	MANCHESTER	0525	RHODES	B.757	3	23.06-08.09
5016/7	1915	MANCHESTER	0425	RHODES	B.757	3	21.07-06.10
5018/9	1625	MANCHESTER	2255	MALAGA	A.320	2	
5040/1	1025	MANCHESTER	2020	TENERIFE	B.757	5	
5052/3	1650	MANCHESTER	2315	MALAGA	A.320	6	
5098/9	0600	MANCHESTER	1230	MALAGA	B.757	6	
5104/5	1000	LIVERPOOL	2235	ALICANTE	A.320	7	

Flight	Dep	Origin	Arr	Destination	Aircraft	Day	Notes
5114/5	0730	LIVERPOOL	1705	TENERIFE	A.320	5	
5128/9	1850	LIVERPOOL	0445	DALAMAN	A.320	5	
5134/5	2255	LIVERPOOL	0835	LAS PALMAS	A.320	6	
5138/9	2350	LIVERPOOL	0800	ZAKINTHOS	A.320	7	
5146/7	0600	LIVERPOOL	2100	ALICANTE	A.320	6	
5154/5	1615	LIVERPOOL	2215	PALMA	A.320	2	
5166/7	1815	LIVERPOOL	0320	LANZAROTE	A.320	4	
5176/7	0825	LIVERPOOL	1500	FARO	A.320	4	
5182/3	2220	LIVERPOOL	0750	BODRUM	A.320	1	
5184/5	2345	LIVERPOOL	0550	PALMA	A.320	2	
5198/9	0840	LIVERPOOL	2255	ALICANTE	A.320	3	
5204/5	0020	GATWICK	0930	RHODES	B.757	4	21.07-06.10
5242/3	0745	GATWICK	1345	ALICANTE	B.757	6	
5244/5	0800	GATWICK	1415	MALAGA	B.757	3	
5246/7	0055	GATWICK	0655	MALAGA	B.757	4	22.07-
5248/9	0700	GATWICK	1550	CHANIA	B.757	2	-12.10
5256/7	2350	GATWICK	0900	ATHENS	B.757	2	
5272/3	0630	GATWICK	1345	CORFU	B.757	1	
5276/7	2255	GATWICK	0445	MALAGA	B.757	5	23.07-01.10
5286/7	2140	GATWICK	0035	MALE, MALDIVES	A.300	7	VIA BAH
5294/5	1055	GATWICK	2030	LAS PALMAS	B.757	1	
5298/9	2130	GATWICK	0655	ANTALYA	A.320	7	
5322/3	2305	GATWICK	0455	PALMA	B.757	6	
5362/3	1330	GATWICK	0030	TEL AVIV	B.757	7	
5364/5	1655	GATWICK	0155	BODRUM	A.320	1	
5376/7	2230	GATWICK	0915	TEL AVIV	B.757	4	
5382/3	0940	GATWICK	2120	TEL AVIV	B.757	2	
5388/9	1115	GATWICK	2045	TENERIFE	B.757	5	
5408/9	1455	LUTON	0055	PAPHOS	A.320	3	
5450/1	0730	LUTON	1355	ALICANTE	A.300	6	
5474/5	0800	LUTON	1435	FARO	A.320	7	
5476/7	2305	LUTON	0615	CORFU	A.320	1	
5494/5	0800	LUTON	1435	FARO	A.300	4	
5516/7	0700	GATWICK	1610	FUERTVENTURA	A.300	3	
5528/9	2130	GATWICK	0440	CORFU	B.757	1	19.07-04.10
5544/5	0645	GATWICK	2030	VERONA	B.757	6	-02.10
5572/3	2335	GATWICK	0710	ZAKINTHOS	B.757	4	
5584/5	0915	GATWICK	1435	MAHON	A.320	5	
5592/3	2335	GATWICK	0540	FARO	B.757	7	18.07-03.10
5598/9	1445	GATWICK	2110	ALMERIA	A.300	4	
5604/5	1355	MANCHESTER	1955	PALMA	B.757	6	
5612/3	2130	MANCHESTER	0720	DALAMAN	A.320	5	
5628/9	1445	MANCHESTER	1200	VERONA	B.757	6	-02.10
5650/1	1550	MANCHESTER	0115	LANZAROTE	A.300	4	
5682/3	2345	MANCHESTER	0710	IBIZA	A.300	6	
5690/1	0815	MANCHESTER	1745	IZMIR	A.320	1	
5692/3	0650	MANCHESTER	1155	SALZBURG	B.757	3	-30.06
	0650	MANCHESTER	1805	SALZBURG	B.757	3	07.07-22.09
5694/5	0845	MANCHESTER	1505	ALICANTE	A.320	2	
5702/3	2315	GATWICK	0540	IBIZA	A300/A320	6	
5708/9	0915	GATWICK	1455	PALMA	B.757	1	
5722/3	0655	GATWICK	2045	MAHON	A.320	4	
5728/9	1030	GATWICK	1940	DALAMAN	B.757	7	
5750/1	0600	GATWICK	1155	FARO	B.757	4	
5770/1	2320	MANCHESTER	0255	MOMBASA	B.757	7	VIA GATWICK
5782/3	1635	GATWICK	0040	AGADIR	B.757	7	
5784/5	2210	GATWICK	0355	IBIZA	B757/A300	3	
5794/5	0900	GATWICK	1525	MALAGA	A.300	7	
5796/7	1610	GATWICK	0135	TENERIFE	A.300	2	
5802/3	0015	GLASGOW	0915	ZAKINTHOS	A.320	7	
5804/5	0700	EDINBURGH	1710	DALAMAN	A.320	5	
5806/7	2130	GLASGOW	0725	BODRUM	A.320	1	
5816/7	2310	GLASGOW	0630	PALMA	A.320	2	
5818/9	1420	EDINBURGH	2305	ZAKINTHOS	A.320	4	
5824/5	1100	GLASGOW	1920	CORFU	A.320	1	
5856/7	2250	EDINBURGH	0900	LAS PALMAS	A.320	6	
5860/1	0615	EDINBURGH	1320	FARO	A.320	4	
5862/3	1015	GLASGOW	2035	HERAKLION	A.320	2	

Flight	Dep	Origin	Arr	Destination	Aircraft			Dates
5866/7	1030	EDINBURGH	2145	LARNACA	A.320		7	
5872/3	0640	EDINBURGH	2140	FARO	A.320		6	
5876/7	0940	GLASGOW	2105	LARNACA	A.320	3		
5878/9	1450	LIVERPOOL	1335	FARO	A.320		6	
5880/1	1830	EDINBURGH	0445	TENERIFE	A.320	5		
5888/9	1310	BRISTOL	1155	SALZBURG	B.757	3		07.07-22.09
5896/7	1445	NEWCASTLE	1230	ALICANTE	A.320		6	
5906/7	0625	GATWICK	1235	OLBIA	B.757		6	-02.10
5926/7	0145	GATWICK	0945	ZAKINTHOS	B.757	1		
5932/3	1030	GATWICK	1645	FARO	B.757		4	
5946/7	1615	GATWICK	2140	MAHON	A.320	5		
5952/3	2300	GATWICK	0655	THESSALONIKI	A.320	5		
5978/9	0030	GATWICK	0620	IBIZA	A.300		7	
5984/5	0900	GATWICK	1445	PALMA	A.300	2		
7018/9	0820	LUTON	1840	LARNACA	B.757	3		
7022/3	1320	LUTON	2115	FUNCHAL	A.320	1		
7040/1	1530	LUTON	0030	FUERTVENTURA	A.320	3		
7056/7	0715	LUTON	1310	MAHON	A.300	5		
7066/7	0045	LUTON	0955	DALAMAN	B.757	2		
7074/5	1600	LUTON	0120	LANZAROTE	B.300	4		
7086/7	1620	LUTON	0220	PAPHOS	A.320		7	
7094/5	2355	LUTON	0610	MALAGA	A.320		6	17.07-25.09
7096/7	0530	LUTON	1310	ZAKINTHOS	A.320	4		
7098/9	1445	LUTON	0020	TENERIFE	A.300	5		
7172/3	2130	MANCHESTER	0345	IBIZA	B.757		6	19.06-02.10
7174/5	1745	MANCHESTER	0120	CORFU	B.757	1		
7180/1	1545	MANCHESTER	2140	VENICE	DC10/A300		7	
7202/3	0630	GATWICK	1525	IZMIR	A.300	1		
7228/9	1730	GATWICK	2345	MALAGA	A.300	4		
7254/5	1715	GATWICK	2215	VERONA	B.757	3		
7256/7	0900	GATWICK	1435	CAGLIARA	A.320		6	
7268/9	2315	GATWICK	0455	REUS	B757/A320	2		EXC.06.07-07.09
7292/3	1555	GATWICK	2210	FARO	A.300		6	
7306/7	0700	MANCHESTER	1335	FARO	A.300		7	
7316/7	2100	MANCHESTER	0655	ANTALYA	A.320		7	
7318/9	1430	MANCHESTER	2045	IBIZA	B.757		7	
7340/1	1900	MANCHESTER	0105	PALMA	A.320	1		
7356/7	1630	EDINBURGH	1510	ALICANTE	A.320	3		
7358/9	0745	MANCHESTER	1415	ALICANTE	A.300		6	
7394/5	1500	MANCHESTER	2225	MONASTIR	A300/DC10		7	
7608/9	0625	GLASGOW	1355	FARO	B.757		6	
7624/5	1655	GLASGOW	1555	REUS	A.320		7	
7628/9	0600	GLASGOW	1610	TENERIFE	B.757	5		
7640/1	1725	GLASGOW	0355	DALAMAN	B.757	5		
7662/3	2255	GLASGOW	0900	LAS PALMAS	B.757		6	
7684/5	1445	GLASGOW	2135	PALMA	B.757		6	
7734/5	1505	MANCHESTER	1250	MAHON	A.320	4		
7736/7	1550	MANCHESTER	2230	ALICANTE	B.757		6	
7782/3	0715	MANCHESTER	1715	RHODES	A.300	3		
7802/3	1215	GATWICK	2115	TENERIFE	B.757	5		
7806/7	2300	GATWICK	0455	IBIZA	B.757		6	
7810/1	0645	GATWICK	1150	FIGARI	B.757		7	
7830/1	1715	GATWICK	2315	MALAGA	A.300		6	
7836/7	1110	GATWICK	2025	RHODES	B.757	3		
7864/5	1555	GATWICK	2140	ALICANTE	B.757	2		
7876/7	2100	GATWICK	0610	TENERIFE	B.757		7	
7886/7	0700	GATWICK	1300	FARO	A.300		4	
7906/7	1700	GATWICK	2245	ALICANTE	B.757	2		
7914/5	2110	GATWICK	0005	MALE	A.300		7	VIA BAHRAIN
7926/7	2345	GATWICK	0545	PALMA	A.320		6	17.07-25.09
7928/9	1540	GATWICK	2200	MALAGA	B.757	3		21.07-29.09

		NAMIBIA		*NAMIB AIR (PTY) LTD.*	*SW/NMB*	*NAMIBIA*	
251		LUSAKA	2110	HEATHROW	B.767	1	
252	2240	HEATHROW		LUSAKA	B.767	1	
273		WINDHOEK	1955	HEATHROW	B.767	2	
274	2115	HEATHROW		LUXEMBOURG	B.767	2	

271		WINDHOEK	1955	HEATHROW	B.767	2	
272	2115	HEATHROW		WINDHOEK	B.767	2	

NEW ZEALAND   AIR NEW ZEALAND   NZ/ANZ   NEW ZEALAND

1	1610	HEATHROW		AUCKLAND	B.747	1234567	
2		AUCKLAND	0920	HEATHROW	B.747	1 34 67	ARR 1200 3
		AUCKLAND	1300	HEATHROW	B.747	2 5	ARR 1105 5
18		LOS ANGELES	1045	FRANKFURT	B.747	56	ARR 1145 6
19	1500	FRANKFURT		LOS ANGELES	B.747	56	

NIPPON CARGO   NIPPON CARGO AIRLINES   KZ/NCA   JAPAN

88	0725	AMSTERDAM	0835	STANSTED	B.747	7	
89	0940	STANSTED	1050	AMSTERDAM	B.747	3 7	1055/1205 7
92		ANCHORAGE	0740	STANSTED	B.747	3	

NITRO   TNT INTERNATIONAL AVIATION   NTR   U.K.

2E	1840	TEESSIDE	1920	EDINBURGH	BAE-146	1	
2G	0005	LIEGE	0115	STANSTED	BAE-146	2	
	0300	STANSTED	0420	BIRMINGHAM	BAE-146	2	
	0255	LIEGE	0420	BIRMINGHAM	B.727	3456	
	0505	BIRMINGHAM	0600	BELFAST	B.727	3456	
2J	2040	BELFAST	2135	BIRMINGHAM	B.727	12345	
	2220	BIRMINGHAM	2359	LIEGE	B.727	12345	
3B	2025	EDINBURGH	2120	LIVERPOOL	BAE-146	1	
	??	LIVERPOOL		LIEGE	BAE-146	1	
3E	0715	TEESSIDE	0810	STANSTED	BAE-146	5	
3F	1530	STANSTED	1640	LIEGE	BAE-146	7	
3G	1750	LIEGE	1900	STANSTED	BAE-146	7	
	1945	STANSTED	2100	DUBLIN	BAE-146	7	
3P	0440	LIVERPOOL	0540	STANSTED	BAE-146	6	
3Y	0310	LIEGE	0420	STANSTED	BAE-146	2345	
	0535	STANSTED	0630	TEESSIDE	BAE-146	2345	
	0535	STANSTED	0650	EDINBURGH	BAE-146	6	
4C	0330	LIEGE	0430	STANSTED	A.300	2345	
	0640	STANSTED	0750	EDINBURGH	A.300	2345	
4F	2045	EDINBURGH	2240	STANSTED	A.300	2345	
	0001	STANSTED	0100	LIEGE	B.727	3456	
6A	0315	LIEGE	0425	STANSTED	BAE-146	6	
	0510	STANSTED	0625	DUBLIN	BAE-146	6	
6X	0145	STANSTED	0255	LIEGE	BAE-146	345	
6Y	0001	LIEGE	0105	STANSTED	BAE-146	345	
9K	0210	LIEGE	0320	STANSTED	BAE-146	2345	-29.06 / 31.08-
9L	0405	STANSTED	0515	LIEGE	BAE-146	2345	-29.06 / 31.08-
12L	0210	LIEGE	0330	BIRMINGHAM	ELECTRA	345	
	0415	BIRMINGHAM	0530	BELFAST	ELECTRA	345	
12Y	1950	BELFAST	2105	BIRMINGHAM	ELECTRA	234	
	2150	BIRMINGHAM	2315	LIEGE	ELECTRA	234	
16A	1910	SHANNON	2040	STANSTED	B.727	5	
	2300	STANSTED	0010	LIEGE	B.727	5	
16Z	0250	LIEGE	0400	STANSTED	B.727	6	
	0445	STANSTED	0540	LIVERPOOL	B.727	6	
776	2235	EDINBURGH	2350	STANSTED	BAE-146	6	
789	0115	STANSTED	0220	LIEGE	BAE-146	7	
789P		BASLE	0655	STANSTED	BAE-146	7	

NORTH FLYING   NORTH FLYING   6Z/NFA   DENMARK

921	1010	NEWCASTLE	1110	ABERDEEN	METRO	12	1210/1310 1
	1130	ABERDEEN		BERGEN	METRO	12	DEP 1330 1
924		BERGEN	1840	ABERDEEN	METRO	12	ARR 2040 1
	1900	ABERDEEN	2000	NEWCASTLE	METRO	12	2100/2200 1

NORTHWEST   NORTHWEST AIRLINES INC.   NW/NWA   U.S.A.

30		PHILADELPHIA	0720	AMSTERDAM	DC-10	1234567	
31	1250	AMSTERDAM		PHILADELPHIA	DC-10	1234567	
32		DETROIT	0955	GATWICK	DC-10	1234567	

33	1300	GATWICK		DETROIT	DC-10	1234567	DEP 1325 14
34		SEATTLE	0740	AMSTERDAM	DC-10	1234567	
35	1000	AMSTERDAM		SEATTLE	DC-10	1234567	
36		WASHINGTON	0645	AMSTERDAM	DC-10	1234567	
37	1035	AMSTERDAM		WASHINGTON	DC-10	1234567	
38		BOSTON	0705	AMSTERDAM	DC-10	1234567	
39	1250	AMSTERDAM		BOSTON	DC-10	1234567	
40		DETROIT	0510	AMSTERDAM	DC-10	1234567	
41	0710	AMSTERDAM		DETROIT	DC-10	1234567	
44		MINNEAPOLIS	0900	GATWICK	DC-10	1234567	
45	1210	GATWICK		MINNEAPOLIS	DC-10	1234567	
46		DETROIT	0745	GATWICK	DC-10	1234567	
47	1510	GATWICK		DETROIT	DC-10	1234567	
48		DETROIT	1015	AMSTERDAM	DC-10	1234567	
49	1530	AMSTERDAM		DETROIT	DC-10	1234567	
50		DALLAS	0605	FRANKFURT	DC-10	1234567	
51	0940	PARIS CDG		DETROIT	DC-10	1234567	
52		DALLAS	0625	FRANKFURT	DC-10	1234567	
53	1250	FRANKFURT		DETROIT	DC-10	1234567	
55	1535	AMSTERDAM		MINNEAPOLIS	DC-10	1234567	
56		MINNEAPOLIS	1115	AMSTERDAM	DC-10	1234567	
57	1030	AMSTERDAM		NEW YORK	DC-10	1234567	
58		NEW YORK	0650	AMSTERDAM	DC-10	1234567	
67	0935	AMSTERDAM		DALLAS	B.747	1234567	
68		DALLAS	0555	FRANKFURT	B.747	1234567	
97	1230	OSLO		MINNEAPOLIS	DC-10	1234567	
98		MINNEAPOLIS	0900	OSLO	DC-10	1234567	

NOSTRU AIR   *AIR NOSTRUM   YW/ANS   SPAIN*

8347	1310	GATWICK		ASTURIAS	F-50	12345 7
8348		ASTURIAS	1720	GATWICK	F-50	12345 7
8564	1810	GATWICK		ZARAGOZA	F-50	12345 7
565		ZARAGOZA	1210	GATWICK	F-50	12345 7

NOUVELAIR   *NOUVEL AIR TUNISIE   LB/LBT   TUNIS*

EVEN NUMBERS - FLIGHTS INTO THE U.K.   UNEVEN NUMBERS - FLIGHTS LEAVING THE U.K.

806/7	1900	EAST MIDLANDS	1800	MONASTIR	MD-83	3	14.07-06.10
824/5	1100	GATWICK	1000	MONASTIR	MD-83	3	
842/3	0130	STANSTED	0030	MONASTIR	MD-83	7	25.07-03.10
842/3	0215	BELFAST	0115	MONASTIR	MD-83	7	
846/7	1915	BIRMINGHAM	1815	MONASTIR	MD-83	7	
882/3	VAR	GATWICK	VAR	MONASTIR	MD-83	5/6	
888/9	1710	GLASGOW	1610	MONASTIR	MD-83	6	12.06-

OLYMPIC   *OLYMPIC AIRWAYS   OA/OAL   GREECE*

259	0745	ATHENS	1120	HEATHROW	A.310	1 3 5
260	1230	HEATHROW	1555	ATHENS	A.310	1234567
261	0720	ATHENS	1120	HEATHROW	A.310	2 4 67
262	1640	HEATHROW	1935	ATHENS	A.310	2 4 67
265	1650	ATHENS	2105	HEATHROW	A.300	1234567
266	2205	HEATHROW	0210	ATHENS	A.300	1234567
269	1140	ATHENS	1520	HEATHROW	B737/A300	1234567
270	1640	HEATHROW	2000	ATHENS	B737/A300	1 3 5
411	1040	ATHENS		NEW YORK	B.747	12 45
412		NEW YORK	0855	ATHENS	B.747	23 56
413	1220	ATHENS		BOSTON	B.747	3
414		NEW YORK	1220	ATHENS	B.747	4
415	1120	ATHENS		NEW YORK	B.747	6
416		BOSTON	1055	ATHENS	B.747	7
417	1300	ATHENS		NEW YORK	B.747	7
418		NEW YORK	1105	ATHENS	B.747	1
423	1040	ATHENS		MONTREAL	B.747	2 6
424		MONTREAL	1105	ATHENS	B.747	3 7

EVEN NUMBERS - FLIGHTS LEAVING THE U.K.   UNEVEN NUMBERS - FLIGHTS INTO THE U.K.

363/4	2150	GATWICK	2100	DALAMAN	MD-88	2	
377/8	2100	MANCHESTER	0915	IZMIR	MD-88	3	
379/0	1010	MANCHESTER	2000	DALAMAN	MD-88	34	1000/0900 4
391/2	2100	GLASGOW	2000	IZMIR	MD-88	4	
400/1	1030	DALAMAN	0935	BRISTOL	MD-80	2	
435/6	1130	GLASGOW	1030	DALAMAN	MD-88	3	
449/0	2030	TEESSIDE	1930	DALAMAN	MD-83	3	
505/6	2025	TEESSIDE	1925	BODRUM	MD-83	3	
507/8	1015	MANCHESTER	0900	BODRUM	MD-88	4	
537/8	2100	EAST MIDLANDS	3000	DALAMAN	MD-88	4	
605/6	2050	EAST MIDLANDS	1950	BODRUM	MD-88	4	
611/2	1130	GLASGOW	1030	BODRUM	MD-88	3	

PAKISTAN   *PAKISTAN INTERNATIONAL AIRWAYS   PK/PIA   PAKISTAN*

701		ISLAMABAD	1055	MANCHESTER	B.747	34	7	
702	1615	MANCHESTER		ISLAMABAD	B.747	34	7	
703	1115	PARIS CDG		NEW YORK	B.747	2		
704		NEW YORK	0910	PARIS CDG	B.747	3		
709		LAHORE	1230	MANCHESTER	B.747	2	56	
710	1615	MANCHESTER		LAHORE	B.747	2	56	
711	1105	PARIS CDG		NEW YORK	B.747		6	
712		NEW YORK	0840	FRANKFURT	B.747		7	
715	1320	ZURICH		NEW YORK	B.747	5		
716		NEW YORK	0900	PARIS CDG	B.747		6	
723	1150	ZURICH		NEW YORK	B.747	3		
724		NEW YORK	0930	ZURICH	B.747	4		
756	2000	HEATHROW		LAHORE	B.747	3	6	DEP 2100 3
757		LAHORE	1130	HEATHROW	B.747	3	6	ARR 1220 3
781		KARACHI	1330	HEATHROW	A.310	3 5		
782	1630	HEATHROW		KARACHI	A.310	3 5		
783		ISLAMABAD	1815	HEATHROW	B.747	2		
784	2105	HEATHROW		ISLAMABAD	B.747	2		
785		ISLAMABAD	1020	HEATHROW	B.747		6	
786	1630	HEATHROW		ISLAMABAD	B.747		6	
787		DUBAI	1655	HEATHROW	B.747		7	
788	2000	HEATHROW		DUBAI	B.747		7	
796		WASHINGTON	0540	FRANKFURT	B.747		6	
797	0535	FRANKFURT		WASHINGTON	B.747	5		
798		WASHINGTON	0540	FRANKFURT	B.747	3		
799	0535	FRANKFURT		WASHINGTON	B.747	2		

PENANT   *COLOR AIR   CLA   NORWAY*

703	1105	OSLO	1300	STANSTED	B.737	12345 7	
704	1355	STANSTED	1550	OSLO	B.737	12345 7	

PICKAIR   *AIR MIDI BIGORRE   BIE   FRANCE*

401		MARSEILLES	0830	SHANNON	B.737	6	29.05-11.09
402	0920	SHANNON		MARSEILLES	B.737	6	29.05-11.09
403		LYONS	1455	SHANNON	B.737	6	29.05-11.09
404	1530	SHANNON		LYONS	B.737	6	29.05-11.09

POLAR TIGER   *POLAR AIR CARGO   PO/PAC   U.S.A.*

602		NEW YORK	1555	MANCHESTER	B.747	1	
	1755	MANCHESTER	1915	AMSTERDAM	B.747	1	
		CHICAGO	1700	PRESTWICK	B.747	4 6	ARR 1800 6
	1900	PRESTWICK		SPL??	B.747	4 6	DEP 2000 6
603	0600	AMSTERDAM		NEW YORK	B.747	6	
604		CHICAGO	1200	SHANNON	B.747	7	
	1400	SHANNON	1530	AMSTERDAM	B.747	7	
605	1030	AMSTERDAM		NEW YORK	B.747	3	
616		CHICAGO	1500	PRESTWICK	B.747	7	
	1700	PRESTWICK		SPL??	B.747	7	
617	1500	AMSTERDAM		NEW YORK	B.747	1 3 7	DEP 0600 1

001	1150	WARSAW		CHICAGO	B.767	1234567	
002		CHICAGO	0900	WARSAW	B.767	1234567	
003	0910	WARSAW		CHICAGO	B.767	12 6	
004		CHICAGO	0615	WARSAW	B.767	2 4	
005	0840	KRAKOW		CHICAGO	B.767	123 7	
006	1210	WARSAW		NEW YORK	B.767	1234567	
007		NEW YORK	0825	WARSAW	B.767	1234567	
008		CHICAGO	0630	KRAKOW	B.767	123 7	
011	1240	WARSAW		NEW YORK	B.767	3 5 7	
012		NEW YORK	0850	WARSAW	B.767	1 4 7	
014		CHICAGO	0925	KRAKOW	B.767	1	
019	1240	WARSAW		NEW YORK	B.767	6	
020		NEW YORK	1045	WARSAW	B.767	7	
021	1220	KRAKOW		NEW YORK	B.767	6	
022		NEW YORK	0910	KRAKOW	B.767	6	
023	1150	WARSAW		CHICAGO	B.767	7	
028	0840	KRAKOW		NEW YORK	B.767	5	
029		NEW YORK	0600	KRAKOW	B.767	5	
031	1015	KRAKOW		TORONTO	B.767	4	
032		TORONTO	0800	KRAKOW	B.767	4	
041	0905	WARSAW		TORONTO	B.767	3 567	DEP 1130 37
042		TORONTO	0630	WARSAW	B.767	1 45	
043	0905	WARSAW		EDMONTON	B.767	5	
044		EDMONTON	0635	WARSAW	B.767	6	
273	0725	KRAKOW	1000	GATWICK	B.737	1234567	0855/1130 3
274	1050	GATWICK	1320	KRAKOW	B.737	2 4 67	
	1145	GATWICK	1415	KRAKOW	B.737	1 3 5	1230/1500 3
279	1350	WARSAW	1630	HEATHROW	B.737	1234567	
280	1730	HEATHROW	1955	WARSAW	B.737	1234567	
281	0700	WARSAW	0940	HEATHROW	B.737	1234567	
282	1050	HEATHROW	1315	WARSAW	B737	1234567	
285	1850	WARSAW	2130	HEATHROW	B.737	1234567	
286	0710	HEATHROW	0935	WARSAW	B.737	1234567	
287		GDANSK	1000	GATWICK	B.737	3	
288	1050	GATWICK		GDANSK	B.737	3	

PORTUGALIA *COMPANIA PORTUGUESA DE TRANSPORTES NI/PGA PORTUGAL*

600		LISBON	1815	MANCHESTER	F-100	12345 7	
601	1900	MANCHESTER		LISBON	F-100	12345 7	
603	1900	MANCHESTER		LISBON	F-100	5	
604		LISBON	1245	MANCHESTER	F-100	6	
605	1325	MANCHESTER		LISBON	F-100	6	

QANTAS *QANTAS AIRWAYS QF/QFA AUSTRALIA*

001		MELBOURNE	0650	HEATHROW	B.747	1234567	VIA BANGKOK
002	1300	HEATHROW		MELBOURNE	B.747	1234567	VIA BANGKOK
009		MELBOURNE	0515	HEATHROW	B.747	1234567	VIA SINGAPORE
010	2230	HEATHROW		MELBOURNE	B.747	1234567	VIA SINGAPORE

QUATARI *QATAR AIRWAYS CO. QR/QTR QATAR*

1		DOHA	1720	HEATHROW	A.300	1234567	
2	2105	HEATHROW		DOHA	A.300	1234567	
5		DOHA	0610	HEATHROW	A.300	1 3 5 7	
6	1030	HEATHROW		DOHA	A.300	1 3 5 7	

RAFAIR *ROYAL AIR FORCE RR/RFR U.K.*

3200	2245	BRIZE NORTON		MT. PLEASANT	L.1011	1	VIA ASCENSION IS.
3201		MT. PLEASANT	0725	BRIZE NORTON	L.1011	4	VIA ASCENSION IS.
3220	2245	BRIZE NORTON		MT.PLEASANT	L.1011	4	VIA ASCENSION IS.
3221		MT.PLEASANT	0725	BRIZE NORTON	L.1011	7	VIA ASCENSION IS.

RAPEX *BAC EXPRESS AIRLINES LTD. RPX U.K.*

233	2130	EDINBURGH	2240	COVENTRY	F-27	12345	
234	0100	COVENTRY	0205	EDINBURGH	F-27	23456	
301	??	LIVERPOOL	??	JERSEY	SH-360	6	-18.09

614	2220	BELFAST	2330	EAST MIDLANDS	F-27	12345	
615	0001	EAST MIDLANDS	0105	BELFAST	F-27	23456	
616	1900	BELFAST	2030	EAST MIDLANDS	SH-360	7	
617	2220	EAST MIDLANDS	2350	BELFAST	SH-360	7	
630	2300	EDINBURGH	2350	LIVERPOOL	F-27	12345	
631	0045	LIVERPOOL	0140	EDINBURGH	F-27	23456	
690	1850	EDINBURGH	2000	EAST MIDLANDS	F-27	7	
691	2150	EAST MIDLANDS	2255	EDINBURGH	F-27	7	
692	2030	STANSTED	2200	EDINBURGH	F-27	7	
692P	1815	EDINBURGH	2000	STANSTED	F-27	7	
693	2100	STANSTED	2245	EDINBURGH	F-27	7	
760	2220	NORWICH	2305	EAST MIDLANDS	SH-360	12345	
761	2330	EAST MIDLANDS	0200	NORWICH	SH-360	12345	
804	1845	EXETER	1950	EAST MIDLANDS	SH-360	7	
807	2200	EAST MIDLANDS	2255	EXETER	SH-360	7	
856	0025	BRISTOL	0125	BELFAST	SH-360	23456	
857	2240	BELFAST	2340	BRISTOL	SH-360	12345	
863	2240	EXETER	2340	EAST MIDLANDS	SH-360	12345	
864	0020	EAST MIDLANDS	0120	EXETER	SH-360	23456	
900	2255	CARDIFF	2345	EAST MIDLANDS	SH-360	12345	
901	0025	EAST MIDLANDS	0115	CARDIFF	SH-360	23456	

REGIONAL AIRLINES — *REGIONAL AIRLINES VM/RGI FRANCE*

211		LE HAVRE	0755	BIRMINGHAM	J'STREAM31	12345	
212	0830	BIRMINGHAM		LE HAVRE	J'STREAM31	12345	
215		LE HAVRE	1805	BIRMINGHAM	J'STREAM31	12345	
216	1845	BIRMINGHAM		LE HAVRE	J'STREAM31	12345	

RIGA LINER — *RIGA AIRLINES GV/RIG LATVIA*

401		RIGA	1325	GATWICK	B.737	12 5 7	
401R		RIGA	1325	GATWICK	B.737	4	
402	1425	GATWICK		RIGA	B.737	12 5 7	
402R	1425	GATWICK		RIGA	B.737	4	

ROY — *ROYAL AIRLINES QN/ROY CANADA*

110		WINNIPEG	1245	STANSTED	A.310	2	22.06-14.09
111	1400	STANSTED		WINNIPEG	A.310	2	22.06-14.09
140		CALGARY	1640	MANCHESTER	A.310	5	25.06-24.09
	1740	MANCHESTER		MUNICH	A.310	5	25.06-24.09
141		MUNICH	1545	MANCHESTER	A.310	5	25.06-24.09
	1645	MANCHESTER		CALGARY	A.310	5	25.06-24.09
150		EDMONTON	1630	GATWICK	A.310	6	26.06-11.09
151	1745	GATWICK		EDMONTON	A.310	6	26.06-11.09
210		TORONTO	1030	MANCHESTER	B.757	2	
211	1145	MANCHESTER		TORONTO	B.757	2	
220		TORONTO	0820	GLASGOW	B.757	3	23.06-15.09
221	0930	GLASGOW		TORONTO	B.757	3	23.06-15.09
228		TORONTO	0930	STANSTED	B.757	3	23.06-08.09
229	1100	STANSTED		TORONTO	B.757	3	23.06-08.09
230		TORONTO	0745	MANCHESTER	B.757	4	24.06-09.09
231	0945	MANCHESTER		TORONTO	B.757	4	24.06-09.09
234		TORONTO	0440	GATWICK	B.757	4	
235	0555	GATWICK		TORONTO	B.757	4	
242		TORONTO	0850	STANSTED	B.757	5	
243	0955	STANSTED		TORONTO	B.757	5	
250		TORONTO	0820	GLASGOW	B.757	6	26.06-
251	0925	GLASGOW		TORONTO	B.757	6	26.06-
262		TORONTO	0710	BELFAST	B757/A310	7	
263	0825	BELFAST		TORONTO	B.757	7	
710		TORONTO	2030	GATWICK	A.310	1	-13.09
711	2135	GATWICK		TORONTO	A.310	1	-13.09
720		TORONTO	2020	STANSTED	A.310	2	22.06-28.09
721	2135	STANSTED		TORONTO	A.310	2	22.06-28.09
722		TORONTO	0925	MANCHESTER	A.310	3	23.06-15.09
723	1045	MANCHESTER		TORONTO	A.310	3	
724		TORONTO	1130	BIRMINGHAM	A.310	3	
725	1245	BIRMINGHAM		TORONTO	A.310	3	

740		TORONTO	2000	GATWICK	A.310	4	
741	2115	GATWICK		TORONTO	A.310	4	
760		TORONTO	0755	GATWICK	B.757	7	20.06-12.09
761	0915	GATWICK		TORONTO	B.757	7	20.06-12.09
770		TORONTO	0945	MANCHESTER	B.757	1	21.06-13.09
771	1100	MANCHESTER		TORONTO	B.757	1	21.06-13.09

ROYAL NEPAL   *ROYAL NEPAL AIRLINES CORP.*   *RA/RNA*   *NEPAL*

229		KATMANDU	1835	GATWICK	B.757	5 7	VIA FRANKFURT
230	1945	GATWICK		KATMANDU	B.757	5 7	VIA FRANKFURT

RUBENS   *VLAAMSE LUCHTTRANSPORT*   *V4/VLM*   *BELGIUM*

101	0700	ANTWERP	0800	LONDON CITY	F-50	123456	
102	0830	LONDON CITY	0930	ANTWERP	F-50	12345	
103	1000	ANTWERP	1100	LONDON CITY	F-50	12345	
104	1130	LONDON CITY	1230	ANTWERP	F-50	123456	
105	1600	ANTWERP	1700	LONDON CITY	F-50	12345 7	
106	1730	LONDON CITY	1830	ANTWERP	F-50	12345 7	
107	1900	ANTWERP	2000	LONDON CITY	F-50	12345 7	
108	2030	LONDON CITY	2130	ANTWERP	F-50	12345 7	
111	1300	ANTWERP	1400	LONDON CITY	F-50	12345	
112	1430	LONDON CITY	1530	ANTWERP	F-50	12345	
201	0800	ROTTERDAM	0900	LONDON CITY	F-50	12345	
202	0830	LONDON CITY	0930	ROTTERDAM	F-50	123456	
203	1000	ROTTERDAM	1100	LONDON CITY	F-50	123456	
204	1130	LONDON CITY	1230	ROTTERDAM	F-50	12345	
205	1600	ROTTERDAM	1700	LONDON CITY	F-50	12345 7	
206	1730	LONDON CITY	1830	ROTTERDAM	F-50	12345 7	
207	1900	ROTTERDAM	2000	LONDON CITY	F-50	12345 7	
208	2030	LONDON CITY	2130	ROTTERDAM	F-50	12345 7	
211	1300	ROTTERDAM	1400	LONDON CITY	F-50	12345	
212	1430	LONDON CITY	1530	ROTTERDAM	F-50	12345	
231	1530	ROTTERDAM	1710	JERSEY	F-50	6	-02.10
232	1750	JERSEY	1930	ROTTERDAM	F-50	6	-02.10
301	0630	DUSSELDORF	0750	LONDON CITY	F-50	123456	
302	0820	LONDON CITY	0940	DUSSELDORF	F-50	123456	
303	1005	DUSSELDORF	1125	LONDON CITY	F-50	123456	
304	1200	LONDON CITY	1315	DUSSELDORF	F-50	123456	
305	1345	DUSSELDORF	1505	LONDON CITY	F-50	12345 7	
306	1535	LONDON CITY	1700	DUSSELDORF	F-50	12345 7	
307	1730	DUSSELDORF	1845	LONDON CITY	F-50	12345 7	
308	1915	LONDON CITY	2030	DUSSELDORF	F-50	12345 7	
431	1200	LONDON CITY	1300	JERSEY	F-50	12345	
432	1330	JERSEY	1430	LONDON CITY	F-50	12345	
701		ROTTERDAM	0730	MANCHESTER	F-50	123456	
702	0815	MANCHESTER		ROTTERDAM	F-50	123456	
703		ROTTERDAM	1245	MANCHESTER	F-50	12345	
706	1510	MANCHESTER		ROTTERDAM	F-50	12345	
707		ROTTERDAM	1840	MANCHESTER	F-50	12345 7	
708	1915	MANCHESTER		ROTTERDAM	F-50	12345 7	

RYANAIR   *RYANAIR*   *FR/RYR*   *IRELAND*

22	0700	DUBLIN	0825	PARIS BEAUVAIS	B.737	1234567	
23	0850	PARIS BEAUVAIS	1020	DUBLIN	B.737	1234567	
24	1045	DUBLIN	1210	PARIS BEAUVAIS	B.737	1234567	
25	1235	PARIS BEAUVAIS	1405	DUBLIN	B.737	1234567	
26	1410	DUBLIN	1535	PARIS BEAUVAIS	B.737	1234567	1200/1325 6
27	1600	PARIS BEAUVAIS	1730	DUBLIN	B.737	1234567	1350/1520 6
28	1755	DUBLIN	1920	PARIS BEAUVAIS	B.737	12345 7	
29	1945	PARIS BEAUVAIS	2115	DUBLIN	B.737	12345 7	
34	0745	STANSTED	0945	OSLO	B.737	1234567	1705/1905 7
35	1010	OSLO	1210	STANSTED	B.737	1234567	1940/2140 7
36	1800	STANSTED	2000	OSLO	B.737	12345 7	
37	2025	OSLO	2225	STANSTED	B.737	12345 7	
42	0655	DUBLIN	0825	BRUSSELS	B.737	123456	0940/1110 6
43	0850	BRUSSELS	1020	DUBLIN	B.737	123456	1135/1305 6

44	1340	DUBLIN	1510	BRUSSELS	B.737	1234567	
45	1535	BRUSSELS	1705	DUBLIN	B.737	1234567	
46	1730	DUBLIN	1900	BRUSSELS	B.737	12345 7	
47	1925	BRUSSELS	2055	DUBLIN	B.737	12345 7	
52	0715	STANSTED	0925	STOCKHOLM	B.737	1234567	
53	1000	STOCKHOLM	1200	STANSTED	B.737	1234567	
54	1035	STANSTED	1245	STOCKHOLM	B.737	1234567	
55	1310	STOCKHOLM	1520	STANSTED	B.737	1234567	
56	1620	STANSTED	1830	STOCKHOLM	B.737	12345 7	
57	1900	STOCKHOLM	2110	STANSTED	B.737	12345 7	
62	0900	PRESTWICK	1035	PARIS BEAUVAIS	B.737	1234567	
63	1100	PARIS BEAUVAIS	1235	PRESTWICK	B.737	1234567	
64	1700	PRESTWICK	1835	PARIS BEAUVAIS	B.737	1234567	1745/1920 6
65	1900	PARIS BEAUVAIS	2035	PRESTWICK	B.737	1234567	1945/2120 6
72	0800	STANSTED	1000	CARCASSONNE (FR)	B.737	67	1010/1210 6
73	1025	CARCASSONNE	1225	STANSTED	B.737	67	1235/1435 6
74	1110	STANSTED	1310	CARCASSONNE	B.737	123456	
75	1325	CARCASSONNE	1525	STANSTED	B.737	123456	
76	1250	STANSTED	1450	CARCASSONE	B.737	12345 7	01.07-
77	1515	CARCASSONE	1715	STANSTED	B.737	12345 7	01.07-
84	1320	STANSTED	1500	ST.ETIENNE(FRANCE)	B.737	1234567	1425/1605 6
85	1530	ST.ETIENNE	1710	STANSTED	B.737	1234567	1640/1815 6
112	0815	DUBLIN	0930	GATWICK	B.737	1234567	
113	1000	GATWICK	1115	DUBLIN	B.737	1234567	
114	1145	DUBLIN	1300	GATWICK	B.737	1234567	
115	1335	GATWICK	1450	DUBLIN	B.737	1234567	
116	1515	DUBLIN	1630	GATWICK	B.737	1234567	
117	1700	GATWICK	1815	DUBLIN	B.737	1234567	
118	1845	DUBLIN	2000	GATWICK	B.737	1234567	
119	2030	GATWICK	2145	DUBLIN	B.737	1234567	
124	1345	STANSTED	1600	ANCONA	B.737	1234567	1720/1935 6
125	1645	ANCONA	1900	STANSTED	B.737	1234567	2010/2235 6
152	0930	DUBLIN	1020	LEEDS	B.737	1234567	
153	1045	LEEDS	1135	DUBLIN	B.737	1234567	
154	1700	DUBLIN	1820	LEEDS	B.737	12345 7	
155	1845	LEEDS	1935	DUBLIN	B.737	12345 7	
156	1510	DUBLIN	1600	LEEDS	B.737	1234567	1625/1715 67
157	1625	LEEDS	1715	DUBLIN	B.737	1234567	1740/1830 67
202	0645	DUBLIN	0805	STANSTED	B.737	1234567	
203	0700	STANSTED	0810	DUBLIN	B.737	123456	
204	0845	DUBLIN	0950	STANSTED	B.737	1234567	
205	0830	STANSTED	0940	DUBLIN	B.737	1234567	
206	0955	DUBLIN	1105	STANSTED	B.737	123456	
207	1015	STANSTED	1120	DUBLIN	B.737	12345 7	
208	1025	DUBLIN	1135	STANSTED	B.737	1234567	
209	1130	STANSTED	1240	DUBLIN	B.737	123456	
221	1200	STANSTED	1310	DUBLIN	B.737	1234567	
222	1045	DUBLIN	1155	STANSTED	B.737	7	
223	1220	STANSTED	1330	DUBLIN	B.737	7	
224	1150	DUBLIN	1300	STANSTED	B.737	12345 7	
225	1435	STANSTED	1545	DUBLIN	B.737	1234567	
226	1300	DUBLIN	1410	STANSTED	B.737	1234567	
227	1535	STANSTED	1645	DUBLIN	B.737	1234567	1450/1600 6
228	1400	STANSTED	1510	DUBLIN	B.737	1234567	1315/1425 6
281	1605	STANSTED	1715	DUBLIN	B.737	5 7	
282	1435	DUBLIN	1545	STANSTED	B.737	5 7	
283	1625	STANSTED	1735	DUBLIN	B.737	12345 7	01.07-
284	1625	DUBLIN	1735	STANSTED	B.737	1234567	
285	1800	STANSTED	1910	DUBLIN	B.737	1234567	
286	1710	DUBLIN	1820	STANSTED	B.737	12345 7	
287	1845	STANSTED	1955	DUBLIN	B.737	1234567	
288	1805	DUBLIN	1915	STANSTED	B.737	12345 7	01.07-
289	2000	STANSTED	2110	DUBLIN	B.737	12345 7	
292	1935	DUBLIN	2045	STANSTED	B.737	1234567	
293	2110	STANSTED	2220	DUBLIN	B.737	1234567	
294	2055	DUBLIN	2205	STANSTED	B.737	567	2015/2125 6
295	2230	STANSTED	2340	DUBLIN	B.737	5 7	
296	2135	DUBLIN	2245	STANSTED	B.737	12345 7	

331	0700	LUTON	0805	DUBLIN	B.737	123456		
332	0830	DUBLIN	0935	LUTON	B.737	1234567		
333	1000	LUTON	1105	DUBLIN	B.737	1234567		
334	1130	DUBLIN	1235	LUTON	B.737	1234567		
335	1300	LUTON	1405	DUBLIN	B.737	1234567		
336	1440	DUBLIN	1545	LUTON	B.737	1234567		
337	1610	LUTON	1715	DUBLIN	B.737	1234567		
338	1740	DUBLIN	1845	LUTON	B.737	12345 7		
341	1910	LUTON	2015	DUBLIN	B.737	12345 7		
342	2040	DUBLIN	2145	LUTON	B.737	12345 7		
372	1610	STANSTED	1800	BIARRITZ	B.737	1234567		
373	1825	BIARRITZ	2030	STANSTED	B.737	1234567		
401	0730	STANSTED	0835	PRESTWICK	B.737	123456		
402	0700	PRESTWICK	0815	STANSTED	B.737	123456		
403	0840	STANSTED	0950	PRESTWICK	B.737	123456		
404	1015	PRESTWICK	1125	STANSTED	B.737	123456		
405	1150	STANSTED	1300	PRESTWICK	B.737	123456		
406	1300	PRESTWICK	1410	STANSTED	B.737	1234567		
407	1530	STANSTED	1640	PRESTWICK	B.737	1234567		
408	1610	PRESTWICK	1720	STANSTED	B.737	12345 7		
409	1745	STANSTED	1855	PRESTWICK	B.737	12345 7		
412	1920	PRESTWICK	2030	STANSTED	B.737	12345 7		
413	2055	STANSTED	2205	PRESTWICK	B.737	12345 7		
414	2105	PRESTWICK	2215	STANSTED	B.737	12345 7	01.07-	
442	0710	DUBLIN	0755	LIVERPOOL	B.737	123456		
443	0820	LIVERPOOL	0905	DUBLIN	B.737	123456		
444	1220	DUBLIN	1305	LIVERPOOL	B.737	12345 7		
445	1330	LIVERPOOL	1415	DUBLIN	B.737	12345 7		
446	2005	DUBLIN	2050	LIVERPOOL	B.737	12345 7	2125/2210 7	
447	2115	LIVERPOOL	2200	DUBLIN	B.737	12345 7	2235/2320 7	
448	1025	DUBLIN	1110	LIVERPOOL	B.737	123456		
449	1135	LIVERPOOL	1220	DUBLIN	B.737	123456		
452	2030	DUBLIN	2105	LIVERPOOL	B.737	7		
453	2130	LIVERPOOL	2215	DUBLIN	B.737	7		
462	0710	STANSTED	0920	TURIN	B.737	1234567	01.07-	
463	0945	TURIN	1155	STANSTED	B.737	1234567	01.07	
464	1745	STANSTED	1945	TURIN	B.737	12345 7	01.07-	
465	2020	TURIN	2230	STANSTED	B.737	12345 7	01.07-	
502	0715	DUBLIN	0815	BRISTOL	B.737	1234567	0805/0900 7	
503	0840	BRISTOL	0935	DUBLIN	B.737	1234567	0925/1020 7	
504	1450	DUBLIN	1545	BRISTOL	B.737	12345 7	1745/1840 7	
505	1610	BRISTOL	1705	DUBLIN	B.737	12345 7	1905/2020 7	
506	2000	DUBLIN	2055	BRISTOL	B.737	12345 7		
507	2120	BRISTOL	2215	DUBLIN	B.737	12345 7		
514	1220	STANSTED	1330	DINARD	B.737	1234567		
515	1355	DINARD	1500	STANSTED	B.737	1234567		
552	0730	DUBLIN	0830	MANCHESTER	B.737	123456		
553	0900	MANCHESTER	0955	DUBLIN	B.737	123456		
554	1025	DUBLIN	1115	MANCHESTER	B.737	7		
555	1145	MANCHESTER	1235	DUBLIN	B.737	7		
558	1745	DUBLIN	1835	MANCHESTER	B.737	1234567	1855/1945 67	
559	1900	MANCHESTER	1950	DUBLIN	B.737	1234567	2010/2100 67	
582	0705	STANSTED	0920	PISA	B.737	1234567		
583	0945	PISA	1205	STANSTED	B.737	1234567		
584	1710	STANSTED	1925	PISA	B.737	12345 7		
585	1950	PISA	2210	STANSTED	B.737	12345 7		
602	1200	DUBLIN	1255	TEESSIDE	B.737	1234567	0700/0755 6	
603	1320	TEESSIDE	1415	DUBLIN	B.737	1234567	0820/0915 6	
634	1010	STANSTED	1230	RIMINI	B.737	1234567	1520/1745 6	
635	1305	RIMINI	1525	STANSTED	B.737	12345 7	1810/2035 6	
662	0700	DUBLIN	0755	BIRMINGHAM	B.737	123456		
663	0820	BIRMINGHAM	0915	DUBLIN	B.737	123456		
664	0940	DUBLIN	1035	BIRMINGHAM	B.737	1234567		
665	1100	BIRMINGHAM	1155	DUBLIN	B.737	1234567		
668	1440	DUBLIN	1535	BIRMINGHAM	B.737	7		
669	1600	BIRMINGHAM	1655	DUBLIN	B.737	7		
672	1535	DUBLIN	1630	BIRMINGHAM	B.737	1234567		
673	1655	BIRMINGHAM	1750	DUBLIN	B.737	1234567		

674	1815	DUBLIN	1910	BIRMINGHAM	B.737	1234567	
675	1935	BIRMINGHAM	2030	DUBLIN	B.737	1234567	
701	1255	STANSTED	1410	KERRY	B.737	1234567	
702	1440	KERRY	1555	STANSTED	B.737	1234567	
703	1925	STANSTED	2045	KERRY	B.737	1234567	1355/1515 6
704	2115	KERRY	2225	STANSTED	B.737	1234567	1540/1655 6
752	0700	STANSTED	0820	HAHN, GERMANY	B.737	1234567	
753	0850	HAHN	1010	STANSTED	B.737	1234567	
756	1910	STANSTED	2030	HAHN	B.737	12345 7	
757	2055	HAHN	2230	STANSTED	B.737	12345 7	
771	1320	PRESTWICK	1405	DUBLIN	B.737	6	
772	0715	DUBLIN	0800	PRESTWICK	B.737	123456	
773	0825	PRESTWICK	0910	DUBLIN	B.737	123456	
774	1235	DUBLIN	1320	STANSTED	B.737	1234567	
775	1345	PRESTWICK	1430	DUBLIN	B.737	1234567	
776	1445	DUBLIN	1530	PRESTWICK	B.737	7	
778	1745	DUBLIN	1830	PRESTWICK	B.737	12345 7	2025/2110 7
779	1855	PRESTWICK	1940	DUBLIN	B.737	12345 7	2135/2220 7
792	0705	STANSTED	0905	VENICE	B.737	1234567	
793	1000	VENICE	1140	STANSTED	B.737	1234567	
796	1750	STANSTED	1940	VENICE	B.737	1234567	
797	2035	VENICE	2225	STANSTED	B.737	1234567	
801	1315	STANSTED	1440	KNOCK	B.737	7	04.07-
802	1505	KNOCK	1625	STANSTED	B.737	7	04.07-
803	1240	STANSTED	1350	KNOCK	B.737	1234567	
804	1430	KNOCK	1550	STANSTED	B.737	1234567	
805	1610	STANSTED	1740	KNOCK	B.737	1234567	1625/1750 6
806	1805	KNOCK	1925	STANSTED	B.737	1234567	1815/1935 6
842	1225	STANSTED	1425	KRISTIANSTAD	B.737	1234567	
843	1450	KRISTIANSTAD	1650	STANSTED	B.737	1234567	
882	1055	DUBLIN	1150	CARDIFF	B.737	1234567	1330/1425 6
883	1215	CARDIFF	1310	DUBLIN	B.737	1234567	1450/1545 6
901	0715	STANSTED	0835	CORK	B.737	1234567	
902	0855	CORK	1015	STANSTED	B.737	1234567	
903	1045	STANSTED	1105	CORK	B.737	1234567	
904	1220	CORK	1340	STANSTED	B.737	1234567	
905	1425	STANSTED	1545	CORK	B.737	1234567	
906	1605	CORK	1725	STANSTED	B.737	1234567	
907	1935	STANSTED	2055	CORK	B.737	1234567	1910/2030 6
908	2120	CORK	2235	STANSTED	B.737	1234567	2055/2210 6
972	0730	STANSTED	0940	GENOA	B.737	12345 7	01.07-
973	1020	GENOA	1230	STANSTED	B.737	12345 7	01.07-
974	1550	STANSTED	1800	GENOA	B.737	1234567	1500/1710 6
975	1825	GENOA	2035	STANSTED	B.737	67	1735/1945 6
976	1625	STANSTED	1835	GENOA	B.737	12345	01.07-
977	1900	GENOA	2110	STANSTED	B.737	123456	
983	1040	GENOA	1250	STANSTED	B.737	7	04.07-
992	0935	DUBLIN	1040	BOURNEMOUTH	B.737	1234567	1430/1535 6
993	1105	BOURNEMOUTH	1210	DUBLIN	B.737	1234567	1600/1705 6
7126	0900	STANSTED	1100	VENICE	B.737	6	
7127	1145	VENICE	1345	STANSTED	B.737	6	
7742	1325	DUBLIN	1420	PRESTWICK	BAC1-11	5	
7743	1455	PRESTWICK	1550	DUBLIN	BAC1-11	5	

		SABENA		*SABENA SN/SAB*	*BELGIUM*		
124		ATLANTA	0730	BRUSSELS	B.767	1234567	DELTA A/C
125	0945	BRUSSELS		ATLANTA	B.767	1234567	DELTA A/C
207	1400	BRUSSELS		TOKYO	A.340	2 45 7	
208		TOKYO	1625	BRUSSELS	A.340	1 3 56	
427	1155	BRUSSELS	1315	JERSEY	AVRO RJ-85	2 6	1330/1450 6
428	1415	JERSEY	1535	BRUSSELS	AVRO RJ-85	2 6	1540/1700 6
429	0910	BRUSSELS	1030	JERSEY	AVRO RJ-85	7	
430	1110	JERSEY	1230	BRUSSELS	AVRO RJ-85	7	
533	140	BRUSSELS		BOSTON	A.340	1234567	
534		BOSTON	0710	BRUSSELS	A.340	1234567	
537	0855	BRUSSELS		NEW YORK	MD-11	1234567	
538		NEW YORK	0450	BRUSSELS	MD-11	1234567	

539	1040	BRUSSELS		CHICAGO	B.747	12 4567	
540		CHICAGO	0640	BRUSSELS	B.747	123 567	
541	1015	BRUSSELS		NEW YORK	B.767	1234567	
542		NEW YORK	1140	BRUSSELS	A.340	1234567	
543	1035	BRUSSELS		CINCINNATI	B.747	1234567	
544		CINCINNATI	0740	BRUSSELS	B.747	1234567	
545	1340	BRUSSELS		ATLANTA	A.340	1234567	
546		ATLANTA	1125	BRUSSELS	A.340	1234567	
547	1830	BRUSSELS		NEW YORK	A.340	1234567	
548		NEW YORK	0725	BRUSSELS	B.767	1234567	
582		MONTREAL	0700	BRUSSELS	MD-11	23 67	
584		PARIS CDG	1700	SHANNON	B.737	6	03.07-28.09
587	1045	BRUSSELS	1145	STANSTED	B.737	1234567	
588	1230	STANSTED	1330	BRUSSELS	B.737	1234567	
591	0845	BRUSSELS	0945	STANSTED	B.737	123456	VIRGIN A/C
592	1030	STANSTED	1130	BRUSSELS	B.737	123456	VIRGIN A/C
593	1305	BRUSSELS	1405	STANSTED	B.737	12345 7	VIRGIN A/C
594	1445	STANSTED	1545	BRUSSELS	B.737	12345 7	VIRGIN A/C
595	1935	BRUSSELS	2035	STANSTED	B.737	12345 7	VIRGIN A/C
596	0650	STANSTED	0750	BRUSSELS	B,737	1234546	VIRGIN A/C
597	0630	BRUSSELS	0740	HEATHROW	B.737	1234567	
598	0740	HEATHROW	0845	BRUSSELS	B.737	1234567	
599	0730	BRUSSELS	0840	HEATHROW	B.737	123456	
600	0830	HEATHROW	0930	BRUSSELS	B.737	123457	
601	0930	BRUSSELS	1040	HEATHROW	B.737	1234567	0950/1100 67
602	0930	HEATHROW	1030	BRUSSELS	B.737	123456	
603	1340	BRUSSELS	1450	HEATHROW	B.737	12345	
604	1125	HEATHROW	1225	BRUSSELS	B.737	1234567	1150/1300 67
605	1530	BRUSSELS	1640	HEATHROW	B.737	1234567	
606	1620	HEATHROW	1720	BRUSSELS	B.737	12345	
607	1630	BRUSSELS	1740	HEATHROW	B.737	12345 7	
608	1730	HEATHROW	1830	BRUSSELS	B.737	1234567	
609	1730	BRUSSELS	1840	HEATHROW	B.737	1234567	
610	1830	HEATHROW	1930	BRUSSELS	B.737	12345 7	
611	1830	BRUSSELS	1940	HEATHROW	B.737	1234567	
612	1930	HEATHROW	2030	BRUSSELS	B.737	1234567	
613	1925	BRUSSELS	2045	HEATHROW	B.737	1234567	
614	0650	HEATHROW	0750	BRUSSELS	B.737	1234567	
615	0840	BRUSSELS	1000	MANCHESTER	B.737	1234567	
616	1055	MANCHESTER	1230	BRUSSELS	B.737	1234567	
617	1345	BRUSSELS	1500	MANCHESTER	B737/A320	12345 7	
618	1615	MANCHESTER	1730	BRUSSELS	B737/A320	12345 7	
619	1755	BRUSSELS	1915	MANCHESTER	B.737	1234567	
620	1955	MANCHESTER	2110	BRUSSELS	B.737	12345 7	
621	2110	BRUSSELS	2230	MANCHESTER	B.737	12345 7	
622	0650	MANCHESTER	0805	BRUSSELS	B.737	1234567	
630	0700	DUBLIN	0830	BRUSSELS	B.737	12345	AER LINGUS A/C
631	0920	BRUSSELS	1110	DUBLIN	B.737	12345	AER LINGUS A/C
632	1140	DUBLIN	1310	BRUSSELS	B.737	12345 7	AER LINGUS A/C
633	1720	BRUSSELS	1905	DUBLIN	B.737	7	
634	1950	DUBLIN	2125	BRUSSELS	B.737	7	
635	1400	BRUSSELS	1550	DUBLIN	B.737	12345 7	AER LINGUS A/C
636	1620	DUBLIN	1800	BRUSSELS	B.737	12345	AER LINGUS A/C
637	1850	BRUSSELS	2025	DUBLIN	B.737	12345	AER LINGUS A/C
638	1145	DUBLIN	1315	BRUSSELS	A.320	6	
639	0915	BRUSSELS	1105	DUBLIN	A.320	6	
641	0645	BRUSSELS	0750	LONDON CITY	DHC-8	12345	SCHREINER A/C
642	0815	LONDON CITY	1015	BRUSSELS	DHC-8	12345	SCHREINER A/C
643	1000	BRUSSELS	1105	LONDON CITY	DHC-8	12345	SCHREINER A/C
644	1130	LONDON CITY	1225	BRUSSELS	DHC-8	12345	SCHREINER A/C
645	1300	BRUSSELS	1405	LONDON CITY	DHC-8	12345	SCHREINER A/C
646	1430	LONDON CITY	1530	BRUSSELS	DHC-8	12345	SCHREINER A/C
647	1600	BRUSSELS	1705	LONDON CITY	DHC-8	12345 7	SCHREINER A/C
648	1730	LONDON CITY	1830	BRUSSELS	DHC-8	12345 7	SCHREINER A/C
649	1900	BRUSSELS	2005	LONDON CITY	DHC-8	12345 7	SCHREINER A/C
650	2030	LONDON CITY	2130	BRUSSELS	DHC-8	12345 7	SCHREINER A/C
651	0700	ANTWERP	0800	LONDON CITY	F-50	123456	VLM A/C
652	0830	LONDON CITY	0930	ANTWERP	F-50	12345	VLM A/C

653	1000	ANTWERP	1100	LONDON CITY	F-50	12345		VLM A/C
654	1130	LONDON CITY	1230	ANTWERP	F-50	123456		VLM A/C
655	1300	ANTWERP	1400	LONDON CITY	F-50	12345		VLM A/C
656	1430	LONDON CITY	1530	ANTWERP	F-50	12345		VLM A/C
657	1600	ANTWERP	1700	LONDON CITY	F-50	12345 7		VLM A/C
658	1730	LONDON CITY	1830	ANTWERP	F-50	12345 7		VLM A/C
659	1900	ANTWERP	2000	LONDON CITY	F-50	12345 7		VLM A/C
660	2030	LONDON CITY	2130	ANTWERP	F-50	12345 7		
661	0950	BRUSSELS	1025	GATWICK	B.737	1234567		VIRGIN A/C
662	1145	GATWICK	1245	BRUSSELS	B.737	1234567		VIRGIN A/C
663	1335	BRUSSELS	1440	GATWICK	B.737	12345 7		VIRGIN A/C
664	1530	GATWICK	1630	BRUSSELS	B.737	12345 7		VIRGIN A/C
667	2055	BRUSSELS	2200	GATWICK	B.737	1234567		VIRGIN A/C
668	0640	GATWICK	0735	BRUSSELS	B.737	1234567		VIRGIN A/C
669	1535	BRUSSELS	1640	GATWICK	B.737	12345 7		VIRGIN A/C
670	1725	GATWICK	1830	BRUSSELS	B.737	12345 7		VIRGIN A/C
671	0840	BRUSSELS	1005	NEWCASTLE	AVRO RJ-85	123456	
672	1055	NEWCASTLE	1210	BRUSSELS	AVRO RJ-85	123456	
673	1400	BRUSSELS	1525	NEWCASTLE	AVRO RJ-85	12345 7	
674	1610	NEWCASTLE	1725	BRUSSELS	AVRO RJ-85	12345 7	
675	1755	BRUSSELS	1920	NEWCASTLE	AVRO RJ-85	1234567	
676	1945	NEWCASTLE	2100	BRUSSELS	AVRO RJ-85	12345 7	
677	2100	BRUSSELS	2225	NEWCASTLE	AVRO RJ-85	12345 7	
678	0650	NEWCASTLE	0805	BRUSSELS	AVRO RJ-85	1234567	
679	0605	BRUSSELS	0725	MANCHESTER	B737/A320	123456	
680	0830	MANCHESTER	0945	BRUSSELS	B737/A320	123456	
681	0825	BRUSSELS	1015	GLASGOW	AVRO RJ-85	123456	
682	1050	GLASGOW	1235	BRUSSELS	AVRO RJ-85	123456	
683	1325	BRUSSELS	1510	GLASGOW	AVRO RJ-85	1234567	
684	1550	GLASGOW	1735	BRUSSELS	AVRO RJ-85	1234567	
685	1105	BRUSSELS	1245	BELFAST	AVRO RJ-85	1234567	
686	1345	BELFAST	1515	BRUSSELS	AVRO RJ-85	1234567	
687	1755	BRUSSELS	1945	GLASGOW	AVRO RJ-85	1234567	
688	0635	GLASGOW	0815	BRUSSELS	AVRO RJ-85	1234567	
689	1735	BRUSSELS	1840	LONDON CITY	AVRO RJ-85	12345 7	
690	0715	LONDON CITY	0815	BRUSSELS	DHC-8	123456	
691	0825	BRUSSELS	1005	EDINBURGH	B.737	1234567	
692	1045	EDINBURGH	1215	BRUSSELS	B.737	1234567	
693	1330	BRUSSELS	1510	EDINBURGH	B.737	12345 7	
694	1555	EDINBURGH	1735	BRUSSELS	B.737	12345 7	
695	1750	BRUSSELS	1935	EDINBURGH	AVRO RJ-85	1234567	
696	0635	EDINBURGH	0815	BRUSSELS	AVRO RJ-85	1234567	
697	0840	BRUSSELS	1005	LEEDS	AVRO RJ-85	123456	
698	1010	LEEDS	1230	BRUSSELS	AVRO RJ-85	123456	
699	1330	BRUSSELS	1500	LEEDS	AVRO RJ-85	12345 7	
700	1540	LEEDS	1700	BRUSSELS	AVRO RJ-85	12345 7	
701	1750	BRUSSELS	1915	LEEDS	AVRO RJ-85	12345 7	
702	1955	LEEDS	2115	BRUSSELS	AVRO RJ-85	12345 7	
703	0820	BRUSSELS	0940	BRISTOL	AVRO RJ-85	123456	
704	1040	BRISTOL	1200	BRUSSELS	AVRO RJ-85	123456	
705	1400	BRUSSELS	1520	BRISTOL	AVRO RJ-85	12345 7	
706	1555	BRISTOL	1710	BRUSSELS	AVRO RJ-85	12345 7	
707	1750	BRUSSELS	1910	BRISTOL	AVRO RJ-85	12345 7	
708	1950	BRISTOL	2110	BRUSSELS	AVRO RJ-85	12345 7	
709	2100	BRUSSELS	2225	BRISTOL	AVRO RJ-85	12345 7	
710	0655	BRISTOL	0815	BRUSSELS	AVRO RJ-85	123456	
711	0820	BRUSSELS	0930	BIRMINGHAM	AVRO RJ-85	1234567	1020/1130 67
712	1055	BIRMINGHAM	1205	BRUSSELS	AVRO RJ-85	1234567	1200/1310 67
713	1340	BRUSSELS	1450	BIRMINGHAM	AVRO-RJ85	12345 7	
714	1530	BIRMINGHAM	1640	BRUSSELS	AVRO RJ-85	12345 7	
715	1725	BRUSSELS	1835	BIRMINGHAM	AVRO RJ-85	12345 7	
716	1920	BIRMINGHAM	2030	BRUSSELS	AVRO RJ-85	12345 7	
717	2115	BRUSSELS	2225	BIRMINGHAM	AVRO RJ-85	1234567	
718	0650	BIRMINGHAM	0805	BRUSSELS	AVRO RJ-85	1234567	
721	1120	BRUSSELS	1250	EDINBURGH	AVRO RJ-85	67	
722	1330	EDINBURGH	1500	BRUSSELS	AVRO RJ-85	67	
729	2120	BRUSSELS	2240	LEEDS	AVRO RJ-85	12345 7	
730	0655	LEEDS	0815	BRUSSELS	AVRO RJ-85	123456	

| 925 | 1110 | BRUSSELS | 1230 | MANCHESTER | B737/RJ-85 | 67 |
| 926 | 1340 | MANCHESTER | 1500 | BRUSSELS | B737/RJ-85 | 67 |

SCILLONIA

ISLE OF SCILLY SKYBUS LTD.   FW/IOS   U.K.

009	0825	LANDS END	0840	ISLE OF SCILLY	BN.ISLAN	123456
010	0845	ISLE OF SCILLY	0900	LANDS END	BN.ISLAN.	123456
017	0920	LANDS END	0935	ISLE OF SCILLY	BN.ISLAN.	123456
018	0940	ISLE OF SCILLY	0955	LANDS END	BN.ISLAN.	123456
061	1525	LANDS END	1540	ISLE OF SCILLY	BN.ISLAN.	123456
062	1545	ISLE OF SCILLY	1600	LANDS END	BN.ISLAN.	123456
100	0815	ISLE OF SCILLY	0905	EXETER	DHC-6	6
101	0940	EXETER	1030	ISLE OF SCILLY	DHC-6	6
102	1045	ISLE OF SCILLY	1135	EXETER	DHC-6	34
103	1210	EXETER	1300	ISLE OF SCILLY	DHC-6	3
104	1100	ISLE OF SCILLY	1150	EXETER	DHC-6	6
105	1225	EXETER	1315	ISLE OF SCILLY	DHC-6	6
106	1545	ISLE OF SCILLY	1635	EXETER	DHC-6	12 456
107	1710	EXETER	1800	ISLE OF SCILLY	DHC-6	12 456
201	0715	NEWQUAY	0745	ISLE OF SCILLY	DHC-6	6
203	0730	NEWQUAY	0800	ISLE OF SCILLY	DHC-6	1 5
204	0830	ISLE OF SCILLY	0900	NEWQUAY	DHC-6	6
205	0815	NEWQUAY	0845	ISLE OF SCILLY	DHC-6	3
206	1330	ISLE OF SCILLY	1400	NEWQUAY	DHC-6	12345
207	0900	NEWQUAY	0930	ISLE OF SCILLY	DHC-6	2 4
208	1345	ISLE OF SCILLY	1415	NEWQUAY	DHC-6	6
209	0935	NEWQUAY	1005	ISLE OF SCILLY	DHC-6	6
210	1035	ISLE OF SCILLY	1105	NEWQUAY	DHC-6	6
211	1135	NEWQUAY	1205	ISLE OF SCILLY	DHC-6	6
213	1445	NEWQUAY	1515	ISLE OF SCILLY	DHC-6	123456
216	1835	ISLE OF SCILLY	1905	NEWQUAY	DHC-6	12 456
218	1715	ISLE OF SCILLY	1745	NEWQUAY	DHC-6	3
220	1435	ISLE OF SCILLY	1505	NEWQUAY	DHC-6	6
221	1535	NEWQUAY	1605	ISLE OF SCILLY	DHC-6	6
222	1635	ISLE OF SCILLY	1705	NEWQUAY	DHC-6	6
223	1735	NEWQUAY	1805	ISLE OF SCILLY	DHC-6	6
300	1035	ISLE OF SCILLY	1120	PLYMOUTH	BN.ISLAN.	1 3 5
301	1200	PLYMOUTH	1245	ISLE OF SCILLY	BN.ISLAN.	1 3 5
400	0835	ISLE OF SCILLY	0945	BRISTOL	DHC-6	1 5
401	1020	BRISTOL	1130	ISLE OF SCILLY	DHC-6	1 5
402	1000	ISLE OF SCILLY	1110	BRISTOL	DHC-6	2 4
403	1145	BRISTOL	1255	ISLE OF SCILLY	DHC-6	2 4

SCOTAIR

EUROSCOT EXPRESS   MY/EUJ   U.K.

120	1540	BOURNEMOUTH	1720	EDINBURGH	ATR-72	5
	1750	EDINBURGH	1820	GLASGOW	ATR-72	5
	1850	GLASGOW	2030	BOURNEMOUTH	ATR-72	5
	1630	BOURNEMOUTH	1810	GLASGOW	ATR-72	7
	1840	GLASGOW	1910	EDINBURGH	ATR-72	7
	1940	EDINBURGH	2120	BOURNEMOUTH	ATR-72	7
121	0700	BOURNEMOUTH	0840	GLASGOW	ATR-72	12345
122	0910	GLASGOW	1050	BOURNEMOUTH	ATR-72	12345
123	1120	BOURNEMOUTH	1300	EDINBURGH	ATR-72	2 4
124	1330	EDINBURGH	1510	BOURNEMOUTH	ATR-72	2 4
125	1630	BOURNEMOUTH	1810	GLASGOW	ATR-72	1234
126	1840	GLASGOW	2020	BOURNEMOUTH	ATR-72	1234
410	0640	INVERNESS	0810	HEATHROW	F-100	1234567
411	0900	HEATHROW	1030	INVERNESS	F-100	1234567
412	1140	INVERNESS	1310	HEATHROW	F-100	1234567
413	1400	HEATHROW	1530	INVERNESS	F-100	1234567
414	1740	INVERNESS	1910	HEATHROW	F-100	1234567
415	2000	HEATHROW	2130	INVERNESS	F-100	1234567

SEYCHELLES

AIR SEYCHELLES   HM/SEY   SEYCHELLES

9	1815	GATWICK		MAHE ISLAND	B.767	7	VIA ZURICH
10		MAHE ISLAND	0810	GATWICK	B.767	7	VIA ZURICH
27	1815	GATWICK		MAHE IS.	B.767	3	VIA DUBAI
28		MAHE IS.	0655	GATWICK	B.767	3	VIA DUBAI

021	0605	KERRY	0655	DUBLIN	BAE-146	123456	
022	1240	DUBLIN	1345	KERRY	F-50	123456	
023	1410	KERRY	1505	DUBLIN	F-50	123456	
026	2200	DUBLIN	2300	KERRY	BAE-146	12345 7	
053	0615	GALWAY	0700	DUBLIN	F-50	123456	
054	1240	DUBLIN	1330	GALWAY	F-50	1234567	
055	1355	GALWAY	1440	DUBLIN	F-50	1234567	
056	1510	DUBLIN	1600	GALWAY	F-50	1234567	
057	1625	GALWAY	1710	DUBLIN	F-50	1234567	
058	2200	DUBLIN	2250	GALWAY	F-50	12345 7	
104		NEW YORK	0620	DUBLIN	A.330	1234567	
105	1200	DUBLIN		NEW YORK	A.330	1234567	
106		NEW YORK	1030	DUBLIN	A.330	1234567	VIA SHANNON
107	1505	SHANNON		NEW YORK	A.330	1234567	VIA SHANNON
111	1115	BELFAST	1205	SHANNON	MD-11	1 4 67	
	1320	SHANNON		NEW YORK	A330/MD11	1234567	
112		NEW YORK	0705	SHANNON	A330/MD11	1234567	
	0815	SHANNON	0910	BELFAST	A330/MD11	1 4 67	
114		NEW YORK	0630	SHANNON	A.330	4567	03.06-02.10
115	1410	SHANNON		NEW YORK	A.330	3456	02.06-01.10
124		CHICAGO	0910	DUBLIN	A.330	1234567	
	0955	DUBLIN	1040	SHANNON	A.330	1234567	
125	1305	SHANNON	1355	DUBLIN	A.330	1234567	
	1455	DUBLIN		CHICAGO	A.330	1234567	
132		BOSTON	0710	SHANNON	A.330	34 6	
	0755	SHANNON	0840	DUBLIN	A.330	34 6	
133	1110	DUBLIN	1155	SHANNON	A.330	23 5	
	1255	SHANNON		BOSTON	A.330	23 5	
134		BOSTON	0810	SHANNON	A.330	12 5 7	30.05-01.10
135	1645	SHANNON		BOSTON	A.330	1 4 67	29.05-30.09
136		BOSTON	0715	DUBLIN	A.330	12 5 7	31.05-01.10
137	1530	DUBLIN		BOSTON	A.330	1 4 67	30.05-30.09
144		LOS ANGELES	1230	DUBLIN	A.330	1 4 6	28.09
	1315	DUBLIN	1400	SHANNON	A.330	1 4 6	28.09
145	1045	SHANNON	1130	DUBLIN	A.330	3 5 7	28.05-
	1230	DUBLIN		LOS ANGELES	A.330	3 5 7	28.05-
151	0745	HEATHROW	0855	DUBLIN	B737/A320	123456	
152	0650	DUBLIN	0805	HEATHROW	A.320	1234567	
153	0905	HEATHROW	1015	DUBLIN	A.320	1234567	
154	0735	DUBLIN	0850	HEATHROW	A.320	1234567	
155	0950	HEATHROW	1100	DUBLIN	A.320	1234567	
156	0835	DUBLIN	0950	HEATHROW	A.320	1234567	
157	1040	HEATHROW	1155	DUBLIN	B737/A320	123456	
158	1000	DUBLIN	1110	HEATHROW	A.320	123456	
159	1205	HEATHROW	1315	DUBLIN	A.320	6	
162	1120	DUBLIN	1235	HEATHROW	A.320	1234567	
163	1335	HEATHROW	1450	DUBLIN	A.320	1234567	
164	1210	DUBLIN	1325	HEATHROW	A.320	1234567	
165	1325	HEATHROW	1440	DUBLIN	A.320	1234567	
166	1245	DUBLIN	1400	HEATHROW	B.737	12345 7	
167	1545	HEATHROW	1700	DUBLIN	B.737	1234567	
168	1305	DUBLIN	1420	HEATHROW	B.737	123456	
169	1650	HEATHROW	1800	DUBLIN	A.320	12345 7	
172	1435	DUBLIN	1550	HEATHROW	A.320	7	
174	1550	DUBLIN	1705	HEATHROW	A.320	1234567	
175	1805	HEATHROW	1920	DUBLIN	A.320	1234567	
176	1700	DUBLIN	1815	HEATHROW	A.320	1234567	
177	1910	HEATHROW	2025	DUBLIN	A.320	1234567	
178	1800	DUBLIN	1915	HEATHROW	A.320	1234567	
179	2010	HEATHROW	2125	DUBLIN	A.320	1234567	
182	1855	DUBLIN	2010	HEATHROW	B737/A320	1234567	
183	2105	HEATHROW	2220	DUBLIN	B737/A320	1234567	
184	1955	DUBLIN	2105	HEATHROW	B.737	1 4	
185	2150	HEATHROW	2305	DUBLIN	B.737	1 4	
186	2005	DUBLIN	2120	HEATHROW	A.320	5	
187	2215	HEATHROW	2330	DUBLIN	A320/B737	5 7	
188	2025	DUBLIN	2140	HEATHROW	B.737	7	
189	2235	HEATHROW	2250	DUBLIN	B.737	1234 7	2235/2345 7

194	2035	DUBLIN	2150	HEATHROW	A.320	1234 7	
195	2240	HEATHROW	2355	DUBLIN	A.320	7	
196	2040	DUBLIN	2155	HEATHROW	B.737	5 7	
197	2245	HEATHROW	2350	DUBLIN	B.737	5 7	
198	2155	DUBLIN	2310	HEATHROW	A.320	7	
202	0715	DUBLIN	0815	MANCHESTER	BAE-146	1234567	
203	0850	MANCHESTER	0950	DUBLIN	BAE-146	1234567	
204	0855	DUBLIN	0955	MANCHESTER	BAE-146	12345	
205	1040	MANCHESTER	1135	DUBLIN	BAE-146	12345	
206	1115	DUBLIN	1215	MANCHESTER	BAE-146	1234567	
207	1300	MANCHESTER	1355	DUBLIN	BAE-146	1234567	
212	1445	DUBLIN	1545	MANCHESTER	BAE-146	12345 7	
213	1630	MANCHESTER	1725	DUBLIN	BAE-146	12345 7	
214	1650	DUBLIN	1745	MANCHESTER	BAE-146	1234567	
215	1825	MANCHESTER	1925	DUBLIN	BAE-146	1234567	
218	1830	DUBLIN	1930	MANCHESTER	BAE-146	1234567	
219	2015	MANCHESTER	2110	DUBLIN	BAE-146	1234567	
222	0735	DUBLIN	0835	GLASGOW	BAE-146	1234567	
223	0920	GLASGOW	1020	DUBLIN	BAE-146	1234567	
224	1135	DUBLIN	1230	GLASGOW	BAE-146	1234567	
225	1315	GLASGOW	1410	DUBLIN	BAE-146	1234567	
228	1505	DUBLIN	1600	GLASGOW	BAE-146	1234567	
229	1645	GLASGOW	1745	DUBLIN	BAE-146	1234567	
234	1830	DUBLIN	1930	GLASGOW	BAE-146	1234567	
235	2015	GLASGOW	2115	DUBLIN	BAE-146	1234567	
244	1040	DUBLIN	1100	EDINBURGH	BAE-146	1234567	
245	1225	EDINBURGH	1325	DUBLIN	BAE-146	1234567	
252	0745	DUBLIN	0845	EDINBURGH	BAE-146	1234567	
253	0930	EDINBURGH	1025	DUBLIN	BAE-146	1234567	
254	1315	DUBLIN	1415	EDINBURGH	BAE-146	12345	
255	1500	EDINBURGH	1600	DUBLIN	BAE-146	12345	
256	1445	DUBLIN	1545	EDINBURGH	BAE-146	1234567	
257	1630	EDINBURGH	1730	DUBLIN	BAE-146	1234567	
258	1825	DUBLIN	1925	EDINBURGH	BAE-146	1234567	
259	2010	EDINBURGH	2110	DUBLIN	BAE-146	1234567	
262	0745	DUBLIN	0845	BIRMINGHAM	BAE-146	1234567	
263	0930	BIRMINGHAM	1030	DUBLIN	BAE-146	1234567	
264	0915	DUBLIN	1015	BIRMINGHAM	BAE-146	6	
265	1100	BIRMINGHAM	1200	DUBLIN	BAE-146	6	
266	1115	DUBLIN	1215	BIRMINGHAM	BAE-146	12345 7	
267	1300	BIRMINGHAM	1400	DUBLIN	BAE-146	12345 7	
268	1230	DUBLIN	1330	BIRMINGHAM	BAE-146	12345	
272	1500	DUBLIN	1600	BIRMINGHAM	BAE-146	1234567	
273	1645	BIRMINGHAM	1745	DUBLIN	BAE-146	1234567	
274	1820	DUBLIN	1920	BIRMINGHAM	BAE-146	1234567	
275	1845	BIRMINGHAM	1945	DUBLIN	BAE-146	1234	
276	1910	DUBLIN	2020	BIRMINGHAM	F-50	7	
277	2005	BIRMINGHAM	2105	DUBLIN	BAE-146	1234567	
278	2000	DUBLIN	2100	BIRMINGHAM	BAE-146	12345	
279	2055	BIRMINGHAM	2205	DUBLIN	F50/BAE146	5 7	2145/2245 5
282	0715	DUBLIN	0825	BRISTOL	F-50	1234567	
283	0850	BRISTOL	1000	DUBLIN	F-50	1234567	
288	1750	DUBLIN	1900	BRISTOL	F-50	1234567	
289	1950	BRISTOL	2100	DUBLIN	F-50	1234567	
302	0750	DUBLIN	0905	NEWCASTLE	F-50	1234567	
303	0950	NEWCASTLE	1105	DUBLIN	F-50	1234567	
308	1815	DUBLIN	1925	NEWCASTLE	F-50	1234567	
309	2015	NEWCASTLE	2120	DUBLIN	F-50	1234567	
314	1355	DUBLIN	1440	KNOCK	BAE-146	7	
	1515	KNOCK	1630	BIRMINGHAM	BAE-146	7	
319	1900	BIRMINGHAM	2015	KNOCK	BAE-146	5	
	2050	KNOCK	2130	DUBLIN	BAE-146	5	
342	1015	DUBLIN	1140	JERSEY	BAE-146	6	29.05-25.09
343	1235	JERSEY	1400	DUBLIN	BAE-146	6	29.05-25.09
364	0750	DUBLIN	0855	LEEDS	F-50	1234567	
365	0945	LEEDS	1055	DUBLIN	F-50	1234567	
368	1820	DUBLIN	1925	LEEDS	F-50	1234567	
369	2020	LEEDS	2130	DUBLIN	F-50	1234567	

371	0650	HEATHROW	0815	SHANNON	B.737	123456	31.05-02.10
372	0900	SHANNON	1015	HEATHROW	B.737	1234567	
373	1050	HEATHROW	1210	SHANNON	B.737	7	
374	1305	SHANNON	1425	HEATHROW	B.737	7	
375	1115	HEATHROW	1230	SHANNON	B.737	1234567	
376	1335	SHANNON	1450	HEATHROW	B.737	1234567	
377	1205	HEATHROW	1320	SHANNON	A.320	12345	
378	1440	SHANNON	1555	HEATHROW	A.320	12345	
381	1515	HEATHROW	1630	SHANNON	B.737	1234567	
382	1735	SHANNON	1850	HEATHROW	B.737	1234567	
383	1940	HEATHROW	2055	SHANNON	B.737	1234567	
384	2155	SHANNON	2310	HEATHROW	B.737	12345 7	30.05-01.10
433	1430	PARIS CDG	1605	SHANNON	B.737	1234567	
434	1720	SHANNON	1900	PARIS CDG	B.737	1234567	
441	0715	STANSTED	0830	DUBLIN	BAE-146	12345	
442	0715	DUBLIN	0830	STANSTED	BAE-146	1234567	
443	0915	STANSTED	1030	DUBLIN	BAE-146	1234567	
444	0915	DUBLIN	1030	STANSTED	BAE-146	1234567	
445	1115	STANSTED	1230	DUBLIN	BAE-146	12345 7	
446	1115	DUBLIN	1230	STANSTED	BAE-146	6	
447	11315	STANSTED	1430	DUBLIN	BAE-146	6	
448	1200	DUBLIN	1315	STANSTED	BAE-146	1234567	
449	1400	STANSTED	1515	DUBLIN	BAE-146	67	
452	1425	DUBLIN	1540	STANSTED	BAE-146	67	
453	1625	STANSTED	1740	DUBLIN	BAE-146	67	
454	1600	DUBLIN	1715	STANSTED	BAE-146	12345	
455	1800	STANSTED	1915	DUBLIN	BAE-146	12345	
456	1810	DUBLIN	1925	STANSTED	BAE-146	1234567	
457	2010	STANSTED	2125	DUBLIN	BAE-146	1234567	
458	2010	DUBLIN	2125	STANSTED	BAE-146	12345 7	
459	2205	STANSTED	2230	DUBLIN	BAE-146	5	
502	0730	DUBLIN	1035	ROME	B.737	12 4	
503	1150	ROME	1505	DUBLIN	B.737	12 4	
504	0905	DUBLIN	1210	ROME	A.320	7	
505	1325	ROME	1640	DUBLIN	B.737	7	
508	1340	DUBLIN	1645	ROME	B.737	6	-25.09
509	1800	ROME	2115	DUBLIN	B.737	6	-25.09
516	1845	DUBLIN	2020	PARIS CDG	B.737	12345 7	
517	2105	PARIS CDG	2245	DUBLIN	B.737	12345 7	
519	0715	PARIS	0855	DUBLIN	B.737	12345	
520	0950	CORK	0630	DUBLIN	B.737	12345	
	0715	DUBLIN	0850	PARIS CDG	B.737	12345	
521	0950	PARIS CDG	1135	DUBLIN	B.737	12345	
	1240	DUBLIN	1325	CORK	B.737	12345	
522	0755	DUBLIN	0930	PARIS	B.737	67	
523	1015	PARIS	1155	DUBLIN	B.737	67	
524	1255	DUBLIN	1430	PARIS	A320/B737	123456	
525	1525	PARIS	1705	DUBLIN	A320/B737	123456	
526	1600	DUBLIN	1735	PARIS	B.737	1234567	
527	1825	PARIS	2005	DUBLIN	B.737	1234567	
528	1715	DUBLIN	1850	PARIS	B.737	12345 7	
529	1935	PARIS	2115	DUBLIN	B.737	5	
530	0945	DUBLIN	1120	PARIS	B.737	7	
531	1205	PARIS CDG	1345	DUBLIN	B.737	7	
532	1500	DUBLIN	1635	PARIS	A.320	6	
533	1730	PARIS	1910	DUBLIN	B.737	6	
538	1810	DUBLIN	1945	PARIS CDG	B.737	6	
539	2030	PARIS	2210	DUBLIN	B.737	6	
594	0900	DUBLIN	1135	MADRID	B.737	3 5	26.05-24.09
595	1225	MADRID	1455	DUBLIN	B.737	3 5	26.05-24.09
601	0735	AMSTERDAM	0910	DUBLIN	B.737	12345	
602	0650	DUBLIN	0830	AMSTERDAM	A320/B737	123456	
603	0920	AMSTERDAM	1055	DUBLIN	A320/B737	123456	
604	1025	DUBLIN	1200	AMSTERDAM	B.737	12345	
605	1255	AMSTERDAM	1430	DUBLIN	B.737	12345	
606	1435	DUBLIN	1610	AMSTERDAM	B.737	12345	

607	1700	AMSTERDAM	1835	DUBLIN	B.737	12345	
608	1405	CORK	1445	DUBLIN	B.737	7	
	1535	DUBLIN	1710	AMSTERDAM	B.737	12345 7	
609	1810	AMSTERDAM	1945	DUBLIN	B.737	12345 7	
612	0705	DUBLIN	0845	AMSTERDAM	B.737	7	
613	1010	AMSTERDAM	1145	DUBLIN	B.737	7	
	1235	DUBLIN	1320	CORK	B.737	7	
614	1800	DUBLIN	1930	AMSTERDAM	B.737	12345 7	
615	2025	AMSTERDAM	2200	DUBLIN	B.737	5	
616	0945	DUBLIN	1115	AMSTERDAM	A.320	7	
617	1205	AMSTERDAM	1340	DUBLIN	A.320	7	
618	1200	DUBLIN	1340	AMSTERDAM	A.320	6	
619	1440	AMSTERDAM	1615	DUBLIN	A.320	6	
622	1245	DUBLIN	1450	COPENHAGEN	B.737	12345	
623	1540	COPENHAGEN	1755	DUBLIN	B.737	12345	
624	1520	DUBLIN	1725	COPENHAGEN	B.737	6	
625	1815	COPENHAGEN	2025	DUBLIN	B.737	6	
626	1445	DUBLIN	1650	COPENHAGEN	B.737	7	
627	1740	COPENHAGEN	1950	DUBLIN	B.737	7	
630	0700	DUBLIN	0835	BRUSSELS	B.737	12345	
631	0920	BRUSSELS	1110	DUBLIN	B.737	12345	
632	1140	DUBLIN	1310	BRUSSELS	B.737	12345 7	
633	1715	BRUSSELS	1855	DUBLIN	B.737	7	
634	1940	DUBLIN	2110	BRUSSELS	B.737	7	
635	1400	BRUSSELS	1550	DUBLIN	B.737	12345 7	
636	1620	DUBLIN	1755	BRUSSELS	B.737	12345	
637	1850	BRUSSELS	2025	DUBLIN	B.737	12345	
638	1145	DUBLIN	1325	BRUSSELS	A.320	6	
639	0915	BRUSSELS	1055	DUBLIN	A.320	6	
650	0700	DUBLIN	0900	FRANKFURT	B.737	123456	
651	0950	FRANKFURT	1155	DUBLIN	B.737	123456	
652	1010	DUBLIN	1215	FRANKFURT	B.737	123456	0955/1155 6
653	1310	FRANKFURT	1515	DUBLIN	B.737	12345	
654	0700	DUBLIN	0900	FRANKFURT	B.737	7	
655	1310	FRANKFURT	1515	DUBLIN	B.737	6	
	1545	DUBLIN	1620	SHANNON	B.737	6	
656	1555	DUBLIN	1800	FRANKFURT	B.737	12345 7	
	1410	CORK	1450	DUBLIN	B.737	6	
	1425	KERRY	1515	DUBLIN	B.737	7	
657	1850	FRANKFURT	2055	DUBLIN	B.737	12345 7	
	2205	DUBLIN	2250	CORK	B.737	12345 7	
658	1325	DUBLIN	1525	FRANKFURT	B.737	6	
659	0950	FRANKFURT	1155	DUBLIN	B.737	67	1610/1815 6
	1235	DUBLIN	1325	KERRY	B.737	7	
660	0815	DUBLIN	1030	ZURICH	B.737	6	
662	1450	SHANNON	1655	ZURICH	B.737	6	
664	1015	DUBLIN	1230	ZURICH	B.737	12345 7	
665	1315	ZURICH	1540	DUBLIN	B.737	12345 7	
667	1115	ZURICH	1350	DUBLIN	B.737	6	
669	1810	ZURICH	2030	DUBLIN	B.737	6	
672	0750	DUBLIN	1025	MILAN	B.737	12345	
673	1110	MILAN	1350	DUBLIN	B.737	12345	
674	1145	DUBLIN	1420	MILAN	B.737	67	
675	1505	MILAN	1745	DUBLIN	B.737	67	
690	1550	SHANNON	1745	DUSSELDORF	B.737	6	
691	1240	DUSSELDORF	1435	SHANNON	B.737	6	
692	0550	CORK	0630	DUBLIN	B.737	6	
	0715	DUBLIN	0910	DUSSELDORF	B.737	123456	
693	1005	DUSSELDORF	1155	DUBLIN	B.737	123456	
	1235	DUBLIN	1320	CORK	B.737	6	
694	1000	DUBLIN	1150	DUSSELDORF	B.737	6	
695	1130	DUSSELDORF	1320	DUBLIN	B.737	7	
	1355	DUBLIN	1445	KERRY	B.737	7	
696	0900	DUBLIN	1045	DUSSELDORF	B.737	7	
697	1835	DUSSELDORF	2025	DUBLIN	B.737	6	
698	1530	KERRY	1620	DUBLIN	B.737	7	
	1640	DUBLIN	1830	DUSSELDORF	B.737	12345 7	
699	1920	DUSSELDORF	2105	DUBLIN	B.737	12345 7	

710	0750	CORK	0905	HEATHROW	A.320	1234567	
711	0955	HEATHROW	1110	CORK	A.320	1234567	
712	1210	CORK	1325	HEATHROW	A.320	1234567	
713	1205	HEATHROW	1320	CORK	A.320	12345	
714	1440	CORK	1555	HEATHROW	A.320	12345	
715	1415	HEATHROW	1530	CORK	A.320	1234567	
717	1445	HEATHROW	1600	CORK	B.737	12345 7	
722	1700	CORK	1815	HEATHROW	A.320	1234567	
723	1910	HEATHROW	2025	CORK	A.320	1234567	
724	2005	CORK	2120	HEATHROW	B.737	12345 7	
744	0815	DUBLIN	0910	CORK	F-50	6	22.05-02.10
	0940	CORK	1145	RENNES	F-50	6	22.05-02.10
745	1300	RENNES	1510	DUBLIN	F-50	6	22.05-02.10
	1535	DUBLIN	1610	CORK	F-50	6	22.05-02.10
761	0700	BIRMINGHAM	0800	DUBLIN	BAE-146	12345	
	0840	DUBLIN	0930	CORK	BAE-146	12345	
763	1415	BIRMINGHAM	1530	CORK	BAE-146	12345	
764	1450	CORK	1605	BIRMINGHAM	BAE-146	6	
765	1715	BIRMINGHAM	1830	CORK	BAE-146	7	
766	1615	CORK	1730	BIRMINGHAM	BAE-146	12345	
767	1730	BIRMINGHAM	1845	CORK	BAE-146	6	
768	1945	CORK	2100	BIRMINGHAM	BAE-146	7	
822	1200	CORK	1335	PARIS CDG	B.737	1234567	
823	1945	PARIS CDG	2125	CORK	B.737	1234567	
840	0650	CORK	0835	AMSTERDAM	B.737	1234567	
841	0920	AMSTERDAM	1105	CORK	B.737	1234567	
851	1430	STANSTED	1600	SHANNON	BAC1-11	1234567	
852	1230	SHANNON	1355	STANSTED	BAC1-11	1234567	
857	1045	BIRMINGHAM	1200	SHANNON	BAC1-11	1234567	
858	0845	SHANNON	1000	BIRMINGHAM	BAC1-11	1234567	

SHUTTLE   *BRITISH AIRWAYS   BA/BAW   U.K.*

2A	0645	HEATHROW	0735	MANCHESTER	B757/A320	12345	BA1382
2E	0745	HEATHROW	0840	MANCHESTER	B.757	1234567	BA1384
2G	1645	HEATHROW	1735	MANCHESTER	B.757	1234567	BA1398
2J	0845	HEATHROW	0940	MANCHESTER	B.757	12345	BA1386
2K	1745	HEATHROW	1840	MANCHESTER	B.757	12345	BA1402
2M	0945	HEATHROW	1035	MANCHESTER	B.757	1234567	BA1388
2P	1545	HEATHROW	1635	MANCHESTER	B.757	12 45	BA1396
	1345	HEATHROW	1440	MANCHESTER	B.757	3	
2R	1845	HEATHROW	1940	MANCHESTER	B.757	1234567	BA1404
2S	1145	HEATHROW	1240	MANCHESTER	B.757	1234567	BA1392
2V	1345	HEATHROW	1440	MANCHESTER	B.757	1234567	BA1394
2W	2045	HEATHROW	2135	MANCHESTER	B.757	1234567	BA1408
3F	1430	MANCHESTER	1520	HEATHROW	B.757	1234567	BA1395
3L	1630	MANCHESTER	1720	HEATHROW	B.757	1234567	BA1399
3M	0640	MANCHESTER	0735	HEATHROW	B.757	12345	BA1383
3N	0730	MANCHESTER	0835	HEATHROW	B.757	1234567	BA1385
3P	0830	MANCHESTER	0935	HEATHROW	B757/A320	1234567	BA1387
3R	0930	MANCHESTER	1030	HEATHROW	B.757	1234567	BA1389
3T	1830	MANCHESTER	1925	HEATHROW	B.757	12345 7	BA1405
	1900	MANCHESTER	1955	HEATHROW	B.757	6	
3U	1030	MANCHESTER	1125	HEATHROW	B757	12345	BA1391
3V	1730	MANCHESTER	1825	HEATHROW	B.757	12345	BA1403
3X	1230	MANCHESTER	1320	HEATHROW	B.757	1234567	BA1393
3Y	1930	MANCHESTER	2030	HEATHROW	B.757	12345	BA1407
4C	1705	HEATHROW	1820	BELFAST INT.	B737/A320	1234567	BA1424
4H	0820	HEATHROW	0935	BELFAST INT.	B737/A320	123456	BA1412
4M	1255	HEATHROW	1410	BELFAST INT.	B737/A320	1234567	BA1418
4N	1900	HEATHROW	2015	BELFAST INT.	B737/A320	1234567	BA1426
4P	1035	HEATHROW	1145	BELFAST INT.	B737/A320	1234567	BA1416
4V	2100	HEATHROW	2210	BELFAST INT.	B737/A320	5	BA1428
4Z	1500	HEATHROW	1615	BELFAST INT.	B737/A320	1234567	BA1422
5A	1300	BELFAST	1410	HEATHROW	B737/A320	1234567	BA1419
5B	0815	BELFAST INT.	0930	HEATHROW	B737/A320	67	BA1415
5J	1500	BELFAST INT.	1610	HEATHROW	B737/A320	1234567	BA1423
5L	0700	BELFAST INT.	0830	HEATHROW	B737/A320	12345	BA1413

5M	1700	BELFAST INT.	1810	HEATHROW	B737/A320	1234567	BA1425
5S	1900	BELFAST INT.	2010	HEATHROW	B737/A320	12345 7	BA1427
5T	1030	BELFAST INT.	1140	HEATHROW	B737/A320	1234567	BA1417
5X	2110	BELFAST INT.	2205	HEATHROW	B737/A320	5	BA1429
6C	0715	HEATHROW	0830	GLASGOW	B.757	12345	BA1472
6E	1515	HEATHROW	1630	GLASGOW	B.757	12345 7	BA1486
6F	1615	HEATHROW	1730	GLASGOW	B.757	1234567	BA1488
6G	0815	HEATHROW	0930	GLASGOW	B.757	123456	BA1474
6J	1715	HEATHROW	1830	GLASGOW	B.757	12345 7	BA1492
6L	0915	HEATHROW	1030	GLASGOW	A.320	12345	BA1476
6M	1815	HEATHROW	1930	GLASGOW	B.757	1234567	BA1494
6N	1015	HEATHROW	1130	GLASGOW	B.757	1234567	BA1478
6P	1915	HEATHROW	2030	GLASGOW	B.757	12345 7	BA1496
6R	1415	HEATHROW	1530	GLASGOW	B757/A320	1234567	BA1484
6T	1215	HEATHROW	1330	GLASGOW	B757/A320	1234567	BA1482
6U	2015	HEATHROW	2130	GLASGOW	B.757	1234567	BA1498
7A	1930	GLASGOW	2045	HEATHROW	B.757	12345 7	BA1497
7B	2030	GLASGOW	2145	HEATHROW	B.757	12345 7	BA1499
7G	1425	GLASGOW	1540	HEATHROW	B.757/A320	1234567	BA1485
7H	1530	GLASGOW	1645	HEATHROW	A.320	12345	BA1487
7P	1630	GLASGOW	1745	HEATHROW	B757/A320	1234567	BA1489
7R	0635	GLASGOW	0800	HEATHROW	B.757	123456	BA1473
7S	0735	GLASGOW	0855	HEATHROW	B.757	1234567	BA1475
7U	1730	GLASGOW	1845	HEATHROW	B.757	12345 7	BA1493
7W	1035	GLASGOW	1150	HEATHROW	B.757	1234567	BA1479
7X	1830	GLASGOW	1945	HEATHROW	B.757	1234567	BA1495
7Y	0930	GLASGOW	1045	HEATHROW	B.757	12345	BA1477
7Z	1230	GLASGOW	1345	HEATHROW	B.757	1234567	BA1483
8A	1500	HEATHROW	1615	EDINBURGH	B.757	1234567	BA1448
8B	0700	HEATHROW	0815	EDINBURGH	B.757	12345	BA1432
8C	1600	HEATHROW	1715	EDINBURGH	B.757	12345	BA1452
8F	0800	HEATHROW	0915	EDINBURGH	B.757	12345	BA1434
8H	1700	HEATHROW	1815	EDINBURGH	B.757	1234567	BA1454
8K	0900	HEATHROW	1015	EDINBURGH	B.757	1234567	BA1438
8L	1800	HEATHROW	1915	EDINBURGH	B.757	12345 7	BA1458
8R	1100	HEATHROW	1215	EDINBURGH	B.757	1234567	BA1442
8S	2000	HEATHROW	2115	EDINBURGH	B.757	12345 7	BA1464
8V	1900	HEATHROW	2015	EDINBURGH	B757/767	1234567	BA1462
8W	1300	HEATHROW	1415	EDINBURGH	B.757	1234567	BA1444
8Y	1400	HEATHROW	1515	EDINBURGH	B.757	12345 7	BA1446
9B	1120	EDINBURGH	1235	HEATHROW	B.757	1234567	BA1443
9C	1915	EDINBURGH	2035	HEATHROW	B.757	1234567	BA1463
9E	2015	EDINBURGH	2130	HEATHROW	B.757	12345 7	BA1465
9J	1315	EDINBURGH	1430	HEATHROW	B.757	1234567	BA1445
9K	1515	EDINBURGH	1630	HEATHROW	B.757	1234567	BA1449
9N	1615	EDINBURGH	1730	HEATHROW	B.757	12345 7	BA1453
9P	1720	EDINBURGH	1835	HEATHROW	B.757	1234567	BA1455
9T	0645	EDINBURGH	0810	HEATHROW	B.767	123456	BA1433
9U	0745	EDINBURGH	0905	HEATHROW	B.757	12345	BA1435
9W	0915	EDINBURGH	1040	HEATHROW	B.757	1234567	BA1439
9Y	1815	EDINBURGH	1935	HEATHROW	B.757	12345	BA1459
9Z	1020	EDINBURGH	1135	HEATHROW	B.757	12345	BA1441

		SINGAPORE		*SINGAPORE AIRLINES*	*SQ/SIA*	*SINGAPORE*	
23		NEW YORK	1025	AMSTERDAM	B.747	123 6	
24	0715	AMSTERDAM		NEW YORK	B.747	12 5 7	
25		NEW YORK	1010	FRANKFURT	B.747	1234567	
26	0730	FRANKFURT		NEW YORK	B.747	1234567	
317	2105	HEATHROW		SINGAPORE	B.747	1234567	DEP 1730 6
318		SINGAPORE	1530	HEATHROW	B.747	1234567	
319	1200	HEATHROW		SINGAPORE	B.747	1234567	
320		SINGAPORE	1900	HEATHROW	B.747	1234567	
321	2215	HEATHROW		SINGAPORE	B.747	1234567	
322		SINGAPORE	0555	HEATHROW	B.747	1234567	
328	0625	AMSTERDAM	0755	MANCHESTER	B.747	34 6	
		SINGAPORE	0740	MANCHESTER	B.747	5 7	

329	0930	MANCHESTER	1100	AMSTERDAM	B.747	45 7	
	0930	MANCHESTER		SINGAPORE	B.747	3 6	
345	0945	MANCHESTER		ZURICH	B.747	1	
346		ZURICH	0820	MANCHESTER	B.747	1	
7356		SHARJAH	1325	DUBLIN	B.747	3 7	ARR 1925 7
7395	0650	HEATHROW		DUBAI	B.747	1 4	DEP 2000 4
7396		DUBAI	1630	HEATHROW	B.747	4 7	ARR 2130 7
7997		NEW YORK	0830	BRUSSELS	B.747	1	
7998	1425	BRUSSELS	1730	NEW YORK	B.747	7	

SIRIOFLY   *EUROFLY S.P.A.   EEZ   ITALY*

EVEN NUMBERS - FLIGHTS INTO THE UK   UNEVEN NUMBERS - FLIGHTS LEAVING THE UK

1550/1	1800	EDINBURGH	1055	ROME	DC-9	4	24.06-02.09
1552/3	1200	EDINBURGH	1700	MILAN	DC-9	4	24.06-02.09
1554/5	1800	EDINBURGH	1710	MILAN	MD-83	4	17.06-09.09
1556/7	2110	EDINBURGH	2020	MILAN	MD-83	4	24.06-02.09
1558/9	1940	EDINBURGH	1850	MILAN	MD-83	5	18.06-10.09
1598		MILAN	2320	STANSTED	MD-83	2	
	0010	STANSTED		URALSK	MD-83	3	
1599		URALSK	1220	STANSTED	MD-83	3	
	1310	STANSTED		MILAN	MD-83	3	

SPEEDBIRD   *BRITISH AIRWAYS   BA/BAW   U.K.*

SEE ALSO   "SHUTTLE"; "BLUE-STAR";   "BRITISH" "BRYMON";   "FLYER" AND "LOGANAIR"

12G	1230	HEATHROW	1340	NEWCASTLE	A320/B757	1234567	BA1332
12H	0925	HEATHROW	1030	NEWCASTLE	B.737	1234567	BA1326
12J	0730	HEATHROW	0835	NEWCASTLE	B.737	12345	BA1324
12N	1645	HEATHROW	1750	NEWCASTLE	VARIES	1234567	BA1334
12Q	1835	HEATHROW	1940	NEWCASTLE	B.757	12345	BA1336
12T	2045	HEATHROW	2150	NEWCASTLE	B.757	1234567	BA1338
13C	0640	NEWCASTLE	0750	HEATHROW	B.757	123456	BA1321
13E	0950	NEWCASTLE	1100	HEATHROW	B737/757	12345	BA1325
13F	1130	NEWCASTLE	1235	HEATHROW	B757/A320	67	BA1327
13J	1600	NEWCASTLE	1705	HEATHROW	B757/1320	1234567	BA1333
13K	1845	NEWCASTLE	1950	HEATHROW	VARIES	1234567	BA1335
13L	2040	NEWCASTLE	2145	HEATHROW	B.757	12345	BA1337
13R	1245	NEWCASTLE	1350	HEATHROW	B737/A320	12345	BA1331
13X	0745	NEWCASTLE	0850	HEATHROW	B.757	7	BA1323
16C	1545	HEATHROW	1640	JERSEY	B737/A320	1234567	BA1372
16E	1205	HEATHROW	1300	JERSEY	B737/A320	1234567	BA1368
16F	2015	HEATHROW	2110	JERSEY	B737/A320	1234567	BA1376
16Q	0755	HEATHROW	0850	JERSEY	B737/A320	1234567	BA1364
17R	0700	JERSEY	0800	HEATHROW	B737/A320	1234567	BA1361
17S	1030	JERSEY	1105	HEATHROW	B737/A320	1234567	BA1365
17T	1350	JERSEY	1445	HEATHROW	B737/A320	1234567	BA1369
17V	1805	JERSEY	1900	HEATHROW	B737/A320	1234567	BA1373
18C	1155	HEATHROW	1320	ABERDEEN	B.757	12345	BA1308
18E	1810	HEATHROW	1935	ABERDEEN	B757/A320	12345 7	BA1316
18F	1400	HEATHROW	1525	ABERDEEN	B757/A320	1234567	BA1312
18V	1630	HEATHROW	1755	ABERDEEN	B.757	1234567	BA1314
18W	2005	HEATHROW	2130	ABERDEEN	B757/A320	1234567	BA1318
18Y	0925	HEATHROW	1050	ABERDEEN	B.757	1234567	BA1306
18Z	0720	HEATHROW	0845	ABERDEEN	B.757	12345	BA1304
19N	0835	ABERDEEN	1005	HEATHROW	B.757	67	BA1303
19Q	0945	ABERDEEN	1115	HEATHROW	B.757	12345	BA1305
19R	1145	ABERDEEN	1310	HEATHROW	B.757	1234567	BA1307
19S	0640	ABERDEEN	0820	HEATHROW	B.757	12345	BA1301
19T	1625	ABERDEEN	1745	HEATHROW	B757/A320	1234567	BA1313
19W	1845	ABERDEEN	2000	HEATHROW	B.757	1234567	BA1315
19X	2035	ABERDEEN	2155	HEATHROW	B757/A320	12345 7	BA1317
19Y	1415	ABERDEEN	1540	HEATHROW	B.757	12345	BA1309
22DL	1730	EDINBURGH	1830	BIRMINGHAM	B.737	12345 7	BA1784
	1910	BIRMINGHAM`	2030	DUSSELDORF	B.737	12345 7	
22DM	0630	EDINBURGH	0730	BIRMINGHAM	EMB/CRJ	123456	BA1768
	0845	BIRMINGHAM	1045	MUNICH	CANADAIR	1234567	
22GL	0655	MANCHESTER	0850	GENEVA	EMB-145	1234567	BA1674

23DM	1120	MUNICH	1325	BIRMINGHAM	CANADAIR	123456	BA1769
	1430	BIRMINGHAM	1530	EDINBURGH	EMB-145	12345	
24DL	1130	EDINBURGH	1230	BIRMINGHAM	B.737	1234567	BA1780
	1330	BIRMINGHAM	1450	MUNICH	B.737	1234567	
4TP	0950	GATWICK	1310	BUCHAREST	B737/757	1234567	BA3894
25DL	0915	DUSSELDORF	1040	BIRMINGHAM	B.737	12345	BA1779
26DL	0710	BIRMINGHAM	0830	DUSSELDORF	B.737	12345	BA1778
28DL	1430	GLASGOW	1545	BIRMINGHAM	BAE-ATP	1234567	BA1896
	1630	BIRMINGHAM	1755	DUSSELDORF	B.737	1234567	BA1782
28EL	1030	GATWICK	1320	BELGRADE	B.737	1 34 7	BA2888
29LE	1320	BELGRADE	1725	GATWICK	B.737	1 34 7	BA2889
32F	0820	GATWICK	1005	ABERDEEN	B.737	1234567	BA2922
32G	1300	GATWICK	1440	ABERDEEN	B.737	123456	BA2924
32J	1525	GATWICK	1700	ABERDEEN	B.737	12345 7	BA2926
32KB	1950	GATWICK	2025	ABERDEEN	B.737	1234567	BA2928
33A	1555	ABERDEEN	1725	GATWICK	B.737	123456	BA2925
33AM	0920	AMSTERDAM	1035	MANCHESTER	B.737	123456	BA1625
33F	1745	ABERDEEN	1925	GATWICK	B.737	12345 7	BA2927
33J	1045	ABERDEEN	1220	GATWICK	B.737	1234567	BA2923
33W	0645	ABERDEEN	0845	GATWICK	B.737	1234567	BA2921
34A	0915	GATWICK	1025	MANCHESTER	B.737	1234567	BA2904
34B	1305	GATWICK	1410	MANCHESTER	B.737	12345	BA2906
34C	0725	GATWICK	0840	MANCHESTER	B.757	1234567	BA2902
34E	2030	GATWICK	2130	MANCHESTER	B.757	1234567	BA2912
34F	1445	GATWICK	1545	MANCHESTER	B.737	12345 7	BA2908
	1600	GATWICK	1700	MANCHESTER	B.737	6	
34G	1710	GATWICK	1805	MANCHESTER	B.737	12345 7	BA2910
35AM	1600	AMSTERDAM	1715	MANCHESTER	B.737	12345 7	BA1629
35B	1630	MANCHESTER	1735	GATWICK	B.737	12345 7	BA2909
	1800	MANCHESTER	1905	GATWICK	B.737	6	
35L	1115	MANCHESTER	1215	GATWICK	B.737	1234567	BA2905
35LH	1800	LISBON	2035	HEATHROW	B.757	1234567	BA503
35R	0625	MANCHESTER	0730	GATWICK	B737/757	1234567	BA2901
35W	1900	MANCHESTER	2000	GATWICK	B.737	12345 7	BA2911
35X	0925	MANCHESTER	1030	GATWICK	B737/757	123456	BA2903
35Y	1500	MANCHESTER	1600	GATWICK	B.737	12345	BA2907
36AM	0715	MANCHESTER	0830	AMSTERDAM	B.737	123456	BA1624
37AM	1945	AMSTERDAM	2055	MANCHESTER	B.737	12345 7	BA1631
37DL	1535	DUSSELDORF	1700	BIRMINGHAM	B.737	1234567	BA1781
	1745	BIRMINGHAM	1845	EDINBURGH	B.737	1234567	
38AM	1410	MANCHESTER	1520	AMSTERDAM	B.737	12345 7	BA1628
39AM	1415	AMSTERDAM	1525	MANCHESTER	B.737	12345 7	BA1627
41BC	0555	BRUSSELS	0655	GATWICK	B.737	1234567	BA2411
42AM	1745	MANCHESTER	1855	AMSTERDAM	B.737	12345 7	BA1630
2412	0840	GATWICK	1000	BRUSSELS	B.737	123456	BA2412
43GL	0930	GENEVA	1130	MANCHESTER	EMB-145	123456	BA1675
	1700	MANCHESTER	1805	EDINBURGH	BAE-ATP	12345 7	
43HJ	1050	BRUSSELS	1150	GATWICK	B.737	123456	BA2413
44AM	1200	MANCHESTER	1310	AMSTERDAM	EMB-145	12345 7	BA1626
44CD	2040	HEATHROW	2145	AMSTERDAM	B.757	12345 7	BA444
44E	2035	BIRMINGHAM	2135	EDINBURGH	B.737	12345	BA1809
44F	1045	PARIS CDG	1200	BIRMINGHAM	B.737	1234567	BA1803
	1310	BIRMINGHAM	1410	GLASGOW	B737/EMB	1234567	
44N	0700	BIRMINGHAM	0800	EDINBURGH	B.737	12345	BA1824
45D	0840	BIRMINGHAM	0950	PARIS CDG	B.737	1234567	BA1802
45F	1500	EDINBURGH	1600	BIRMINGHAM	B.737	1234567	BA1808
45H	1915	EDINBURGH	2015	BIRMINGHAM	B.737	12345	BA1825
45K	1320	BIRMINGHAM	1440	DUSSELDORF	B.737	1234567	BA1780
45MP	1600	BRUSSELS	1710	GATWICK	B.737	345 7	BA2415
46G	1335	HAMBURG	1510	BIRMINGHAM	B.737	12345	BA1753
	1600	BIRMINGHAM	1700	GLASGOW	B.737	12345	
46H	1600	PARIS CDG	1710	BIRMINGHAM	B.737	12345 7	BA1807
	1800	BIRMINGHAM	1900	GLASGOW	B.737	12345 7	
46JK	1555	GATWICK	1700	BRUSSELS	B.737	12345	BA2416
46Q	0700	BIRMINGHAM	0800	GLASGOW	B.737	12345	BA1820
46T	0835	BIRMINGHAM	0935	GLASGOW	B.737	12345	BA1902
46V	2040	BIRMINGHAM	2140	EDINBURGH	B.737	12345 7	BA1783
	1835	DUSSELDORF	2000	BIRMINGHAM	B.737	1234567	

46W	1000	BIRMINGHAM	1115	GLASGOW	BAE-ATP	123456	BA1801
46X	0720	DUSSELDORF	0850	BIRMINGHAM	B.737	123456	BA1777
	0935	BIRMINGHAM	1035	EDINBURGH	B.737	1234567	
46Y	1700	BIRMINGHAM	1815	GLASGOW	BAE-ATP	123457	BA1912
46Z	1410	FRANKFURT	1545	BIRMINGHAM	B.737	12345	BA1761
47B	0830	GLASGOW	0930	BIRMINGHAM	B.737	12345	BA1752
	1030	BIRMINGHAM	1255	HANOVER	B.737	12345	
47C	1930	GLASGOW	2030	BIRMINGHAM	B.737	12345 7	BA1913
47E	0700	GLASGOW	0800	BIRMINGHAM	B.737	123456	BA1802
	0840	BIRMINGHAM	0950	PARIS CDG	B.737	123456	
47F	1145	BIRMINGHAM	1320	FRANKFURT	B.737	12345	BA1760
47G	1230	GLASGOW	1330	BIRMINGHAM	B.737	12345 7	BA1806
	1410	BIRMINGHAM	1520	PARIS CDG	B.737	12345 7	
47H	0730	GLASGOW	0845	BIRMINGHAM	BAE-ATP	12345 7	BA1903
47K	1730	GLASGOW	1830	BIRMINGHAM	B.737	12345	BA1911
47R	1600	GLASGOW	1700	BIRMINGHAM	EMB-145	6	BA1810
	1745	BIRMINGHAM	1855	PARIS CDG	B.737	12345 7	
47TV	1750	BRUSSELS	1850	GATWICK	B.737	12345	BA2417
48LM	1325	GATWICK	1425	BRUSSELS	B.737	345 7	BA2414
49DL	0905	BRUSSELS	1030	MANCHESTER	B.737	1234567	BA1617
52CD	1930	GATWICK	2030	BRUSSELS	B.737	1234567	BA2420
52D	1350	MANCHESTER	1455	EDINBURGH	DHC-8	12345	BA1868
52G	1300	ROME	1555	MANCHESTER	B.737	12345 7	BA1655
	1700	MANCHESTER	1805	EDINBURGH	BAE-ATP	12345 7	
52R	0620	FRANKFURT	0810	MANCHESTER	B.737	123456	BA1705
	0850	MANCHESTER	0940	EDINBURGH	DHC-8	123456	
52RF	0755	HEATHROW	1020	ROME	B.767	1234567	BA552
52W	0705	MANCHESTER	0810	EDINBURGH	DHC-8	12345	BA1864
53E	0705	EDINBURGH	0755	MANCHESTER	B.737	6	BA1654
	0900	MANCHESTER	1155	ROME	B.737	12345 7	
53K	1900	MANCHESTER	2055	FRANKFURT	B.737	12345	BA1714
53M	1835	EDINBURGH	1940	MANCHESTER	DHC-8	12345	BA1873
53N	1655	EDINBURGH	1755	MANCHESTER	DH8/EMB4	12345 7	BA1714
53RF	1115	ROME	1400	HEATHROW	B.767	1234567	BA553
54L	0700	MANCHESTER	0810	GLASGOW	DHC-8	12345	BA1840
54M	1230	MADRID	1500	MANCHESTER	B.737	12345	BA1641
	1525	MANCHESTER	1630	GLASGOW	DHC-8	12345 7	
54N	0700	BRUSSELS	0920	MANCHESTER	B.737	123456	BA1615
	0900	MANCHESTER	1005	GLASGOW	DHC-8	123456	
54PT	1830	HEATHROW	2105	LISBON	B.767	1234567	BA504
54R	1700	MANCHESTER	1805	GLASGOW	DHC-8	12345	BA1848
54S	1915	MANCHESTER	2010	GLASGOW	B.737	12345 7	BA1661
55H	1150	GLASGOW	1255	MANCHESTER	DHC-8	6	BA1660
55T	0840	GLASGOW	0945	MANCHESTER	DHC-8	12345	BA1843
55X	1905	GLASGOW	2010	MANCHESTER	DHC-8	12345	BA1849
56E	1510	PARIS CDG	1630	MANCHESTER	B.737	1234567	BA1607
	1715	MANCHESTER	1840	ABERDEEN	DHC-8	12345	
57F	1605	MANCHESTER	1730	PARIS CDG	B.737	12345 7	BA1600
57RF	1735	ROME	2020	HEATHROW	B.767	1234567	BA557
58RF	1745	HEATHROW	2010	ROME	B.767	1234567	BA558
59LL	1400	BOLOGNA	1605	HEATHROW	B.757	1234567	BA593
62GL	1430	GLASGOW	1530	BIRMINGHAM	B.737	123456	BA1808
	1635	BIRMINGHAM	1745	PARIS CDG	B.737	1234567	
62PG	0635	BIRMINGHAM	0740	PARIS CDG	B.737	123456	BA1800
63KL	1600	BRUSSELS	1720	MANCHESTER	B.737	12345	BA1619
65YZ	1905	BRUSSELS	2015	MANCHESTER	B.737	12345 7	BA1621
67FG	0645	BIRMINGHAM	0800	BRUSSELS	B.737	123456	BA1744
69WX	1840	BRUSSELS	1950	BIRMINGHAM	B.737	12345 7	BA1749
72AR	1850	GATWICK	2120	STOCKHOLM	B.737	1234567	BA2772
72YZ	0700	MANCHESTER	0825	BRUSSELS	B.737	123456	BA1616
74DL	0740	MANCHESTER	0905	DUSSELDORF	B.737	1234567	BA1682
74MT	1700	GLASGOW	1750	MANCHESTER	B737/DH8	12345 7	BA1622
	1850	MANCHESTER	2010	BRUSSELS	B.737	12345 7	
74PL	0955	GATWICK	1205	NAPLES	B.737	1234567	BA2606
75DL	1000	DUSSELDORF	1130	MANCHESTER	B.737	1234567	BA1683
76AT	0825	GATWICK	1225	ATHENS	B.757	1234567	BA2640
76EF	1700	MANCHESTER	1820	BRUSSELS	B.737	12345	BA1620
76PL	1825	GATWICK	2040	NAPLES	B.737	1234567	BA2608

77AT	1325	ATHENS	1725	GATWICK	B.737	1234567	BA2641
77DL	1920	DUSSELDORF	2050	MANCHESTER	B.737	12345 7	BA1689
78PX	1250	GATWICK	1510	VERONA	B.737	1234567	BA2596
79EM	1530	DUSSELDORF	1700	MANCHESTER	B.737	12345 7	BA1687
79WW	1305	VIENNA	1535	GATWICK	B.737	1234567	BA2695
82MJ	1825	GATWICK	2030	GENOA	B.737	1234567	BA2618
82WW	1000	GATWICK	1220	VIENNA	B.737	1234567	BA2694
83GG	0700	GENEVA	0845	GATWICK	B.737	1234567	BA2735
83MJ	1300	GENOA	1500	GATWICK	B.737	1234567	BA2615
83PX	0645	VERONA	0855	GATWICK	B.737	1234567	BA2595
84WW	1810	GATWICK	2030	VIENNA	B.737	1234567	BA2698
85MJ	0750	GENOA	1000	GATWICK	B.737	1234567	BA2613
85PX	1555	VERONA	1800	GATWICK	B.737	1234567	BA2597
86CK	1325	MANCHESTER	1450	DUSSELDORF	B.737	12345 7	BA1686
86DL	1710	MANCHESTER	1835	DUSSELDORF	B.737	12345 7	BA1688
86GA	0945	GATWICK	1200	ZAGREB	B.737	1234567	BA2886
86GG	0740	GATWICK	0920	GENEVA	B.737	1234567	BA2736
86WX	0825	BRUSSELS	0945	BIRMINGHAM	B.737	123456	BA1745
87GA	1200	ZAGREB	1530	GATWICK	B.737	1234567	BA2887
88GG	1455	GATWICK	1630	GENEVA	B.737	1234567	BA2738
88GH	1645	BIRMINGHAM	1755	BRUSSELS	B.737	12345 7	BA1748
88PX	1810	GATWICK	2030	VERONA	B.737	1234567	BA2598
89MT	1500	MONTPELLIER	1700	GATWICK	B.737	1234567	BA2329
92GG	1915	GATWICK	2115	GENEVA	B.737	12345 7	BA2740
93RL	1000	DUSSELDORF	1130	HEATHROW	B757/767	1234567	BA937
94EL	0725	HEATHROW	0840	DUSSELDORF	B.767	1234567	BA936
94MT	1200	GATWICK	1405	MONTPELLIER	B.737	1234567	BA2328
95GG	1025	GENEVA	1200	GATWICK	B.737	1234567	BA2737
95VE	0820	PARIS CDG	0930	BIRMINGHAM	B.737	123456	BA1801
	1000	BIRMINGHAM	1100	GLASGOW	B737/EMB	123456	
95XC	1600	PARIS CDG	1710	BIRMINGHAM	B.737	12345 7	BA1807
95YB	1825	PARIS CDG	1935	BIRMINGHAM	B.737	1234567	BA1809
	2040	BIRMINGHAM	2140	GLASGOW	B.737	12345 7	
97PL	0630	NAPLES	0930	GATWICK	B.737	1234567	BA2605
99GG	1715	GENEVA	1855	GATWICK	B.737	12345 7	BA2739
99PL	1350	NAPLES	1700	GATWICK	B.737	1234567	BA2607
463J	0640	MADRID	0910	GATWICK	B.757	1234567	BA2463
464M	0930	GATWICK	1200	MADRID	B.737	1234567	BA2464
466M	1335	GATWICK	1605	MADRID	B.737	1234567	BA2466
470M	1950	GATWICK	2215	MADRID	B.737	1234567	BA2470
001	1030	HEATHROW		NEW YORK	CONCORDE	1234567	
002		NEW YORK	1725	HEATHROW	CONCORDE	1234567	
003	1900	HEATHROW		NEW YORK	CONCORDE	1234567	
004		NEW YORK	2225	HEATHROW	CONCORDE	1234567	
005	1325	HEATHROW		TOKYO	B.747	1234567	
006		TOKYO	1530	HEATHROW	B.747	1234567	
007	1545	HEATHROW		TOKYO	B.747	1234567	
008		TOKYO	1740	HEATHROW	B.747	1234567	
009	2215	HEATHROW		BANGKOK	B.747	1234567	
010		BANGKOK	0520	HEATHROW	B.747	1234567	
011	1200	HEATHROW		SINGAPORE	B.747	1234567	
012		SINGAPORE	0655	HEATHROW	B.747	1234567	
015	2210	HEATHROW		SINGAPORE	B.747	1234567	
016		SINGAPORE	0555	HEATHROW	B.747	1234567	
025	1530	HEATHROW		HONG KONG	B.747	1 4 6	
026		HONG KONG	0525	HEATHROW	B.747	1 3 6	
027	2130	HEATHROW		HONG KONG	B.747	1234567	
028		HONG KONG	0545	HEATHROW	B.747	1234567	
031	1525	HEATHROW		HONG KONG	B.747	23 5 7	
032		HONG KONG	0515	HEATHROW	B.747	2 45 7	
033	1915	HEATHROW		KUALA LUMPUR	B.747	234 67	DEP 2225 347
034		KUALA LUMPUR	0550	HEATHROW	B.747	1 34567	
035	1435	HEATHROW		MADRAS	B.747	2 6	DEP 1455 2
036		MADRAS	1425	HEATHROW	B.747	3 7	
037	1250	HEATHROW		SHANGHAI	B.747	2	
038		BEIJING	1505	HEATHROW	B.747	2 4 67	
039	1630	HEATHROW		BEIJING	B.747	1 3 56	

048		SEATTLE	1130	HEATHROW	B.747	1234567	
049	1330	HEATHROW		SEATTLE	B.747	1234567	
052		SEATTLE	1335	HEATHROW	B.747	1 4 6	
053	1110	HEATHROW		SEATTLE	B.747	3 56	
054		JOHANNESBURG	0805	HEATHROW	B.747	123 567	
055	2205	HEATHROW		JOHANNESBURG	B.747	1 34567	
056		JOHANNESBURG	0620	HEATHROW	B.747	1234567	
057	2100	HEATHROW		JOHANNESBURG	B.747	1234567	
058		JOHANNESBURG	0740	HEATHROW	B.747	12 4567	ARR 0805 5
059	2115	HEATHROW		JOHANNESBURG	B.747	234567	
066		PHILADELPHIA	0625	HEATHROW	B.777	1234567	
067	1125	HEATHROW		PHILADELPHIA	B.777	1234567	
068		PHILADELPHIA	0850	HEATHROW	B.777	1234567	
069	1600	HEATHROW		PHILADELPHIA	B.777	1234567	
072		ABU DHABI	0550	HEATHROW	B.777	1234567	
073	0945	HEATHROW		ABU DHABI	B.777	1234567	
084		VANCOUVER	1315	HEATHROW	B.747	1234567	
085	1630	HEATHROW		VANCOUVER	B.747	1234567	
092		TORONTO	0620	HEATHROW	B.747	1234567	
093	1155	HEATHROW		TORONTO	B.747	1234567	
094		MONTREAL	0905	HEATHROW	B.747	1234567	
095	1705	HEATHROW		MONTREAL	B.747	1234567	
096		TORONTO	2205	HEATHROW	CONCORDE	2345	DATES VARY
097	0900	HEATHROW		TORONTO	CONCORDE	2345	DATES VARY
098		TORONTO	1100	HEATHROW	B.747	1 3 567	ARR 1015 7
099	1610	HEATHROW		TORONTO	B.747	2 4 67	
102		TEHRAN	1215	HEATHROW	B.777	1 3 5 7	
103	2020	HEATHROW		TEHRAN	B.777	2 4 67	
106		DUBAI	0620	HEATHROW	B.777	1234567	
107	1230	HEATHROW		DUBAI	B.777	1234567	
112		NEW YORK	0600	HEATHROW	B.747	1234567	
113	1700	HEATHROW		NEW YORK	B.747	1234567	
116		NEW YORK	0945	HEATHROW	B.747	1234567	
117	0845	HEATHROW		NEW YORK	B.747	1234567	
118		ALMATA	1245	HEATHROW	B.777	2 4 6	ARR 1300 4
119	2015	HEATHROW		ALMATA	B.777	1 3 5	DEP 2115 3
124		BAHRAIN	0625	HEATHROW	B.777	1234567	
125	1025	HEATHROW		BAHRAIN	B.777	1234567	
126		DUBAI	0620	HEATHROW	B.777	1234567	
127	1230	HEATHROW		DUBAI	B.777	1234567	
128		ISLAMABAD	1355	MANCHESTER	B.747	1 4 6	ARR 1230 1
	1500	MANCHESTER	1555	HEATHROW	B.747	1 4 6	1335/1430 1
129	1750	HEATHROW	1850	MANCHESTER	B.747	3 5 7	1555/1655 7
	1950	MANCHESTER		ISLAMABAD	B.747	3 5 7	DEP 1755 7
132		JEDDAH	0620	HEATHROW	B.777	1 34 6	ARR 0650 6
133	1455	HEATHROW		JEDDAH	B.777	23 5 7	DEP 2040 3
138		BOMBAY	0725	HEATHROW	B.747	1234567	
139	0955	HEATHROW		BOMBAY	B.747	1234567	
142		DELHI	0455	HEATHROW	B.747	3 7	
143	2155	HEATHROW		DELHI	B.747	1 5	
144		DELHI	0455	HEATHROW	B.747	12 456	
145	2155	HEATHROW		DELHI	B.747	234 67	
154		CAIRO	1205	HEATHROW	B.777	1234567	
155	1645	HEATHROW		CAIRO	B.777	1234567	
156		KUWAIT	0700	HEATHROW	B.777	1234567	
157	1420	HEATHROW		KUWAIT	B.777	1234567	
162		TEL AVIV	1130	HEATHROW	B.777	1234567	
163	2240	HEATHROW		TEL AVIV	B.777	1234567	
164		TEL AVIV	1405	HEATHROW	B.777	7	
165	1835	HEATHROW		TEL AVIV	B.777	56	DEP 0925 5
174		NEW YORK	0705	HEATHROW	B.747	1234567	
175	1100	HEATHROW		NEW YORK	B.747	1234567	
176		NEW YORK	0830	HEATHROW	B.747	1234567	
177	1400	HEATHROW		NEW YORK	B.747	1234567	
178		NEW YORK	2100	HEATHROW	B.747	1234567	
179	1830	HEATHROW		NEW YORK	B.747	1234567	
184		NEW YORK	0830	HEATHROW	B.747	1234567	
185	1505	HEATHROW		NEW YORK	B.747	1234567	

Flight	Dep	From	Arr	To	Aircraft	Days	Notes
188		NEW YORK	0635	HEATHROW	B.777	1234567	
189	0940	HEATHROW		NEW YORK	B.777	1234567	
202		DETROIT	0700	HEATHROW	B.747	1234567	
203	1235	HEATHROW		DETROIT	B.747	1234567	
208		MIAMI	0910	HEATHROW	B.747	1234567	
209	1235	HEATHROW		MIAMI	B.747	1234567	
212		BOSTON	0455	HEATHROW	B.747	1234567	
213	1050	HEATHROW		BOSTON	B.747	1234567	
214		BOSTON	0735	HEATHROW	B.747	1234567	
215	1600	HEATHROW		BOSTON	B.747	1234567	
216		WASHINGTON	0625	HEATHROW	B.747	1234567	
217	1215	HEATHROW		WASHINGTON	B.747	1234567	
222		WASHINGTON	0940	HEATHROW	B.747	1234567	
223	1530	HEATHROW		WASHINGTON	B.747	1234567	
238		BOSTON	2010	HEATHROW	B.777	1234567	
239	1835	HEATHROW		BOSTON	B.777	1234567	
242		MEXICO	1450	HEATHROW	B.747	2 4 67	
243	1340	HEATHROW		MEXICO	B.747	1 3 56	
262		RIYADH	0640	HEATHROW	B.777	2 4 7	
263	1350	HEATHROW		RIYADH	B.777	1 3 6	DEP 1255 6
268		LOS ANGELES	1530	HEATHROW	B.747	1234567	
269	1535	HEATHROW		LOS ANGELES	B.747	1234567	
273K	0635	STOCKHOLM	0900	GATWICK	B.737	1234567	BA2773
278		LOS ANGELES	0915	HEATHROW	B.747	1234567	02/06-
279	0925	HEATHROW		LOS ANGELES	B.747	1234567	02.06-
282		LOS ANGELES	1200	HEATHROW	B.747	1234567	
283	1215	HEATHROW		LOS ANGELES	B.747	1234567	
284		SAN FRANCISCO	1005	HEATHROW	B.747	1234567	
285	1040	HEATHROW		SAN FRANCISCO	B.747	1234567	
286		SAN FRANCISCO	1230	HEATHROW	B.747	1234567	
287	1315	HEATHROW		SAN FRANCISCO	B.747	1234567	
294		LOS ANGELES	1630	HEATHROW	B.747	1 3 5	
295	2225	HEATHROW		LOS ANGELES	B.747	2 4 7	
296		CHICAGO	1005	HEATHROW	B.747	1234567	
297	1515	HEATHROW		CHICAGO	B.747	1234567	
298		CHICAGO	0720	HEATHROW	B.747	1234567	
299	1115	HEATHROW		CHICAGO	B.747	1234567	
301	0640	PARIS CDG	0805	HEATHROW	B.757	1234567	
304	0715	HEATHROW	0830	PARIS CDG	B.757	1234567	
305	0945	PARIS CDG	1100	HEATHROW	B.757	1234567	
306	0915	HEATHROW	1020	PARIS CDG	B.757	12345	
307	1120	PARIS CDG	1240	HEATHROW	B.757	12345	
308	1150	HEATHROW	1255	PARIS CDG	B.757	1234567	
309	1355	PARIS CDG	1500	HEATHROW	B.757	1234567	
316	1410	HEATHROW	1515	PARIS CDG	B.757	1234567	
317	1620	PARIS CDG	1735	HEATHROW	B.757	1234567	
318	1615	HEATHROW	1720	PARIS CDG	B.757	12345 7	
319	1825	PARIS CDG	1935	HEATHROW	B.757	12345 7	
324	1840	HEATHROW	1950	PARIS` CDG	B.757	1234567	
325	2045	PARIS CDG	2155	HEATHROW	B.757	12345 7	
326	2100	HEATHROW	2205	PARIS CDG	B.757	12345 7	
332	0640	HEATHROW	0800	PARIS ORLY	B.757	1234567	
333	0850	PARIS ORLY	1010	HEATHROW	B.757	1234567	
334	1230	HEATHROW	1350	PARIS ORLY	B.757	1234567	
335	1440	PARIS ORLY	1600	HEATHROW	B.757	1234567	
338	1830	HEATHROW	1945	PARIS ORLY	B.757	12345 7	
339	2110	PARIS ORLY	2215	HEATHROW	B.757	12345 7	
341	0800	NICE	1000	HEATHROW	B.767	1234567	
342	0840	HEATHROW	1035	NICE	B.767	1234567	
343	1145	NICE	1340	HEATHROW	B.767	1234567	
344Z	1315	HEATHROW	1510	NICE	B.767	1234567	
345	1605	NICE	1810	HEATHROW	B.767	1234567	
346	0725	HEATHROW	0920	NICE	A320/B757	56	0955/1150 5
347	1015	NICE	1215	HEATHROW	A320/B757	56	1250/1455 5
348	1500	HEATHROW	1700	NICE	B737/A320	1234567	
349	1750	NICE	1950	HEATHROW	B737/A320	1234567	
352	1950	HEATHROW	2145	NICE	B.767	1234567	
353L	0705	LYON	0850	HEATHROW	B.757	1234567	

354	0950	HEATHROW	1120	LYON	B.757	1234567		
355	1225	LYON	1405	HEATHROW	B737/757	1234567		
356	1515	HEATHROW	1650	LYON	A320/B757	1234567		
357	1750	LYON	1925	HEATHROW	A320/B757	1234567		
358	1900	HEATHROW	2035	LYON	A320/B757	1234567		
388	0725	HEATHROW	0835	BRUSSELS	B.757	12345		
389R	0650	BRUSSELS	0805	HEATHROW	B757/A320	1234567		
391R	1100	BRUSSELS	1210	HEATHROW	A320/B757	12345		
392	0855	HEATHROW	1015	BRUSSELS	B.757	1234567		
393R	1145	BRUSSELS	1250	HEATHROW	B.757	1234567		
394	1220	HEATHROW	1325	BRUSSELS	B.757	6		
395	1425	BRUSSELS	1525	HEATHROW	B.757	6		
396	1415	HEATHROW	1520	BRUSSELS	B.757	1234567		
397R	1630	BRUSSELS	1735	HEATHROW	B.757	1234567		
398	1620	HEATHROW	1730	BRUSSELS	B737/A320	12345 7		
399R	1820	BRUSSELS	1925	HEATHROW	B737/A320	12345 7		
404	1915	HEATHROW	2015	BRUSSELS	B757/A320	1234567		
418	1725	HEATHROW	1835	LUXEMBOURG	A.320	12345 7		
419X	1940	LUXEMBOURG	2100	HEATHROW	A.320	12345 7		
423	0620	AMSTERDAM	0735	HEATHROW	B.757	123456		
426	0640	HEATHROW	0810	AMSTERDAM	B.757	123456		
427	0920	AMSTERDAM	1025	HEATHROW	B.757	1234567		
430	0840	HEATHROW	0955	AMSTERDAM	B.757	1234567		
431	1100	AMSTERDAM	1210`	HEATHROW	B.757	1234567		
434	1130	HEATHROW	1245	AMSTERDAM	B.757	1234567		
435	1340	AMSTERDAM	1450	HEATHROW	B.757	1234567		
438	1330	HEATHROW	1435	AMSTERDAM	B.757	1234567		
439	1540	AMSTERDAM	1645	HEATHROW	B.757	1234567		
440	1610	HEATHROW	1715	AMSTERDAM	B.757	1234567	16135/1740 3 5
441	1815	AMSTERDAM	1920	HEATHROW	B.757	1234567	1840/1945 35
442	1750	HEATHROW	1855	AMSTERDAM	B.757	1234567		
443	2015	AMSTERDAM	2120	HEATHROW	B.757	12345 7		
455C	0745	MADRID	1000	HEATHROW	B.767	1234567		
456	0800	HEATHROW	1015	MADRID	B.767	1234567		
457C	1120	MADRID	1330	HEATHROW	B.767	1234567		
458	0955	HEATHROW	1210	MADRID	B.757	1234567		
459C	1315	MADRID	1530	HEATHROW	B.757	1234567		
460	1410	HEATHROW	1625	MADRID	B767/757	1234567		
461C	1730	MADRID	1945	HEATHROW	B.767	1234567		
462	1900	HEATHROW	2115	MADRID	B767	1234567		
474	0825	HEATHROW	1025	BARCELONA	B.757	67		
475	1320	BARCELONA	1520	HEATHROW	B.757	67		
477	0800	BARCELONA	1015	HEATHROW	B.767	1234567		
478	0925	HEATHROW	1135	BARCELONA	B757/767	1234567		
479	1225	BARCELONA	1435	HEATHROW	B757/767	1234567		
480	1430	HEATHROW	1630	BARCELONA	B.757	1234567		
481	1755	BARCELONA	2010	HEATHROW	B.757	1234567		
482	1900	HEATHROW	2100	BARCELONA	B.767	1234567		
484B	1050	HEATHROW	1235	BILBAO	A.320	1234567		
485	1400	BILBAO	1545	HEATHROW	A.320	1234567		
486B	1620	HEATHROW	1805	BILBAO	A.320	1234567		
487	1910	BILBAO	2055	HEATHROW	A.320	1234567		
496	0825	HEATHROW	1030	LISBON	B.757	6		
497	1235	LISBON	1500	HEATHROW	B.757	6		
499	0830	LISBON	1105	HEATHROW	B.767	1234567		
500	0940	HEATHROW	1210	LISBON	B.767	1234567		
501	1310	LISBON	1545	HEATHROW	B.767	1234567		
502	1410	HEATHROW	1645	LISBON	B.757	1234567		
551	0720	ROME	1000	HEATHROW	B.767	1234567		
554	1125	HEATHROW	1345	ROME	B.767	1234567		
555	1455	ROME	1730	HEATHROW	B.757	1234567		
556	1410	HEATHROW	1635	ROME	B.767	1234567		
558	1740	HEATHROW	2000	ROME	B.767	1234567		
560	0645	HEATHROW	0920	ROME	B.757	1234567		
561	1020	ROME	1250	HEATHROW	B.757	1234567		
562	1020	HEATHROW	1250	ROME	B.737	1234567		
563	0730	MILAN	0930	HEATHROW	B.767	123456		
564	0745	HEATHROW	0940	MILAN	B.767	12345		

565	1050	MILAN	1240	HEATHROW	B.767	12345	
566	1215	HEATHROW	1410	MILAN	B.767	12345	
567	1510	MILAN	1705	HEATHROW	B.767	12345	
568	1530	HEATHROW	1725	MILAN	B.767	12345	
569	1835	MILAN	2035	HEATHROW	B.767	12345	
570	1755	HEATHROW	1945	MILAN	B.767	12345 7	
573	0730	MILAN	0930	HEATHROW	B.767	7	
574	0745	HEATHROW	0945	MILAN	B.767	67	
575	1045	MILAN	1240	HEATHROW	B.767	67	
576	1020	HEATHROW	1220	MILAN	B.757	1234567	
577	1325	MILAN	1520	HEATHROW	B.757	1234567	
578	1210	HEATHROW	1410	MILAN	B.767	67	
579	1515	MILAN	1710	HEATHROW	B.767	67	
580	1530	HEATHROW	1725	MILAN	B.767	67	
581	1835	BOLOGNA	2035	HEATHROW	B.767	67	
582	1755	HEATHROW	1945	MILAN	B.757	6	
585	1740	VENICE	1950	HEATHROW	B.757	6	
586	1435	HEATHROW	1645	VENICE	B.757	6	
587	0840	VENICE	1105	HEATHROW	B.757	1234567	
588	1040	HEATHROW	1250	VENICE	B.767	1234567	
589	1350	VENICE	1605	HEATHROW	B.767	1234567	
590	2015	HEATHROW	2225	VENICE	B.757	1234567	
592	1055	HEATHROW	1255	BOLOGNA`	B.757	1234567	
594	1315	HEATHROW	1520	BOLOGNA	A320/B757	1 34567	1250/1455 1 4
595	1620	BOLOGNA	1830	HEATHROW	A320/B737	1 34567	1555/1755 2
631	0705	ATHENS	1000	HEATHROW	B.767	123456	
632	1205	HEATHROW	1650	ATHENS	B.767	1234567	
633	1700	ATHENS	2050	HEATHROW	B.767	1234567	
634	2245	HEATHROW	0225	ATHENS	B.767	1234567	
662	0655	HEATHROW	1155	LARNACA	B.767	67	
663	1620	LARNACA	2130	HEATHROW	B.767	67	
664	2000	HEATHROW	0040	LARNACA	B.767	1234567	
665	0200	LARNACA	0650	HEATHROW	B.767	1234567	
675	0705	ISTANBUL	1100	HEATHROW	B757/767	1234567	
676	0910	HEATHROW	1245	ISTANBUL	B.757	1234567	
677	1410	ISTANBUL	1805	HEATHROW	B.757	1234567	
680	1655	HEATHROW	2035	ISTANBUL	B757/767	1234567	
699	0700	VIENNA	0930	HEATHROW	B.767	1234567	
700V	0855	HEATHROW	1110	VIENNA	B.757	1234567	
701	1210	VIENNA	1430	HEATHROW	B.757	1234567	
704V	1500	HEATHROW	1710	VIENNA	B.757	1234567	
705	1800	VIENNA	2025	HEATHROW	B.757	1234567	
706V	1820	HEATHROW	2030	VIENNA	B.767	1234567	
709Q	0710	ZURICH	0900	HEATHROW	B.757	1234567	
710	0745	HEATHROW	0925	ZURICH	B757/767	1234567	
711Q	1035	ZURICH	1215	HEATHROW	B757/767	`1234567	
712	1010	HEATHROW	1150	ZURICH	B.757	12345 7	
713	1255	ZURICH	1435	HEATHROW	B.757	12345 7	
714	1200	HEATHROW	1340	ZURICH	B.757	1234567	
715Q	1445	ZURICH	1630	HEATHROW	B.757	1234567	
718	1505	HEATHROW	1640	ZURICH	B.757	1234567	
719Q	1740	ZURICH	1925	HEATHROW	B.757	12345 7	
720	1835	HEATHROW	2025	ZURICH	B.757	12345 7	
723	0750	GENEVA	0930	HEATHROW	B.757	1234567	
724	0830	HEATHROW	1000	GENEVA	B.757	1234567	
725	1105	GENEVA	1240	HEATHROW	B.757	1234567	
726	0720	HEATHROW	0850	GENEVA	B.757	67	1040/1210 6
	0950		1120	GENEVA	B.757	12345	
727	0950	GENEVA	1120	HEATHROW	B.757	67	1310/1435 6
	1355	GENEVA	1525	HEATHROW	B.757	12345	
728	1250	HEATHROW	1420	GENEVA	B.767	1234567	
729	1515	GENEVA	1705	HEATHROW	B.767	1234567	
730	1535	HEATHROW	1705	GENEVA`	B757/767	1234567	
731	1820	GENEVA	2000	HEATHROW	B.767	12345 7	
732	1925	HEATHROW	2055	GENEVA	B.757	12345 7	
742J	0850	HEATHROW	1030	BASLE	A.320	1234567	
743	1140	BASLE	1320	HEATHROW	A.320	1234567	
746J	1550	HEATHROW	1720	BASLE	A320/B737/757	1234567	

Flight	Dep	From	Arr	To	Aircraft	Days	Extra
747J	1830	BASLE	2005	HEATHROW	A320/B737/757	1234567	
761	0710	OSLO	0930	HEATHROW	B.757	1234567	
762	0750	HEATHROW	0950	OSLO	B.757	1234567	
763	1100	OSLO	1310	HEATHROW	B.757	1234567	
764	0950	HEATHROW	1200	OSLO	B737/767	1234567	
765	1325	OSLO	1535	HEATHROW	B737/767	1234567	
766	1435	HEATHROW	1635	OSLO	B.757	1234567	
767	1645	OSLO	1850	HEATHROW	B757/767	1234567	
768	1410	HEATHROW	1615	OSLO	B.757	1234567	
769	1715	OSLO	1920	HEATHROW	B.757	1234567	
770	1755	HEATHROW	2000	OSLO	B.757	1234567	
772	0655	HEATHROW	0855	STOCKHOLM	B757/A320	1234567	0720/0925 67
773	1100	OSLO	1310	HEATHROW	B757/A320	1234567	
775C	0625	STOCKHOLM	0910	HEATHROW	B.767	1234567	
776F	0755	HEATHROW	1025	STOCKHOLM	B757/A320	1234567	0855/1125 67
777C	1125	STOCKHOLM	1405	HEATHROW	B757/A320	1234567	1240/1510 67
778F	1035	HEATHROW	1300	STOCKHOLM	B.757	1234567	
779C	1450	STOCKHOLM	1730	HEATHROW	B.757	1234567	
780	1340	HEATHROW	1605	STOCKHOLM	B.757	1234567	
781C	1730	STOCKHOLM	2000	HEATHROW	B.757	1234567	
782	1750	HEATHROW	2015	STOCKHOLM	B.767	1234567	
794H	1150	HEATHROW	1445	HELSINKI	B.757	1234567	
795L	0540	HELSINKI	0850	HEATHROW	B.757	1234567	
798H	1720	HEATHROW	2020	HELSINKI	B.757	1234567	
799L	1540	HELSINKI	1850	HEATHROW	B.757	1234567	
811	0740	COPENHAGEN	0935	HEATHROW	B.757	1234567	
813	1315	COPENHAGEN	1510	HEATHROW	B.757	1234567	
812	0950	HEATHROW	1145	COPENHAGEN	B757/A320	1234567	
814	0830	HEATHROW	1025	COPENHAGEN	B.757	1234567	
815	1115	COPENHAGEN	1310	HEATHROW	B.757	1234567	
816	1215	HEATHROW	1410	COPENHAGEN	B.757	1234567	
817	1505	COPENHAGEN	1700	HEATHROW	B.757	1234567	
818	1430	HEATHROW	1625	COPENHAGEN	B.757	1234567	
819	1715	COPENHAGEN	1910	HEATHROW	B.757	12345 7	
820	1840	HEATHROW	2035	COPENHAGEN	B.757	12345 7	
849	0925	WARSAW	1155	HEATHROW	B.757	1234567	
850	1140	HEATHROW	1400	WARSAW	B.757	1234567	
851	1510	WARSAW	1745	HEATHROW	B.757	1234567	
852	1835	HEATHROW	2100	WARSAW	B.757	1234567	
855	0650	PRAGUE	0900	HEATHROW	B.767	1234567	
856	1105	HEATHROW	1300	PRAGUE	B.767	1234567	
857	1355	PRAGUE	1555	HEATHROW	B.767	1234567	
858	1755	HEATHROW	2000	PRAGUE	B.767	1234567	
865	0745	BUDAPEST	1005	HEATHROW	B.757	1234567	0840/1100 67
868	1015	HEATHROW	1250	BUDAPEST	B.767	1234567	
869	1345	BUDAPEST	1615	HEATHROW	B.767	1234567	
870	1935	HEATHROW	2205	BUDAPEST	B.757	1234567	1800/2030 67
872	0920	HEATHROW	1255	MOSCOW	B.767	1234567	
873	1435	MOSCOW	1835	HEATHROW	B.767	1234567	
901U	0635	FRANKFURT	0820	HEATHROW	B.767	1234567	
902N	0725	HEATHROW	0900	FRANKFURT	B.767	1234567	
903U	1020	FRANKFURT	1200	HEATHROW	B.767	1234567	
904N	1200	HEATHROW	1330	FRANKFURT	B757/767	1234567	
905U	1425	FRANKFURT	1600	HEATHROW	B757/767	1234567	
908N	1500	HEATHROW	1630	FRANKFURT	B757/767	1234567	
909U	1740	FRANKFURT	1915	HEATHROW	B.767	12345 7	
910N	1845	HEATHROW	2015	FRANKFURT	B.757	12345 7	
911U	2110	FRANKFURT	2240	HEATHROW	B.757	12345 7	
914N	2020	HEATHROW	2155	FRANKFURT	B.767	12345 7	
919	0655	STUTTGART	0900	HEATHROW	A.320	1234567	
920	0820	HEATHROW	0950	STUTTGART	B.757	1234567	
921	1105	STUTTGART	1250	HEATHROW	A.320	1234567	
922	1400	HEATHROW	1545	STUTTGART	B.757	1234567	
923	1710	STUTTGART	1850	HEATHROW	B.757	1234567	
924	1720	HEATHROW	1855	STUTTGART	A.320	1234567	
926	0850	HEATHROW	1010	COLOGNE	B757/A320	1234567	
927	1155	COLOGNE	1315	HEATHROW	A.320	1234567	
928	1610	HEATHROW	1730	COLOGNE	B757/A320	1234567	

929	1825	COLOGNE	1945	HEATHROW	B757/1320	1234567		
935	0625	DUSSELDORF	0755	HEATHROW	B.757	1234567		
936	0725	HEATHROW	0855	DUSSELDORF	B.767	1234567		
937	1000	DUSSELDORF	1130	HEATHROW	B757/767	1234567	1025/1155	67
940	1330	HEATHROW	1445	DUSSELDORF	B.767	1234567		
941	1540	DUSSELDORF	1710	HEATHROW	B.767	1234567		
942	1600	HEATHROW	1715	DUSSELDORF	B767/B767	1234567		
943	1815	DUSSELDORF	1940	HEATHROW	B767/B757	12345 7		
946	1905	HEATHROW	2015	DUSSELDORF	B.757	12345 7		
947	0655	MUNICH	0900	HEATHROW	B757/B767	1234567		
948M	0815	HEATHROW	1000	MUNICH	B767/B757	1234567		
949L	1105	MUNICH	1300	HEATHROW	B757/767	1234567		
950M	1130	HEATHROW	1315	MUNICH	B.767	1234567		
951	1435	MUNICH	1630	HEATHROW	B.767	1234567		
952M	1330	HEATHROW	1515	MUNICH	B.757	1234567		
953	1610	MUNICH	1810	HEATHROW	B757/A320	1234567		
954M	1725	HEATHROW	1910	MUNICH	B757/767	1234567		
955	2010	MUNICH	2205	HEATHROW	B757/767	12345 7		
956M	2015	HEATHROW	2155	MUNICH	B.757	12345 7		
963	0610	HAMBURG	0750	HEATHROW	B.357	1234567		
964	0655	HEATHROW	0825	HAMBURG	B.757	1234567	0930/1100	67
965F	1005	HAMBURG	1145	HEATHROW	B.757	1234567	1150/1325	67
970	1420	HEATHROW	1550	HAMBURG	B757/767	1234567		
971	1650	HAMBURG	1830	HEATHROW	B757/767	1234567		
972	2005	HEATHROW	2135	HAMBURG	B.757	1234567		
975	0635	HANOVER	0815	HEATHROW	A.320	12 4567		
976V	0725	HEATHROW	0850	HANOVER	B.757	12345		
977	2140	HANOVER	2310	HEATHROW	A.320	2		
979	1125	HANOVER	1255	HEATHROW	B.757	12345		
980	1940	HEATHROW	2115	HANOVER	A.320	1234567	1925/2055	2
981	0625	BERLIN	0835	HEATHROW	B.757	1234567		
982G	0755	HEATHROW	0940	BERLIN	B.757	1234567		
983	1055	BERLIN	1245	HEATHROW	B.757	1234567		
984G	1245	HEATHROW	1430	BERLIN	B757/A320	1234567		
985	1605	BERLIN	1800	HEATHROW	B757/A320	1234567		
986G	1540	HEATHROW	1725	BERLIN	B.757	1234567		
987	1835	BERLIN	2030	HEATHROW	B.757	1234567		
988G	1945	HEATHROW	2130	BERLIN	B.757	1234567		
990G	0655	BERLIN	0840	HEATHROW	B757/A320	1234567	0910/1055	67
991	1000	BERLIN	1200	HEATHROW	B757/A320	1234567	1155/1350	67
994	0955	HEATHROW	1140	BERLIN	A.320	6		
995	1300	BERLIN	1455	HEATHROW	A.320	6		
1038		SHANGHAI	1300	HEATHROW	B.747	3 5		
1502		NEW YORK	0620	MANCHESTER	B.767	1234567		
1503	1000	MANCHESTER		NEW YORK	B.767	1234567		
1601	0630	PARIS CDG	0750	MANCHESTER	EMB-145	123456		
1602	0715	MANCHESTER	0835	PARIS CDG	B.737	123456		
1603	0915	PARIS CDG	1045	MANCHESTER	B.737	123456		
1604	0845	MANCHESTER	1005	PARIS CDG	B.737	12345 7		
1605	1045	PARIS CDG	1215	MANCHESTER	B.737	12345 7		
1606	1305	MANCHESTER	1425	PARIS CDG	B.737	1234567		
1609	1825	PARIS CDG	1945	MANCHESTER	B.737	12345 7		
1610	1810	MANCHESTER	1930	PARIS CDG	B.737	12345 7		
1611	2015	PARIS CDG	2135	MANCHESTER	B.737	12345 7		
1612	1910	MANCHESTER	2030	PARIS CDG	EMB-145	12345 7		
1618	1400	MANCHESTER	1520	BRUSSELS	B.737	12345		
1632	1535	MANCHESTER	1645	AMSTERDAM	EMB-145	12345		
1633	1720	AMSTERDAM	1830	MANCHESTER	EMB-145	12345		
1640	0700	GLASGOW	0750	MANCHESTER	B.737	123456		
	0915	MANCHESTER	1145	MADRID	B.737	123456		
1642	1550	MANCHESTER	1820	MADRID	B.737	12345 7		
1643	1855	MADRID	2135	MANCHESTER	B.737	12345 7		
1657	0625	MILAN	0845	MANCHESTER	EMB-145	123456		
1658	0745	MANCHESTER	0955	MILAN	B.737	123456		
1659	1045	MILAN	1300	MANCHESTER	B.737	123456		
1660	1150	GLASGOW	1255	MANCHESTER	DHC-8	12345		
	1330	MANCHESTER	1540	MILAN	B.737	12345 7		

1661	1620	MILAN	1840	MANCHESTER	B.737	12345 7	
	0655	MANCHESTER	0850	GENEVA	EMB-145	123456	
1662	1750	MANCHESTER	2000	MILAN	EMB-145	12345 7	
1676	1600	MANCHESTER	1755	GENEVA	EMB-145	12345 7	
1677	1830	GENEVA	2035	MANCHESTER	EMB-145	12345 7	
1694	0700	MANCHESTER	0855	OSLO	EMB-145	123456	01.06-
1695	0930	OSLO	1130	MANCHESTER	EMB-145	123456	01.06-
1696	1700	MANCHESTER	1855	OSLO	EMB-145	12345 7	01.06-
1697	1930	OSLO	2130	MANCHESTER	EMB-145	12345 7	01.06-
1706	0725	MANCHESTER	0915	FRANKFURT	B.737	1234567	
1707	1000	FRANKFURT	1150	MANCHESTER	B.737	1234567	
1708	1200	MANCHESTER	1345	FRANKFURT	EMB-145	12345	
1709	1430	FRANKFURT	1620	MANCHESTER	EMB-145	12345	
1712	1600	MANCHESTER	1745	FRANKFURT	B.737	1234567	
1713	1700	EDINBURGH	1750	MANCHESTER	DH8/EMB4	12345 7	1710/1815 7
	1835	FRANKFURT	2020	MANCHESTER	B.737	1234567	
1720	0955	MANCHESTER	1230	WARSAW	B.737	2 5 7	1105/1340 7
1721	1420	WARSAW	1655	MANCHESTER	B.737	12345 7	
1750	1820	BIRMINGHAM	1930	BRUSSELS	CANADAIR	12345	
1751	2000	BRUSSELS	2110	BIRMINGHAM	CANADAIR	12345	
1757	0615	FRANKFURT	0755	BIRMINGHAM	B.737	123456	
1758	0700	GLASGOW	0800	BIRMINGHAM	B737/EMB4	123456	
	0840	BIRMINGHAM	1020	FRANKFURT	B.737	1234567	
1759	1100	FRANKFURT	1235	BIRMINGHAM	B.737	1234567	
	1325	BIRMINGHAM	1430	EDINBURGH	B.737	1234567	
1762	1615	BIRMINGHAM	1755	FRANKFURT	B.737	12345 7	
1763	1840	FRANKFURT	2035	BIRMINGHAM	B.737	12345 7	
1764	1910	BIRMINGHAM	2045	FRANKFURT	CANADAIR	12345 7	
1770	1230	EDINBURGH	1330	BIRMINGHAM	EM4/CRJ	12345 7	
1771	1635	MUNICH	1840	BIRMINGHAM	CANADAIR	12345 7	
1779	0915	DUSSELDORF	1040	BIRMINGHAM	B.737	12345	
1792	0830	EDINBURGH	0930	BIRMINGHAM	B.737	1234567	
1793	1300	MADRID	1520	BIRMINGHAM	B.737	1234567	
	1600	BIRMINGHAM	1700	EDINBURGH	B.737	1234567	
1796	1035	BIRMINGHAM	1245	BARCELONA	B.737	1234567	0905/1110 6
1797	1330	BARCELONA	1545	BIRMINGHAM	B.737	1234567	1200/1420 6
1811	1945	PARIS CDG	2045	BIRMINGHAM	B.737	12345 7	
1847	1525	GLASGOW	1630	MANCHESTER	DHC-8	12345	
1849	1905	GLASGOW	2010	MANCHESTER	DHC-8	12345	
1867	0840	EDINBURGH	0945	MANCHESTER	DHC-8	12345	
1869	1525	EDINBURGH	1625	MANCHESTER	DHC-8	12345	
1872	2025	MANCHESTER	2115	EDINBURGH	B.737	12345 7	
1874	1530	MANCHESTER	1635	EDINBURGH	DH8/B737	5 7	
1875	1355	EDINBURGH	1445	MANCHESTER	B737/DHC8	123456	
1891	0830	BIRMINGHAM	0930	EDINBURGH	EMB-145	12345	
1914	1900	BIRMINGHAM	2000	GLASGOW	B.737	5	
2006		CHARLOTTE	0605	GATWICK	B.777	1234567	
2007	1135	GATWICK		CHARLOTTE	B.777	1234567	
2018		DENVER	0725	GATWICK	B.777	1234567	
2019	1020	GATWICK		DENVER	B.777	1234567	
2024		HOUSTON	0715	GATWICK	B.747	1234567	
2025	1000	GATWICK		HOUSTON	B.747	1234567	
2028		BAKU	0700	GATWICK	B.767	3 5 7	
2029	1030	GATWICK		BAKU	B.767	2 456	DEP 1645 5
2036		ORLANDO	0640	GATWICK	B.747	45	
2037	1055	GATWICK		ORLANDO	B.747	1234567	
2048		CARACAS	1230	GATWICK	B.747	1 4 6	
2049	1015	GATWICK		CARACAS	B.747	3 5 7	
2052		HARARE	0555	GATWICK	B.747	1 3 5 7	
2053	2130	GATWICK		HARARE	B.747	1 3 56	
2062		MAURITIUS	0450	GATWICK	B.747	7	
2063	2205	GATWICK		MAURITIUS	B.747	5	
2066		ENTEBBE	0455	GATWICK	B.747	3 6	
2067	2300	GATWICK		ENTEBBE	B.747	1 4	
2068		NAIROBI	0515	GATWICK	B.747	1234567	
2069	2225	GATWICK		NAIROBI	B.747	1234567	
2074		LAGOS	0550	GATWICK	B.747	1234567	
2075	1100	GATWICK		LAGOS	B.747	1234567	

2078		ACCRA	0540	GATWICK	B.777	2 4	ARR 0625 4
		ACCRA	0630	GATWICK	B.777	56	ARR 0730 5
2081	1415	GATWICK		ACCRA	B.777	1 4 7	DEP 1250 4
2142		BALTIMORE	0635	GATWICK	B.767	1234567	
2143	1315	GATWICK		BALTIMORE	B.767	1234567	
2148		DHAHRAN	0540	GATWICK	B.777	12 4567	
2149	1320	GATWICK		DHAHRAN	B.777	1 34567	
2154		BRIDGETOWN	0830	GATWICK	B.747	2 7	ARR 1015 2
2155	1045	GATWICK		BRIDGETOWN	B.747	1234567	
2156		BRIDGETOWN	0845	GATWICK	B.747	1 3456	
2166		TEL AVIV	2025	GATWICK	B.777	1234567	
2167	0900	GATWICK		TEL AVIV	B.777	1234567	
2172		NEW YORK	0630	GATWICK	B.767	1234567	
2173	0930	GATWICK		NEW YORK	B.767	1234567	
2176		WASHINGTON	2355	GATWICK	B.777	4	
2192		DALLAS	0640	GATWICK	B.777	1234567	
2193	0945	GATWICK		DALLAS	B.777	1234567	
2198		PITTSBURGH	0555	GATWICK	B.767	5	
2199	1215	GATWICK		PITTSBURGH	B.767	1234567	
2226		ATLANTA	0625	GATWICK	B.747	1234567	
2227	1115	GATWICK		ATLANTA	B.777	1234567	
2232		BERMUDA	0625	GATWICK	B.777	3 567	
2233	1425	GATWICK		BERMUDA	B.777	2 456	
2244		RIO DE JANEIRO	1450	GATWICK	B.747	5 7	
2245	1015	GATWICK		RIO DE JANEIRO	B.747	4 6	
2246		RIO DE JANEIRO	1515	GATWICK	B.747	12 6	
2247	1015	GATWICK		SAO PAULO	B.747	1 5 7	
2266		BUENOS AIRES	1115	GATWICK	B.747	1234567	
2267	2205	GATWICK		BUENOS AIRES	B.747	1234567	
2288		PHOENIX	1600	GATWICK	B.747	1234567	
2289	1130	GATWICK		PHOENIX	B.747	1234567	
2294		MIAMI	0615	GATWICK	B.747	1234567	
2295	1010	GATWICK		MIAMI	B.747	1234567	
2330	1615	GATWICK	1805	MONTPELLIER	B.737	6	
2331	1905	MONTPELLIER	2055	GATWICK	B.737	6	
2361	0610	MARSEILLES	0820	GATWICK	B.757	1234567	
2362	0940	GATWICK	1140	MARSEILLES	B.737	1234567	
2363	1240	MARSEILLES	1435	GATWICK	B.737	1234567	
2364	1400	GATWICK	1600	MARSEILLES	B.737	1234567	
2365	1700	MARSEILLES	1855	GATWICK	B.737	1234567	
2366	1900	GATWICK	2055	MARSEILLES	B737/757	1234567	
2368	1100	GATWICK	1255	MARSEILLES	B.737	567	1630/1825 5
2369	1420	MARSEILLES	1615	GATWICK	B.737	567	1930/2125 5
2465	1250	MADRID	1505	GATWICK	B.737	1234567	
2467	1805	MADRID	2020	GATWICK	B.737	1234567	
2485	0700	BARCELONA	0910	GATWICK	B.737	1234567	
2488	1325	GATWICK	1535	BARCELONA	B.737	1234567	
2489	1620	BARCELONA	1835	GATWICK	B.737	1234567	
2490	1830	GATWICK	2035	BARCELONA	B.737	1234567	
2539	0625	ROME	0915	GATWICK	B.737	1234567	
2540	1305	GATWICK	1545	ROME	B.737	1234567	
2541	1640	ROME	1915	GATWICK	B.737	1234567	
2542	1825	GATWICK	2110	ROME	B.737	1234567	
2569	0715	MILAN	0930	GATWICK	B.737	1 34567	
2570	0845	GATWICK	1100	MILAN	B.737	1234567	
2571	1145	MILAN	1345	GATWICK	B.737	1234567	
2578	1845	GATWICK	2045	MILAN	B.737	234567	
2580	1215	GATWICK	1425	TRIESTE	B.737	1234567	
2581	1510	TRIESTE	1720	GATWICK	B.737	1234567	
2590	1030	GATWICK	1245	VERONA	B.737	1234 6	
2591	1330	VERONA	1540	GATWICK	B.737	1234 6	
2598	1810	GATWICK	2020	VERONA	B.737	1234567	
2599	0750	PISA	1000	GATWICK	B.737	1234567	
2600	1040	GATWICK	1245	PISA	B.757	1234567	
2601	1450	PISA	1700	GATWICK	B.757	1234567	
2604	1825	GATWICK	2040	PISA	B.737	1234567	
2618	1825	GATWICK	2030	GENOA	B.737	1234567	
2691	0615	VIENNA	0850	GATWICK	B.737	1234567	0730/1010 5

2713	0650	FRANKFURT	0840	GATWICK	B.737	1234567		
2714	0950	GATWICK	1210	FRANKFURT	B.737	1234567		
2715	1020	FRANKFURT	1200	GATWICK	B.737	1234567		
2716	1345	GATWICK	1520	FRANKFURT	B737/757	123456		
2717	1615	FRANKFURT	1750	GATWICK	B737/757	12345 7		
2718	1915	GATWICK	2050	FRANKFURT	B.737	12345 7		
2770	0820	GATWICK	1100	STOCKHOLM	B.737	1234567	0915/1155 6	
2771	1240	STOCKHOLM	1440	GATWICK	B.737	1234567		
2776	1240	GATWICK	1505	STOCKHOLM	B.737	1234567		
2777	1600	STOCKHOLM	1855	GATWICK	B.737	1234567		
2781	0635	GOTHENBURG	0845	GATWICK	B.737	1234567		
2782	0725	GATWICK	0930	GOTHENBURG	B.737	1234567		
2783	1015	GOTHENBURG	1225	GATWICK	B.737	1234567		
2784	1455	GATWICK	1700	GOTHENBURG	B.737	1234567		
2785	1815	GOTHENBURG	2025	GATWICK	B.737	1234567		
2786	1835	GATWICK	2040	GOTHENBURG	B.737	1234567		
2789	0625	OSLO	0845	GATWICK	B.737	123456		
2790	0840	GATWICK	1100	OSLO	B.737	1234567		
2791	1155	OSLO	1405	GATWICK	B.737	1234567		
2792	1910	GATWICK	2125	OSLO	B.737	12345 7		
2817	0600	PARIS CDG	0715	GATWICK	B.737	1234567		
2820	0700	GATWICK	0820	PARIS CDG	B.737	123456		
2821	0910	PARIS CDG	1015	GATWICK	B.737	123456		
2826	0925	GATWICK	1035	PARIS CDG	B.737	1234567		
2827	1115	PARIS CDG	1225	GATWICK	B.737	1234567		
2832	1350	GATWICK	1450	PARIS CDG	B.737	1234567		
2833	1540	PARIS CDG	1640	GATWICK	B.737	1234567		
2838	1645	GATWICK	1745	PARIS CDG	B.737	1234567		
2839	1825	PARIS CDG	1930	GATWICK	B.737	12345 7		
2844	2020	GATWICK	2120	PARIS CDG	B.737	12345 7		
2846	0930	GATWICK	1210	KRAKOW	B.737	1		
2848	1755	GATWICK	2035	KRAKOW	B.737	2		
2853		VILNUIS	0835	GATWICK	B.737	1234 6		
2856	1845	GATWICK	2140	VILNUIS	B.737	123 5 7		
2861	0640	GDANSK	0915	GATWICK	B.737	3 5		
2862	0930	GATWICK	1150	GDANSK	B.737	1		
2863	1305	GDANSK	1535	GATWICK	B.737	1		
2864	1755	GATWICK	2015	GDANSK	B.737	2 4		
2865	1450	LJUBLJANA	1710	GATWICK	B.737	2		
2866	1115	GATWICK	1330	LJUBLJANA	B.737	2 6		
	1845	GATWICK	2100	LJUBLJANA	B.737	1 3 2	015/2325 3	
2867	0540	LJUBLJANA	0800	GATWICK	B.737	2 4	0805/1030 4	
	1420	LJUBLJANA	1640	GATWICK	B.737	6		
2871	0540	RIGA	0845	GATWICK	B.737	1234567	0615/0915 12	
2874	1735	GATWICK	2125	RIGA	B.737	1234	1850/2200 13	
	1845	GATWICK	2225	RIGA	B.737	567	1910/2255 7	
2878	1005	GATWICK	1525	LENINGRAD	B.737	1 3 567		
2879	1530	LENINGRAD	1805	GATWICK	B.757	1 3 567		
2880	1335	GATWICK	1720	MOSCOW	B.757	1234567	0740/1130 57	
2881	1825	MOSCOW	2225	GATWICK	B.757	1234567	1240/1640 57	
2884	1040	GATWICK	1410	KIEV	B.737	12 45 7		
2885	1515	KIEV	1900	GATWICK	B.737	12 45 7		
2890	1015	GATWICK	1435	SOFIA	B.737	2 5 7		
2891	1515	SOFIA	1800	GATWICK	B.737	2 5 7		
2892	1845	GATWICK	2205	SOFIA	B.737	1 3 7		
2893	0555	SOFIA	0830	GATWICK	B.737	12 4	0525/0800 4	
2894	0955	GATWICK	1325	BUCHAREST	B.737	1234567		
2895	1430	BUCHAREST	1800	GATWICK	B.737	1234567		
2896	1740	GATWICK	2055	BUCHAREST	B.737	5 7	1810/2130 5	
2897	0510	BUCHAREST	0845	GATWICK	B.737	1 6	0535/0915 6	
2931	0625	EDINBURGH	0800	GATWICK	B.737	1234567		
2934	0705	GATWICK	0830	EDINBURGH	B.737	12345		
2935	0910	EDINBURGH	1040	GATWICK	B.737	12345		
2936	0845	GATWICK	1005	EDINBURGH	B.737	1234567		
2937	1125	EDINBURGH	1300	GATWICK	B.737	1234567		
2938	1120	GATWICK	1250	EDINBURGH	B.737	123456		
2939	1330	EDINBURGH	1500	GATWICK	B.737	123456		
2940	1400	GATWICK	1525	EDINBURGH	B.737	1234567		

SPEEDBIRD (Cont.)

2941	1615	EDINBURGH	1740	GATWICK	B.737	1234567	
2942	1615	GATWICK	1735	EDINBURGH	B.737	12345 7	
2943	1845	EDINBURGH	2015	GATWICK	B.737	12345 7	
2946	1955	GATWICK	2125	EDINBURGH	B.737	1234567	
2953	0610	GLASGOW	0740	GATWICK	B.737	1234567	
2956	0730	GATWICK	0855	GLASGOW	B.737	12345	
2957	0955	GLASGOW	1125	GATWICK	B.737	12345	
2958	1015	GATWICK	1145	GLASGOW	B.737	1234567	
2959	1245	GLASGOW	1355	GATWICK	B.737	1234567	
2962	1400	GATWICK	1530	GLASGOW	B.737	1234567	
2963	1610	GLASGOW	1735	GATWICK	B.737	1234567	
2964	1615	GATWICK	1740	GLASGOW	B.737	12345 7	
2965	1835	GLASGOW	2000	GATWICK	B.737	12345 7	
2966	1710	GATWICK	1835	GLASGOW	B.737	1234567	
2967	1915	GLASGOW	2040	GATWICK	B.737	1234567	
2968	2000	GATWICK	2145	GLASGOW	B.737	1234567	
3571	1015	STANSTED		HONG KONG	B.747	3 5 7	DEP 0700 7
3572		DELHI	1900	STANSTED	B.747	1 4 6	
3595	2230	STANSTED	0320	CAIRO	A.300	6	
3596	0505	TEL AVIV	1330	STANSTED	A.300	7	
4502		CANCUN	1315	GATWICK	B.777	2 6	ARR 1025 6
4503	1530	GATWICK		CANCUN	B.777	1 5	DEP 1240 5
4504		NASSAU	1045	GATWICK	B.777	2 4	ARR 1145 4
		NASSAU	1405	GATWICK	B.777	7	
4505	1100	GATWICK		NASSAU	B.777	1 3	DEP 1200 3
	1420	GATWICK		NASSAU	B.777	6	
4508		SAN JUAN	0710	GATWICK	B.777	1 7	ARR 1035 7
4509	1125	GATWICK		SAN JUAN	B.777	67	DEP 1030 6
4516		TAMPA	0855	GATWICK	B.777	5 7	ARR 1010 5
		TAMPA	1140	GATWICK	B.777	234	ARR 1310 2
4517	1300	GATWICK		TAMPA	B.777	4 6	DEP 1415 6
	1545	GATWICK		TAMPA	B.777	123	DEP 1715 1
4520		KINGSTON	0915	GATWICK	B.777	56	ARR 1145 6
		KINGSTON	1315	GATWICK	B.777	1 3	ARR 1255 1
4521	0920	GATWICK		KINGSTON	B.777	45	DEP 1155 5
	1305	GATWICK		KINGSTON	B.777	2 7	DEP 1325 2

9010C - 9099C   ONE OFF CHARTER FLIGHTS TO/FROM HEATHROW TO VARIOUS DESTINATIONS WITH CONCORDE

9653		BERMUDA	0625	GATWICK	B.777	3 567	BA2232
9669		ATLANTA	0625	GATWICK	B.777	1234567	BA2226
9672		DALLAS	0640	GATWICK	B.777	1234567	BA2192
9683	1020	GATWICK		MIAMI	B.777	1234567	BA2295
9684		MIAMI	0615	GATWICK	B.777	1234567	BA2294

SPEEDWAY   _DEUTSCHE BA_   _DI/BAG_   _GERMANY_

A LETTER IS ADDED AFTER THE FLIGHT NUMBER - 'H' TO/FROM HAMBURG, 'M' TO/FROM MUNICH, ETC.

640	0600	HAMBURG	0740	GATWICK	B.737	1234567	DI4640
641	0840	GATWICK	1020	HAMBURG	B.737	1234567	DI4641
642	1115	HAMBURG	1255	GATWICK	B.737	1234567	1400/1545 7
643	1340	GATWICK	1525	HAMBURG	B.737	1234567	1610/1755 67
644	1700	HAMBURG	1840	GATWICK	B.737	12345 7	DI4644
645	1940	GATWICK	2115	HAMBURG	B.737	12345 7	DI4645
714	0545	MUNICH	0740	GATWICK	B.737	1234567	DI4714
715	0840	GATWICK	1035	MUNICH	B.737	1234567	DI4715
716	1050	MUNICH	1245	GATWICK	B.737	1234567	
717	1320	GATWICK	1515	MUNICH	B.737	1234567	
718	1650	MUNICH	1840	GATWICK	B.737	12345 7	DI4718
719	1930	GATWICK	2125	MUNICH	B.737	12345 7	DI4719
950	0550	STUTTGART	0735	GATWICK	B.757	1234567	
951	0840	GATWICK	1025	STUTTGART	B.757	1234567	
954	1645	STUTTGART	1830	GATWICK	B.737	12345 7	
955	1920	GATWICK	2105	STUTTGART	B.737	12345 7	

EVEN NUMBERS - FLIGHTS TO SHANNON   UNEVEN NUMBERS - FLIGHTS LEAVING SHANNON

8430/1	1935	BERLIN	1255	SHANNON	B.737	6	-25.09
8432/3	1335	LEIPZIG	1855	SHANNON	B.737	6	-25.09
8434/5	1900	DUSSELDORF	1145	SHANNON	B.737	6	-25.09

8436/7	1235	STUTTGART	1815	SHANNON	B.737	6	-25.09
8438/9	1900	HAMBURG	1815	SHANNON	B.737	6	-25.09
8440/1	1900	SHANNON	1815	MUNICH	B.737	6	-25.09
8442/3	1625	SHANNON	1540	MUNICH	B.737	6	-25.09
8444/5	1600	SHANNON	1515	MUNICH	B.737	6	-02.10

SPRINGBOK — *SOUTH AFRICAN AIRWAYS   SA/SAA   SOUTH AFRICA*

212		JOHANNESBURG	0625	HEATHROW	B.747	1 3 6	
215	1930	HEATHROW		JOHANNESBURG	B.747	4 67	
217	1930	HEATHROW		JOHANNESBURG	B.747	1 3 6	DEP 2130 6
220		JOHANNESBURG	0630	HEATHROW	B.747	1 3 5 7	
221	2115	HEATHROW		JOHANNESBURG	B.747	1 3 5 7	DEP 1815 3
222		JOHANNESBURG	0625	HEATHROW	B.747	2 45	
226		JOHANNESBURG	0625	HEATHROW	B.747	7	
227	2030	HEATHROW		JOHANNESBURG	B.747	2 45	DEP 1945 5
229	2130	HEATHROW		JOHANNESBURG	B.747	123 5 7	
231	1800	HEATHROW		CAPE TOWN	B.747	6	
232		CAPE TOWN	0620	HEATHROW	B.747	2 4 6	
233	1905	HEATHROW		JOHANNESBURG	B.747	2	
234		JOHANNESBURG	0700	HEATHROW	B.747	123456	
237	1800	HEATHROW		CAPE TOWN	B.747	4	
238		JOHANNESBURG	0700	HEATHROW	B.747	7	

STERLING — *STERLING EUROPEAN AIRWAYS   NB/SNB   DENMARK*

795		STOCKHOLM	1030	GLASGOW	B.737	5	11.06-10.09
796	1130	GLASGOW		STOCKHOLM	B.737	5	11.06-10.09

STREAMLINE — *STREAMLINE AVIATION   SSW   U.K.*

300	1815	MANCHESTER	1920	STANSTED	SH-360	1234
300P	1600	LUTON	1645	MANCHESTER	SH-360	1234
340P	2030	STANSTED	2100	LUTON	SH-360	1234
380		DUSSELDORF	1945	STANSTED	SH-360	1234
390P	2015	STANSTED	2045	LUTON	SH-360	1234

SUCKLING — *SUCKLING AIRWAYS   CB/SAY   U.K.*

001	0700	CAMBRIDGE ·	0800	AMSTERDAM	DO-228	12345	
002	0825	AMSTERDAM	0925	CAMBRIDGE	DO-228	1234	
005	1625	AMSTERDAM	1730	CAMBRIDGE	DO-228	12345	
007	1745	CAMBRIDGE	1850	AMSTERDAM	DO-228	12345 7	1645/1750 7
008	1905	AMSTERDAM	2010	CAMBRIDGE	DO-228	12345 7	1805/1910 7
009	1000	CAMBRIDGE	1100	AMSTERDAM	DO-228	1	
010	1500	CAMBRIDGE	1605	AMSTERDAM	DO-228	2345	
014	1245	AMSTERDAM	1345	CAMBRIDGE	DO-228	5	
201	0650	NORWICH	0745	MANCHESTER	DO-228	12345	
202	0815	MANCHESTER	0905	NORWICH	DO-228	12345	
203	1620	NORWICH	1715	MANCHESTER	DO-228	12345	
204	1740	MANCHESTER	1835	NORWICH	DO-228	12345	
310	0705	GLASGOW	0830	LONDON CITY	DO-328	123456	
312	1050	GLASGOW	1210	LONDON CITY	DO-328	12345	
314	1440	GLASGOW	1605	LONDON CITY	DO-328	12345	
316	1805	GLASGOW	1925	LONDON CITY	DO-328	12345 7	
313	1235	LONDON CITY	1350	GLASGOW	DO-328	12345	
315	1630	LONDON CITY	1745	GLASGOW	DO-328	12345	
317	1940	LONDON CITY	2055	GLASGOW	DO-328	12345 7	
311	0855	LONDON CITY	1015	GLASGOW	DO-328	123456	
401	0700	LUTON	0810	PARIS CDG	DO-328	12345	
402	0845	PARIS CDG	0955	LUTON	DO-328	1234	
	0845	PARIS CDG	1035	NORWICH	DO-328	5	VIA LUTON
403	1020	LUTON	1125	PARIS CDG	DO-328	1234	
404	1200	PARIS CDG	1350	NORWICH	DO-328	1234	VIA LUTON
405	1410	NORWICH	1605	PARIS CDG	DO-328	12345	VIA LUTON
406	1635	PARIS CDG	1740	LUTON	DO-328	12345	
407	1810	LUTON	1915	PARIS CDG	DO-328	12345	
408	1950	PARIS CDG	2055	LUTON	DO-328	12345	
453	1055	NORWICH	1245	PARIS CDG	DO-328	5	VIA LUTON
454	1325	PARIS CDG	1430	LUTON	DO-328	5	

SUCKLING (Cont.)

Flt	Dep	Origin	Arr	Destination	Aircraft	Days	Notes
475	1410	LUTON	1515	PARIS CDG	DO-328	7	
476	1545	PARIS CDG	1735	NORWICH	DO-328	7	VIA LUTON
477	1750	NORWICH	1935	PARIS CDG	DO-328	7	VIA LUTON
478	2000	PARIS CDG	2105	LUTON	DO-328	7	
501	1030	LUTON	1200	WATER FORD	DO-228	123456	0815/0935 6
502	1220	WATER FORD	1345	LUTON	DO-228	123456	1005/1125 6
507	1345	LUTON	1510	WATER FORD	DO-228	7	
508	1535	WATER FORD	1700	LUTON	DO-228	7	
811	0930	NORWICH	1055	EDINBURGH	DO-228	12345	
812	1115	EDINBURGH	1245	NORWICH	DO-228	12345	
813	1850	NORWICH	2015	EDINBURGH	DO-228	12345	
814	2040	EDINBURGH	2205	NORWICH	DO-228	12345	
815	1700	NORWICH	1825	EDINBURGH	DO-228	7	
816	1850	EDINBURGH	2015	NORWICH	DO-228	7	
886	1030	SOUTHAMPTON	1145	AMSTERDAM	DO-328	12345 7	1345/1500 7
887	1230	AMSTERDAM	1345	SOUTHAMPTON	DO-328	12345 7	1530/1645 7
888	1815	SOUTHAMPTON	1930	AMSTERDAM	DO-328	2345	
889	1955	AMSTERDAM	2110	SOUTHAMPTON	DO-328	2345	
910	0610	DUNDEE	0725	LONDON CITY	DO-328	12345	
911	0740	LONDON CITY	0855	DUNDEE	DO-328	12345	
912	0925	DUNDEE	1040	LONDON CITY	DO-328	12345	
913	1110	LONDON CITY	1225	DUNDEE	DO-328	12345	
914	1415	DUNDEE	1530	LONDON CITY	DO-328	12345	
915	1600	LONDON CITY	1715	DUNDEE	DO-328	12345	
916	1800	DUNDEE	1915	LONDON CITY	DO-328	12345 7	1745/1900 7
917	1935	LONDON CITY	2050	DUNDEE	DO-328	12345 7	1920/2035 7
3881	0850	AMSTERDAM	1005	SOUTHAMPTON	DO-328	123456	0930/1045 6
3882	0645	SOUTHAMPTON	0800	AMSTERDAM	DO-328	123456	0730/0845 6
3884	1445	SOUTHAMPTON	1600	AMSTERDAM	DO-328	12345	1515/1630 1
	1715	SOUTHAMPTON	1830	AMSTERDAM	DO-328	7	
3885	1630	AMSTERDAM	1745	SOUTHAMPTON	DO-328	12345	1750/1905 1
	1915	AMSTERDAM	2030	SOUTHAMPTON	DO-328	7	

SABRE   *SABRE AIRWAYS SBE U.K.*

EVEN NUMBERS - FLIGHTS LEAVING THE UK   UNEVEN NUMBERS - FLIGHTS INTO THE UK

Flt	Dep	Origin	Arr	Destination	Aircraft	Days	Notes
1002/3	0540	GATWICK	1255	CORFU	B.737	1	
1004/5	0640	GATWICK	0030	KEFALLINIA	B.737	2	
1006/7	0555	GATWICK	2200	DUBROVNIK	B.727	5	-09.07 ARR 2000
1008/9	1430	GATWICK	2010	SPLIT	B.737	1	
1010/1	1615	GATWICK	2135	FARO	B.737	6	
1012/3	1030	GATWICK	1940	KEFALLINIA	B.727	6	
1014/5	2145	GATWICK	0500	CORFU	B.737	1	19.07-05.10
1016/7	2245	GATWICK	0435	PALMA	B.737	6	24.07-03.10
1018/9	0540	GATWICK	1500	SAMOS	B.737	4	
1020/1	0555	GATWICK	1140	NAPLES	B.737	5	-08.10
1022/3	0600	GATWICK	1515	ZAKYNTHOS	B.737	7	-03.10
1024/5	1300	GATWICK	1850	IBIZA	B.727	7	-03.10
1026/7	1600	GATWICK	1445	CORFU	B.727	1	-11.10
1028/9	0555	GATWICK	1500	CHANIA	B.727	2	-05.10
1030/1	1630	GATWICK	2240	ZAKYNTHOS	B.737	7	-03.10
1036/7	2015	GATWICK	0205	IBIZA	B.737	7	25.07-27.09
1038/9	1350	GATWICK	0115	SHARM EL SHEIKH	B.737	5	
1040/1	2045	GATWICK	0400	CORFU	B.727	6	18.07-04.10
1048/9	1530	GATWICK	2240	KEFALLINIA	B.737	4	07.10-28.10
1056/7	0555	GATWICK	1225	ALICANTE	B.727	4	
1058/9	1600	GATWICK	0255	HURGHADA	B.737	4	
1062/3	0600	GATWICK	1150	IBIZA	B.727	7	
1092/3	2000	GATWICK	2300	PALMA	B.727	2	13.07-05.10
1094/5	1615	GATWICK	0115	FUERTVENTURA	B.727	3	26.05-07.10
1096/7	2030	GATWICK	2220	FARO	B.727	4	
2000/1	1325	MANCHESTER	1215	DUBROVNIK	B.727	5	
2002/3	0600	MANCHESTER	1935	REUS	B.737	3	
2004/5	1400	GLASGOW	1240	IBIZA	B.727	7	12.06-18.07
2006/7	1530	MANCHESTER	2230	MALAGA	B.737	5	-08.10
2008/9	2000	MANCHESTER	0355	MALTA	B.737	6	-10.10
2010/1	1415	BIRMINGHAM	1310	KEFALLINIA	B.737	7	-10.10
2012/3	0510	MANCHESTER	2220	KEFALLINIA	B.737	7	

2014/5	0500	MANCHESTER	1300	CORFU	B.737	1	-04.10
2016/7	0740	MANCHESTER	1615	FUNCHAL	B.737	2	
2018/9	0715	MANCHESTER	1415	NAPLES	B.737	5	
2020/1	1745	MANCHESTER	0300	HERAKLION	B.737	2	
2022/3	2245	MANCHESTER	0635	CORFU	B.737	1	19.07-05.10
2024/5	2330	MANCHESTER	0755	ATHENS	B.737	5	-08.10
2028/9	1415	MANCHESTER	2115	SPLIT	B.737	1	
2030/1	1325	GLASGOW	1210	REUS	B.737	3	21.07-06.10
2030/1	1540	GLASGOW	1425	REUS	B.737	3	-14.07
2032/3	1720	BIRMINGHAM	1620	TENERIFE	B.727	5	
2034/5	2050	MANCHESTER	0610	KOS	B.737	3	21.07-
2036/7	0915	MANCHESTER	1955	SAMOS	B.737	4	
2038/9	2100	MANCHESTER	0330	ALICANTE	B.737	4	
2056/7	0920	MANCHESTER	1900	KEFALLINIA	B.737	6	-02.10
3000/1	0745	STANSTED	1450	CORFU	B.727	1	
3002/3	0730	STANSTED	1645	HERAKLION	B.727	2	
3004/5	0730	STANSTED	1400	FARO	B.727	4	
3006/7	0655	STANSTED	1330	FARO	B.727	6	
3010/1	0700	STANSTED	0235	TENERIFE	B.727	5	
3012/3	1530	STANSTED	0040	LANZAROTE	B.727	4	
3014/5	0745	STANSTED	1615	RHODES	B.727	3	
3018/9	0600	GATWICK	1415	PREVEZZA	B.737	6	
3022/3	1500	STANSTED	2130	MALAGA	B.727	6	
3026/7	0755	STANSTED	2230	FARO	B.727	7	
5029/0	0630	GATWICK	1430	HASSI MESSAOUD	B.727	3	
5031/2	0540	GATWICK	1430	HASSI MESSAOUD	B.727	1	

	SATA			*SERVICO ACOREANO DE TRANSPORTES SP/SAT PORTUGAL*			
9450		FARO	1740	NORWICH	B.737	7	
9451	1830	NORWICH		FARO	B.737	7	

	SAUDIA			*SAUDIA ARABIAN AIRLINES SV/SVA SAUDIA ARABIA*			
020		NEW YORK	0840	JEDDAH	B.747	6	
021	2115	JEDDAH		NEW YORK	B.747	1234	
022		NEW YORK	1140	JEDDAH	B.747	3	
034		NEW YORK	1340	JEDDAH	B.747	5	
035	2115	JEDDAH		NEW YORK	B.747	3	
038		NEW YORK	1205	RIYADH	B.747	1	
101		RIYADH	1650	HEATHROW	B.777	7	
102	1230	HEATHROW		RIYADH	B.777	4	
103		RIYADH	0625	HEATHROW	B.777	4	
104	2155	HEATHROW		RIYADH	B.777	4	
105		JEDDAH	1550	HEATHROW	B.777	4	
106	1600	HEATHROW		RIYADH	B.777	5	
107		RIYADH	0700	HEATHROW	B.777	5	
108	2045	HEATHROW		RIYADH	B.777	1	
109		RIYADH	1805	HEATHROW	B.777	1	
110	1230	HEATHROW		DHARHAN	B.777	7	
111		DHARHAN	0715	HEATHROW	B.777	7	
112	1230	HEATHROW		JEDDAH	B.777	12 5	
113		JEDDAH	0620	HEATHROW	B.747	12 5	
115		JEDDAH	1740	HEATHROW	B.777	3 67	
116	2045	HEATHROW		JEDDAH	B.777	3 67	
117		DHARAN	1650	HEATHROW	B.777	4	
118	2200	HEATHROW		DHARAN	B.777	7	
120	2115	HEATHROW		JEDDAH	B.777	4	
900		NEW YORK	1055	BRUSSELS	B.747	7	
901	1530	BRUSSELS		NEW YORK	B.747	6	
902		NEW YORK	1005	BRUSSELS	B.747	5	
903	1530	BRUSSELS		NEW YORK	B.747	4	
904		NEW YORK	1005	BRUSSELS	MD-11	3	
905	1530	BRUSSELS		NEW YORK	MD-11	2	
906		NEW YORK	1005	BRUSSELS	MD-11	6	
907	1530	BRUSSELS		NEW YORK	MD-11	5	

500	0650	HEATHROW	0835	COPENHAGEN	MD-81	1234567	
501	0800	COPENHAGEN	0955	HEATHROW	B767/MD90	1234567	
502	1120	HEATHROW	1310	COPENHAGEN	B767/MD90	1234567	
503	1630	COPENHAGEN	1825	HEATHROW	MD-81	1234567	
504	1820	HEATHROW	2010	COPENHAGEN	MD-81	1234567	
505	1355	COPENHAGEN	1550	HEATHROW	MD-81	1234567	
506	1655	HEATHROW	1840	COPENHAGEN	MD-81	1234567	
507	0940	COPENHAGEN	1140	HEATHROW	MD-81	1234567	
508	1240	HEATHROW	1430	COPENHAGEN	MD-81	1234567	
509	1400	OSLO	1610	HEATHROW	MD-90	1234567	
510	1755	HEATHROW	1935	OSLO	MD-90	1234567	
511	0635	OSLO	0850	HEATHROW	MD-90	1234567	
512	1030	HEATHROW	1300	OSLO	MD-90	1234567	
513	1600	OSLO	1820	HEATHROW	MD81/MD90	1234567	
514	1920	HEATHROW	2120	OSLO	MD81/MD90	1234567	
515	0725	STAVANGER	0920	HEATHROW	DC-9	1234567	
516	1015	HEATHROW	1200	STAVANGER	DC-9	1234567	
517	1715	OSLO	1935	HEATHROW	MD-87	12345 7	
518	2105	HEATHROW	2330	OSLO	MD-87	12345 7	2130/2350 5
519	1600	STAVANGER	1755	HEATHROW	DC-9	1234567	
520	1900	HEATHROW	2045	STAVANGER	DC-9	1234567	
521	1550	GOTHENBURG	1755	HEATHROW	MD-81	1234567	
522	1900	HEATHROW	2055	GOTHENBURG	MD-81	1234567	
523	0610	GOTHENBURG	0825	HEATHROW	MD-81	1234567	
524	1020	HEATHROW	1115	GOTHENBURG	MD-90	1234567	
525	0630	STOCKHOLM	0905	HEATHROW	MD-90	1234567	
526	0920	HEATHROW	1145	STOCKHOLM	MD-81	1234567	
527	1400	STOCKHOLM	1635	HEATHROW	MD-90	1234567	
528	1755	HEATHROW	1920	STOCKHOLM	MD-90	1234567	
529	1600	STOCKHOLM	1835	HEATHROW	MD-90	1234567	
530	1935	HEATHROW	2155	STOCKHOLM	MD-97	1234567	
531	1010	STOCKHOLM	1245	HEATHROW	MD-87	1234567	
532	1445	HEATHROW	1640	STOCKHOLM	MD-87	1234567	
533	1700	STOCKHOLM	1935	HEATHROW	MD-87	12345 7	
534	2105	HEATHROW	2345	STOCKHOLM	MD-87	12345 7	2130/0005 5
535	1450	AARHUS	1655	HEATHROW	MD-81	1234567	
536	1930	HEATHROW	2110	AARHUS	MD-81	1234567	
537	0805	COPENHAGEN	1010	DUBLIN	B.737	1234567	
538	1100	DUBLIN	1300	COPENHAGEN	B.737	1234567	
539	0805	COPENHAGEN	0955	MANCHESTER	B.737	1234567	
540	1040	MANCHESTER	1225	COPENHAGEN	B.737	1234567	
541	1525	COPENHAGEN	1715	MANCHESTER	B.737	1234567	
542	1815	MANCHESTER	1955	COPENHAGEN	B.737	1234567	
901	1845	COPENHAGEN		NEW YORK	B.767	1234567	
902		NEW YORK	1225	COPENHAGEN	B.767	1234567	
903	0945	STOCKHOLM		NEW YORK	B.767	1234567	
904		NEW YORK	0650	STOCKHOLM	B.767	1234567	
907	1000	OSLO		NEW YORK	B.767	1234567	
908		NEW YORK	0730	OSLO	B.767	1234567	
911	0940	COPENHAGEN		NEW YORK	B.767	1234567	
912		NEW YORK	0655	COPENHAGEN	B.767	1234567	
937	0935	COPENHAGEN		SEATTLE	B.767	1234567	
938		SEATTLE	0655	COPENHAGEN	B.767	1234567	
943	0945	COPENHAGEN		CHICAGO	B.767	1234567	
944		CHICAGO	1210	COPENHAGEN	B.767	1234567	
945	0900	STOCKHOLM		CHICAGO	B.767	1234567	
946		CHICAGO	0640	STOCKHOLM	B.767	1234567	
983	1440	COPENHAGEN		TOKYO	B.767	123 567	
984		TOKYO	1520	COPENHAGEN	B.767	1234567	
1501	1925	COPENHAGEN	2120	HEATHROW	MD-81	12345 7	
1510	0740	HEATHROW	0940	OSLO	MD-81	123456	
1511	1840	OSLO	2100	HEATHROW	MD-81	12345 7	
1513	0910	OSLO	1205	HEATHROW	MD-87	1234567	
1514	1310	HEATHROW	1510	OSLO	MD-87	1234567	
1516	2150	HEATHROW	0105	TROMSO	MD-81	4 7	30.05-26.08
1517	0315	TROMSO	0625	HEATHROW	MD-81	1 5	31.05-27.08
1527	1900	STOCKHOLM	2135	HEATHROW	MD-81	12345 7	
1530	0650	HEATHROW	0915	STOCKHOLM	MD-81	123456	

1533	0820	OSLO	1020	MANCHESTER	DC-9	12345 7	
1534	1100	MANCHESTER	1250	OSLO	DC-9	12345 7	
1539	1830	COPENHAGEN	2020	MANCHESTER	MD-81	12345 7	
1540	0650	MANCHESTER	0835	COPENHAGEN	MD-81	123456	
1541	0810	STOCKHOLM	1035	MANCHESTER	DC-9	12345 7	
1542	1125	MANCHESTER	1345	STOCKHOLM	DC-9	12345 7	
2501		COPENHAGEN	1515	STANSTED	DC-9	1234567	
2502	1600	STANSTED		COPENHAGEN	DC-9	1234567	
2503		COPENHAGEN	0900	STANSTED	DC-9	1234567	
2504	0945	STANSTED		COPENHAGEN	DC-9	1234567	
2507		COPENHAGEN	2015	STANSTED	DC-9	12345 7	
2508	2100	STANSTED		COPENHAGEN	DC-9	12345 7	
2509		OSLO	0825	STANSTED	DC-9	1234567	16.08-
2510	0910	STANSTED		OSLO	DC-9	1234567	16.08-
2511		OSLO	1710	STANSTED	B.737	1234567	16.08-
2512	1810	STANSTED		OSLO	DC-9	1234567	16.08-
2525	1500	STOCKHOLM	1730	STANSTED	DC-9	1234567	
2526	1830	STANSTED	2045	STOCKHOLM	DC-9	12345 7	
2527	0600	STOCKHOLM	0825	STANSTED	DC-9	123456	
2528	0935	STANSTED	1140	STOCKHOLM	DC-9	1234567	
2529	0635	STOCKHOLM	0900	STANSTED	DC-9	7	
2530	1000	STANSTED	1210	STOCKHOLM	DC-9	7	
2537	1525	COPENHAGEN	1730	DUBLIN	B.737	1234567	
2538	1820	DUBLIN	2020	COPENHAGEN	B.737	1234567	
2841	0610	STAVANGER	0715	ABERDEEN	DC-9	123456	
2842	0800	ABERDEEN	0900	STAVANGER	DC-9	123456	
2843	1000	STAVANGER	1105	ABERDEEN	DC-9	1234567	
2844	1145	ABERDEEN	1245	STAVANGER	DC-9	1234567	
2845	1600	STAVANGER	1705	ABERDEEN	DC-9	12345 7	
2846	1750	ABERDEEN	1850	STAVANGER	DC-9	12345 7	
2547	1520	STOCKHOLM	1730	EDINBURGH	MD-90	6	
2548	1830	EDINBURGH	2040	STOCKHOLM	MD-80	6	

SUDANAIR   *SUDAN AIRWAYS   SD/SDA   SUDAN*

| 130 | | CAIRO | 1850 | HEATHROW | A.310 | 7 |
| 131 | 2100 | HEATHROW | | CAIRO | A.310 | 7 |

SUNSCAN   *SUN-AIR OF SCANDINAVIA   EX/SUS   DENMARK*

BRITISH AIRWAYS EXPRESS GROUP

8245		BILLUND	0830	MANCHESTER	J'STREAM41	12345
8246	0900	MANCHESTER		BILLUND	J'STREAM41	12345
8247		BILLUND	1745	MANCHESTER	BAE-ATP	12345 7
8248	1820	MANCHESTER		BILLUND	BAE-ATP	12345 7

SUNTURK   *PEGASUS HAVA TASIMACILIGI A.S.   PGT   TURKEY*

EVEN NUMBERS - FLIGHTS LEAVING THE U.K.   UNEVEN NUMBERS - FLIGHTS INTO THE U.K.

435/6	1025	GLASGOW	0940	BODRUM	B.737	1	
445/6	0030	GATWICK	2335	DALAMAN	B.737	4	
447/8	2100	GATWICK	2015	DALAMAN	B.737	3	
463/4	2145	MANCHESTER	2055	BODRUM	B.737	6	
465/6	0930	BIRMINGHAM	0825	BODRUM	B.737	6	
471/2	1100	LEEDS	1000	BODRUM	B.737	1	
473/4	1120	EAST MIDLANDS	1025	BODRUM	B.737	1	
477/8	2150	GATWICK	2100	DALAMAN	B.737	1	
477/8	2230	GLASGOW	2130	DALAMAN	B.737	1	14.06-19.07
479/0	1210	GATWICK	1115	BODRUM	B.737	1	
489/0	2150	GATWICK	2100	DALAMAN	B.737	5	
495/6	1045	MANCHESTER	0955	ANTALYA	B.737	7	

SUNWING   *SPANAIR   JK/JKK   SPAIN*

EVEN NUMBERS - FLIGHTS LEAVING THE U.K.   UNEVEN NUMBERS - FLIGHTS INTO THE U.K.

3101/2	2355	CARDIFF	2305	PALMA	MD-83	1
3103/4	2355	CARDIFF	2255	TENERIFE	MD-83	2
3105/6	2355	CARDIFF	2255	LAS PALMAS	MD-83	6

Flight	Dep	From	Arr	To	Aircraft	Days	Notes
3107/8	0050	BELFAST	2355	PALMA	MD-83	7	
3107/8	2355	BIRMINGHAM	2305	PALMA	MD-83	6	
3111/2	1315	BELFAST	1215	LAS PALMAS	MD-83	1	
3113/4	2355	BELFAST	2255	LAS PALMAS	MD-83	1	-09.08
3115/6	1220	MANCHESTER	1115	TENERIFE	MD-83	5	
3117/8	0020	EDINBURGH	2320	TENERIFE	MD-83	6	
3117/8	2340	CARDIFF	2240	TENERIFE	MD-83	5	
3119/0	2355	EDINBURGH	2255	LAS PALMAS	MD-83	6	
3121/2	2340	TEESSIDE	2245	PALMA	MD-83	5	
3123/4	1250	BELFAST	1200	REUS	MD-83	3	-29.09
3125/6	1920	BELFAST	1830	REUS	MD-83	3	-29.09
3127/8	2350	BELFAST	2250	TENERIFE	MD-83	7	
3141/2	0955	MANCHESTER	0900	PALMA	MD-83	5	
3153/4	1605	BRISTOL	1510	MAHON	MD-80	4	
3155/6	2220	BRISTOL	2125	PALMA	MD-80	4	
3157/8	2350	BIRMINGHAM	2255	PALMA	MD-83	1	
3161/2	1300	EAST MIDLANDS	1205	PALMA	MD-83	3	
3163/4	2310	EAST MIDLANDS	2215	FUERTVENTURA	MD-83	3	
3167/8	1350	MANCHESTER	1255	PALMA	MD-83	4	
3169/0	2045	MANCHESTER	1950	MAHON	MD-83	4	
3177/8	1015	BIRMINGHAM	0915	IBIZA	MD-83	5	
3179/0	1640	BIRMINGHAM	1550	PALMA	MD-83	5	
3191/2	1705	MANCHESTER	1610	PALMA	MD-83	6	
3193/4	2355	MANCHESTER	2305	PALMA	MD-83	6	
3203/4	1050	ABERDEEN	1000	PALMA	MD-83	4	
3211/2	??	LIVERPOOL	??	PALMA	MD-83	4	
3213/4	1145	TEESSIDE	1045	TENERIFE	MD-83	7	
3221/2	1305	EDINBURGH	1310	PALMA	MD-83	6	
3223/4	2100	EDINBURGH	2005	REUS	MD-83	6	
3255/6	2055	ABERDEEN	1200	PALMA	MD-83	6	
3257/8	1255	ABERDEEN	1955	IBIZA	MD-83	6	
3301/2	??	LIVERPOOL	??	PALMA	MD-83	2	
3305/6	0915	BIRMINGHAM	0815	PALMA	MD-83	6	
3307/8	1530	GLASGOW	1430	PALMA	MD-83	6	
3321/2	1215	STANSTED	1115	TENERIFE	MD-83	5	
3323/4	2320	GLASGOW	2220	TENERIFE	MD-83	5	
3323/4	2335	EAST MIDLANDS	2255	TENERIFE	MD-83	5	
3325/6	1510	BIRMINGHAM	1410	TENERIFE	MD-83	2	
3335/6	1400	STANSTED	1250	LANZAROTE	MD-83	4	
3337/8	1215	EAST MIDLANDS	1115	TENERIFE	MD-83	5	
3339/0	2335	MANCHESTER	2235	TENERIFE	MD-83	5	
3343/4	2245	MANCHESTER	2145	TENERIFE	MD-83	5	
3343/5	2305	GLASGOW	2205	TENERIFE	MD-83	5	11.06-30.07
3353/4	2345	GATWICK	2250	IBIZA	MD-83	7	
3367/8	2115	LEEDS	2020	PALMA	MD-83	6	
3371/2	2300	GLASGOW	2200	PALMA	MD-83	6	
3381/2	1640	MANCHESTER	1545	PALMA	MD-83	6	
3381/2	1725	BRISTOL	1630	PALMA	MD-80	6	
3385/6	0145	BELFAST	0045	LAS PALMAS	MD-83	7	
3385/6	0145	MANCHESTER	0045	LAS PALMAS	MD-83	7	
3391/2	1930	MANCHESTER	1815	IBIZA	MD-83	3	
3393/4	0010	GATWICK	2315	PALMA	MD-83	6	
5135/6	2355	MANCHESTER	2305	PALMA	MD-83	5	
7261/2	0200	EDINBURGH	0100	MADRID	MD-83	3	
8607/8	1725	GATWICK	1625	MADRID	MD-83	4 7	1405/1305 4

		SWISSAIR		*SWISSAIR SR/SWR*	*SWITZERLAND*		
100	1130	ZURICH		NEW YORK	MD-11	1234567	
101		NEW YORK	0700	ZURICH	MD-11	1234567	
102	0930	ZURICH		NEW YORK	MD-11	1 34567	
103		NEW YORK	0915	ZURICH	MD-11	12 4567	
104	1725	ZURICH		NEW YORK	A.330	1234567	
105		NEW YORK	1215	ZURICH	A.330	1234567	
106	0900	ZURICH		LOS ANGELES	MD-11	1234567	
107		LOS ANGELES	1010	ZURICH	MD-11	1234567	
108	1520	ZURICH		SAN FRANCISCO	MD-11	2345 7	
109		SAN FRANCISCO	1620	ZURICH	MD-11	1 3456	

116	0940	ZURICH		MIAMI	MD-11	1 3456
117		MIAMI	0715	ZURICH	MD-11	2 4567
118	1055	BASLE		NEW YORK	A.310	12 4567
119		NEW YORK	0915	BASLE	A.310	123 567
120	0900	ZURICH		ATLANTA	B.747	1234567
121		ATLANTA	0715	ZURICH	B.747	1234567
124	0920	ZURICH		CHICAGO	B747/MD11	1234567
125		CHICAGO	0640	ZURICH	B747/MD11	1234567
126	0915	ZURICH		BOSTON	B747/MD11	1234567
127		BOSTON	0700	ZURICH	B747/MD11	1234567
134	1150	ZURICH		MONTREAL	MD11/A330	1234567
135		MONTREAL	0515	ZURICH	MD11/A330	1234567
138	1115	GENEVA		NEW YORK	MD-11	1234567
139		NEW YORK	0830	GENEVA	MD-11	1234567
162	1300	ZURICH		OSAKA	MD-11	123 567
163		OSAKA	1715	ZURICH	MD-11	1234 67
168	1300	ZURICH		TOKYO	MD-11	1 4567
169		TOKYO	1625	ZURICH	MD-11	12 567
800	0635	ZURICH	0820	HEATHROW	MD-11	1234567
801R	0810	HEATHROW	0955	ZURICH	A.321	1234567
802	1115	ZURICH	1300	HEATHROW	A.321	1234567
803	0945	HEATHROW	1120	ZURICH	MD-11	1234567
804	1505	ZURICH	1640	HEATHROW	A.321	1234567
805	1350	HEATHROW	1525	ZURICH	A.321	1234567
806	1640	ZURICH	1825	HEATHROW	A.321	1234567
807	1725	HEATHROW	1900	ZURICH	A.321	1234567
808	1855	ZURICH	2040	HEATHROW	A.321	1234567
809	1915	HEATHROW	2050	ZURICH	A.321	1234567
810	1955	ZURICH	2140	HEATHROW	A.321	1234567
811	0630	HEATHROW	0805	ZURICH	A.321	1234567
830	0650	GENEVA	0840	HEATHROW	A.321	1234567
831	0955	HEATHROW	1130	GENEVA	A.321	1234567
832	1235	GENEVA	1415	HEATHROW	A.321	1234567
833	1505	HEATHROW	1635	GENEVA	A.321	1234567
836	1730	GENEVA	1915	HEATHROW	A.321	1234567
837	2000	HEATHROW	2130	GENEVA	A.321	1234567
838	1905	GENEVA	2045	HEATHROW	A.320	1234567
839	0800	HEATHROW	0930	GENEVA	A.320	1234567
842	1910	ZURICH	2115	MANCHESTER	A.320	1234567
843	0635	MANCHESTER	0835	ZURICH	A.320	1234567
844	1330	ZURICH	1525	MANCHESTER	A.320	234567
845	1615	MANCHESTER	1810	ZURICH	A.320	234567
846	0915	ZURICH	1105	MANCHESTER	A.320	1234567
847	1205	MANCHESTER	1405	ZURICH	A.320	1234567
3814	1730	ZURICH	1915	HEATHROW	BAE-146	1234567
3815	2115	HEATHROW	2250	ZURICH	BAE-146	1234567
3844	1330	ZURICH	1525	MANCHESTER	BAE-146	1
3845	1615	MANCHESTER	1805	ZURICH	BAE-146	1
5760		ZURICH	0845	STANSTED	BAE-146	1234567
5763	1320	STANSTED		ZURICH	BAE-146	1234567
5764		ZURICH	1735	STANSTED	BAE-146	1234567
5765	1820	STANSTED		ZURICH	BAE-146	1234567
7000	1100	BASLE	1315	SHANNON	DC-10	5 7	1615/1830 7
	1415	SHANNON		CHICAGO	DC-10	5 7	DEP 1930 7
7001		CHICAGO	0910	BASLE	DC-10	56	ARR 1245 6

		SYRIANAIR		*SYRIAN ARAB AIRLINES*	*RB/SYR*	*SYRIA*
409		DAMASCUS	1700	HEATHROW	B.727	6
410	1005	HEATHROW		DAMASCUS	B.727	7
411		DAMASCUS	1900	HEATHROW	B.747	1
412	1105	HEATHROW		DAMASCUS	B.747	2
413		DAMASCUS	1950	HEATHROW	B.727	3
414	1100	HEATHROW		DAMASCUS	B.727	4

		TANGO LIMA		*TRANS MEDITERRANEAN AIRWAYS*	*TL/TMA*	*LEBANON*
141		BEIRUIT	1500	HEATHROW	B.707	4
142	1700	HEATHROW		BEIRUIT	B.707	4

171		BEIRUT	1500	HEATHROW	B.707	7	
172	1700	HEATHROW		BEIRUT	B.707	7	

TAROM

TAROM   RO/ROT   ROMANIA

003	1040	BUCHAREST		NEW YORK	A.310	1 5	
004		NEW YORK	1015	BUCHAREST	A.310	2 6	
005	0855	TIMISOARA		NEW YORK	A.310	3	
006		NEW YORK	1100	TIMISOARA	A.310	4	
007	1500	AMSTERDAM		CHICAGO	A.310	5	
008		CHICAGO	1210	AMSTERDAM	A.310	6	
391		BUCHAREST	1130	HEATHROW	B.737	1234567	
392	1250	HEATHROW		BUCHAREST	B.737	1234567	
395		BUCHAREST	2120	HEATHROW	B.737	5	
396	0730	HEATHROW		BUCHAREST	B.737	6	

TAT

TAT EUROPEAN AIRLINES   IJ/TAT   FRANCE

3142	0840	GATWICK		TOULOUSE	F-100	1234567	
3143		TOULOUSE	1045	GATWICK	F-100	1234567	
3144	1450	GATWICK		TOULOUSE	F-100	1234567	
3145		TOULOUSE	1300	GATWICK	F-100	1234567	
3146	2000	GATWICK		TOULOUSE	F-100	1234567	
3147		TOULOUSE	1910	GATWICK	F-100	1234567	
3224	1825	GATWICK		BORDEAUX	F-100	1234567	
3225		BORDEAUX	1740	GATWICK	F-100	1234567	
3236	1350	GATWICK		BORDEAUX	F-100	1234567	
3237		BORDEAUX	1400	GATWICK	F-100	1234567	
3238	1145	GATWICK		BORDEAUX	F-100	1234567	
3239		BORDEAUX	0735	GATWICK	F-100	1234567	
3260	0820	HEATHROW	0930	PARIS ORLY	B.737	1234567	
3261	0625	PARIS ORLY	0735	HEATHROW	B.737	1234567	
3262	1605	HEATHROW	1715	PARIS ORLY	B.737	1234567	
3263	1350	PARIS ORLY	1500	HEATHROW	B.737	1234567	
3264	2010	HEATHROW	2020	PARIS ORLY	B.737	1234567	
3265	1820	PARIS ORLY	1930	HEATHROW	B.737	1234567	

TEE AIR

TOWER AIR   FF/TOW   U.S.A.

30		NEW YORK	1245	TEL AVIV	B.747	12345 7	ARR 0420 5
31	2000	TEL AVIV		NEW YORK	B.747	1234 67	
34		NEW YORK	0815	PARIS CDG	B.747	4 7	
35	1330	PARIS CDG		NEW YORK	B.747	4 7	
86		NEW YORK	0715	ATHENS	B.747	1	TO TEL AVIV
87	1725	ATHENS		NEW YORK	B.747	1	EX TEL AVIV

THAI

THAI AIRWAYS INT.   TG/THA   THAILAND

910		BANGKOK	0715	HEATHROW	B.747	1234567	
911	1200	HEATHROW		BANGKOK	B.747	1234567	DEP 1050 356
916		BANGKOK	1815	HEATHROW	B.747	2 4 6	
917	2130	HEATHROW		BANGKOK	B.747	2 4 6	

TRANSAT

AIR TRANSAT   TS/TSC   CANADA

200		TORONTO	0630	GLASGOW	B.757	6	
201	0815	GLASGOW		TORONTO	B.757	6	
202		TORONTO	1015	GLASGOW	L-1011	4	
203	1215	GLASGOW		TORONTO	L-1011	4	
204		TORONTO	0955	LEEDS	B.757	2	
205	1055	LEEDS	1135	BIRMINGHAM	B.757	2	
	1305	BIRMINGHAM		TORONTO	B.757	2	
206		TORONTO	0545	BELFAST	L-1011	6	-19.06 / 04.09-
	0840	BELFAST	0940	BIRMINGHAM	L-1011	6	-19.06 / 04.09-
207	1140	BIRMINGHAM	1240	BELFAST	L-1011	6	-19.06 / 04.09-
	1350	BELFAST		TORONTO	L-1011	6	-19.06 / 04.09-
218		HALIFAX	1000	GATWICK	L-1011	1	
219	1225	GATWICK		HALIFAX	L-1011	1	
228		TORONTO	1115	GATWICK	B.757	2	29.06-14.09
229	1400	GATWICK		TORONTO	B.757	2	29.06-14.09

Flight	Dep	From	Arr	To	Aircraft	Days	Dates
230		TORONTO	0710	CARDIFF	B.757	4	
231	0840	CARDIFF		TORONTO	B.757	4	
247	1245	EXETER	1345	STANSTED	B.757	3	
248		MONTREAL	0710	GATWICK	L-1011	4	-30.09
249	1145	GATWICK		MONTREAL	L-1011	4	-30.09
252		TORONTO	0815	EDINBURGH	L-1011	5	
253	1015	EDINBURGH		TORONTO	L-1011	5	
254		TORONTO	0645	MANCHESTER	B.757	6	
255	0815	MANCHESTER		TORONTO	B.757	6	
256		TORONTO	0655	MANCHESTER	B.757	5	-01.10
257	0915	MANCHESTER		TORONTO	B.757	5	-01.10
258		TORONTO	0650	GATWICK	L-1011	5	25.06-10.09
259	0850	GATWICK		TORONTO	L-1011	5	25.06-10.09
268		TORONTO	1130	GATWICK	L-1011	6	
269	1325	GATWICK		TORONTO	L-1011	6	
270		TORONTO	1415	STANSTED	B.757	1	
271	1605	STANSTED		TORONTO	B.757	1	
278		MONTREAL	1105	GATWICK	L-1011	7	
279	1255	GATWICK		MONTREAL	L-1011	7	
304		TORONTO	0845	BIRMINGHAM	B.757	6	26.06-28.08
305	1015	BIRMINGHAM		TORONTO	B.757	6	26.06-28.08
306		TORONTO	0900	DUBLIN	B.757	5	
	1000	DUBLIN	1045	SHANNON	B.757	5	
307	1230	SHANNON		TORONTO	B.757	5	
314		TORONTO	0905	MANCHESTER	B.757	1	28.06-13.09
315	1035	MANCHESTER		TORONTO	B.757	1	28.06-13.09
400		TORONTO	0715	ABERDEEN	B.757	1	21.06-13.09
401	0815	ABERDEEN	0905	NEWCASTLE	B.757	1	21.06-13.09
	1035	NEWCASTLE		TORONTO	B.757	1	
822		CALGARY	1655	GATWICK	A.330	1	-04.10
823	2015	GATWICK		CALGARY	A.330	1	-04.10
832		CALGARY	0725	MANCHESTER	A.330	3	
833	0955	MANCHESTER		CALGARY	A.330	3	
852		VANCOUVER	0925	MANCHESTER	A.330	5	25.06-17.09
	1030	MANCHESTER	1145	PARIS CDG	A.330	5	25.06-17.09
853	1330	PARIS CDG	1455	MANCHESTER	A.330	5	25.06-17.09
	1555	MANCHESTER		VANCOUVER	A.330	5	25.06-17.09
862		CALGARY	1415	GATWICK	A.330	6	
863	1545	GATWICK		VANCOUVER	A.330	6	
944		CALGARY	1015	GATWICK	L-1011	4	24.06-30.09
945	1315	GATWICK		CALGARY	L-1011	4	24.06-30.09
974		CALGARY	1545	GLASGOW	L-1011	7	
975	1745	GLASGOW		CALGARY	L-1011	7	

TRANSAVIA

TRANSAVIA HOLLAND B.V.   HV/TRA   NETHERLANDS

Flight	Dep	From	Arr	To	Aircraft	Days	Dates
215	1305	AMSTERDAM	1445	SHANNON	B.737	7	-17.10
216	1535	SHANNON	1710	AMSTERDAM	B.737	7	-17.10
601	0645	AMSTERDAM	0750	GATWICK	B.737	123456	
602	0835	GATWICK	0935	AMSTERDAM	B.737	123456	
603	1110	AMSTERDAM	1215	GATWICK	B.737	1234567	
604	1300	GATWICK	1400	AMSTERDAM	B.737	1234567	
605	1515	AMSTERDAM	1615	GATWICK	B.737	12345 7	
606	1700	GATWICK	1800	AMSTERDAM	B.737	12345 7	
609	1845	AMSTERDAM	1945	GATWICK	B.737	12345 7	
610	2030	GATWICK	2130	AMSTERDAM	B.737	12345 7	

TRANSBRASIL

TRANSBRASIL SA LINHAS AEREAS   TR/TBA   BRASIL

Flight	Dep	From	Arr	To	Aircraft	Days	Dates
872		RIO DE JANERIO	1615	GATWICK	B.767	3	
	1715	GATWICK	1820	AMSTERDAM	B.767	3	
873	1930	AMSTERDAM	2035	GATWICK	B.767	3	
	2200	GATWICK		RIO DE JANERIO	B.767	3	

TRANSLIFT

TRANSLIFT AIRWAYS LTD   TLA   IRELAND

Flight	Dep	From	Arr	To	Aircraft	Days	Dates
200/1	0655	GATWICK	1140	MAHON	A.300	1	-04.10
202/3	1410	GATWICK	2105	MALAGA	A.300	1	19.07-04.10
212/3	0640	GATWICK	1330	FARO	A.300	4	22.07-07.10

TRANSLIFT (Cont.)

214/5	1600	GATWICK	0040	LANZAROTE	A.300		4	22.07-28.10
216/7	0555	GATWICK	1530	TENERIFE	A.300		5	
218/9	1705	GATWICK	2245	MAHON	A.300		5	11.06-10.09
220/1	0640	GATWICK	1500	MALAGA	A.300		6	
222/3	1700	GATWICK	2350	ALICANTE	A.300		6	
226/7	1755	GATWICK	0045	MALAGA	A.300		7	
228/9	0630	GATWICK	1320	MALAGA	A.300	2		20.07-05.10
236/7	1630	GATWICK	0210	TENERIFE	A.300	2		20.07-06.10
238/9	1705	GATWICK	0245	TENERIFE	A.300		5	
532/3	2335	GLASGOW	2235	HERAKLION	A.320		5	
664/5	1040	GLASGOW	0940	RHODES	A.320		6	
668/9	2155	BIRMINGHAM	2140	RHODES	A.320		6	
572/3	2040	BELFAST	1940	HERAKLION	A.320	2		-05.10

TRANSOVIET — *TRANSAERO AIRLINES UN/TSO RUSSIA*

321	1210	MOSCOW		LOS ANGELES	B.767		7	
322		LOS ANGELES	0430	MOSCOW	B.767	2		
341		MOSCOW	2100	GATWICK	B.737	1234567		ARR 1325 23
342	2315	GATWICK		MOSCOW	B.737	1234567		DEP 1430 23

TUNAIR — *TUNIS AIR TU/TAR TUNISIA*

790		TUNIS	1625	HEATHROW	A.320	2	567	ARR 1705 67
791	1810	HEATHROW		TUNIS	A.320	2	567	
792		DJERBA	1950	HEATHROW	B.737		4	
793	2105	HEATHROW		DJERBA	B.737		4	

TURKAIR — *TURKISH AIRLINES TK/THY TURKEY*

1481	0755	ISTANBUL		CHICAGO	A.340	3 5 7	
1482		CHICAGO	0830	ISTANBUL	A.340	1 4 6	
1491	0700	ISTANBUL		NEW YORK	A.340	1234567	
1492		NEW YORK	0845	ISTANBUL	A.340	1234567	
1979		ISTANBUL	1025	HEATHROW	A.310	1234567	
1980	1230	HEATHROW		ISTANBUL	A.310	1234567	
1981		ISTANBUL	2110	HEATHROW	B.737	1234567	
1982	0640	HEATHROW		ISTANBUL	B.737	1234567	DEP 0750 167
1991		ISTANBUL	1550	HEATHROW	A.310	1234567	
1992	1655	HEATHROW		ISTANBUL	A.310	1234567	
1993		ISTANBUL	1115	MANCHESTER	B.737	2 45 7	
1994	1215	MANCHESTER		ISTANBUL	B.737	2 45 7	
1997		IZMIR	1230	HEATHROW	A.310	1 6	
1998	1330	HEATHROW		IZMIR	A.310	1 6	

TWA — *TWA TRANS WORLD AIRLINES INC. TW/TWA U.S.A.*

720		ST. LOUIS	0930	GATWICK	B.767	1234567	
721	1155	GATWICK		ST. LOUIS	B.767	1234567	
722		ST LOUIS	1155	GATWICK	B.767	1234567	
723	1515	GATWICK		ST. LOUIS	B.767	1234567	
840		NEW YORK	0800	ROME	B.767	1234567	
841	0945	ROME		NEW YORK	B.767	1234567	
842		NEW YORK	0745	MILAN	B.767	1234567	
843	1005	MILAN		NEW YORK	B.767	1234567	
884		NEW YORK	1300	TEL AVIV	B.767	1234567	
885	2205	TEL AVIV		NEW YORK	B.767	1234567	
888		NEW YORK	1235	CAIRO	B.767	2 4 6	
891	2305	CAIRO		NEW YORK	B.767	2 4 6	
924		NEW YORK	0715	PARIS	B.767	1234567	
925	1120	PARIS		NEW YORK	B.767	1234567	

TYROLEAN — *TYROLEAN AIRWAYS VO/TYR AUSTRIA*

753		VIENNA	1240	EDINBURGH	F70/CRJ	2 4 7	
754	1320	EDINBURGH		VIENNA	F70/CRJ	2 4 7	
933		INNSBRUCK	1235	BIRMINGHAM	CANADAIR	6	12.06-11.09
934	1315	BIRMINGHAM		INNSBRUCK	CANADAIR	6	12.06-11.09
935		INNSBRUCK	1310	EDINBURGH	CANADAIR	6	12.06-18.09
936	1350	EDINBURGH		INNSBRUCK	CANADAIR	6	12.06-18.09

10M	1640	STANSTED	1740	AMSTERDAM	F100/BAE146	1234567	UK2010
11M	1700	AMSTERDAM	1800	STANSTED	F-100	12345 7	UK2011
11Z	1555	STANSTED	1720	ABERDEEN	BAE-146	12345 7	UK2411
12M	1840	STANSTED	1940	AMSTERDAM	F-100	12345 7	UK2012
12Z	1345	ABERDEEN	1515	STANSTED	BAE-146	12345 7	UK2412
13E	0850	AMSTERDAM	1000	LEEDS	F100/BAE146	1234567	UK2113
13M	1830	AMSTERDAM	1930	STANSTED	F100/BAE146	1234567	UK2013
14E	0610	LEEDS	0720	AMSTERDAM	F-100	1234567	UK2114
14M	2040	STANSTED	2140	AMSTERDAM	F-100	12345 7	UK2014
15B	1500	HUMBERSIDE	1610	AMSTERDAM	F-100	12345 7	UK2110
15E	1320	AMSTERDAM	1430	LEEDS	F-100	1234567	UK2115
15K	2045	AMSTERDAM	2145	STANSTED	F-100	12345 7	UK2015
15Z	1045	ABERDEEN	1210	STANSTED	BAE-146	12345	UK2410
16E	1040	LEEDS	1150	AMSTERDAM	F100/BAE146	1234567	UK2116
16Z	1800	ABERDEEN	1930	STANSTED	BAE-146	12345 7	UK2416
17E	1840	AMSTERDAM	1950	LEEDS	F-100	1234567	UK2117
17Y	0905	LONDON CITY	1025	EDINBURGH	BAE-146	12345	UK2317
	1000	LONDON CITY	1120	EDINBURGH	BAE-146	6	
17Z	2005	STANSTED	2130	ABERDEEN	BAE-146	12345 7	UK2415
18E	1520	LEEDS	1635	AMSTERDAM	F-100	1234567	UK2118
18Y	0705	EDINBURGH	0835	LONDON CITY	BAE-146	12345	UK2318
	0810	EDINBURGH	0930	LONDON CITY	BAE-146	6	
19Z	1245	STANSTED	1405	GLASGOW	BAE-146	12345	UK2409
20Y	1100	EDINBURGH	1225	LONDON CITY	BAE-146	12345	UK2320
21C	0615	AMSTERDAM	0740	MANCHESTER	F-100	1234567	UK2021
21G	1200	GUERNSEY	1350	LEEDS	F-50	6	UK2541
21L	0635	AMSTERDAM	0735	LONDON CITY	BAE-146	1234 6	UK2221
21Y	1405	LONDON CITY	1525	EDINBURGH	BAE-146	12345	UK2321
	1645	LONDON CITY	1805	EDINBURGH	BAE-146	7	
22C	0825	MANCHESTER	0950	AMSTERDAM	F-100	1234567	UK2022
22G	1430	LEEDS	1620	GUERNSEY	F-50	6	UK2542
22L	0815	LONDON CITY	0925	AMSTERDAM	BAE-146	1234 6	UK2222
22Y	1450	EDINBURGH	1610	LONDON CITY	BAE-146	7	UK2322
23K	0835	AMSTERDAM	0935	NORWICH	ATR-72	1234567	UK2123
23L	1015	AMSTERDAM	1115	LONDON CITY	BAE-146	12345	UK2223
23Y	1830	LONDON CITY	1950	EDINBURGH	BAE-146	12345	UK2323
	2040	LONDON CITY	2200	EDINBURGH	BAE-146	7	
24C	1050	MANCHESTER	1215	AMSTERDAM	F100/BAE146	1234567	UK2024
24E	0620	NORWICH	0720	AMSTERDAM	ATR-72	1234567	UK2124
24L	1150	LONDON CITY	1255	AMSTERDAM	BAE-146	12345	UK2224
24Y	1630	EDINBURGH	1755	LONDON CITY	BAE-146	12345	UK2324
	1840	EDINBURGH	2005	LONDON CITY	BAE-146	7	
251	1135	BERGEN	1325	ABERDEEN	F-50	12345	UK2325
25C	1035	AMSTERDAM	1150	MANCHESTER	F-100	123456	UK2025
25L	1345	AMSTERDAM	1450	LONDON CITY	BAE-146	12345	UK2225
26A	0930	ABERDEEN	1105	BERGEN	F-50	12345	UK2326
26C	1225	MANCHESTER	1340	AMSTERDAM	F-100	123456	UK2026
26E	1010	NORWICH	1110	AMSTERDAM	ATR-72	1234567	UK2126
26L	1525	LONDON CITY	1625	AMSTERDAM	BAE-146	12345	UK2226
27A	1750	BERGEN	1930	ABERDEEN	F-50	7	UK2327
27C	1250	AMSTERDAM	1410	MANCHESTER	F-100	1234567	UK2027
27E	1250	AMSTERDAM	1350	NORWICH	ATR-72	1234567	UK2127
27L	1450	AMSTERDAM	1600	LONDON CITY	BAE-146	2345 7	UK2227
28A	1545	ABERDEEN	1720	BERGEN	F-50	7	UK2328
28C	1510	MANCHESTER	1625	AMSTERDAM	F-100	1234567	UK2028
28L	1630	LONDON CITY	1745	AMSTERDAM	BAE-146	2345 7	UK2228
29C	1530	AMSTERDAM	1645	MANCHESTER	F-100	12345 7	UK2029
29E	1700	AMSTERDAM	1800	NORWICH	ATR-72	12345	UK2129
	1830	AMSTERDAM	1930	NORWICH	ATR-72	67	
29L	1715	AMSTERDAM	1820	LONDON CITY	BAE-146	12345 7	UK2229
29M	1715	MILAN	1920	STANSTED	BAE-146	6	UK2309
30C	1740	MANCHESTER	1905	AMSTERDAM	F-100	12345 7	UK2030
30E	1525	NORWICH	1625	AMSTERDAM	ATR-72	1234567	UK2130
30L	1855	LONDON CITY	2000	AMSTERDAM	BAE-146	12345 7	UK2230
31C	1815	AMSTERDAM	1930	MANCHESTER	F-100	1234567	UK2031
31E	2010	AMSTERDAM	2110	NORWICH	ATR-72	12345	UK2131
32C	2010	MANCHESTER	2120	AMSTERDAM	F-100	12345 7	UK2032
32E	1835	NORWICH	1935	AMSTERDAM	ATR-72	12345	UK2132

32E	1835	NORWICH	1935	AMSTERDAM	ATR-72	12345	UK2132
32T	0705	ABERDEEN	0830	STAVANGER	F-50	12345	UK2332
33A	0630	AMSTERDAM	08155	NEWCASTLE	F-50	1234567	UK2133
33C	2020	AMSTERDAM	2135	MANCHESTER	F-100	12345 7	UK2033
33T	0900	STAVANGER	1035	ABERDEEN	F-50	12345	UK2333
34Z	0635	NEWCASTLE	0745	AMSTERDAM	F-100	1234567	UK2134
35T	1310	STAVANGER	1445	ABERDEEN	F-50	12345	UK2335
35Z	0835	AMSTERDAM	0950	NEWCASTLE	F-100	1234567	UK2135
36A	0850	NEWCASTLE	1025	AMSTERDAM	F-50	1234567	UK2136
36L	1215	EDINBURGH	1335	STANSTED	BAE-146	67	UK2362
36M	0715	MILAN	0920	STANSTED	F-100	67	UK2306
36T	1115	ABERDEEN	1240	STAVANGER	F-50	12345	UK2336
37Z	1300	AMSTERDAM	1420	NEWCASTLE	F-100	1234567	UK2137
385T	1630	ABERDEEN	1755	STAVANGER	F-50	12345 7	UK2338
38A	1035	NEWCASTLE	1155	AMSTERDAM	F-100	1234567	UK2138
38E	0855	EDINBURGH	1015	STANSTED	BAE-146	123456	UK2358
39A	1530	AMSTERDAM	1715	NEWCASTLE	F-50	12345 7	UK2139
39R	0715	STANSTED	0835	NEWCASTLE	F-50	12345	UK2399
39T	1825	STAVANGER	2000	ABERDEEN	F-50	12345 7	UK2339
40D	0610	BIRMINGHAM	0725	AMSTERDAM	F-100	1234567	UK2040
41B	0625	AMSTERDAM	0740	BIRMINGHAM	BAE146/F100	12345 7	UK2041
41R	1155	STANSTED	1315	NEWCASTLE	F-50	12345	UK2401
41T	0630	NORWICH	0820	ABERDEEN	F-50	12345	UK2341
41Z	1830	AMSTERDAM	1945	NEWCASTLE	F-100	1234567	UK2141
42A	1805	NEWCASTLE	1940	AMSTERDAM	F-50	12345 7	UK2142
42B	0815	BIRMINGHAM	0930	AMSTERDAM	BAE146/F100	12345 7	UK2042
42N	0720	ABERDEEN	0905	NORWICH	F-50	12345	UK2342
42R	0910	NEWCASTLE	1030	STANSTED	F-50	12345	UK2402
42Z	1505	NEWCASTLE	1625	AMSTERDAM	F-100	1234567	UK2140
43D	0830	AMSTERDAM	0940	BIRMINGHAM	F-100	1234567	UK2043
43G	0845	LONDON CITY	0950	MANCHESTER	F-50	12345	UK2443
43N	1630	NORWICH	1815	ABERDEEN	F-50	7	UK2343
43R	1630	STANSTED	1750	NEWCASTLE	F-50	12345 7	UK2403
44D	1035	BIRMINGHAM	1150	AMSTERDAM	F-100	1234567	UK2044
44G	0655	MANCHESTER	0805	LONDON CITY	F-50	12345	UK2444
44N	1515	ABERDEEN	1700	NORWICH	F-50	12345	UK2344
44R	1400	NEWCASTLE	1520	STANSTED	F-50	12345	UK2404
45A	0830	AMSTERDAM	0945	TEESSIDE	F-100	1234567	UK2145
45D	1250	AMSTERDAM	1415	BIRMINGHAM	F-100	1234567	UK2045
45N	1530	NORWICH	1715	ABERDEEN	F-50	12345	UK2345
46A	0730	TEESSIDE	0730	AMSTERDAM	F-100	1234567	UK2146
46D	1500	BIRMINGHAM	1620	AMSTERDAM	F-100	1234567	UK2046
46G	1025	MANCHESTER	1135	LONDON CITY	F-50	12345	UK2446
46R	1825	NEWCASTLE	1945	STANSTED	F-50	12345 7	UK2406
47A	1320	AMSTERDAM	1435	TEESSIDE	F-100	1234567	UK2147
47D	1705	AMSTERDAM	1820	BIRMINGHAM	F-100	123456	UK2047
47G	1515	LONDON CITY	1620	MANCHESTER	F-50	12345	UK2449
47N	1740	NORWICH	1930	ABERDEEN	F-50	12345	UK2347
48A	1040	TEESSIDE	1150	AMSTERDAM	F-100	1234567	UK2148
48D	1900	BIRMINGHAM	2020	AMSTERDAM	F-100	12345	UK2048
48N	1930	ABERDEEN	2115	NORWICH	F-50	12345 7	UK2348
49A	1845	AMSTERDAM	2000	TEESSIDE	F-100	12345 7	UK2149
49D	1820	AMSTERDAM	1940	BIRMINGHAM	F-100	1234567	UK2049
49L	1030	ROME	1315	STANSTED	F-100	1234567	UK2349
50A	1525	TEESSIDE	1635	AMSTERDAM	F-100	12345 7	UK2150
50D	2020	AMSTERDAM	2140	BIRMINGHAM	F-100	1234567	UK2050
51A	0850	BRUSSELS	1010	STANSTED	F-50	123456	UK2251
51D	2100	AMSTERDAM	2210	BIRMINGHAM	F-100	12345 7	UK2051
	1900	AMSTERDAM	2010	BIRMINGHAM	F-100	7	
51G	1840	LONDON CITY	1955	MANCHESTER	F-50	12345 7	UK2451
51M	0615	AMSTERDAM	0715	STANSTED	F-100	123456	UK2001
51V	1000	MILAN	1220	STANSTED	F-100	12345	UK2301
52A	0700	STANSTED	0820	BRUSSELS	F-50	123456	UK2252
52G	1700	MANCHESTER	1810	LONDON CITY	F-50	12345 7	UK2452
52M	0840	STANSTED	0940	AMSTERDAM	F-100	12345	UK2002
52V	1310	STANSTED	1510	MILAN	F-100	1234567	UK2302
53A	1255	BRUSSELS	1410	STANSTED	F-50	12345	UK2253
53B	0840	AMSTERDAM	0950	HUMBERSIDE	F-100	1234567	UK2103

53L	1755	ROME	2040	STANSTED	F-100	1234567	UK2353
53V	1550	MILAN	1810	STANSTED	F-100	1234567	UK2303
54A	1040	STANSTED	1150	BRUSSELS	F-50	12345	UK2254
54G	1050	STANSTED	1150	AMSTERDAM	BAE146/F100	1234567	UK2004
54L	1420	STANSTED	1710	ROME	F-100	1234567	UK2354
54V	1700	STANSTED	1900	MILAN	F-100	12345 7	UK2304
55A	1640	BRUSSELS	1755	STANSTED	F-50	12345 7	UK2255
55C	0710	JERSEY	0800	SOUTHAMPTON	ATR-72	123456	UK2455
	0830	JERSEY	0920	SOUTHAMPTON	ATR-72	7	
55E	0840	AMSTERDAM	1615	BELFAST INT.	F-100	1234567	UK2155
55H	1130	JERSEY	1305	HUMBERSIDE	ATR-72	6	UK2505
55K	0650	STANSTED	0810	EDINBURGH	BAE-146	12345	UK2355
55M	1040	AMSTERDAM	1140	STANSTED	F-100	12345	UK2005
	1020	AMSTERDAM	1120	STANSTED	F-100	7	
55V	0720	STANSTED	0930	MILAN	F-100	12345	UK2300
56A	1455	STANSTED	1610	BRUSSELS	F-50	12345 7	UK2256
56B	1030	HUMBERSIDE	1145	AMSTERDAM	F-100	1234567	UK2106
56C	0835	SOUTHAMPTON	0925	JERSEY	ATR-72	123456	UK2456
	0955	SOUTHAMPTON	1045	JERSEY	ATR-72	7	
56E	0610	BELFAST INT.	0750	AMSTERDAM	F-100	1234567	UK2156
56H	1345	HUMBERSIDE	1525	JERSEY	ATR-72	6	UK2506
56L	0630	EDINBURGH	0750	STANSTED	BAE-146	12345	UK2356
56M	1240	STANSTED	1340	AMSTERDAM	F100/BAE146	1234567	UK2006
57C	1000	JERSEY	1050	SOUTHAMPTON	ATR-72	123456	UK2457
57L	1320	AMSTERDAM	1500	BELFAST INT.	F-100	1234567	UK2157
57Z	0840	STANSTED	1010	ABERDEEN	BAE-146	12345	UK2407
	1020	STANSTED	1150	ABERDEEN	BAE-146	6	
58C	1125	SOUTHAMPTON	1215	JERSEY	ATR-72	123456	UK2458
58E	1055	BELFAST INT.	1230	AMSTERDAM	F-100	1234567	UK2158
58Z	0630	ABERDEEN	0805	STANSTED	BAE-146	12345	UK2408
	0800	ABERDEEN	0935	STANSTED	BAE-146	6	
59B	0630	HUMBERSIDE	0735	AMSTERDAM	F-100	1234567	UK2104
59E	1845	AMSTERDAM	2025	BELFAST INT.	F-100	12345 7	UK2159
59K	2015	BRUSSELS	2125	STANSTED	F-50	12345 7	UK2259
59L	0840	STANSTED	1000	EDINBURGH	F100/BAE146	123456	UK2359
59M	1440	AMSTERDAM	1540	STANSTED	F100/BAE146	123456	UK2009
60L	1535	BELFAST INT.	1710	AMSTERDAM	F-100	12345 7	UK2160
61A	1830	STANSTED	1945	BRUSSELS	F-50	12345 7	UK2260
61E	1100	STANSTED	1220	EDINBURGH	F100/BAE146	1234567	UK2361
61Z	0630	AMSTERDAM	0815	ABERDEEN	F-100	1234567	UK2061
62L	1040	EDINBURGH	1200	STANSTED	F100/BAE146	1234567	UK2360
62M	0620	ABERDEEN	0805	AMSTERDAM	BAE-146	123456	UK2060
	0650	ABERDEEN	0825	AMSTERDAM	BAE-146	7	
62Z	0910	ABERDEEN	1055	AMSTERDAM	F-100	1234567	UK2062
63L	1240	STANSTED	1400	EDINBURGH	BAE-146	12345 7	UK2363
63M	0920	AMSTERDAM	1100	ABERDEEN	BAE-146	1234567	UK2063
64C	1415	SOUTHAMPTON	1505	JERSEY	ATR-72	1234567	UK2464
64E	1300	EDINBURGH	1420	STANSTED	F100/BAE146	1234567	UK2364
64Z	1550	ABERDEEN	1725	AMSTERDAM	BAE-146	1234567	UK2064
65C	1250	JERSEY	1340	SOUTHAMPTON	ATR-72	1234567	UK2465
65E	1500	STANSTED	1620	EDINBURGH	BAE-146	123456	UK2365
65M	1325	AMSTERDAM	1500	ABERDEEN	BAE146/F100	1234567	UK2065
65V	1940	MILAN	2150	STANSTED	F-100	12345 7	UK2305
66L	1440	EDINBURGH	1600	STANSTED	BAE-146	12345 7	UK2366
66M	1745	ABERDEEN	1920	AMSTERDAM	BAE146/F100	1234567	UK2066
67C	1725	JERSEY	1810	SOUTHAMPTON	F-100	6	UK2467
67L	1700	STANSTED	1820	EDINBURGH	BAE-146	12345 7	UK2367
67M	1245	AMSTERDAM	1345	STANSTED	F-100	1234567	UK2007
67Z	1645	AMSTERDAM	2020	ABERDEEN	BAE-146	1234567	UK2067
68C	1850	SOUTHAMPTON	1935	JERSEY	F-100	6	UK2468
68E	1700	EDINBURGH	1820	STANSTED	BAE-146	12345	UK2368
68G	0640	STANSTED	0740	AMSTERDAM	F-100	1234567	UK2000
68K	0700	STANSTED	0940	ROME	F-100	1234567	UK2350
68M	1430	STANSTED	1530	AMSTERDAM	F-100	12345 7	UK2008
69E	1900	STANSTED	2020	EDINBURGH	BAE-146	12345 7	UK2369
71G	2130	STANSTED	2245	EDINBURGH	BAE-146	5	UK2371
71J	1040	JERSEY	1130	SOUTHAMPTON	ATR-72	7	UK2471
72C	1705	SOUTHAMPTON	1755	JERSEY	ATR-72	1234567	UK2472

72H	0620	EDINBURGH	0755	AMSTERDAM	BAE-146	1234567	UK2072
73C	1540	JERSEY	1630	SOUTHAMPTON	ATR-72	1234567	UK2473
73H	1020	AMSTERDAM	1155	EDINBURGH	BAE-146	12345	UK2073
73L	2010	STANSTED	2130	EDINBURGH	BAE-146	6	UK2373
74C	1955	SOUTHAMPTON	2045	JERSEY	ATR-72	1234567	UK2474
74H	1230	EDINBURGH	1405	AMSTERDAM	BAE-146	12345	UK2074
75B	0825	STANSTED	0940	GLASGOW	BAE146/F100	123456	UK2375
	1030	STANSTED	1150	GLASGOW	F-100	7	
75H	0810	AMSTERDAM	0945	EDINBURGH	F100/BAE146	123456	UK2075
	0850	AMSTERDAM	1025	EDINBURGH	F100	7	
75W	0615	MANCHESTER	0735	AMSTERDAM	F-100	1234567	UK2020
76B	0630	GLASGOW	0750	STANSTED	BAE-146	123456	UK2376
	0830	GLASGOW	0950	STANSTED	BAE-146	7	
76H	1025	EDINBURGH	1205	AMSTERDAM	F100/BAE146	1234567	UK2076
76J	1205	SOUTHAMPTON	1250	JERSEY	ATR-72	7	UK2476
77B	1310	AMSTERDAM	1420	HUMBERSIDE	F-100	1234567	UK2107
77C	1830	JERSEY	1920	SOUTHAMPTON	ATR-72	1234567	UK2475
77H	1315	AMSTERDAM	1445	EDINBURGH	BAE146/F100	1234567	UK20775
77L	1900	EDINBURGH	2020	STANSTED	BAE-146	12345 7	UK2370
77M	1000	MILAN	1220	STANSTED	F-100	67	UK2307
78H	1535	EDINBURGH	1710	AMSTERDAM	BAE146/F100	1234567	UK2078
78M	1425	STANSTED	1425	MILAN	BAE-146	6	UK2308
79H	1835	AMSTERDAM	2010	EDINBURGH	BAE-146	1234567	UK2079
80B	1020	GLASGOW	1140	STANSTED	BAE146/F100	123456	UK2380
	1230	GLASGOW	1350	STANSTED	F-100	7	
81H	1500	AMSTERDAM	1640	EDINBURGH	F-100	6	UK2081
81L	0855	DUSSELDORF	1040	STANSTED	ATR-72	123456	UK2281
81S	0830	AMSTERDAM	1000	SHEFFIELD	F-50	123456	UK2181
82H	1830	EDINBURGH	2000	AMSTERDAM	F-100	12345 7	UK2082
82S	0630	SHEFFIELD	0800	AMSTERDAM	F-50	123456	UK2182
83B	1220	STANSTED	1340	GLASGOW	BAE-146	123456	UK2383
	1430	STANSTED	1550	GLASGOW	BAE146/F100	67	1550/1710 6
83H	1620	AMSTERDAM	1750	EDINBURGH	F-100	12345 7	UK2083
83L	0635	STANSTED	0810	DUSSELDORF	ATR-72	123456	UK2280
83M	0845	AMSTERDAM	0945	STANSTED	BAE146/F100	1234567	UK2003
83S	1310	AMSTERDAM	1450	SHEFFIELD	F-50	1234567	UK2183
84L	1140	STANSTED	1330	DUSSELDORF	ATR-72	1234567	UK2284
84S	1030	SHEFFIELD	1200	AMSTERDAM	F-50	1234567	UK2184
85L	1405	DUSSELDORF	1545	STANSTED	ATR-72	1234567	UK2285
85S	1840	AMSTERDAM	2015	SHEFFIELD	F-50	12345 7	UK2185
85T	0700	JERSEY	0815	STANSTED	ATR-72	12345	UK2485
	0740	JERSEY	0855	STANSTED	ATR-72	6	
86L	1620	STANSTED	1800	DUSSELDORF	ATR-72	12345 7	UK2286
86S	1530	SHEFFIELD	1700	AMSTERDAM	F-50	12345 7	UK2186
86T	0700	STANSTED	0800	JERSEY	F100/BAE146	6	UK2486
	1230	STANSTED	1330	JERSEY	F-100	6	
87B	1610	STANSTED	1730	GLASGOW	BAE-146	12345 7	UK2387
87L	1835	DUSSELDORF	2020	STANSTED	ATR-72	12345 7	UK2287
87T	0840	JERSEY	0940	STANSTED	F-100	7	UK2487
88B	1415	GLASGOW	1535	STANSTED	BAE146/F100	12345	UK2388
	1630	GLASGOW	1750	STANSTED	F-100	7	
88H	1730	EDINBURGH	1905	AMSTERDAM	F-100	6	UK2080
88T	0900	STANSTED	1015	JERSEY	ATR-72	12345	UK2488
	0930	STANSTED	1045	JERSEY	ATR-72	6	
89B	2010	STANSTED	2130	GLASGOW	BAE-146	12345 7	UK2389
89T	1230	JERSEY	1345	STANSTED	ATR-72	12345	UK2489
	1325	JERSEY	1440	STANSTED	ATR-72	7	
90B	1805	GLASGOW	1930	STANSTED	BAE-146	12345 7	UK2390
90J	1050	STANSTED	1205	JERSEY	F-50	6	UK2490
91A	0910	FRANKFURT	1105	STANSTED	F-100	123456	UK2291
91G	1745	JERSEY	1905	STANSTED	F-50	6	UK2491
91L	0820	AMSTERDAM	1005	GLASGOW	F-100	1234567	UK2091
92A	1205	STANSTED	1340	FRANKFURT	F-100	1234567	UK2292
92J	0830	STANSTED	0930	JERSEY	F-100	6	UK2492
92L	0610	GLASGOW	0750	AMSTERDAM	BAE-146	1234567	UK2092
93A	1420	FRANKFURT	1600	STANSTED	F-100	1234567	UK2293
93C	0840	AMSTERDAM	1000	MANCHESTER	F100/BAE146	1234567	UK2023
93L	1305	AMSTERDAM	1450	GLASGOW	BAE-146	1234567	UK2093

93T	1725	JERSEY	1840	STANSTED	ATR-72	1234567	UK2493
94A	1635	STANSTED	1810	FRANKFURT	F-100	12345 7	UK2294
94L	1045	GLASGOW	1225	AMSTERDAM	F-100	1234567	UK2094
94T	1515	STANSTED	1630	JERSEY	ATR-72	12345 7	UK2494
95A	1850	FRANKFURT	2030	STANSTED	F-100	12345 7	UK2295
95J	2015	JERSEY	2115	STANSTED	F-100	6	UK2495
96A	0655	STANSTED	0835	FRANKFURT	F-100	123456	UK2290
96L	1530	GLASGOW	1715	AMSTERDAM	BAE-146	1234567	UK2096
96T	1915	STANSTED	2030	JERSEY	ATR-72	1234567	UK2496
97L	1835	AMSTERDAM	2020	GLASGOW	F100/BAE146	1234567	UK2097
97T	1410	JERSEY	1510	STANSTED	BAE-146	6	UK2497
99B	2030	AMSTERDAM	2135	HUMBERSIDE	F-100	12345 7	UK2109
269	0850	PARIS CDG	1010	STANSTED	ATR-72	1234567	UK2269
271	1240	PARIS CDG	1405	STANSTED	ATR-72	1234567	UK2271
272	0655	STANSTED	0820	PARIS CDG	ATR-72	1234567	UK2272
274	1045	STANSTED	1205	PARIS CDG	ATR-72	1234567	UK2274
275	1625	PARIS CDG	1745	STANSTED	ATR-72	1234567	UK2275
276	1440	STANSTED	1555	PARIS CDG	ATR-72	1234567	UK2276
277	2005	PARIS CDG	2130	STANSTED	ATR-72	1234567	UK2277
278	1815	STANSTED	1935	PARIS CDG	ATR-72	1234567	UK2278
603		GUERNSEY	0955	NORWICH	ATR-72	6	-18.09
604	1125	NORWICH		GUERNSEY	ATR-72	6	-18.09
608		JERSEY	1505	NORWICH	BAE-146	6	-25.09
609	1545	NORWICH		JERSEY	BAE-146	6	-25.09
611	0700	STANSTED		CALVI	BAE-146	7	
613	1515	STANSTED		ALICANTE	BAE-146	6	
614		ALICANTE	2055	STANSTED	BAE-146	6	
617	1700	STANSTED		ALICANTE	F-100	6	
618		ALICANTE	2255	STANSTED	F-100	6	
638		JERSEY	1455	TEESSIDE	F-50	6	
639	1530	TEESSIDE		JERSEY	F-50	6	
753		NORWICH	2230	GLASGOW	BAE-146	1	
754	2105	STANSTED		AMSTERDAM	BAE-146	5	
756	2100	GLASGOW		AMSTERDAM	F-100	1	

UNITED   *UNITED AIRLINES*   *UA/UAL*   *U.S.A.*

904		NEW YORK	0905	HEATHROW	B.767	1234567	
905	1355	HEATHROW		NEW YORK	B.767	1234567	
906		NEW YORK	0725	HEATHROW	B.777	1234567	
907	0955	HEATHROW		NEW YORK	B.777	1234567	
911	1600	PARIS CDG		WASHINGTON	B.777	1234567	
912		WASHINGTON	0955	PARIS CDG	B.777	1234567	
914		WASHINGTON	0615	PARIS	B.777	1234567	
915	1200	PARIS		WASHINGTON	B.777	1234567	
916		WASHINGTON	0615	FRANKFURT	B.747	1234567	
917	1135	FRANKFURT		WASHINGTON	B.747	1234567	
918		WASHINGTON	0555	HEATHROW	B.777	1234567	
	0640	HEATHROW	0750	AMSTERDAM	B.767	1 56	0740/0850 6
919	1250	HEATHROW		WASHINGTON	B.777	1234567	
920		WASHINGTON	0730	HEATHROW	B.777	1234567	
921	1125	HEATHROW		WASHINGTON	B.747	1234567	
924		WASHINGTON	0955	HEATHROW	B.777	1234567	
925	1640	HEATHROW		WASHINGTON	B.777	1234567	
928		WASHINGTON	0655	HEATHROW	B.777	1234567	
929	1055	HEATHROW		CHICAGO	B.777	1234567	
930		SAN FRANCISCO	0625	HEATHROW	B.777	1234567	
	0755	HEATHROW	0900	BRUSSELS	B.767	1234567	
931	1100	BRUSSELS	1205	HEATHROW	B.767	1234567	
	1445	HEATHROW		SAN FRANCISCO	B.777	1234567	
933	0930	HATHROW		LOS ANGELES	B.777	1234567	
934		LOS ANGELES	1245	HEATHROW	B.777	1234567	
935	1000	AMSTERDAM	1100	HEATHROW	B.767	4 7	
	1155	HEATHROW		LOS ANGELES	B.777	1234567	
936		LOS ANGELES	0710	HEATHROW	B.777	1234567	
938		CHICAGO	1040	HEATHROW	B.777	1234567	
939	0755	HEATHROW		CHICAGO	B.777	1234567	
940		CHICAGO	1105	FRANKFURT	B.777	1234567	

941	1255	FRANKFURT		CHICAGO	B.777	1234567	
942		CHICAGO	0730	PARIS	B.777	1234567	
943	1100	PARIS		CHICAGO	B.777	1234567	
944		CHICAGO	0500	FRANKFURT	B.777	1234567	
945	0740	FRANKFURT		CHICAGO	B.777	1234567	
946		WASHINGTON	0605	AMSTERDAM	B.777	1234567	
947	1130	AMSTERDAM		WASHINGTON	B.777	1234567	
950		WASHINGTON	0625	BRUSSELS	B.767	1234567	
951	1145	BRUSSELS		WASHINGTON	B.767	1234567	
952		CHICAGO	1105	DUSSELDORF	B.767	1234567	
953	1445	DUSSELDORF		CHICAGO	B.767	1234567	
954		SAN FRANCISCO	1125	HEATHROW	B.777	1234567	
955	0855	HEATHROW		SAN FRANCISCO	B.777	1234567	
956		NEW YORK	0655	HEATHROW	B.767	1234567	
957	0855	HEATHROW		NEW YORK	B.767	1234567	
958		CHICAGO	0855	HEATHROW	B.777	1234567	
959	1100	AMSTERDAM	1205	HEATHROW	B.767	1234567	1200/1310 2
	1355	HEATHROW		CHICAGO	B.777	1234567	
960		SAN FRANCISCO	0900	PARIS	B.777	1234567	
961	1010	PARIS CDG		SAN FRANCISCO	B.777	1234567	
962		WASHINGTON	0655	MUNICH	B.767	1234567	
963	1110	MUNICH		WASHINGTON	B.767	1234567	
970		WASHINGTON	0640	MILAN	B.767	1234567	
971	1050	MILAN		WASHINGTON	B.767	1234567	
976		NEW YORK	2115	HEATHROW	B.767	1234567	
977	1610	FRANKFURT		WASHINGTON	B.747	1234567	
978		WASHINGTON	1025	FRANKFURT	B.777	1234567	
979 ●	1800	HEATHROW		NEW YORK	B.767	1234567	
998		BOSTON	0625	HEATHROW	B.767	1234567	
999	1040	HEATHROW		BOSTON	B.767	1234567	

		UPS		*UNITED PARCEL SERVICE CO.*		*5X/UPS*	*U.S.A.*	
6070	2220	STANSTED	2345	COLOGNE	B.767	5	
6077		PHILADELPHIA	2050	COLOGNE	B.747	2345	
6080	0200	COLOGNE		PHILADELPHIA	B.747	23456	DEP 0300 6
6083		PHILADELPHIA	2030	PARIS CDG	B.767	2345	
6084	0530	PARIS CDG		PHILADELPHIA	B.767	23456	
6570	0205	COLOGNE	0330	STANSTED	B.767	12345	0045/0210 1
6571		PHILADELPHIA	2010	EAST MIDLANDS	B.767	2345 7	ARR 2300 7
	2230	EAST MIDLANDS	2350	COLOGNE	B.767	2345	
6572	0215	COLOGNE	0330	EAST MIDLANDS	B.767	23456	
	2045	EAST MIDLANDS		LOUISVILLE	B.767	1234	

		U.S.AIR		*U.S. AIR*	*US/USA*	*U.S.A.*	
2		PHILADELPHIA	0840	ROME	B.767	1234567	
3	1110	ROME		PHILADELPHIA	B.767	1234567	
14		PHILADELPHIA	0700	MUNICH	B.767	1234567	
15	1135	MUNICH		PHILADELPHIA	B.767	1234567	
16		PHILADELPHIA	0830	PARIS CDG	B.767	1234567	
23	1145	PARIS CDG		PHILADELPHIA	B.767	1234567	
42		PHILADELPHIA	0845	AMSTERDAM	B.767	1234567	
43	1120	AMSTERDAM		PHILADELPHIA	B.767	1234567	
48		PITTSBURG	0655	PARIS CDG	B.767	1234567	
49	1115	PARIS CDG		PITTSBURG	B.767	1234567	
94R		CHARLOTTE	0755	GATWICK	B.767	1234567	
95R	1115	GATWICK		CHARLOTTE	B.767	1234567	
98		PHILADELPHIA	0555	GATWICK	B.767	1234567	
99	1225	GATWICK		PHILADELPHIA	B.767	1234567	
126		PHILAPELPHIA	1030	GATWICK	B.767	1234567	ARR 0930 4
127	1115	GATWICK		PHILADELPHIA	B.767	1234567	
730		BOSTON	0725	HEATHROW	B.767	1234567	
731	1420	HEATHROW		BOSTON	B.767	1234567	
732		CHARLOTTE	0755	HEATHROW	B.767	1234567	
733	1055	HEATHROW		CHARLOTTE	B.767	1234567	
734		PHILADELPHIA	0615	HEATHROW	B,767	1234567	
735	1045	HEATHROW		PHILADELPHIA	B.767	1234567	

736		PHILADELPHIA	0810	HEATHROW	B.767	1234567
737	1210	HEATHROW		PHILADELPHIA	B.767	1234567
738		PITTSBURG	0600	HEATHROW	B.767	1234567
739	1135	HEATHROW		PITTSBURG	B.767	1234567
781	1025	FRANKFURT		PITTSBURGH	B.767	1234567
782		PITTSBURGH	0600	FRANKFURT	B.767	1234567
893	1120	FRANKFURT		PHILADELPHIA	B.767	1234567
894		PHILADELPHIA	0850	FRANKFURT	B.767	1234567

UZBEK   *UZBEKISTAN AIRWAYS   HY/UZB   UZBEKISTAN*

235	1330	TASHKENT	2000	HEATHROW	B.767	23 567	ARR	1400	6
236	2130	HEATHROW	0520	TASHKENT	B.767	23 567	DEP	1530	6

VARIG   *VARIG   RG/VRG   BRAZIL*

756		SAO PAULO	1320	HEATHROW	MD-11	3 5 7
	1415	HEATHROW	1615	COPENHAGEN	MD-11	3 5 7
757	1905	COPENHAGEN	2100	HEATHROW	MD-11	3 5 7
	2200	HEATHROW		SAO PAULO	MD-11	3 5 7
760		RIO DE JANEIRO	1325	HEATHROW	MD-11	6
761	2200	HEATHROW		RIO DE JANEIRO	MD-11	4
762		SAO PAULO	1335	HEATHROW	MD-11	4
763	2200	HEATHROW		SAO PAULO	MD-11	6

VARNA AIR   *AIR VIA BULGARIAN AIRLINES   VIM   BULGARIA*

EVEN NUMBERS - FLIGHTS LEAVING THE U.K.   UNEVEN NUMBERS - FLIGHTS INTO THE U.K.

??	1640	CARDIFF	1540	BOURGAS	TU-154	7	23.05-26.09
101/2	??	LIVERPOOL	??	BOURGAS	TU-154	1	
105/6	0810	PRESTWICK	0710	VARNA	TU-154	1	
111/2	1755	MANCHESTER	1655	BOURGAS	TU-154	1	31.05-20.09
123/4	0640	EDINBURGH	0540	BOURGAS	TU-154	1	31.05-20.09
603/4	1630	EAST MIDLANDS	1530	VARNA	TU-154	6	22.05-25.09
607/8	0930	MANCHESTER	0725	VARNA	TU-154	6	
609/0	0800	BIRMINGHAM	0700	VARNA	TU-154	6	
621/2	1700	GATWICK	1600	VARNA	TU-154	6	
623/4	1710	EDINBURGH	1610	VARNA	TU-154	6	22.05-25.09
701/2	1115	GATWICK	0945	BOURGAS	TU-154	7	
703/4	1830	EAST MIDLANDS	1730	BOURGAS	TU-154	7	23.05-26.09
705/6	1640	CARDIFF	1540	BOURGAS	TU-154	7	23.05-26.09
711/2	1810	MANCHESTER	1710	BOURGAS	TU-154	7	
719/0	0830	GLASGOW	0730	BOURGAS	TU-154	7	
721/2	0830	BIRMINGHAM	0725	BOURGAS	TU-154	7	
723/4	0815	LEEDS	0715	BOURGAS	TU-154	7	

VIKING   *PREMIAIR .   DK/VKG   DENMARK*

71		STOCKHOLM	2035	STANSTED	DC-10	4	-10.06 / 02.09-
72	2205	STANSTED		STOCKHOLM	DC-10	4	-10.06 / 02.09-
75		STOCKHOLM	2020	STANSTED	DC-9	7	-13.06 / 05.09-
		STOCKHOLM	1820	STANSTED	A.320	7	20.06-29.09
76	2200	STANSTED		STOCKHOLM	DC-9	7	-13.06 / 05.09-
	1945	STANSTED		STOCKHOLM	A.320	7	20.06-29.08
495		COPENHAGEN	1510	STANSTED	A.320	4	
496	1635	STANSTED		COPENHAGEN	A.320	4	
497		COPENHAGEN	1520	STANSTED	A.320	7	-06.06 / 05.09-
498	1635	STANSTED		COPENHAGEN	A.320	7	-06.06 / 05.09-
888	2100	STANSTED		OSLO	A.320	4	23.09-
889		OSLO	1930	STANSTED	A.320	7	12.09-
890	2100	STANSTED		OSLO	A.320	7	12.09-

VIRGIN   *VIRGIN ATLANTIC AIRWAYS   VS/VIR   U.K.*

001	1600	HEATHROW	0905	NEW YORK	B.747	1234567
002		NEW YORK	0905	HEATHROW	B.747	1234567
003	1400	HEATHROW		NEW YORK	B.747	1234567
004		NEW YORK	0710	HEATHROW	B.747	1234567
005	1030	HEATHROW		MIAMI	B.747	1234567

Flight					Aircraft	Days	Notes
006		MIAMI	0655	HEATHROW	B.747	1234567	
007	1200	HEATHROW		LOS ANGELES	B.747	1234567	
008		LOS ANGELES	1145	HEATHROW	B.747	1234567	
009	1835	HEATHROW		NEW YORK	A.340	1234567	
010		NEW YORK	1050	HEATHROW	A.340	1234567	
011	1115	GATWICK		BOSTON	B.747	1234567	
012		BOSTON	0750	GATWICK	B.747	1234567	
015	1230	GATWICK		ORLANDO	B.747	1234567	
016		ORLANDO	0815	GATWICK	B.747	1234567	
017	1300	GATWICK		NEW YORK	B.747	1234567	
018		NEW YORK	0610	GATWICK	B.747	1234567	
019	1100	HEATHROW		SAN FRANCISCO	B.747	1234567	
020		SAN FRANCISCO	1030	HEATHROW	B.747	1234567	
021	1130	HEATHROW		WASHINGTON	A340/B747	1234567	
022		WASHINGTON	0705	HEATHROW	A340/B747	1234567	
023	1505	HEATHROW		LOS ANGELES	A.340	1234567	
024		LOS ANGELES	1535	HEATHROW	A.340	1234567	
025	2130	HEATHROW		NEW YORK	A.340	234567	08.06-
026		NEW YORK	2200	HEATHROW	A.340	1 34567	07.06-
027	1400	GATWICK		ORLANDO	B.747	1234567	
028		ORLANDO	0940	GATWICK	B.747	1234567	ARR 1015 2
029	1045	GATWICK		BRIDGETOWN	B.747	1 4 6	
030		BRIDGETOWN	0630	GATWICK	B.747	2 4 7	
031	1045	GATWICK		ST. LUCIA	B.747	7	
032		ST. LUCIA	0630	GATWICK	B.747	1	
033	1045	GATWICK		ANTIGUA	B.747	3 5	DEP 1130 5
034		ANTIGUA	0630	GATWICK	B.747	4 6	ARR 1030 6
037	0640	HEATHROW		MOSCOW	A.340	1234567	DEP 0750 4-7
038		MOSCOW	1650	HEATHROW	A.340	1234567	ARR 1725 1346
039	1500	GATWICK		NEW YORK	A.340	1234567	
040		NEW YORK	0630	GATWICK	A.340	1234567	
051	1100	GATWICK		NEW YORK	B.747	1234567	
052		NEW YORK	0810	GATWICK	B.747	1234567	
053	1130	GATWICK		SAN FRANCISCO	B.747	1234567	DEP 1030 6
054		SAN FRANCISCO	0915	GATWICK	B.747	1234567	ARR 1015 7
055	1430	GATWICK		LAS VEGAS	B.747	4567	
056		LAS VEGAS	1400	GATWICK	B.747	1 567	
069	1130	GATWICK		BOSTON	B.747	1234567	
070		BOSTON	0750	GATWICK	B.747	1234567	
075	1030	MANCHESTER		ORLANDO	B.747	234567	
076		ORLANDO	0620	MANCHESTER	B.747	1 34567	
200	2100	HEATHROW		HONG KONG	A.340	1234567	
201		HONG KONG	0555	HEATHROW	A.340	1234567	
250	1615	HEATHROW		SHANGHAI	A.340	1 6	
251		SHANGHAI	1750	HEATHROW	A.340	2 7	
501	2200	HEATHROW		KUALA LUMPUR	B.747	1 5	
502		KUALA LUMPUR	0605	HEATHROW	B.747	1 4	
503	1200	HEATHROW		KUALA LUMPUR	B.747	4	
504		KUALA LUMPUR	1710	HEATHROW	B.747	5	
601	2115	HEATHROW		JOHANNESBURG	A.340	1234567	
602		JOHANNESBURG	0635	HEATHROW	A.340	1234567	
603	1715	HEATHROW		CAPE TOWN	A.340	5 7	
604		CAPE TOWN	1930	HEATHROW	A.340	1 6	
900	1300	HEATHROW		TOKYO	A.340	1234567	DEP 1150 3
901		TOKYO	1605	HEATHROW	A.340	1234567	
1000	2115	HEATHROW		ATHENS	A.320	1234567	
1001	1600	ATHENS	2000	HEATHROW	A.320	1 34567	0800/1200 2
1002	1100	GATWICK	1445	ATHENS	A.320	1 34567	
1003	0545	ATHENS	0945	GATWICK	A.320	1 34567	
1005	0800	ATHENS	1200	HEATHROW	A.320	2	
6150		KUALA LUMPUR	1630	HEATHROW	MD-11	3	
6151	2155	HEATHROW		KUALA LUMPUR	MD-11	3	

UNEVEN NUMBERS - FLIGHTS LEAVING THE UK   EVEN NUMBERS - FLIGHTS INTO THE UK

6103/4	0640	GATWICK	1550	LAS PALMAS	A.320		1
6105/6	1700	GATWICK	0015	CORFU	A.320		1
6203/4	0600	GATWICK	1500	HERAKLION	A.320		2
6205/6	1600	GATWICK	2220	MALAGA	A.320		2

6207/8	2330	GATWICK	0520	PALMA	A.320	2	
6303/4	0640	GATWICK	1415	KAVALA	A.320	3	
6305/6	1640	GATWICK	2240	IBIZA	A.320	3	
6403/4	0610	GATWICK	1230	MAHON	A.320	4	
6405/6	1255	GATWICK	1930	FARO	A.320	4	
6407/8	2030	GATWICK	0530	RHODES	A.320	4	
6503/4	0555	GATWICK	1530	TENERIFE	A.320	5	
6505/6	2030	GATWICK	0530	HERAKLION	A.320	5	
6515/05	2120	MANCHESTER	0705	BODRUM	A.320	6	
6603/4	0630	GATWICK	1220	ALICANTE	A.320	6	
6605/6	1545	GATWICK	1940	PALMA	A.320	6	
6607/8	2040	GATWICK	0540	BODRUM	A.320	6	
6703/4	0640	GATWICK	1440	VOL??	A.320	7	
6705/6	1545	GATWICK	0045	DALAMAN	A.320	7	
8107/8	0640	MANCHESTER	1555	LAS PALMAS	A.320	1	
8111/2	1800	MANCHESTER	0145	CORFU	A.320	1	
8211/2	0600	MANCHESTER	1530	HERAKLION	A.320	2	
8213/4	1620	MANCHESTER	2300	MALAGA	A.320	2	
8215/6	0005	MANCHESTER	0610	PALMA	A.320	3	
8307/8	0830	MANCHESTER	1400	SALZBURG	A.320	3	
8311/2	1825	MANCHESTER	0050	IBIZA	A.320	3	
8411/5	0600	MANCHESTER	1220	MAHON	A.320	4	
8413/4	1320	MANCHESTER	2000	FARO	A.320	4	
8415/6	2100	MANCHESTER	0645	RHODES	A.320	4	
8507/8	0745	MANCHESTER	1700	TENERIFE	A.320	5	
8511/2	1900	MANCHESTER	0415	TENERIFE	A.320	5	
8611/2	0655	MANCHESTER	1320	ALICANTE	A.320	6	
8613/4	1420	MANCHESTER	2020	PALMA	A.320	6	
8707/8	0835	MANCHESTER	1435	MAHON	A.320	7	
8711/2	1535	MANCHESTER	0135	DALAMAN	A.320	7	

WEST INDIAN — *BRITISH WEST INDIAN AIRWAYS   BW/BWA   TRINIDAD & TOBAGO*

900		BARBADOS	1010	HEATHROW	L-1011	1234567	
901	1215	HEATHROW		BARBADOS	L-1011	1234567	

WHITE STAR — *STAR AIR AS   DO/SRR   DENMARK*

6567	2115	EDINBURGH		COLOGNE	B.727	1234	
6568		COLOGNE	0110	EAST MIDLANDS	B.727	1	
	0430	EAST MIDLANDS	0530	EDINBURGH	B.727	1	
		COLOGNE	1900	EDINBURGH	B.727	234	

WIDEROE — *WIDEROE'S FLYVESELSKAP A/S   WF/WIF   NORWAY*

380		STAVANGER	1005	GLASGOW	SH-330	12345	
381	1130	GLASGOW		STAVANGER	SH-330	12345	
382		STAVANGER	1650	GLASGOW	DHC-8	7	
383	1815	GLASGOW		STAVANGER	DHC-8	7	

WOODAIR — *WOODGATE AIR CHARTER   WOD   UK*

211	2300	BELFAST	2359	EDINBURGH	TRISLANDER	12345	
212	0030	EDINBURGH	0130	BELFAST	TRISLANDER	23456	

YEMENI — *YEMEN AIRWAYS   IY/IYE   YEMEN*

742		SANAA	1655	GATWICK	A.310	7	VIA ROME
743	1755	GATWICK		SANAA	A.310	7	VIA ROME
744		SANAA	1655	GATWICK	A.310	3	VIA PARIS CDG
745	1845	GATWICK		SANAA	A.310	3	VIA PARIS CDG

25P	2150	STANSTED		LIVERPOOL	ATR-42	123456
25S		LIVERPOOL	0055	STANSTED	ATR-42	234567
129A	0230	STANSTED		DUSSELDORF	ATR-142	123456
129B		DUSSELDORF	0615	STANSTED	ATR-142	123456
700A	1955	STANSTED	2040	EAST MIDLANDS	SH-360	7
700B	2135	EAST MIDLANDS	2220	STANSTED	SH-360	7

ZENA *ORBI GEORGIAN AIRWAYS   NQ/DVU   GEORGIA*

701		TBILSI	0540	HEATHROW	L.1011	1
702	2115	HEATHROW		TBILSI	L.1011	4
703		TBILSI	1305	HEATHROW	L.1011	5
704	2215	HEATHROW		TBILSI	L.1011	5
707		TBILSI	0740	HEATHROW	L.1011	7
706	2115	HEATHROW		TBILSI	L.1011	7